# ALFRED E. SMITH

# Alfred E. Smith

## THE HAPPY WARRIOR

*Christopher M. Finan*

 HILL AND WANG

*A division of Farrar, Straus and Giroux*

*New York*

Hill and Wang
A division of Farrar, Straus and Giroux
19 Union Square West, New York 10003

Distributed in Canada by Douglas & McIntyre Ltd.
Printed in the United States of America
First edition, 2002

Library of Congress Cataloging-in-Publication Data
Finan, Christopher M., 1953–
    Alfred E. Smith : the happy warrior / Christopher M. Finan.—
1st ed.
        p.   cm.
    Includes bibliographical references (p.    ) and index.
    ISBN 0-8090-3033-0 (alk. paper)
    1. Smith, Alfred Emanuel, 1873–1944.   2. Presidential candidates—
United States—Biography.   3. Governors—New York (State)—
Biography.   4. New York (State)—Politics and government—1865–1950.
5. United States—Politics and government—1901–1953.   6. Presidents—
United States—Election—1928.   7. Irish Americans—Biography.
8. Catholics—United States—Biography.   I. Title.

E748.S63 F56 2002
973.91'5'092—dc21

                                                                          2002019476

Designed by Jonathan D. Lippincott

www.fsgbooks.com

1 3 5 7 9 10 8 6 4 2

*For the three people who made this possible,*
*Sally Seidman, Joseph Finan,*
*and Pat Willard*

# CONTENTS

# ACKNOWLEDGMENTS

I started this book when my oldest son was two. Today he's six-two. My youngest son wasn't even born then. A high school sophomore, he worries that his father will go crazy now that his book is done. When you have been working on something that long even the people who have helped you no longer remember what they did and are embarrassed when you bring it up. So I will keep this short.

The book began as a history dissertation under the direction of Walter P. Metzger of Columbia University. I doubt that I would have continued past the master's degree without the support of Professor Metzger, who did not think there was anything wrong with a journalist pursuing a Ph.D. I am also grateful to Professor Kenneth Jackson at Columbia, who gave me the benefit of his comments on both my dissertation and portions of this book.

After graduate school, I worked for two years under the skillful guidance of agent Diane Cleaver creating a proposal to transform my academic study into a trade book. Sadly, Diane died suddenly shortly after she had sent out the proposal. When the book failed to find a publisher, I wrote to almost everyone who I thought would have an interest in Al Smith. Geoffrey Ward responded by offering encouragement as well as useful criticism of several chapters. Simon Michael Bessie gave me the advice that framed the final work.

I am grateful to Michael A. Bamberger of Media Coalition and Oren Teicher of the American Booksellers Association, former employers who became good friends and supporters of this book. My current employer is the American Booksellers Foundation for Free Expression, whose directors are mainly independent booksellers. A would-be author could not find more understanding and supportive bosses.

I also want to thank Dan Cullen, who has read so many of my drafts over the years that he earns the dubious distinction of being my first editor. Anne Depue picked up the pieces after Diane's death. She not only sold the proposal, she read each chapter as it was completed and made many important suggestions. The greatest credit for the shape of the book belongs to Lauren Osborne at Hill and Wang, the editor I always dreamed of. She was assisted by Catherine Newman, who guided the book through the last stages with enthusiasm and skill.

Finally, I want to express my deep appreciation to my sons, Sam and Al, who grew up thinking it normal for a father to disappear into his study on weekends, and to my wife, Pat Willard. Marrying a writer was brilliant planning on my part. With seeming effortlessness, Pat has published three books in the time it has taken me to finish one. She has read and commented on everything I have written for over twenty-five years. Yet I never appreciated her more than during the difficult weeks when I was finishing and she was resisting her very strong desire to strangle me. This book could not have been written if it hadn't been as important to Pat as it was to me.

# ALFRED E. SMITH

# PROLOGUE

Alfred E. Smith committed political suicide on January 25, 1936. In the depths of the Depression, before an audience of elegantly dressed members of the American Liberty League, he delivered a slashing attack on the New Deal, accusing President Franklin Roosevelt of making the federal government so powerful that it threatened political and economic freedom. "There can be only one capital, Washington or Moscow," Smith thundered. "There can be only one atmosphere of government, the clear, pure, fresh air of free America, or the foul breath of Communistic Russia." Democrats had heard Smith criticize the administration before, but they were shocked by his statement that he was ready "to take a walk" out of the Democratic Party rather than support Roosevelt in the upcoming presidential campaign. It seemed unthinkable: Smith and Roosevelt had worked closely together since 1920; it was Roosevelt who called Smith "the Happy Warrior" in nominating him for president at the 1924 Democratic National Convention; when Smith won the nomination in 1928, he chose Roosevelt to be his successor as governor of New York and warmly supported his reelection in 1930. But what was most surprising about the Liberty League speech was that Smith appeared to have turned his back on the people of small means whom he had always proudly championed as "the rank and file." "I just can't understand it," Roosevelt told Frances Perkins. "Practically all the things we've done in the Federal Government are like things Al Smith did as Governor of New York. They're things he would have done if he had been President of the United States. What in the world is the matter?"

No one has provided a satisfactory answer to this question. Some have argued that Smith fell under the influence of the wealthy men who became his friends after he entered business in 1929. Others believe that Smith was jealous of Roosevelt, who had defeated him for the presidential nomination in 1932. Historians are divided between those who see Smith as a liberal who lost his way and those who believe that he was at most a compassionate conservative. What is most remarkable, however, is not that historians have disagreed about him but that they ignored him. Although there were several popular biographies of him, the first full study of his career by a historian was not published until 2001, seventy-three years after he became the first Catholic to run for president. Part of the problem is that Smith left almost no personal papers. But the absence of scholarly interest also reflects the fact that in his Liberty League speech he destroyed his reputation as one of the great political leaders of his time.

In the 1920s there was no more powerful spokesman for liberalism in the United States than Al Smith. The struggle began in the aftermath of the terrible Triangle Shirtwaist fire in 1911, when Smith, as a member of the New York Assembly, led the fight for bills to make factories safer, to limit the working hours of women and children, and to support workers injured on the job. When business groups objected that he was threatening the free enterprise system, Smith's answer was simple. "What did we set up government for?" he asked. "My idea of law and democracy is the expression of what is best, what fits the present day needs of society, what does the greatest good for the greatest number." When he was elected governor in 1918, Smith continued to push for government regulation of business. He wanted to end child labor and establish a minimum wage for women. (It was presumed that men would be protected by their unions.) He believed that government should own and operate electrical generating plants and that it should play a role in building housing for the poor. As a candidate for president, Smith proposed federal intervention to solve the problem of the agricultural surpluses that were depressing farm prices.

But Smith was different from other liberals. Born in 1873, he grew up in a country that was deeply divided between natives and immigrants. Over 30 million immigrants entered the United States in the seventy years before the country's traditional "open door" was finally slammed shut in 1921. Smith, who was born on the Lower East Side of New York City, was a product of this great immigrant wave. His mother's parents were Irish; his father's, German and Italian. Smith entered politics as a cog in the political machine called Tammany Hall, which drew its greatest support from the immigrants and their children. While Tammany was a powerful and often dominating force in New York City, however, it had little power in state affairs. As a result of a provision in the New York State Constitution, the residents of New York and the state's other cities were deprived of the political power to which they were entitled. State government was dominated by Republicans representing the rural sections of "upstate" New York. They didn't control state government alone. In the absence of laws guaranteeing cities the right of home rule, Republicans also dictated the smallest details of how life was lived in the cities, including the forms of recreation that workers could enjoy on Sundays. When Smith was elected to the Assembly in 1903, his first objective was to win political equality for the immigrant population of New York City. His experience as the leader of an oppressed minority played a crucial role in shaping his political outlook. As governor, he demonstrated a special sensitivity to the importance of protecting individual rights. He also pushed through the legislature a program of government reorganization that helped democratize New York.

Smith soon became the first Catholic political leader with a national following. By 1920 the overwhelming majority of people living in cities in the East and Midwest were first- and second-generation immigrants. When nativism blossomed in the early 1920s in the form of a revived Ku Klux Klan, immigrant Americans rallied behind Smith. They cheered his opposition to Prohibition and made him their candidate in 1924 against William Gibbs McAdoo, the front-runner for the Democratic presidential nomination, who was backed by the Klan. But most of all, they supported Smith because he was one of them. "They have belonged for 75 years to a secondary order of citizenship," Walter Lippmann wrote in 1925. "Perhaps he will breach the walls. They have been tolerated but not accepted. Perhaps he, who is one of them, will be accepted."

Smith didn't think of himself solely as an immigrant leader. He had united New York Democrats, winning the support of both upstate "reformers" and the urban machines. Protestants had always figured prominently in his campaigns, and his success had depended on the support of many New York City Republicans. He saw his life as a uniquely American success story, a symbol of how well American institutions assimilated newcomers from every land. Consequently, Smith was completely unprepared for the outpouring of anti-Catholic bigotry that greeted his nomination for president. The campaign changed the way he looked at his country, but he denied the accusation that he had turned his back on his own people. On the contrary, his opposition to the New Deal was based on the lessons of his long fight for equal rights, he said. The story of Al Smith can only be understood against the background of the struggle over who could call themselves Americans and participate fully in the nation's political and social life.

# 1 ✳ GREAT EXPECTATIONS

It was the kind of hot and muggy July day that has always made New Yorkers want to murder each other. In 1863 there was no place for the nearly 500,000 impoverished Irish and German immigrants living below Fourteenth Street to escape the heat. They crowded into tenement apartments without running water; 15,000 lived in basements. Some turned to crime to escape these conditions, but the overwhelming majority labored almost without pause in an effort to rise. On Monday, July 15, however, thousands of honest men and women put down their tools and picked up weapons.

The violence began on the outskirts of town, at the corner of Third Avenue and Forty-sixth Street. On Saturday, officials in the Ninth District office of the U.S. provost marshal had begun drawing the names of the local men who would be drafted into the Union Army, then mired in the third year of the bloody and stalemated Civil War. A large crowd and a detail of watchful police had gathered in front of the provost marshal's office. The conscription law was hated in the poorer districts of the city, particularly the provision that allowed a draftee to present a substitute or pay $300 to escape military service. The poor believed that the rich would buy exemptions for themselves and their sons, forcing workers to do the fighting. Some sort of violent protest against the draft seemed inevitable. When the doors of the draft office opened, however, the crowd entered peacefully and the selection of names began. Its completion was scheduled for Monday.

The authorities believed that the threat of violence had passed, but they were wrong. On Monday, many men failed to show up for work at the city's railroads, machine shops, shipyards, and iron foundries. Some of them were seen walking up Eighth and Ninth Avenues on their way to a meeting in Central Park, stopping at shops, factories, and construction sites to urge other workers to join them. After a brief meeting, a crowd began to march downtown to the provost marshal's office. As the size of the crowd on Third Avenue grew, the police called for reinforcements, and the lottery resumed. Only fifty-six names had been called when a volunteer fire company, the Black Joke, arrived with a hose truck loaded with stones. One of its members had been drafted, and the men were determined to destroy the records containing his name. Their barrage of rocks shattered the windows of the draft office, and the firemen rushed the building. They smashed the selection wheel, poured kerosene on the floor, and set the office on fire. The chief engineer of the fire department had just persuaded the crowd to let his men try to save the homes of innocent workers in neighboring buildings when a new group of rioters arrived and drove the firefighters away. These New Yorkers weren't just trying to stop the draft. They wanted to see the city burn.

The anger at the ruling class revealed itself in attacks on the police. The rioters had already assaulted several uniformed policemen when Superintendent John A. Kennedy arrived. A former policeman spotted Kennedy. "Here comes the son of a bitch Kennedy," he shouted. "Let's finish him!" Kennedy was knocked out with a club, dragged through the mud, and punched in the face so many times that he became unrecognizable. The rioters sent a force of forty-five police officers running for their lives. They captured Officer William H. Travis, knocked him out, and jumped up and down on his body, breaking his jaw and knocking his teeth out. He was left lying naked in the gutter.

By that afternoon, the authorities realized they were in danger of losing control of the city. Two weeks earlier, Robert E. Lee's forces had invaded Pennsylvania, and New York's regiments had been rushed to Gettysburg, leaving a skeletal military force in the city. If the police could not restore order, anarchy would reign. Inspector Daniel Carpenter, who was put in command of three hundred men, asked Police Commissioner Thomas C. Acton what to do with any prisoners. "Prisoners? Don't take any! Kill! Kill! Kill! Put down the mob. Don't bring a prisoner in till the mob is put down," Acton ordered. The rioting continued for three more days.

With the police virtually powerless to stop them, the rioters turned their anger against blacks. Not only did immigrants share the racist attitudes of other white Americans, they were in competition with blacks for the city's lowest-paying jobs and had seen blacks used to break their strikes. In addition, the issuance of the Emancipation Proclamation on January 1 seemed to support the idea that the Civil War was being fought not to save the Union, as Lincoln claimed, but to end slavery. Blacks were a symbol of the war and the hated draft. A fruit vendor became the first black victim on Monday when he was beaten by a mob that had just torched a nearby draft office. A couple of hours later, the Colored Orphans Asylum on Fifth Avenue was set on fire. On Tuesday, James Costello, a black shoemaker, was beaten and hanged. The body was cut down, dragged through the street, smashed with heavy stones and finally burned. At least nine other black men, a dark-skinned Mohawk Indian, and a white woman, Ann Derrickson, who was married to a black man, were killed in the rioting.

Alfred Emanuel Smith was at work three miles downtown when smoke on the horizon gave the first hint of trouble. Smith had a lot in common with the rioters. His parents were poor immigrants. He had little education: like most of the children in the heavily immigrant Fourth Ward, he had gone to work at an early age. He was a Catholic and a Democrat. Over six feet tall and weighing 225 pounds, he was a powerful man who valued courage and had demonstrated it himself. He was a member of Liberty Hose Company Number 10, one of the volunteer fire companies whose loyalty seemed doubtful after the Black Joke's attack. At twenty-three, he was eligible for the draft.

But Alfred Smith had no sympathy for the men who attacked the Weehawken and Fulton ferries and attempted to burn the Harlem and McComb's dam bridges. Although not wealthy, he owned property. As a young man working in a grindstone yard on Front Street, he had learned the valuable skill of driving a team of horses. He had purchased a team and wagon and gone to work as a truck driver. A few months after the riots he would enlist in the Union Army. He may have been attracted by the large bonuses paid to volunteers, or perhaps he was simply looking for new adventures, but it is possible that Smith's enlistment also reflected devotion to the Union cause.

It is clear that Smith did not share the prejudices of his more bigoted neighbors—partly because he was a minority member himself in the largely Irish Fourth Ward. His father, Emanuel, had come to the United States from northern Italy as a boy of twelve; his mother was German. Smith may not have been a liberal, but he was a firm believer that the United States was "the best poor man's country," a place where a man could raise himself by his own efforts. He saw his fate as tied to the fate of his city and country. He could not remain indifferent as rioting engulfed the Fourth Ward.

There was fighting all over the neighborhood. The headquarters of his fire company was located at the corner of Dover and Pearl Streets, only a block from Roosevelt Street, where boardinghouses that were home to black sailors were under attack. He told his daughter, Mary, about two incidents. He had saved a black man just as he was being strung up by a mob. He had also helped two black men who were being chased and stoned by hiding them in barrels and then using his wagon and team to carry the barrels onto a ferry and across the river to safety in Brooklyn. He told Mary that his motive was humanitarian. "They are the children of God and they have a right to live," he said. Alfred's love of storytelling was well known, but even if the stories are untrue, they reveal his sympathy for the underdog. They are lent additional credibility by the ample evidence of Smith's physical courage. A man who swam regularly in the swift currents of the East River was not a man who backed down, even in the face of a mob.

On Thursday night, soldiers returning from Gettysburg finally restored peace in New York. The city had been badly damaged during the worst civil disturbance in American history. A historian of the riots has concluded that 112 people died. Although many Americans blamed the immigrants, this was simplistic. German workers opposed the draft, but they generally refrained from violence. The Irish were divided: a majority of the rioters were Irish after the first day, but most Irish policemen and firemen remained loyal. The gap between rich and poor in New York was so wide that many in the working class felt that they had nothing to lose. The riots at least offered them the opportunity to settle scores with those they blamed for their predicament.

When Alfred Smith returned from the war, he went back to driving his truck. The life of a "cartman" was not easy. In all kinds of weather, he had to contend with the terrible jumble of wagons, omnibuses, and horse-drawn streetcars that clogged New York's streets from early morning until late afternoon. There were nearly 20,000 vehicles a day traveling in both directions on Broadway by the early 1870s. A contemporary guidebook described the scene:

> Carriages, wagons, carts, omnibuses, and trucks are packed together in the most helpless confusion. . . . In a few minutes, however . . . a squad of gigantic policemen dash into the throng of vehicles. They are the masters of the situation, and woe to the driver who dares disobey their sharp and decisive commands. The shouts and curses cease, the vehicles move one at a time in the routes assigned to them, and soon the street is clear again. . . .

But the worst part of the job may have been the fear of unemployment. The 1855 census listed 5,498 cartmen, draymen, and teamsters in the city, and the competition for work was ferocious. A trucker could never stop hustling. One of Al Smith's clearest memories of his father was of his return from work "grimy with dust of the streets—more neglected then than now—wet with streaky sweat, peeling off garment after garment, plunging his neck, hands, and arms into cold water to cool off." Like most New Yorkers, he worked a six-day week, and even on Sunday he had to tend the horses.

But Smith enjoyed his work. He was a man who loved company, and driving a truck brought him into contact with people all day long. Because he lived and worked in the neighborhood where he was born, he had known many of the same people all of his life. Smith was always making new friends: whether during work or in a bar later, men were attracted by his open manner and the stories that he told so well. He knew how to keep the friends he made. "A man who cannot do a favor for a friend is not a man," he told his son.

Alfred married for the first time after the war. Not much is known about his wife except that her name was Donnelly and that she came from a "respectable" family that lived in Brooklyn. Alfred might have chosen her in part because her background was more distinguished than his own. She gave birth to a daughter but died soon after of an unknown illness. Alfred sent his daughter to live with her maternal grandmother and soon began looking for a second wife. His next choice was a girl from his own Fourth Ward.

Alfred met Catherine Mulvehill because the stable where he kept his horses adjoined the building at the corner of Dover and Water Streets, where her family lived. Catherine's parents, Thomas and Maria Mulvehill, had left Westmeath, Ireland, for New York in 1841. Traveling on one of the sailing ships of the Black Ball line, the first company to provide regular passenger service between Europe and the United States, they sailed from Liverpool to New York. Unlike later immigrants, who would disembark at the immigrant receiving stations at Castle Garden and Ellis Island, the Mulvehills did not have to go through any formalities when they arrived. Their ship sailed directly up the East River to a pier at the foot of Beekman Street. They walked just three blocks before spotting a sign advertising rooms for rent in the building at Dover and Water and took an apartment on the second floor. Catherine was born there nine years later. When Alfred Smith met Catherine, she was twenty-one years old and an apprentice in an umbrella factory.

Catherine's family was unusual. Her mother, Maria Marsh, had been raised as a Protestant. Maria's father was a wealthy barrister who owned a property in the village of Moate large enough to be called "Marshland." Maria was well educated and could write in an elegant script; she was also trained in embroidery and other types of needlework. When Maria fell in love with Thomas, a Catholic tailor, she converted to Catholicism so that she could marry him. The Mulvehills were a stable, happy family. When Alfred Smith came calling on their daughter, they had been living in the same apartment for thirty years. They were faithful parishioners of the St. James Roman Catholic Church, and Catherine graduated from its school. Catherine may have been more handsome than beautiful: the Mulvehills were characterized by long, narrow faces; and Catherine's nose may have been a little too large. But she was a steady girl and well educated for her class. Alfred Smith could hardly have found a better woman to help him start over.

Catherine was also taken with Alfred. He was much taller than the Mulvehill men and better-looking: his brow was broad and his large mustache grew to the jaw line, framing a firm chin; his deep tan suggested good health and a life lived out of doors. He had friends everywhere. As the son of a German, he was also entirely at home in the heavily German neighborhood to the north known as Kleindeutschland, "Little Germany." There was something very attractive about a man who was so secure about himself and his place in the world.

The Mulvehills must have been pleased when Alfred finally proposed. Smith had his own business and was making a good living. Alfred and Catherine were married in St. James Church in September 1872. They took a five-room apartment nearby that rented for $15 per month, a substantial sum. Other families in the neighborhood may have been paying as much, but the Smiths were unusual in planning to live without boarders to help pay the rent. The apartment also featured the rare luxury of a tub in the kitchen. It was above a barber shop in a small brick building at 174 South Street, and the Smiths' windows looked out on the sailing ships that were moored along the East River. "This is like the view from an ocean liner," a visitor remarked. Between the masts of the ships they could see the river and the hills of Brooklyn as well as the first tower of the Brooklyn Bridge, the only evidence of the great bridge that would one day pass almost directly over the Smiths' apartment. At the age of thirty-five, Alfred Smith had achieved much of his dream. With strong arms he had raised himself by his bootstraps. He had every reason to be optimistic about life.

New York City was probably the best place in the world for an ambitious young man. In 1876 Joshua H. Beal stood 276 feet above the swirling East River to take its picture. From the top of the still-incomplete Brooklyn Bridge, he looked down on a city that had yet to be revolutionized by the birth of the skyscraper. Only the spire of Trinity Church at the intersection of Broadway and Wall Street was as tall as the towers of the bridge. Most of the buildings had four or five stories and were lower than the masts of the sailing ships that lined the wharves like a forest of blackened trunks. This was old New York, an island city defined by the spacious bay to the south and the great rivers that bordered it on the east and west, meeting again thirteen miles north of the Battery. It was a city that had been dominated by the maritime trade, but this was changing. Beal's photos also showed evidence of a new New York: the narrow berths for sailing ships interspersed with wide-mouthed ferry slips that received boats bulging with commuters from the city of Brooklyn. New York had become the nation's financial and business capital and an important manufacturing center. The 1880 census revealed that New York and Brooklyn had a population of nearly 1.8 million. When the Brooklyn Bridge was completed in 1883, it made possible the consolidation of Manhattan, Brooklyn, the Bronx, Queens, and Staten Island into a new, greater New York. By 1930 New York encompassed nearly seven million people. It had become one of the wonders of the modern world.

The speed of New York's growth was amazing. In 1800 its population of 79,000 made it a small town compared to London and Tokyo. The biggest city in the United States was Philadelphia. So sure were the city fathers that New York would not grow rapidly that when they built a new City Hall in 1811 near the intersection of Broadway and Chambers Street, they installed marble on only three sides of the building. They covered the north side in common brownstone, which they assumed few people would see. This seemed entirely reasonable at a time when Broadway came to a dead end at a farmer's picket fence a mile north at Astor Place, and Greenwich Village was a rural hamlet that lay along a dirt road, one of the city's first suburbs.

New Yorkers watched the city being remade before their eyes. Wealthy residential districts were invaded by commerce, leading their inhabitants to flee north. They never seemed to get far enough away: in the course of a single lifetime, the wealthy left their homes on Bowling Green and moved to new quarters on Broadway, then to Washington Square and lower Fifth Avenue before coming to a rest on upper Fifth Avenue. The three-story brick residences that first lined Broadway were replaced by commercial buildings that rose to five stories. "The spirit of pulling down and building up is abroad," Philip Hone, a businessman and former mayor, observed of the Wall Street district in 1839. "Brickbats, rafters, and slates are showering down in every direction. There is no safety on the sidewalks." Hone summed up the spirit of his times. "Overturn, overturn, overturn is the maxim of New York," he said. In 1856 *Harper's Monthly* acknowledged that the residents of New York did not love their city. "Why should it be loved as a city?" *Harper's* asked. "It is never the same city for a dozen years altogether." If they didn't love it, they were at least proud of its dynamism.

There was a dark side to New York's rapid growth. In 1877 Jacob Riis, a Danish immigrant who had been unemployed for many months, finally landed a job as the police reporter for the *New York Tribune*. He moved into an office on Mulberry Street, less than a mile from the apartment where Alfred and Catherine Smith lived. Over the next twelve years Riis would come to know the area intimately. "For years I walked every morning between two and four o'clock the whole length of Mulberry Street, through the Bend, across the Five Points down to Fulton Ferry," he recalled. At Fulton Ferry he was only a stone's throw from the Brooklyn

Bridge. The bridge was beautiful, but the area he had passed through was a terrible slum. "It was not fit for Christian men and women, let alone innocent children, to live in," he said. As the city expanded rapidly to the north, it became known as the Lower East Side. In 1890 Riis published his classic exposé of living conditions on the Lower East Side, *How the Other Half Lives*.

New York had grown too quickly. In 1845 the entire European potato crop failed, hitting Ireland the hardest but also affecting the Continent, particularly southern Germany. In that year the number of immigrants exceeded 100,000 for the first time; there were 200,000 in 1847, 300,000 in 1850, and 427,833 in 1854. Within a generation, New York's population quadrupled, reaching over 813,000 in 1860. There was nowhere to put the newcomers. On the Lower East Side, when the cellars and attics of the existing houses were full, developers built "rear houses" in the backyards. These began as two-story buildings, but additional floors were soon added. The front houses were also expanded until their foundations could not stand another floor. Then barracks-like tenement houses of five and even six stories were built side-to-side and back-to-back. At 290,000 people per square mile, the Lower East Side easily surpassed the densest London or Peking slum by 1855.

Alfred Emanuel Smith, Jr., was born on December 30, 1873, in the South Street apartment that Catherine and Alfred had rented the year before. Two years later Mary was born on the same day. The Smiths lived within a short walk of many of the worst parts of the Lower East Side. The Five Points, which took its name from the five-cornered intersection created by Worth, Baxter, and Park Streets, had become a slum long before the Civil War. Its wooden buildings, located on streets that were crooked, narrow, and dirty, were so old and poorly maintained that many of them sagged in upon themselves and seemed on the verge of collapse. They housed hundreds of the poorest families as well as alcoholics, prostitutes, and criminals. Bars, pawn shops, and dance halls provided the main forms of commerce in the Points. Even the grocery stores sold liquor by the glass. According to one guidebook, the reputation of the Five Points was so lurid—and alluring—that tourists demanded to see it even "before they visit Fifth Avenue or the Central Park." Junius Henri Browne, the author of a 1869 guide to New York City, described the experience of walking there:

Your senses ache, and your gorge rises, at the scenes and objects before you. Involuntarily your handkerchief goes to your nostrils, and your feet carry you away from the social carrion into which you have stepped. . . . Those boys and girls have no childhood, no youth, no freshness, no sweetness, no innocence. . . . Hardness, and grimness, and filthiness are in the people and the places, spread up, and down, and across every visible thing.

Different people drew different boundaries in determining the extent of the Five Points. One guidebook writer included all of the Fourth and Sixth Wards, "the most wretched and criminal of all in the city." Browne was more precise. "Within half to three-quarters of a mile to the north and southeast of the Points, poverty and depravity, ignorance and all uncleanliness, walk hand in hand with drunken gait and draggled skirt," he said. Both estimates place Alfred Smith's apartment within the perimeter of the slum.

In later life, Al Smith never tried to hide the seamy side of the neighborhood in which he was raised. A reporter who interviewed him wrote this about his childhood:

His earliest memories are dotted with pictures of fighting men and screaming women being dragged through the streets to the police station. As a toddler ranging away from the doorstep of his house he heard and was curious about the tinkle of piano music and the shuffle of dancing feet behind windows painted red and screen doors that swung continuously during the long summer evenings. Thousands of rigidly respectable families in the Fourth Ward lived in that environment, but at the same time far apart from it.

Some blocks of Water Street, which was next to South Street, were almost entirely given over to prostitution: the prostitutes met their customers in basement dives and took them upstairs to rooms above the street-level shops. Catherine Smith knew the dangers in the neighborhood and tried to get her children to play in the attic above their apartment as much as possible. When they went out alone, they were warned to avoid a section of Water Street where prostitution was the worst. Catherine also took great care in dressing her children to ensure that no one would mistake them for slum children.

Despite the neighborhood's problems, Alfred had no desire to leave the Fourth Ward, and even turned down at least one opportunity to move. While hauling equipment for a machinery firm, he became friends with one of its senior partners. The man did not live in the neighborhood, and he did not believe that the waterfront was any place to raise children. He told Smith that he would sell him a small farm in south Brooklyn for modest payments of $15 per month, the same amount he was paying in rent. Smith could not have dismissed such a generous offer out of hand. (As his son later noted, the property became enormously valuable as farmland was converted to residential use.) He still declined. Brooklyn was too far away from his business. Trucking depended on personal contacts, and many of these came from people living in the neighborhood. Besides, Alfred loved living in New York. "[H]e himself would not be contented in the country," his son remembered.

What outsiders failed to understand was that the Lower East Side contained many neighborhoods. The people who lived in the parish served by St. James Church did not consider themselves slum dwellers. Almost everyone worked, and the neighborhood had a small middle class of shopkeepers and bar owners who lived around the corner from their businesses. Although the construction of large residential flats was destroying the natural beauty of the area, there were still a number of tree-lined streets with private houses. Henry Campbell, a wealthy grocer who was a friend of Alfred Smith, lived in a house on Madison Street in the heart of the Lower East Side. Convenience may have been one reason middle-class people stayed, but they also valued what Al Smith called "neighborhood spirit":

When I was growing up everybody downtown knew his neighbors—not only people who were immediate neighbors but everybody in the neighborhood. Every new arrival in the family was hailed not by the family alone but by the whole neighborhood. Every funeral and wake was attended by the whole neighborhood. Neighborly feelings extended to the exchange of silverware for events in the family that required some extraordinary celebration.

St. James Church was at the center of community life. Built to house an Episcopal congregation, it had been purchased by the Catholic Church in 1827 to meet the needs of a rapidly increasing stream of immigrants from Ireland. By 1883 the parish of St. James had 16,000 communicants, making it the largest in the city. It operated a school and an orphanage and provided space for the meetings of at least fifteen clubs and other organizations, including the St. James Total Abstinence Benevolent Society, St. James Rifle Corps, the Longshoremen's Protective Society, the St. James Dramatic Society, and a ladies' sodality. The pastor of St. James, the Rev. John Kean, was known as a strict priest: he was particularly hard on drinkers, banning alcoholic beverages from all church functions and declaring war on bars that served women. Father Kean's parishioners accepted the importance of firmness in a place that was so full of temptation. The parish also knew that he kept a sharp eye on its children. In seasonable weather, Father Kean stuck his head out of the window of the rectory at 9 p.m. and shouted, "Everybody home."

The church was only one part of a system of social interaction that seems intense by today's standards. On New Year's Day, people exchanged calling cards with neighbors they hadn't met yet. It was on such a visit that Al Smith as a young man met the future mayor of New York, James J. Walker, who was only a small boy at the time. On Washington's Birthday, men who belonged to martial organizations donned borrowed uniforms and paraded to a park where they competed at target shooting and feasted. During Smith's childhood, the St. Patrick's Day parade marched up the Bowery and Fourth Avenue to Twenty-third Street. There was also a competition on Thanksgiving Day when neighborhood groups dressed up in fancy costumes for the "ragamuffins" parade. A fancy-dress ball followed several days later.

The question in Alfred Smith's mind was not why he stayed in the Fourth Ward but why anyone would want to leave. New York was one of the world's great ports, and South Street was its heart. From Market Street, which was four blocks to the north of the Smith home, to the Battery, which lay less than a mile south, the East River waterfront was the busiest in the city. The East Side was where the big clipper ships docked after their journeys from places around the world: the tea ships from China and India landed at the foot of Market Street; the Port Line and Black Ball line brought passengers from Europe to the Smiths' front door; below Fulton Street were the ships engaged in the trade of the West Indies and South and Central America. There were no playgrounds, but the children didn't miss them. "No gymnasium that was ever built . . .

could offer to anybody the opportunities given to the small boy along the water front," Al Smith insisted. Boys used the bowsprits of heavily laden ships to climb into their rigging and pretended to be at sea or acrobats in the circus. Al and his friends learned to swim in the East River with ropes tied around their waists or in the large tanks behind Fulton Fish Market that held live fish during the day. The waterfront was also an inexhaustible source of pets brought to port by sailors. At one time Al kept a West Indian goat, four dogs, a parrot, and a monkey in the attic of his building.

New York had more theaters than any city in the country. It also had summer gardens, concerts, lectures, operas, plays, and melodramas. Alfred took his family to the Atlantic Garden in Little Germany, where hundreds of other families sat at tables listening to the all-women band playing on the balcony. Later, variety entertainers told jokes and danced in wooden clogs. Al and his sister were "given chocolate to drink and huge slices of cake, while the elders drank their beer, gossiped and listened to the entertainment." Although New York's theaters had a well-deserved reputation for lewdness and violence earlier in the century, by the time Al Smith was born in 1873 producers were trying to rehabilitate the stage. One of the first had been P. T. Barnum, who made a landmark of his American Museum, which was located on Broadway just south of City Hall. Barnum gave the exhibits in his museum verve by emphasizing live acts: a Chinese juggler, a serpent charmer, rope dancers, glass blowers, ventriloquists, flea circuses, Indian chiefs, and a knitting machine operated by a dog. He searched the world for human oddities: an "Albino lady," a tattoo-covered man, a hairy child billed as "The Wild Boy," giants, midgets, and an armless man who could use his feet to do anything.

As the demand for popular entertainment continued to grow, New York rapidly developed two theater districts. The "legitimate" theater, featuring the works of Shakespeare and other plays favored by the upper classes, soon moved up Broadway to Fourteenth Street and beyond; popular theater was headquartered on the Bowery. In 1873 an economic depression cleared the Bowery of hundreds of retail stores and small businesses. They were replaced by saloons that sold five-cent whiskey, gambling houses, shooting galleries, variety halls, and theaters. Some of the variety halls were nothing more than "dumps, slabs and honky-tonks."

A gang operated the Grand Duke's Concert Hall in the basement of a tenement, stealing whatever props the performers needed.

The Bowery was not all bad. Dime museums provided family entertainment for people who could not have afforded any otherwise. Standing in front, the "outside talker" attempted to persuade the passing throng to step inside. Al Smith, who lived within walking distance of the Bowery, memorized the patter: "I went to the Dime Museum so often that, at a moment's notice, I could have taken the place of the announcer as he described the mysteries of the India-rubber man; Jojo, the dog-faced boy; Professor Coffey, the skeleton dude, the sword-swallower, the tattooed man and the snake charmer." It was in the museums that Smith saw theater for the first time. For an extra nickel, patrons could watch a variety bill of four to seven acts and an after piece, a comedy sketch in which all the entertainers performed, often in blackface. A typical bill at the National Theater ran over four hours. The Bowery crowds were hard audiences. Liquor was sold in most theaters, which meant that there were always drunks in the house. But everyone joined in razzing the talent. To keep order, Henry Miner employed guards on each level of his Bowery Theater. The one on the ground floor stood with his back to the pit, eyeing the customers. The man in the balcony carried a rattan cane that he slapped against the wall to establish order at the end of the overture. "Hats off, youse," he would demand. "Hats off, all o' youse!" Boisterous laughs, wisecracks, and foot stomping were not punished, but Miner drew the line at tobacco spitting, throwing paper wads, fighting, and molesting females. Misbehaving patrons were told to "cheese it."

By the late 1870s life in New York was improving in ways that were noticeable to the residents of the Fourth Ward. The congestion that had plagued the city for decades began to ease with the construction of elevated trains. Soon, "els" ran up Second, Third, and Ninth Avenues as far as the Harlem River, opening vast new areas of Manhattan for residential development. One el ran up the Bowery, casting the street in shadow, but it did not remain dark for long. In 1882 Thomas Edison established an electrical generating station to light buildings in the Wall Street area. More than a mile of the Bowery was transformed by electric signs and streetlights into New York's first "Great White Way." New York was also expanding skyward. The first skyscraper district in New York grew up next to the Fourth Ward. In 1873 the *New York Tribune* built a nine-story structure with a clock tower that rose to 260 feet across from City Hall. The *New York Times* constructed a thirteen-story skyscraper around the shell of its old building on Printing House Square. A block away stood the eighteen-story *New York World* Building.

The invention in 1874 of the "safety" bicycle had a dramatic impact on the lives of the residents of the Fourth Ward. Easier to ride than its predecessors, the new bicycle created a biking craze that even working-class families could join by renting bikes by the hour. On summer evenings the neighbors could be found wobbling up and down Wall Street, which was one of the few streets in the area that was paved with asphalt instead of cobblestones. The bicycle was a symbol of personal freedom. No longer limited by the routes of the stages and streetcars, people rode off into the wilds of upper Manhattan, the Bronx, and Westchester County. They could ride out to the Rockaways for a swim or to Coney Island, whose beaches and popular amusements attracted so many people from the Lower East Side that some called it "the Bowery by the Sea." The paths were quickly jammed, Al Smith said. "On a warm night in summer the cyclists were so numerous that they rode elbow to elbow on the Parkway. The lights on the wheels at night, and the bells which riders were required to carry, made a fascinating picture of flashing lights accompanied by tinkling bells of all sorts and descriptions." New York could be magical even for the lower classes.

The construction of the Brooklyn Bridge provided much of that magic during the 1870s and early 1880s. New Yorkers watched as giant wooden caissons were towed into place and sunk in the East River to become the foundations for the towers of the bridge. Air was pumped into the caissons to empty them of water, enabling men to stand on the river floor. Reading long accounts in the newspapers, New Yorkers tried to imagine the workers as they labored in the blue-white glare of calcium lamps, their voices sounding pinched and high in the compressed air, using picks and shovels to dig out mud and rocks that blocked the caissons' descent toward bedrock. Towers rose from the water, and anchorages were built to hold the four main cables, which were spun from wires only an eighth of an inch thick. No one was more enthralled than Alfred Smith. While others fretted that the bridge would never be completed, he saw evidence almost every day that the great work was progressing. In May 1875, when he and Catherine had been living on South Street for almost three years, work began on the New York anchorage. Entire blocks were demolished to make way for the gigantic masonry ramp that rose to meet the bridge.

From the beginning there had been questions about the safety of the bridge's design and its enormous cost. The construction involved considerable risk to the workers, many of whom lived in the neighborhood. Catherine Smith may have been one of those with doubts. She told her son that the bridge might never have been built if people had known how many men would lose their lives in its construction. The project was plagued by dishonest contractors and unscrupulous politicians. To the bridge's supporters, however, it was a symbol of man's indomitable will. There was also the pure thrill of walking 200 feet above the East River. Alfred longed to be among the first to cross the bridge, and his opportunity came with the construction of a footbridge made of wooden planks that were four feet long. Even with gaps between the planks to allow the wind to blow through, preventing excessive sway, the footbridge rocked slightly as it climbed 200 feet at a thirty-five-degree angle from the anchorage to the top of the first tower, descended to about 180 feet, then climbed again to the top of the other tower and down the other side. A reporter described the experience:

> The undulating of the bridge caused by the wind, which was blowing a gale, the gradually increasing distance between the apparently frail support and the ground, the houses beneath bristling all over with chimneys, looking small enough to impale a falling man, the necessity of holding securely to the handrail, to prevent being blown off, produce the sensations in the reporter's head — and stomach — never experienced before.

For a time, the bridge managers allowed ordinary citizens to use the footbridge, requiring only that they obtain a ticket first. While rejecting the request of an actress who wanted to ride a horse across, they did give a ticket to a couple and their newborn baby. Alfred Smith probably crossed at this time and later repeated the trip with his son, who was around nine. Catherine was terrified. "I remember Mother sitting at home, saying 10 rosaries all the time they were gone," Mary Smith said. On opening day, Alfred crossed the Brooklyn Bridge again, this time with his whole family, and returned without incident by the Fulton Street ferry.

Al Smith didn't mention the trip across the footbridge with his father in his 1928 autobiography. What he did remember was the accident that occurred a week after the bridge opened. It was a warm and sunny Memorial Day, and as many as 20,000 people were on the bridge at around 4 p.m. The pedestrian traffic was so heavy on the New York end that people were having difficulty moving up and down a stairway leading from the roadway to the promenade. Suddenly, a woman lost her footing and fell, causing another woman to scream. The scream caused a panic, perhaps worsened by lingering doubts about the safety of the bridge. (Later there were reports that someone had shouted that the bridge was falling.) The crush of people around the stairway became so great that clothes were torn off and hats, umbrellas, and pocketbooks fell through the bridge, hitting the pavement of South Street where nine-year-old Al Smith happened to be standing with some of his friends. The boys didn't know what was going on until they learned that ambulances were being called to the New York terminal of the bridge. They rushed there in time to see bodies being loaded into the ambulances. Twelve people had been killed and hundreds were injured. As darkness fell, Al watched the police piling up their belongings. "That was my first view of a great calamity," Smith said. "I did not sleep for nights."

One reason that Al Smith may have been so shocked by the disaster at the bridge is that there was no room for accidents or tragedy in his father's view of life. Alfred was certainly aware of the possibility of failure, but he kept his fears at bay with a positive attitude and a relentless commitment to making good. He was always working, sometimes supplementing his income from trucking by working as a watchman. If working so hard meant that Alfred did not see much of Catherine and the children except on Sundays, he had the satisfaction of knowing that he was a good provider. "We had good food and good clothes, and we even had toys and toys weren't so common in those days," Mary Smith said.

The Smiths' livelihood depended on Alfred's health, however, and ultimately it began to fail. He developed an ulcer and suffered from chronic gastritis. In 1885 it became impossible for him to drive a truck. The pressure of feeding and housing his family forced him to begin selling his horses and wagons. They moved to cheaper lodgings next to the anchorage of the Brooklyn Bridge. In 1886 Alfred's condition took a turn for the worse, and he was no longer able to work even as a watchman. In late October, a new doctor began to visit the second-floor apartment on

Dover Street, but there was little he could do. On the way home from the polls on Election Day, Alfred became so weak that he had to rest on the steps to his apartment. Catherine brought pillows and a blanket to make him comfortable. He died a week later at the age of forty-six. Catherine was thirty-six; Mary was ten and Alfred was twelve. Alfred's friends paid for his funeral.

Catherine was not alone. Although her mother had died the year before, she could count on the support of her brother, a fireman, and her sister, who was now living with her. But she knew this wouldn't be enough. Mary Smith said her mother momentarily gave in to despair. "I don't know where to turn," she said. Until the adoption of the "widow's pension" in 1915, widows without resources were routinely separated from their children, who were raised in orphanages. The family's survival depended on Catherine's getting a job. There was one possibility. Catherine had learned the trade of umbrella making before her marriage, and the forelady of the factory was a woman from the neighborhood. She put on her coat and, taking Al with her, set out for the woman's apartment. The woman was willing to help.

For the next year and a half, Catherine Smith worked at the umbrella factory during the day and brought work home with her at night. Al had been selling newspapers since his father became ill. For two hours after school, he delivered the city's seven major dailies to regular customers along a route that ran from his home to the Fulton Ferry. But her husband's long illness and death had taken a heavy toll on Catherine's health. Working day and night proved impossible. The woman who owned their building offered to help by letting them run a small combination candy and grocery store on the ground floor. After school, Mary watched the store until Al had finished delivering newspapers, then he waited on customers until bedtime. By the spring of 1888 it was clear that the earnings from the grocery store and the paper route were not going to be enough to support the family. Al was fourteen and about to graduate from seventh grade, the final primary school grade. He was not much of a student. He was not especially interested in his studies and sometimes disrupted class. A teacher once called him "a great mischief" and ordered Mary to tell her mother that "it was useless to keep the boy in school any longer." Catherine had done everything she could to keep her son in school, but the family budget could not stand the strain any longer. With graduation in sight, Al left school and became a truck chaser for $3 per week. It was his job to run along the waterfront looking for his employer's trucks and tell the drivers where to go next. Slowly, things began to improve. The Smiths began attending the theater again. In 1890 Al got a new job as an office boy making $8 per week.

Al wasn't going to be an office boy forever, but it was not immediately clear what else he could do. He faced handicaps his father hadn't. He was not tall and strapping. Physically, he took after the Mulvehills. He was short and thin and not at all handsome. As he grew into manhood, he developed a long narrow face whose most distinguishing feature was the prominent Mulvehill nose.

What Al did have was a remarkable verbal ability. He had inherited his father's love of talk and trading stories. He also loved the theater: he and his friends staged their own productions of the popular plays of the day in the attic on South Street. Adults began to notice Al's gift when he was still in school. In sixth grade, his recitation on the life of Robespierre won him a medal at a citywide competition among parochial school students. As he grew older, he developed a deep, booming voice that carried to the furthest corners of the auditorium. Smith's voice was so loud that he was hired to read to a crowd the blow-by-blow description of the heavyweight championship fight between John L. Sullivan and James J. (Gentleman Jim) Corbett as it came across the teletype machine from New Orleans. Sullivan was a hero to the New York Irish, and Smith needed every decibel he possessed to be heard over the bellowing crowd as Sullivan was defeated in twenty-one rounds.

But Al longed to be more than an announcer. He felt he could be a leader. His teacher may have despaired of the future of someone who would "crack wise" for the amusement of his friends. But Al was far more than a class clown. One of his childhood friends recalled, "If anybody made a hostile demonstration against Al—and many did because he had a caustic tongue and used sarcasm—he would talk that hostile party into a pacific state of mind. I saw him do it dozens of times. His humor was our kind of humor. A boy or man can't fight and laugh, at the same time, and Al Smith could make anyone laugh." Al could make fun of the strongest boy and get away with it. Throughout his political career, he would use humor to disarm his opponents and tie his friends to him more closely. Even as a young man, he knew this made him special. At times it also made him insufferable. A woman who grew up with Smith recalled:

He was talking all the time, at parties, or reciting or dancing. He was quite a boy at jigs, and he thought he could sing, too. One day some of us girls were making plans for a picnic. For some reason we hadn't invited Alfred—no one called him Al in those days— but while we were talking it over he happened along and chimed in. "You haven't been asked to go," one of us said. "Oh, you'll ask me," he answered. "You won't be able to get along without the talent."

Like his father, he believed that popularity was a key to success. Acquiring it became Al Smith's goal.

Although he was a little hard to take at times, Al had a lot of friends, and his friends were content to follow him. When he and his friends staged their juvenile productions in his attic, Al was the director. As he grew up he became a power in the affairs of the St. James' Union, the parish club. Once he intervened to help Father Kean, who wanted to expel from the Union several boys he had seen drinking during a dance. The priest demanded that the Union bylaws be changed to allow him to expel anyone he believed to be unfit, but many of the boys were opposed. Smith had been raised to respect the authority of priests. He was also smart enough to know the importance of pleasing Father Kean, so he persuaded the other boys to allow the priest to explain his position. Later they voted unanimously to amend the bylaws.

Smith also founded a bicycling club, the St. James Wheelmen, which had over one hundred members. The sport of "coasting," which involved racing bicycles down hills, had become so popular that the New York Athletic Club had begun to hold competitions. Smith was an expert coaster, according to a clipping in his scrapbook. "On Sundays, he pedals up to Westchester where he spends the day in rolling down steep hills," it reported. Some of Smith's friends called him the "Coasting King," but he really liked all kinds of bicycle races. He also achieved the distinction of membership in the Century Club by cycling over one hundred miles in one day. He and his friends left the Lower East Side at 9 a.m. on a Sunday and rode all the way to the beach at Far Rockaway, where they swam and ate dinner before riding back.

In 1892 Smith took a job at the Fulton Fish Market. The market later became a symbol of Smith's remarkable rise, but there was nothing ro-

mantic about it at the time. Although he was paid well—$12 per week—
Smith had to report to work at 4 a.m. and worked until 4 p.m. On Fridays
he was expected to start at 3 a.m. One of the advantages of the job was
that employees were entitled to take as much free fish as they wanted. After a while, though, the Smiths couldn't eat any more: "I think I may well
say that for a long time we had such a complete fish diet that the entire
family developed a fear of them. A live one might at some time or other
wreak his vengeance for the devoured members of his finny family." In
1893 Smith turned twenty. He had reached his full height of five feet
seven inches, and was strong enough to command the wages of a man
who could do heavy physical labor. He took a higher-paying job at the
Davison Steam Pump Works in Brooklyn. Smith said he was a shipping
clerk, but the authors of his 1928 campaign biography maintained that
he was actually a "receiving clerk," a euphemism for a common laborer.

There must have been times on the new job when Al Smith felt
deeply frustrated. His father had believed deeply in the American dream.
Alfred Smith had gambled everything on his ability to handle a team of
horses, and he imbued his son with a belief that he, too, would one day
be the master of his own destiny. But Alfred's death seemed to have
robbed Al of the opportunity to pursue his dream. As long as he was the
main breadwinner, there seemed to be no hope of seeking more education or raising the capital to go into business for himself. Smith knew that
he was talented. He burned to do bigger things. Yet he still had to get up
every morning, eat the big breakfast prepared by his mother, and go to
work.

# 2 ✳ MAKING IT

I t was usually late when Al Smith left the home of his girlfriend in the Bronx to return to Manhattan. Catherine Dunn's home was on Third Avenue near 170th Street. To reach it, Al had to take the elevated train that ran from South Ferry to Chatham Square, then along Third Avenue to the Harlem Bridge, where he changed to an older-style steam train pulled by a locomotive. The trip was often fun—the train ran above the Bowery, past theaters and variety houses that Smith knew well, and Al could even call down to friends walking on the street thirty feet below. Even though the els were three times faster than horsecars, it took an hour and a half to make the ten-mile trip. At the end of a long day, Smith often found himself being rocked to sleep by the rhythm of the train. One day he woke to find that someone had taken his umbrella. Umbrellas were not cheap, and when Smith's mother gave him a new one for Christmas, he was determined he would not be fooled again. So he was prepared one night when some of his friends boarded the southbound el at Fifty-ninth Street and spotted him sleeping in his suit and straw boater. The young men were returning from a fair at the Catholic Club on Fifty-ninth Street. One of them sneaked up on Smith and snatched the umbrella, only to find that Al had used a piece of twine to tie it to his suspenders. Al Smith proved that he was wide awake, even when napping. It was just the quality that Henry Campbell needed.

Campbell lived on Madison Street in the heart of the Fourth Ward. He owned a large retail and wholesale grocery business on Vesey Street as well as twenty-five apartment buildings in the neighboring Seventh Ward, a house by the water in Bath Beach, Brooklyn, and a large farm in Dutchess County. People were probably not far wrong when they called Campbell a millionaire, but he refused to leave what most wealthy men would have considered a slum. He was an active member of St. James, and every summer he brought the kids in the church orphanage to his home in Bath Beach to enjoy the ocean. Campbell had a reputation for kindness and was said to be an understanding landlord. "Unfortunate tenants, families without means of support or in difficulties, are given material help instead of being molested and troubled for rentals," one newspaper reported.

He was also an important figure outside the Fourth Ward. He was a trustee of St. Patrick's Cathedral, the beautiful Gothic cathedral that had been completed in 1879 and stood as a symbol of the rising fortunes of the Catholic church and the Irish and German immigrants who formed the overwhelming majority of its members. A major contributor to the Democratic Party, Campbell was a friend of President Grover Cleveland. (Cleveland was reportedly so grateful to Campbell for his support that he gave him a chair made from a cherry tree that had stood on the White House grounds.) Campbell was a prominent member of Tammany Hall, the political organization that met in a large brownstone building on Fourteenth Street. Tammany Hall took its name from the Tammany Society, a social club founded at the conclusion of the Revolutionary War. At the time, there were no political parties, and Tammany was one of many political clubs in New York City. But its identification with the interests of the workingman gave it a growing political base. Its power was symbolized by its mascot, the tiger. Tammany was eventually recognized as the official Democratic Party organization in Manhattan and operated as the New York County Democratic Committee. Tammany Hall had no formal connection to the Tammany Society, although there was a great deal of overlap between the memberships of the two groups. Campbell was a member of the Tammany Hall General Committee of the Second Assembly District, a working-class district that included the Fourth Ward and was one of the main cogs in the Tammany "machine."

Campbell was a bachelor who spent a lot of money helping orphans, and Smith was a fatherless boy who could use all the help he could get. Their relationship grew so close that Al eventually ate all his Sunday dinners at Campbell's house. Mealtime conversation probably revolved around local events and their common interest in bicycling, although Campbell was a heavy man who preferred to ride in the country where there was more room. Surely they talked a good deal about Smith's future as well. Campbell knew that Smith was intended for something better than carrying pipe. He could have offered him a job in the grocery business or taught him how to manage real estate. Instead, Campbell asked Smith to help him fight Tammany Hall.

Evidence of Tammany wrongdoing was growing. In 1892 the Rev. Charles Parkhurst, the pastor of the Madison Square Presbyterian Church, had launched a crusade against Tammany, which he accused of protecting prostitution, gambling, and saloon keepers who openly flouted the law against selling liquor on Sundays. Many refused to believe his claims that the police were receiving kickbacks from these illegal activities and that the criminal justice system as a whole had been corrupted. Ignoring the criticisms of some of the members of his own congregation, Parkhurst disguised himself and toured some of the city's brothels in the company of a private detective. When he returned to the pulpit, he had proof that almost everyone was on the take. For a time, Tammany was able to successfully deny Parkhurst's charges. By the end of 1893, however, even some Tammany members were beginning to believe that Boss Richard Croker had lost control of the city.

Campbell was not unconcerned with conditions outside the Fourth Ward but his main objective was the overthrow of Patrick ("Paddy") Divver, the man whom Croker had installed as the leader of the Second Assembly District. Like many of the men who rose to the top in Tammany, Paddy Divver began his political career as a saloon keeper. Beginning with one bar on Park Row across from City Hall, Divver eventually owned several saloons and a sailors' boardinghouse. It was not Divver's profession that made him controversial but his ties to the criminal element in the Fourth Ward. When he was appointed a police magistrate in 1890, the *New York Tribune* observed:

> If [Mayor Grant] had instituted a search for the unfittest man in all this vast city to exercise the immense power over crime and criminals that a Police Justice possesses, he could not have succeeded better than he has in the selection of "Paddy" Divver. Here is a vulgar, illiterate, ginmillkeeper, by his very profession a

breeder of vice and a maker of criminals, as ignorant of the law as a kangaroo, whose saloons are the hanging-out places of gambler and sharper, elevated to the bench of that court wherein all the virtue and charity and wisdom of which man is capable would often be severely tested. Could anything be more shameful or more disgusting?

Later, the Lexow commission, which investigated Parkhurst's charges, would hear testimony that Paddy actually acted as a bank for a group of gamblers and con men who used his saloon as its headquarters. In the early 1890s, however, newspaper criticism made no dent in Divver's popularity in his district.

Campbell knew that the fight against Divver required organized support, so in 1894 he founded the Seymour Club. Even after Tammany became the dominant Democratic faction, there were other Democratic clubs that coexisted with it, sometimes allying themselves with "the Hall," sometimes opposing it. Tammany's great advantage over its rivals was its ability in normal times to elect the mayor and reward its followers with city jobs. Without any patronage to dispense, Campbell was determined to spend lavishly to provide a home for the district's rebels. The club opened a headquarters on Market Street but soon moved to a building on Madison Street near Campbell's home. It was as a member of the Seymour Club that Al Smith fought his first political battles. Campbell's friendship enabled the young man to play a leading role in the club from the beginning. Smith became the secretary of the club, but his gift for public speaking soon gave him the unofficial title of club "orator."

Campbell had joined the New York State Democracy, one of the factions of dissident Democrats that were working with the Republicans in support of the candidacy of William L. Strong for mayor. Campbell and his colleagues struggled to convince the workingmen on the Lower East Side that Tammany was not their friend. Anti-Tammany speakers tried to show how corruption hurt the workingman. One speaker for the State Democracy, Otto Kempner, told them that they might have been hired to clean snow from the streets if Tammany hadn't been bribed to hire Italian immigrants. But denunciations of corruption meant little to poor laborers who knew that they could turn to Tammany for help in hard times. The reformers were winning few converts until Tammany made the mistake of denying renomination to the district's Congressman, Timothy J. Campbell.

In normal times, Tammany's decision to replace Tim Campbell as Congressman for the Ninth District of New York would have caused little distress to anyone except the Congressman himself and his closest friends. In Tammany's view, election to office was a reward for party service, and elected officials were expected to give way to new men after a short period of time. Since the days of the Jacksonian revolution, the Democrats had advocated the view that democracy did not depend on the election of the best man but on a regular rotation of offices among many men. It was on this understanding that Tammany had elected Tim Campbell, and after three terms in office he was asked to give way to a new man, Henry Miner. Miner was well known. A native of the Bowery, he had an outgoing manner that made him popular, and his popularity helped him win the leadership of the Third Assembly District. Miner had made good in business, too. He opened a theater on the Bowery where he helped shape the form that variety entertainment maintained for the next fifty years. It was in his theater in 1879 that a spoof of Gilbert and Sullivan's recent show, *H.M.S. Pinafore*, launched a tradition of burlesquing musicals that made Miner and many other theater owners rich. By 1894 Miner owned four of the most popular theaters in New York and another in Newark. It is not surprising that Tammany would want to reward such a wealthy party contributor. And in 1892, Tim had agreed to step aside at the end of his next term.

Two years later, however, Tim Campbell had changed his mind. Possibly emboldened by his popularity and Tammany's weakness, he tried to get the district leaders in his area, including Divver, to nominate him for another term. When they refused and nominated Miner, Campbell announced that he would run for reelection on an independent ticket. "I'm going to be elected, me boy," he told a reporter. What could justify such a dramatic break with Tammany? Tim Campbell said that there was nothing less at stake than the principle of home rule—for Miner no longer lived in the Ninth Congressional District but in a house on Madison Avenue.

> [T]his campaign of mine is a sort of uprisin' of the people. The people of this Congressional district wants home rule, you see? No

carpet baggers; no Tammany millionaires from Madison Avenue. Why, me boy, I've lived in this district for 46 years and they all know me. If anybody gets in a scrape they're after me to pull them out of it. . . . Why, every man, woman and child in this district knows me.

The Ninth Congressional District was "the most peculiar district in the city," Campbell insisted. "Nobody but a man who's lived in it knows what it is. Why, we're like a big family; we all know each other's affairs. . . . Does he know us? Do our people want him mixing himself up in their domestic affairs? Not a bit of it."

The next day, Al Smith and Henry Campbell were present at a meeting of the Oriental Club in Grand Street when Tim Campbell kicked off his independent campaign. It was Smith's first political meeting, and he could hardly have hoped for a more memorable introduction to politics. The Oriental Club was located in a Chinese section bordered by an Italian neighborhood. The meeting room was on the second floor in the front, but most of the men had been drinking in the bar at the back when the Congressman arrived. When the meeting began, the front room was "jammed with sweltering but hopeful politicians," a *New York Herald* reporter noted. They "howled and waxed exceeding glad" at the conclusion of a nominating speech. An unofficial speaker rose to second.

One individual, who had interviewed the bar too assiduously, clambered upon a chair and insisted on making a speech. He had partially cleared his throat, and had made a vague preliminary flourish, when the chair broke and he sunk into oblivion and the arms of his friends. From far down in the depths his voice could be heard arising, like incense, in praise of "Tim" Campbell.

The Congressman then departed for a meeting at the Cleveland Club on East Broadway, drawing his followers behind him. "Everybody tagged on, and by the time the club was reached the human kite, of which Mr. Campbell was the body, had a fine long serrated tail that stretched all the way around into Grand Street," the *Herald* reported. A drawing in the newspaper pictured Campbell as a handsome man with a fine head of hair and a handlebar mustache. He was wearing a double-breasted cutaway coat and a white tie, which he straightened as he prepared to speak. Campbell promised a clean campaign. "There will be no billingsgate and no vituperation, even though my opponent has stated that my promises are like pie crusts—easily broken," Campbell said. "I have made up my mind to fill the bill gentlemen, and if I can't fill it, you can go uptown and get a Congressman." With another round of cheers, the meeting was adjourned, although the partying went on through the night. "Then they all went to bed with their boots on, and it is probable that the average east side hat is much too small today," the *Herald* said.

The campaign that followed was as colorful as the first night promised. To the charge that Miner was an outsider, Tammany answered that Campbell was an ingrate. At Miner headquarters in the People's Theater, a spokesman called "Doc" explained:

> Why that man's been to Congress enough, ain't he? Does he want to die in Congress, what? Won't he give no other son of a gun a chance to blow off in the national legislater? Why, Miner's stood off for that man for two consecutive terms, and now, when he wants to get into business, this feller Campbell tries to block his game. Am I right? Tell me, am I right?

Friend turned against friend as the Ninth District dissolved in civil war.

> "It's Miner sure!" cried Candidate for Assembly Philip Lessig yesterday. "Do I look like a shouter or a bean eater, or am I full of booze? No, sir! Miner's got 'em dead!"
>
> "Rats!" roared Sullivan, "not while the woters of this 'deestrict' kin git a loaf of bread, a herrin' and a schooner o' beer fer tree cents. I tell ye, it's Campbell. Not that I love you less, Phil, but that I love Campbell more."

With cockney eloquence employed on both sides, the battle quickly became a contest over who could spend the most money on the voters. A messenger brought Campbell the news that Miner was planning a benefit at his theater for the striking cloakmakers.

> "Ully smoke!" cried the messenger, "that ain't the worst of it. He's givin' away free tickets and bill board tickets, an' the hull destrict is

chantin' his praises." Tim was lost in a brown study for several moments on the receipt of this news. "That, that is a good play," he
said after a moment, with admiration in his tones, "but I'll double
discount it, see! I'll appeal to the home lovin' instincts of this district, and keep open house for a month!"

But this was a fight not only over home rule and candidates but over
the principles by which the machine operated. Croker had put Divver in
charge of the Second Assembly District, a man whom Henry Campbell
considered little better than a criminal. He was determined to oust
Divver and he was prepared to fight Tammany to do it. Al Smith joined
him in speaking not only for Tim Campbell, but for the entire anti-
Tammany ticket, including mayoral candidate William Strong, a Republican.

Henry Miner's defeat of Tim Campbell was not a shock. The only surprise was how close Campbell came to victory: he received 7,113 votes to
Miner's 7,992. More important, New Yorkers had rejected Mayor Hugh
Grant, the Tammany candidate, giving Strong nearly 60 percent of the
vote. In part the victory was the result of the Rev. Charles Parkhurst's
campaign to spur the respectable classes to action, but there had also
been a serious erosion of support for Tammany in its traditional strong-
holds on the Lower East Side. Strong received 45 percent of the votes of
the men in the Second Assembly District, although Smith was not among
them because he did not turn twenty-one for another two months. Grant
almost lost the Third Assembly District, another strongly working-class
constituency, which split 3,903 to 3,901.

Tammany's defeat changed Smith's life. When he took the stump
against Tammany, he was still carrying pipe at a steam factory. But Henry
Campbell used his connections in the new administration to get Al a job
as a process server for the commissioner of jurors. When Smith was offered the patronage job, he recalled, "I had a choice of hard labor at a
small wage of $10 a week, or $12 at the most, in the kind of jobs that were
open to me, or easier work at a greater wage." The work was not physically taxing, it was conducted during normal working hours, and there
was no predawn commute to Brooklyn. On January 15, 1895, the reformers celebrated the inauguration of William Strong, and Al Smith and his
family celebrated his new salary of $15 per week.

Smith's new job was to track down people who had refused to appear for jury duty and hand them summonses that threatened them with contempt of court. "[F]or $60 a month you were required, day after day, to take a shower of abuse," Smith said. "The subpoena server in the office of a busy businessman was about as welcome as a safety-razor manufacturer would be at a barbers' convention." But the job took him to places he had never been—into businesses and banks. As Smith's knowledge of the world grew, so did his responsibilities. He was promoted and given the job of checking out the excuses that people gave for being unable to serve on a jury. On one occasion he asked a woman why she had ignored her summonses and received a lecture on the injustice of requiring women to serve on juries when they were denied the right to vote. "She told me to take the subpoena back and tell the Supreme Court, the commissioner of jurors or anybody else who, in my opinion, should hear it, that she had frankly said she would not serve on the jury until she was admitted to her full rights of citizenship," Smith remembered. Meanwhile, his sense of humor helped him deal with the abuse. A supervisor remembered Smith entertaining his co-workers by sticking a feather duster in his hat and bellowing the Toreador Song from *Carmen*. Smith was not only the most entertaining of the investigators in the office, he was also the smartest, and he eventually became a supervisor.

He had enjoyed his first experience in politics. "I had a fondness for politics and I liked the excitement of public life," he explained later. But there was a major obstacle to any hope that he may have entertained for a career in politics—Paddy Divver. In a desperate effort to save the candidacy of Mayor Grant, Boss Croker had forced some of the worst Tammany leaders to resign, including Divver. He blamed his enemies in the district for his defeat, and he was eager for revenge. "I propose to do what I can for those who have been my friends, and to do what I can against those who went against me when they should have remained my friends when they look for political advancement," Divver told a reporter. His hit list must have included the secretary and "orator" of the Seymour Club, Al Smith.

Smith may not have been overly concerned by Divver's threats, however, because he had discovered another possible career. Four years earlier, he had agreed to take a small part in a play produced by the St. James Dramatic Society, which put on two shows every year in the 800-seat auditorium in the basement of the church. Although the players were amateurs and their performances were benefits that supported the parish orphanage, the spring and fall shows were big events in the neighborhood. Because playwrights were willing to waive their royalties for charity, the plays put on at St. James were often the same ones being performed professionally around town. Every performance in the two-week runs was sold out, with adults in the chairs and children sitting on the floor around the apron of the stage. Smith had become one of the company's stars. Although he was too short, homely, and high-spirited for romantic leads, he was a natural character actor and played villains with such zest that he always drew a large, hostile reaction from his audiences. He quickly learned that the enthusiastic booing and hissing was a tribute to his acting ability. At one performance, Smith's gun was knocked out of his hand by the hero and accidentally fell off the stage onto the floor where the small children sat during the performances. One of them picked up the gun and handed it back to Smith. "Here you are, Al," the boy said in a voice loud enough to be heard by everyone.

Smith was "dead stuck on acting," and it is not hard to understand why. The people of the Lower East Side were surrounded by theater. The Bowery shows infused daily life, providing the jokes, the songs, and the drama that filled daily conversation. The culture a century ago was more verbal than it is today, and Smith had a special talent for memorization. Al learned the Declaration of Independence, the preamble to the Constitution, and plenty of poetry, and he was honored for his excellent recitations at school assemblies. After he left school, he continued to hone his histrionic gift. He appeared on several programs put on by Catholic social clubs outside his parish during the 1890s.

The high points of Smith's theatrical career came as a member of the St. James Dramatic Society. The company had great success with its production of Dion Boucicault's play *The Shaughraun*, which was revived twice and included a two-night run at a theater on the Bowery. But the members' greatest thrill came in 1899, when they were invited to perform at the Catholic Summer School of America in Cliff Haven, New York, which was located on Lake Champlain near the Canadian border. Neither Smith nor many of the other members of the company had ever traveled so far. They boarded the night boat to Albany, where they transferred to a train north. Arriving in Cliff Haven, the troupe moved into the Red Swan Inn. Smith marked the occasion of his first stay in a hotel by saving one of the complimentary postcards, which he later pasted into his scrapbook.

While the appointments of the Red Swan Inn were decidedly modest, Cliff Haven itself was a well-known resort that attracted many well-heeled vacationers. The theater on the Champlain assembly grounds was not far from the Hotel Champlain, a first-class hotel that was then playing host to President William McKinley. Some of the prominent guests at the hotel took in the performances at the summer theater. One night, after the members of the company had performed William J. Florence's *The Mighty Dollar*, an army general came backstage to congratulate the cast. The general had seen the play when it had been a hit in Washington with Florence himself in the leading role, but he insisted that the St. James production—with Al Smith in the lead—was just as good as the original.

Far from home, Smith and the other young members of the troupe were on their own for the first time in their lives. Yet they were never far from the sheltering arms of the Catholic church. Many priests and nuns vacationed in Cliff Haven, and Father Kean took the opportunity to visit. His players met him at the train station and escorted him to the assembly grounds, singing as they went. It had been a memorable trip, and there must have been some regret when it came time to return to New York, but Smith had things to attend to back in the city. The most important was Katie Dunn.

The Dunns knew what they were doing when they moved to the Bronx. They had originally lived on the Lower East Side, where Katie's father had operated a sailors' supply store. But they had long since left the crowds behind and moved to the wide-open spaces of the Bronx and now lived in a single-family home at the edge of Crotona Park. While some natives of the Lower East Side, including Al's sister, Mary, had tried the Bronx and found it to be too lonely and removed, the Dunns seem to have welcomed the distance. According to some accounts, Katie's father had left the retail business to become a contractor. There was money to be made in construction in a city that was growing so rapidly, and many Irish-Americans were benefiting from the opportunities. There is no question that the Dunns were middle-class and determined that their children would enjoy every advantage. Katie was educated at a convent school. She cultivated womanly arts, including singing. And, like his father, Smith was attracted to refinement.

Despite the Dunns' best efforts, the Lower East Side came to reclaim their daughter in the figure of Al Smith. The Dunns still had family on the Lower East Side. Mrs. Dunn's nephew, John Heaviside, was a friend of Al Smith's. One day in 1894, John had been asked to get his aunt's signature on some papers relating to the family plot in Calvary Cemetery, and Smith had agreed to keep him company on the long trip. After meeting sixteen-year-old Katie, a slim and pretty girl with dark hair, Al prevailed on Heaviside to take him back to the Bronx. Later, Katie made several visits to John's family on Catherine Street, perhaps by prearrangement with Smith.

Money was an obstacle to their romance. When Al first met Katie Dunn, he was not in a position to court her. Smith had been helping to support his mother, sister, and aunt since his father's death in 1886. His sister's marriage lightened his burden, but the day when Smith would earn enough to start a family of his own was not in sight. More than a year passed before the relationship became serious, and even then there were difficulties, including the concerns of Katie's parents. They liked the young man; he was funny and entertaining. Obviously, a boy who was taking care of his mother was also responsible. But they could not help feeling disappointed that their daughter had chosen to favor a poor boy.

By 1899 Smith was growing impatient. He had been courting Katie for so long it had become routine. On weekends he traveled to the Bronx. Many evenings, they joined the rest of the family in the parlor, where Katie would play the sentimental ballads of the period—"Sweet Violets," "Only a Pansy Blossom," "Say Au Revoir but Not Goodbye." Smith undoubtedly offered funny songs from his vast store of Bowery show tunes. Katie would travel back to the Lower East Side for the Seymour Club balls or join Al at Harry Campbell's house at Bath Beach for the club picnics. But Smith wanted Katie with him all the time. Before agreeing to the marriage, however, her parents had to be assured that he had abandoned his dream of a career in the theater and that he intended to stick to his city job. Although the Dunns had hoped for better, they accepted this security for their daughter. Katie later said that she couldn't have cared less about her fiancé's job. "If Al had gone on being a clerk, it would have been all right with me," she said.

Before Smith could consummate his romantic relationship, he had to fulfill his obligation to the first woman in his life—his mother. Now twenty-five, Smith could not start his own family until he was able to arrange a new home for her. A solution appeared in 1898 when Smith's sister, Mary, and her husband, John Glynn, decided to move. They had been living with the Smiths since their abortive move to the Bronx, but the arrival of a second child led them to seek an apartment for themselves. Rents continued to climb, so they followed the path of many other "old-timers" and began looking in Brooklyn. One of Catherine Smith's sisters had moved to the area surrounding the Brooklyn Navy Yard, which was just north of the Brooklyn Bridge. The Glynns found a house on the edge of Brooklyn Heights, which commanded a sweeping view of lower New York, and moved there with Smith's aunt. The new house had room for Mrs. Smith, and in 1900 she joined the rest of her family there. Smith walked across the Brooklyn Bridge to visit his mother every Sunday. On May 6, 1900, Al and Katie were finally married at a church in the Bronx. With the summer coming, they moved temporarily to Bath Beach in Brooklyn, but they moved back to the old neighborhood in the fall.

Smith and his bride established their household at 83 Madison Street, conveniently only three doors up from the Seymour Club and a short walk from Henry Campbell's house. A career in politics remained a possibility, for the Seymour Club had continued to grow. Henry Campbell opened a new headquarters for the club at 77 Madison Street in 1897. He spared no expense. On the ground floor, expensive carpet imported from Brussels covered the floor of the smoking and conversation room. The main meeting room upstairs featured an elegant Turkish carpet and was fitted with furniture and appointments of the "highest order." Like the local Tammany organization, the Seymour Club sponsored events for its members several times a year. In the summer Campbell threw a party at the Ocean Villa in Bath Beach, where the concrete-bound residents of the district could participate in water, barrel, and potato races in the fresh air and sunshine. In the winter the club sponsored a ball. The 1899 event attracted 176 couples, which made it more than half as big as the St. James ball that embraced the whole district, both Tammany and dissident. In 1901 it was said that the Seymour Club controlled the votes of nearly two thousand men in the Second Assembly District, nearly a third of the electorate.

Paddy Divver was still blocking Smith's path, however. In 1897 the voters of New York had returned Tammany to power, and Divver had resumed the post of district leader. His return meant that he would once again use his power to advance the interests of those who would pay for his favor—gamblers, prostitutes, swindlers, and thieves—and he still craved revenge. It was clear that Divver would strike at the Seymour Club when he could, but open warfare did not break out immediately. Both sides sought to win the support of the other influential men of the district. Two of the most important men were saloon keepers, Thomas F. Foley and Lawrence Kaine, who between them were said to be able to swing half the vote of the Second Assembly District. With the support of the Seymour Club, either Foley or Kaine might have become leader himself, but both men were longtime Divver supporters. Foley was described as one of Divver's closest advisers.

Yet Foley seemed like a good prospect. Born in Williamsburg, Brooklyn, and apprenticed as a blacksmith, he abandoned his trade in 1872 when he moved to Manhattan and opened a saloon at the corner of Oliver and Water Streets, only a few blocks from where Al Smith was born the following year. Foley was a young man and Smith was a small boy when the two men met for the first time. Smith remembered "an enormous big man with a jet-black mustache." The saloon keeper often crossed paths with Smith and his childhood friends. It was usually good news when they did, for Foley frequently gave each of them a nickel. "In those days a penny looked big, but when you got a nickel you thought it was Sunday," Smith recalled. Street urchins were not the only ones to benefit from Foley's generosity. A man of resources who did business in a poor neighborhood, Foley often helped those in trouble. His Tammany connections could find a job for a man who was out of work, legal help for a boy in trouble, or coal for a widow. Foley does not appear to have cultivated relations with the criminal element in the neighborhood. As Divver's problems grew in 1894, many wondered why Foley did not step forward as the next district leader.

Foley didn't really want the job. He was not interested in getting rich, and the position entailed many headaches. Despite the urging of Campbell and others, Foley remained loyal to Divver for another three years. In the meantime, police corruption returned with a vengeance, and reformers were preparing to make a new assault on Tammany in the 1901 mayoral election. A new reform group, the Citizens Union, was working to re-create the coalition of Republicans and independent Democrats that had triumphed in 1894.

Although Tom Foley was not a reformer, he finally agreed on the importance of more honest leadership in the district in 1901 and declared his candidacy for district leader. He made a special promise to the young men of his district, telling them that if they helped him become district leader, he would give them a chance to run for office. The Seymour Club would have supported almost anyone against Divver, but Foley's promise created an additional incentive for ambitious young men like Al Smith. "Prior to that time, nominations to the Board of Aldermen or to the Assembly were made largely on the ability of the candidate to control votes, and in most instances, he was a saloon keeper," Smith explained. Foley's promise involved a subtle but definite shift in how politics would be played in the Second Assembly District. No longer would wealth be the primary consideration in the choice of candidates. There would be no more rotation in office, allowing each rich man his moment in the spotlight. The day when Henry Miner could impose himself on the people at the expense of a popular leader like Tim Campbell was past. Under Foley's rule, men would advance strictly on merit.

The Foley-Divver race was close. As both sides prepared for competing Labor Day picnics, there were no clear indications of who was ahead. There were prominent men on both sides, and the public did not know for certain who Timothy D. Sullivan was supporting. "Big Tim" represented the Bowery in the State Senate and exercised a strong influence over politics all over the Lower East Side. Much would be revealed when Foley and Divver and their supporters marched to the East River to board their respective ferries. Newspapers reported that four thousand people marched in Foley's parade through streets where partisans hanging from windows and mobbing the streets cheered so loudly that few could hear the marching band, the drum-and-fife corps, or the bagpipe players. Every building showed some sort of decoration. The *New York Times* reported: "It was not only the Stars and Stripes that did honor to the day. The green flag, with the harp, fluttered from many windows, and banners and drapings of green hung from door posts and housetops. But there were German flags, too, and at one point the yellow flag of the Chinese, with the big dragon, fluttered in the breeze." The cheering increased as the crowd saw that one of the men marching with Foley was Big Tim. "Big Tim's wid us. How kin we lose?" shouted a man in a white fedora. Not all of the spectators were Foley supporters. A reporter heard one Divverite grumble at the sight of Chinese in the Foley parade. "It's hard times, sure, when they've got to muster in the chinks," he muttered. But Divver was also seeking support from minority groups. Charlie Bacigalupo, a Chinatown undertaker, and three hundred Italians marched in his entourage of 2,500.

The Divverites charged that Foley did not live in the district. True, Foley and his wife did live in a house on Thirty-fourth Street, but it was impossible to make the charge of carpetbagging stick against a man who had been in business in the Fourth Ward since 1872. Divver was far more vulnerable to attack. In 1893 Divver had offered prizes to the precinct captains who brought in the biggest vote, spurring them into a frenzy of fraud. The indictment of eighteen election workers followed, and Divver fled to California to avoid arrest. Divver later returned when it became clear that the authorities lacked the evidence to indict him, but many in the neighborhood were outraged that he had left poor men holding the bag. The Foley parade featured a float with large paintings on either side: one showed Divver drinking wine in a California palm garden above the sign "California—here's where Divver was in 1894"; the other depicted a cell in Sing Sing with the three election inspectors imprisoned for committing fraud at Divver's invitation, "You go hunt—I'll stick to you." The moral of the story was drawn in a third painting showing Divver running for a receding express train: "He who quits and runs away will be beat on primary day."

Foleyites and Divverites exchanged words as their ferries passed on their way to different picnic grounds, but then politics was adjourned. Although the whole neighborhood had participated in the demonstrations, only men were invited to board the boats. The Foley party was looking forward to a steak dinner, and once it reached the picnic grounds more than a thousand men pushed and hammered at the doors of the eating hall until they were admitted and had their fill. They then proceeded outside for various games and competitions. "I'm satisfied with the showing," Foley told a reporter. "The boys have turned out all right and they'll stick." The party had a triumphal return to the neighborhood, where its march was illuminated by torches and fireworks.

The primary itself two weeks later was something of an anticlimax. By then it was clear that Foley had the endorsement of the most influential men in the district as well as those of the mayor, Robert Van Wyck, and former police chief "Big Bill" Devery. Divver appears to have feared the worst, for in addition to bringing men into the district to vote illegally, he created a paper ballot that was intended to fool Foley voters into choosing a slate of Divver men to the committee that would make the actual choice of leader. Foley was expecting this kind of subterfuge. He, too, had imported voters and employed "repeaters" who would vote more than once for their man. "[A]t no time since the days of William M. Tweed has such an assemblage of offscourings of society appeared to exercise the right of franchise," the *New York Times* reported. In the end, Foley had more men than Divver, and he used them better. His crowning stroke was to get his supporters to the polls long before opening time so that they could repel the expected invasion of Divver's army. Divver conceded less than two hours after the polls opened, and Foley was elected by a better than three-to-one margin. In one of the more remarkable examples of the pot calling the kettle black, Divver claimed that he was beaten by "crooks and repeaters and the police."

At a time when government took little responsibility for the welfare of its poorest citizens, it was the district leaders who tried to find solutions for their problems. Tom Foley needed help, and Al Smith was one of the men he turned to. Smith had become the leader of one of the election districts that made up the Assembly district and had helped get out the vote on primary day. Now that Divver had been ousted, the rebels of the Seymour Club had no reason to oppose Tammany, and Smith became part of the political establishment. Every night after dinner he picked his way through the crowded streets to the Downtown Tammany Club on Madison Street. Although not significantly larger than its neighbors, the structure looked like a headquarters: a long, wide set of stairs carried the visitor into the building through an arch flanked by torchlike lamps. The arch featured an intricate iron grill, decorative stonework around the windows, the stone head of a man near the pinnacle, and a large flagpole projecting above a roof line. The Downtown Tammany Club must almost have seemed like a cathedral to the plain people who brought their problems to Foley every night. To Smith it became a second home. He was there every night socializing with other party workers until Foley called them into his office and gave them their assignments, telling them how to help a family that had been burned out of their apartment, about a man who needed a job on the Metropolitan Railroad or at Consolidated Gas, and about the drunks in jail who needed their fines paid.

Foley kept his promise to promote a new kind of man for office. Within weeks of his defeat of Divver, the new district leader chose Joseph P. Bourke to run for the New York Assembly. Bourke was young and popular: he had been a classmate of Smith's at St. James School who had managed to obtain a college education. Bourke won easily in 1901 and was reelected in 1902. In 1903, however, Foley decided to replace him. Foley never spoke publicly of his reasons for dissatisfaction, but there were reports that he felt that Bourke did not spend enough time helping him at the club. Continuing his commitment to youth; Foley offered the job next to Pat Whalen, a clerk who was working on the staff of District Attorney William Travers Jerome. This nomination would have had symbolic importance: Whalen was not only young, he was working for Jerome, who had impressed people in the Fourth Ward by being one of the few reformers in 1901 to open a headquarters on the Lower East Side. But when Whalen asked Jerome's advice, the district attorney discouraged him, and Whalen declined Foley's offer.

There probably were a number of young men on Foley's list after Whalen dropped out, and Al Smith was one of them. In September 1903, Smith was twenty-nine years old. In their three years of marriage, Al and Katie had lived in three different apartments. Their first apartment on Madison Street had become too small with the birth of their first child, Alfred. They moved to another apartment on Madison on the top floor of an old three-story building, where a daughter, Emily, was born the following year. But this building was sold to people who planned to demolish it to make way for another building. So, in the fall of 1903, the Smiths moved to an apartment on Peck Slip within smelling distance of the Fulton Fish Market. Smith had a good city job that paid $900 per year; he was comfortable before an audience and popular with his neighbors. At the Seymour Club picnic in 1901, he had nearly stolen the show as he performed a minstrel song and dance with his newborn son in his arms. What most distinguished Smith from the other potential candidates on Foley's list, however, was the support of Henry Campbell, who had been an important ally in Foley's fight against Divver. It was reported that when Campbell heard a rumor that Bourke was out, he went to Foley to urge him to select Smith, and it was Campbell who found Smith in the offices of the commissioner of jurors to tell him that Foley had chosen him.

Smith had dreamed of the Assembly job for many years. Nevertheless, he was very surprised when Campbell gave him the news. It wasn't just that he had no inkling of Foley's unhappiness with Bourke. He wasn't nearly as qualified as the other men. Bourke had been to high school and college. Whalen was going to be a lawyer one day. Smith's boss, the commissioner of jurors, thought that his lack of education was probably an insurmountable obstacle to his success, and he warned Smith against taking the job: "He said that a man who went to the legislature who was not a lawyer had very little chance, and that there were blocks and blocks of ex-aldermen and ex-assemblymen walking the streets of New York; a great many of whom seemed to have done nothing for the rest of their lives." Smith was determined to take the job anyway. A member of the Assembly made $1,500 per year, and Smith needed the money: he already had two children, and he and Katie wanted more. Election to the Assembly also gave him a foothold in Tammany that might lead to other jobs like an appointment in the building department or a position with a contractor with strong Tammany ties. As for his lack of education, Smith was sure he was smart enough.

After telling his wife, Smith's first thought was to notify his mother in Brooklyn Heights. Neither family had a telephone, so Smith sent a friend on foot to tell her the news. Then he prepared for an official notification ceremony. While it was Foley who selected Smith, it was the delegates to the district convention who formally bestowed the nomination. Tradition required a committee of two men from the convention to find the candidate and notify him. The purpose of the tradition was probably to perpetuate the fiction that the candidate had never actually sought the office, which would have been undignified. In practice, the candidate and his supporters pondered long and hard about where would be the best place to be "found." Smith and his people decided the best place would be the St. James' Union, the club that had nurtured Smith's political gifts.

Once he had been surprised by the notification committee, the candidate was supposed to accompany the committee back to the convention hall and express his appreciation to the delegates. Smith's problem was that he had only two suits. His winter suit was still in mothballs, and he was wearing the other one. "[S]o that while contemplating my coming nomination, I was in the kitchen of the Peck Slip house wearing my wife's apron while I pressed my blue serge in order to be presentable to the convention," he later remembered. The young man in the freshly pressed suit received a standing ovation as he entered the convention hall with his escorts. Many of the delegates had known him his whole life, and they cheered the triumph of Alfred's boy. Soon his picture appeared on campaign posters throughout the district. "I believed I had reached the very zenith of my political fortunes when I saw my picture in the windows of the shopkeepers of the district."

Smith's election required practically no effort on his part. The Democratic nominee for Assembly always won in the Second Assembly District, but Smith still went through the motions. Because there were almost no places in the district capable of holding large crowds, the campaign was mostly conducted out of doors. Smith's loud voice gave him a natural advantage over the opposition, which included a Republican, a Socialist, and—what was even rarer in the district—a Prohibitionist. "I am told I could be heard a block away, over the rattle of the horse cars on Madison Street," Smith recalled. The returns showed the usual dominance of the Democratic Party. Smith received almost 5,000 votes to the Republican's 1,472; the Socialist polled 106 votes, and the Prohibitionist, 5. Smith was willing to concede to a reporter for the *New York Morning Telegraph* that his victory did not owe much to his campaigning. "It was like rolling off a log," he told a reporter. "I could have sat at home and been elected, but I took the stump a bit and did a bit of talking. I like it, you see." It had been too easy. Smith was smart enough to know that what Foley had given, he could just as easily take away. But he shoved aside all thoughts of failure. While speaking to a reporter he used boasting to help cover his nervousness:

You see it's this way. Acting is a lot harder work than helping make the laws. That's why I'm booked for Albany for the season. The footlights for your Irvings and your Mansfields, but the comfortable and cozy seats of the State Capitol for mine. The fact is, politics pays better than the wig-paste profession, and, if I'm not exactly a star in the House as yet, this is my first venture, I guess I'll get the center of the stage and bask in the political limelight before I get through.

Smith's first encounter with the press must have given Tom Foley indigestion. He had replaced Bourke because the man believed he was so popular that he no longer had to work for the people's approval. But

Smith sounded ten times more conceited. Foley took his new protégé aside and gave him some advice. "Don't speak until you have something to say. Men who talk just for the pleasure of it do not get very far."

Not long after the election, Henry Campbell took Smith uptown to Brooks Brothers so that "the old neighborhood would have as well dressed an assemblyman as the uptown folks have." Campbell bought Smith a cutaway for everyday use and formal clothes, including a spike-tail dress suit and top hat. Smith was already looking forward to the reception for legislators that would be held by Governor Benjamin Odell at the Executive Mansion. "Al went up to Albany on his first trip to the Assembly just as cocksure of himself as he has ever been in his life," Tom Foley later recalled. Smith was headed for disappointment, however. He would soon wish he had listened to the commissioner of jurors.

# 3 ❋ STRANGERS AT THE DOOR

W hen Al Smith set out for Albany on January 5, 1904, the eastern United States was firmly in the grip of a great cold wave. It wasn't easy for him to leave his family. Members of the legislature didn't earn enough to enable them to relocate their households to Albany during the legislative sessions. It was the custom for a legislator to share rooms with a colleague during the week and return home on the weekend. Although Al and Katie would grow used to these separations over the next twelve years, the first time was hard. The Smith family was growing rapidly. Alfred III was three, Emily, two; and Katie was six months pregnant. In addition, this would be Smith's first extended separation from the city he loved. The wind was whistling down the river, producing bone-numbing temperatures, not making it any easier to depart.

The weather was worse in Albany. The streets of the capital were snow-packed on the evening Smith arrived and checked into the Keeler Hotel. But it wasn't the storm that worried Smith. Less than a week before, a brand-new, supposedly fireproof theater in Chicago, the Iroquois, had caught fire, killing more than five hundred people. As Smith sat in his room reading about the disaster in the newspaper, he thought about the roaring fire in the open hearth of the hotel lobby. He went to look for a fire escape; finding none, he decided not to go to sleep. Instead, he persuaded his roommate, Tom Caughlan, a grocer and Tammany man who represented one of the Assembly districts that adjoined his, to play pinochle all night.

Neither fear nor homesickness got the better of Smith. Hardly showing the effects of no sleep, he presented himself the next day at the caucus of Democratic members of the Assembly and helped choose the leadership for the new session. Later, the Democrats joined the Republicans in the ornate Assembly chamber and Smith was formally sworn in as a member of the legislature. He was looking forward to the governor's reception for the legislature. Smith imagined that the reception was only for the two hundred members of the legislature and their families, and so prepared carefully for what he imagined would be his real debut as a man of influence. That evening he jumped into a sleigh with four of his colleagues and traveled to the Executive Mansion, where his dream was promptly shattered. Smith entered to find five thousand people. A soldier led Smith and his friends to Governor Benjamin Odell, who shook hands with them pleasantly, then introduced them to his wife, who introduced them to the secretary of state. Smith shook hands with a whole line of officials and their wives and was on his way back to the cloakroom to retrieve his top hat in less than three minutes. He did not hide his irritation from his colleagues. "I casually observed that if I was ever governor and gave a reception to the legislature, it would be for members and their families only, so that they might receive the full attention of their host," Smith recalled in his autobiography. But the governor's reception was only one in a string of disappointments that would convince Smith that being an assemblyman was just another dead-end job.

The first inauspicious sign had been the caucus of Democratic members of the Assembly that met on Smith's first full day in the legislature. The Democratic Assembly leader, George M. Palmer, had given his troops a rousing speech about the rosy prospects of the Democratic Party in New York. In November, a Democrat, George B. McClellan, had defeated the reform mayor Seth Low. "The great metropolis of our State has been reclaimed, and Democracy is again in the ascendancy there," Palmer said. While it was true that the party had lost seats in the Assembly, Palmer pointed out that the Democrats were a majority of the voters "if our people will only come to the polls and vote their principles." "It is with confidence, then, that we may look for victory when the next political test is waged," he said. But Palmer's cheering words were at odds with the facts. Only 53 of the 150 members of the Assembly were Democrats in 1904. The 97 Republican assemblymen caucused in the Assembly chamber itself, while the Democrats fit comfortably in the Assembly parlor. The Republicans also controlled the Senate by a comfortable margin.

Republicans had dominated the legislature since 1896, when they elected 103 of the 150 members of the Assembly. In 1898 and 1899 the Republican majority slipped below 100, but William McKinley's landslide victory the next year restored their better than two-to-one advantage over the Democrats. The edge in the Senate was much smaller, but the Republicans had a secure majority there too. When Smith arrived in Albany, Republican rule was entering its eighth year and, despite Palmer's prediction, showed little prospect of being broken soon. Even if the Republicans lost the Senate, their control of the Assembly seemed unassailable. "So consistently have the Republicans controlled the Assembly since its membership was increased to 150 that it is a mooted question whether, as the districts are now erected, the Democrats will ever elect a majority," the *New York Times* correspondent in Albany observed in 1904.

Al Smith would serve in the New York Assembly for the next twelve years. During that period the Democrats would control the legislature twice and only for one year each time. At first glance, there is nothing surprising about this. The Republican Party had dominated the nation's politics since the Civil War. When Grover Cleveland was elected in 1884, he was the first Democratic president in over twenty years, and there would not be another until Woodrow Wilson in 1912. Historians have noted the fact that Smith spent almost his entire legislative career as a member of the minority and that the Republican Party was dominated by upstate conservatives who attempted to thwart the progressive measures he advocated after 1911. However, they have not paid enough attention to the fact that the Republican advantage was the consequence of an act of constitutional legerdemain intended to preserve the dominance of the Republican Party after it had lost the allegiance of a majority of New Yorkers. New York politics was not just highly partisan, it was undemocratic and corrupt. Consequently, it has not been understood that before Smith fought for factory safety, a limitation on the hours worked by women and children, and the other measures for which he is remembered, he battled to give Democrats the basic right of equal representation. Smith's struggle to make New York politics democratic would continue after he left the legislature, becoming one of the central themes of his governorship. It is also a key to understanding how he evaluated the New Deal. It is important, therefore, to look closely at how New York politics was practiced when Smith entered the legislature.

By 1894 it was becoming clear that the question was not if but when the Democrats would represent a majority of the state's residents. In the 1880s, five million immigrants had entered the United States to find jobs in the booming manufacturing industries. Most new factories were built in cities, so the immigrants settled there, spurring rapid urban growth all over the country. Nowhere was this process clearer than in New York. The state's rural population had begun to decline in the years after 1870. By 1880 New York and Brooklyn, which were then independent cities, contained 34 percent of the state's five million residents. Ten years later, their populations had grown to over three million, or 55 percent. The other cities of the state were growing almost as fast. The populations of Buffalo, Rochester, Syracuse, Utica, Yonkers, and Schenectady would all double or triple by 1910. This growth strengthened the Democrats, who had been far more successful than Republicans in recruiting the immigrants by defending them from nativist attack and providing material relief at a time when government accepted little responsibility for the poor.

The Republicans devised a solution for their problem during the 1894 New York State Constitutional Convention. The convention met during a time of financial crisis. A panic in 1893 had caused the bankruptcy of almost five hundred banks and more than 15,000 businesses. As unemployment surged, so did demands for government relief. Jacob Coxey, an Ohioan, announced that he would lead a march of the unemployed on Washington. Socialist Eugene Debs tied up railroads in the Midwest with a strike against the Pullman Car Company. To the Republican majority at the constitutional convention, it was only too obvious that socialism and other foreign ideas were being propagated by immigrant radicals in the nation's cities. The fear of radicalism provided a wonderful rationale for pushing through an apportionment scheme that effectively disenfranchised millions of New Yorkers who lived in urban areas. Under the proposal, the Assembly, presumably the more representative branch, became the cornerstone of rural domination. Because every county in the state would receive at least one Assembly member, no matter how small its population, upstate New York would have almost as many representatives as New York City. In 1910 this would mean that Republican counties with less than a third of the state's population had nearly the same voting strength as New York City, which contained more than half. Under the new system, as long as the Republicans could elect even a small number of assemblymen in the city, they would control the Assembly.

Challenged to defend the curb on the power of New York City, Henry J. Cookinham, a Republican from Utica, gave a remarkably candid reply. More power was reserved to rural voters because they were better people, he said.

> The average citizen in the rural district is superior in intelligence, superior in morality, superior in self-government, to the average citizen in the great cities. . . . [Y]our government will be better, your government will be safer in his hands than in the hands of the average citizen of the great cities.

The Democratic delegates protested the blatantly undemocratic plan that deprived them of almost any hope of controlling state government. "We of the minority will have little interest in the governing of the State thereafter," De Lancey Nicoll, a delegate from New York City, complained. "Our occupation will be gone. Those of us who do not like it can leave it." Almet F. Jenks of Brooklyn charged the Republicans with betraying the principles upon which the country had been founded. "There are men here whose sires fought for rights like these you brush away. There are men here who stood in battle for the freedom which you bind in chains of party gain," he said. But the convention adopted the amendment, and it was approved by the voters that fall.

The 1894 apportionment article accomplished its purpose. Over the next thirty years, the Democrats would capture control of both houses only in 1910 and 1912. The consequences were indisputable. In 1922 John Godfrey Saxe, a former Democratic member of the Assembly, said:

> Thirty years of Republican Assemblies means that the partisans who framed the Constitution, through the Assembly provisions alone, guaranteed to the Republican Party thirty years of Republican statutes, Republican policies, Republican patronage and thirty years of continuous pandering to the Republican vote. A Democratic Assembly is unconstitutional.

Writing a generation later, social scientist Gordon E. Baker was even more emphatic: "The state constitution of 1894 placed virtually permanent control of both houses in the upstate region."

The Republican domination of state government might have been less irksome to New York City Democrats if they had been able to govern the affairs of their municipality, but this was also denied them. Even the infamous Tammany boss William Marcy Tweed couldn't exercise absolute control during the 1860s. No New York City politician could aspire to so much power. The city's charter had been written by the legislature, and it reserved to the legislature so much control over city affairs that the residents lacked the ability to make crucial decisions affecting the future of their community. While Tammany usually controlled the vote in New York City and succeeded in electing the mayor and other officials, the Republicans in the legislature intervened to stymie its efforts to govern. In 1857 the legislature virtually took the city out of the hands of Tammany mayor Fernando Wood by creating state commissions to oversee the police, fire, and health departments and the construction of Central Park. The British Parliament passed fewer acts to regulate its empire between 1835 and 1850 than the New York legislature passed to regulate municipalities between 1867 and 1870. The legislature enacted more than 1,300 municipal laws in New York in the 1880s. The problem of legislative interference in municipal affairs grew so great that many reformers who were just as adamant in their opposition to Tammany Hall as rural legislators joined the call for home rule. The constitutional convention of 1894 made a token effort to address these complaints by giving mayors the right to veto legislation that affected their cities, but the legislature could override these vetoes by a simple majority. In essence, the mayor had gained only the right to protest his powerlessness.

The legislature had good reason to maintain its control of New York City: the Republicans had figured out a way to make it pay like a bank. In 1896 they used their newly secured control of the Assembly and Senate to pass the Raines law. Named for State Senator John Raines, an upstate Republican, the law overhauled the state system of liquor regulation. At the time, local governments issued liquor licenses and both set and collected the license fees. The Raines law abolished 964 local excise boards and placed the power for issuing licenses and setting fees in the hands of a commissioner appointed by the governor. To compensate the state for its new role of oversight, the law also gave it one-third of the license fee, which it hiked to an exorbitant $1,200. Support for temperance legislation was strong upstate, and one of the arguments for the bill was that it would reduce the consumption of alcohol, particularly in the intemperate cities. The bill also reenacted a ban on the sale of liquor on Sundays, which appealed to upstate moralists. Urban representatives saw it for what it was—a $12 million annual tax on the city.

While many upstate legislators saw the advantage to their constituents of imposing a new tax on urban areas, many of the supporters of the Raines law were sincere in their desire to uplift the urban masses. There was a long tradition in the New York legislature of enacting legislation to enforce morality in the city. The law banning the sale of liquor on Sundays had been on the books for thirty years. Applied as intended, it would have shut all the bars in the city on the only day of leisure in the urban laborer's week—and for that reason it was not applied as intended. Protestants and Catholics differed over Sunday observance. To Protestants, the sale of alcohol was only one of a number of activities that violated the commandment to keep the Sabbath holy. Performing nonreligious music and playing games on Sundays were also violations. Militant Protestants even wanted to stop the streetcars, trains, and mail steamers. In New York they prohibited both professional and amateur baseball games. While the Catholic church did not want to compete with secular recreations on Sunday mornings any more than the Protestants did, it did not prohibit its members from pursuing them after church. Consequently, every Sunday, the largely Catholic population of New York City broke the law by drinking in bars that should have been closed and playing games that were forbidden.

The interference of upstate Republicans in both the administration of New York City and the social life of its citizens was deeply resented. Senator George Washington Plunkitt is remembered today primarily as a result of the classic *Plunkitt of Tammany Hall*, a slim book produced by journalist William L. Riordan in 1905 to record the philosophy of one of Tammany's leading representatives. Plunkitt admitted that Tammany politicians accepted graft, although he insisted that they only took "honest graft," not the "dishonest graft" that came from saloon keepers, prostitutes, and gamblers who paid bribes for the right to break the law. Plunkitt was an Assembly district leader who saw nothing wrong with growing rich by exploiting inside knowledge. He wanted his epitaph to read, "George W. Plunkitt. He seen his opportunities, and he took 'em." Plunkitt was also one of the longest-serving members of the legislature when Al Smith arrived there. In *Plunkitt of Tammany Hall*, the senator exhausted his considerable creativity in finding comparisons to the relationship between New York City and upstate New York. To upstate New Yorkers, he maintained, residents of New York City were not citizens at all.

> The hayseeds think we are like the Indians to the National Government—that is, sort of wards of the State, who don't know how to look after ourselves and have to be taken care of by the Republicans of St. Lawrence, Ontario, and other backwoods counties. . . . They put on a sort of patronizing air, as much as to say, "These children are an awful lot of trouble." . . . And if you try to argue with them, they'll smile in a pitin' sort of way as if they were humorin' a spoiled child.

The motives of the Republican government were mainly mercenary, Plunkitt claimed. "It says right out in the open: 'New York City is a nice big fat Goose. Come along with your carvin' knives and have a slice,'" he said.

As a New York City resident and a Tammany man, Al Smith shared Plunkitt's resentment. The issue of home rule came up frequently in New York politics and was raised again within days of Smith's arrival in Albany. To the surprise of everyone, it was the Republican governor, Benjamin Odell, who broached the subject this time. Reportedly convinced that the people of New York and other cities believed themselves to be badly treated in Albany, the governor announced that he would hold a conference with Republican leaders to consider granting home rule. The announcement was so out of step with Republican practice that the newspaper reporters did not know what to make of it. They went to the Democratic leaders of the legislature for their reaction. "I cannot conceive of the Republican Party granting home rule to New York or any other city. . . . I don't believe the proposition is advanced in good faith," Senator Victor H. Dowling said. To call the governor's alleged bluff, Dowling introduced a bill repealing state regulation of liquor and special election rules that applied only to New York City. "It abolishes everything except the Harlem and the Bronx rivers and may be amended in that respect," a Tammany senator observed. Democratic skepticism was soon justified.

Senator Raines didn't even pretend to favor home rule, and the initiative died quietly shortly after.

It was not long before Al Smith discovered that whatever new celebrity he might enjoy in his neighborhood, in Albany there were few things lower than a freshman Democrat. Besides, he had no training to be a lawmaker. The legislature was changing. At one time a large number of representatives had been farmers. But there were only a dozen farmers in the Assembly of 1904. Lawyers were now the largest group, and many of the rest had been to college.

By mid-January the realities of his new position were apparent. The Republican Speaker of the Assembly had already announced that in order to find places for the new Republican members, he was reducing the number of Democrats on the legislative committees that carried on the work of the Assembly. The committees would include ten Republicans and only three Democrats. The Democratic leaders protested but were forced to parcel out their allotment. Because committee memberships were assigned on the basis of seniority, it appears that Al Smith had no committee assignments during his first year in the legislature. He sat with other freshmen Democrats in the last row of the Assembly, so far from the Speaker's desk that it was hard to distinguish them from the visitors milling in the lobby at the back. Nor did the Speaker go out of his way to meet the new Democratic members. When Smith did finally shake his hand, it was three and a half months later, shortly before adjournment.

What bothered Smith most was that he had no idea of what was going on. The complicated rules of procedure made it practically impossible for a newcomer to understand what was happening on the floor. At first, Smith took bills home to study. But the bills were framed as amendments to laws he didn't even know existed. Smith confessed his confusion to his roommate on several occasions. "I can tell a haddock from a hake by the look in its eye, but in 200 years I could not tell these things from a bale of hay," he told his roommate, Tom Caughlan.

The one thing that Smith excelled at was socializing. Service in the legislature was like a temporary return to bachelorhood, and the members were free to entertain themselves without any concern for checking in with wife and family at the end of the day. Albany did everything it could to assist them. Although city government was ruled by Republicans, it followed New York in giving virtually free rein to prostitution.

Carl H. Stubig, a former Albany newspaper reporter, claimed there were as many as 1,200 prostitutes working in the city, including 400 streetwalkers. Stubig may have been exaggerating—this would be an astronomical number for a town of Albany's size. Nevertheless, there were so many brothels in one part of town that it became known as "the Tenderloin." While the ready availability of prostitutes may have fluttered the hearts of rural legislators, they were nothing new to someone who had grown up in the Fourth Ward. Smith was never known as a frequenter of brothels. In fact, there has been no hint of his ever committing a sexual indiscretion. A devout Catholic, he appears to have absorbed his church's teaching on the importance of sexual self-discipline.

But if Smith abjured brothels, he loved bars. Saloons were one of the centers of social life in New York, and he visited them regularly. He may have started as young as fifteen, when he took his first full-time job. This is when he started smoking cigars, and it is not hard to believe that he began drinking beer at the same age. Although by contemporary standards Smith was only an adolescent, he was shouldering the responsibilities of an adult and probably leaped at the chance to demonstrate his manliness. Saloons also offered male companionship to a young man who had lost his father at twelve and who was surrounded by women at home. The habits of drinking and smoking would stay with Smith for the rest of his life. Cigars became a part of his daily routine. Later in life when expense was no obstacle, Smith smoked as many as twelve to fifteen per day, and it was rare to see him without one. One of the earliest portraits of Assemblyman Smith shows him in top hat and tails with a cigar clamped between his teeth.

By the time Smith reached Albany, the saloon had become his stage. He loved singing popular songs, though the sound he made was not very musical. His voice was deep and powerful. Perhaps as the result of so many cigars, it sounded as if it had been poured through gravel. It was also slightly nasal. But there was no one better at telling stories. His campaign biographers noted that, like the best performers on the Bowery stage, he could mimic all of the accents heard on the Lower East Side: "[H]e has stories today that involve long stretches of the kind of Neapolitan Italian heard on the East Side. Naturally, in the character sketches and anecdotes involving his own nationality and its fascinating brogue, he is at his best. He knows enough Yiddish to picture Jewish characters with vividness." The good times that Smith spent in the Albany bars brought at least some consolation for the many hours of confusion and disappointment that he experienced during his first year in the legislature.

Smith was not so discouraged that he rejected renomination in the fall. Confident of his reelection, he cast his ballot on Election Day and then returned home to Peck Slip, where movers were waiting with a horse and wagon to relocate the Smith family to 28 Oliver Street. There were five Smiths now, including the baby, Catherine, who had been born in April, but they would have the entire third floor to themselves. Smith's confidence in his election was entirely justified: he was returned to the legislature by an even larger majority than the year before.

Smith returned to Albany to confront the same dismal situation. The Democrats remained a hopeless minority, and their inability to control the circumstances under which liquor was sold in New York City symbolized their impotence. At first, Tammany had been alone in its opposition to the ban on Sunday liquor sales, but after the turn of the century, even many reformers began to recognize that the prohibition was doing more harm than good. In 1901 William Travers Jerome, a candidate for district attorney on the reform ticket, pointed out that the rampant corruption in New York City life had much to do with efforts to enforce laws against Sunday sale of liquor, gambling, and prostitution that were for the most part unenforceable. It was inevitable that most policemen would accept bribes to look the other way.

Corruption was not the worst consequence of upstate control of liquor. Far from having advanced the cause of morality, the Raines law had actually contributed to a spreading epidemic of sexual vice. While it had continued the general ban on the Sunday sale of alcoholic beverages, the law had made an exception for hotels of more than ten rooms, which were allowed to sell liquor in their restaurants. What was a logical exemption on its face soon became a nightmare, as nearly every bar in town attempted to convert itself into a hotel. Unfortunately, the people who rented the closet-sized rooms that were created in back rooms and upper stories of the bar were prostitutes. The Raines law "hotels" spread prostitution to almost every city block and even to prestigious restaurant-bars like Lüchow's. "If there is such a thing as hell, it is right here in New York," the Rev. Lee W. Beattie of Madison Square Church House observed.

By 1905 the problem of the Raines law hotels had grown so severe that New York City reformers joined together to demand that it be amended. They carried to the legislature a bill that would require Raines law hotels to be fireproof. The city already had an ordinance requiring hotels of more than three stories to be fireproof, but the application of this requirement to small hotels entailed so much added expense that it was expected to put the phony Raines law hotels out of business. When the bill reached the Senate floor, it provided Tammany senator Thomas Grady with an opportunity to excoriate the Raines law as a whole. The law had not only spread prostitution, it had caused the suicides of saloon keepers who had been put out of business by its high license fees, Grady said. But the debate only measured the vast difference between the Democrats and the Republicans in New York State. Senator Raines was unmoved. The death of saloon keepers was a good thing, he said. "Was it not better that they should take their own lives than continue to drive others to destruction?" he asked. Raines refused to take any responsibility for the evil consequences of his law. The legislature did adopt the bill applying stricter building standards to the Raines law hotels, which helped to put them out of business. It refused to learn the lesson, however, that errors could be prevented by letting the people of New York City adopt the laws and regulations that affected them on a daily basis.

When the 1905 session opened, Al Smith still wished that the whole, puzzling mess that was the Assembly would suddenly make sense. He hoped to be assigned to committees where he would find work that he could understand, but his appointment to the Committee on Banks and the Committee on Public Lands and Forestry only underlined his ignorance. "I knew nothing about banking laws and had never been in a bank except to serve a jury notice, and I had never seen a forest," Smith said later. Smith was convinced that he had made a mistake. After the session ended, he began to think about quitting the Assembly. In the summer he met Tom Foley for breakfast at a downtown restaurant to discuss the future. Foley was convinced that Smith should return to Albany. Foley knew that Smith had a large ego, and he exploited it. He talked about the position that the Assembly job gave him in the neighborhood and challenged Smith to prove that he was smarter than the average Tammany man. After thinking about it for several weeks, Smith agreed to run again. "I just hated the idea that I should have to admit there was anything I could not understand," he explained.

Smith resolved to be more serious and systematic in his approach to learning his job. "I worked very hard during the winter of 1906," he recalled. "By working hard I mean to say that I went back to the Capitol at night and devoted every minute of my time to a study of what was taking place." He was developing an approach to knowledge that would guide him for the rest of his life. As the light of understanding came on during those nights at the Capitol and his understanding of the state's legislative and political history grew, Smith became convinced that the first step to solving any problem was to get "the facts." Later, he would become well known for insisting, "Let's look at the record." His commitment to inductive reasoning meant that he would try to consider every problem objectively, free of any ideology that might obstruct the solution.

Implicit in Smith's approach was a distrust of theory. "I would sooner have a short shakehand with the fellow who knows how to do it than listen for a week to the fellow who knows how to tell you what the trouble is," he would say later. He discovered that there was no need to feel inferior to the members of the legislature who had attended college. The important question was not where did you go to college, it was how much did you know. Several years later, Smith gently mocked some of his college-educated brethren who had interrupted an Assembly debate to discuss sporting results:

> Mr. Wende said, "Mr. Speaker, I have just heard that Cornell won the boat race." Merritt said, "That doesn't mean anything to me. I'm a Yale man." Hammond said, "It doesn't mean anything to me. I'm a Harvard man." Phillips said, "It doesn't mean anything to me. I am a U. of M. man." I was all alone, the only one of the quartet left standing, so I said, "It doesn't mean anything to me because I am an F.F.M. man." Assemblyman Hoey shouted out, "What is that, Al?" I said, "Fulton Fish Market. Let's proceed with the debate."

Once the FFM graduate felt that he was competing on an equal footing with the other members of the legislature, there were no more thoughts of retirement.

Meanwhile, dramatic changes were about to rock New York State politics, opening undreamed-of possibilities to Smith and his party. After decades of rapid and unregulated economic growth, the United States was being forced to confront the consequences. New voices were decrying the problems of an industrial and urban society. In 1902 journalist Lincoln Steffens, on assignment for *McClure's*, one of the many new magazines that appealed to an urban middle class, began a tour of major American cities in an attempt to explain the corruption he found there. What Steffens discovered was that corruption was not confined to any particular class. Steffens called his series *The Shame of the Cities* because he believed that the people themselves had become corrupt through their selfish desire to enjoy privileges at the expense of others. This intensely self-critical spirit was soon being applied by other journalists, who set themselves the task of examining every American institution with the objective of exposing whatever was evil. They would be called "muckrakers" by President Theodore Roosevelt, who was irritated by the ceaseless criticism. The muckrakers, however, were critically important in identifying the problems that Roosevelt and other politicians, working at all levels of government, would work to eliminate over the next ten years.

In New York, the Progressive era began in 1905 with a series of exposures of corruption in the gas and insurance industries. In New York City, the Consolidated Gas Company had succeeded in obtaining a monopoly on the sale of gas, which was still the primary means of lighting the city's streets, businesses, and homes. Everyone suspected that the company was overcharging for gas, covering its tracks with dishonest bookkeeping that inflated production costs. But it was only after a legislative committee was appointed to investigate the subject in the spring of 1905 that the suspicion was confirmed. During six weeks of hearings in New York City's aldermanic chamber, Charles Evans Hughes, the committee counsel, proved that Consolidated Gas was charging a rate that was at least 25 percent more than could be justified by its costs. (He also showed that Consolidated Gas had secured control of the New York Edison Company and was charging four times more for electricity than it cost to produce.) Hughes recommended that the legislature immediately reduce the cost of gas and create a commission to regulate utility rates.

The New York gas investigation produced a great deal of public indignation, but the inquiry into the insurance industry conducted later in the year was a national sensation. In 1904 Thomas W. Lawson, a prominent stock speculator, began a series of stories in *Collier's* that revealed how John D. Rockefeller and a handful of millionaire financiers had gained control of much of the country's industry by placing men loyal to them on the boards of directors of the leading companies. Once in control, the financiers gained access to hundreds of millions of dollars to which they had no right. Besides paying themselves high salaries, these men, whom Lawson called "the System," used shareholders' money to invest in risky speculations that they hoped would pay them a fortune but that, as often as not, cost the public everything they had invested. What was shocking was Lawson's claim that the System had extended its control into the insurance industry and that it was speculating in funds that were supposed to be conservatively invested so that they would be available to pay claims. Every American who owned an insurance policy felt threatened by the exposures of Lawson and the journalists who followed up his revelations. They demanded a government investigation.

Since the three largest insurance companies in the country were New York corporations, it was natural that the investigation would be conducted there. Once again, Hughes was enlisted as the counsel for a legislative investigative committee. Throughout the fall of 1905, he called the leaders of the insurance industry to the chamber of the New York City Board of Aldermen, where they revealed that company executives routinely overpaid themselves and were not averse to tax evasion when they could get away with it. The insurance companies had engaged in political corruption as well. Hughes showed that the insurance companies had been paying bribes to influence legislation and taxation in most of the states throughout the nation. In New York, Mutual Life operated a "house of mirth" where key legislators lived during the legislative session and where less critical men were entertained at the appropriate time. Former Republican boss Thomas Platt testified that the insurance companies had given his party large campaign contributions to ensure its cooperation.

The gas and insurance investigations shook the New York political order to its core. The voters were outraged at leaders who had allowed the gas companies to rob them and the insurance companies to undermine their financial security. The first manifestation of this anger came in the 1905 elections, when candidates of a new party, the Municipal Ownership League, challenged members of the Assembly and Senate who had not moved swiftly enough to enact Hughes's recommendations for solving the gas problem. Newspaper publisher William Randolph Hearst, a candidate for mayor of New York and an advocate of public ownership of utilities, charged Tammany with being a tool of Consolidated Gas, and was nearly elected. It was the Republican Party, however, that was most vulnerable to attack. To protect itself, it nominated Charles Evans Hughes for governor in 1906. Hughes ran on a platform that promised to follow Theodore Roosevelt's policy of using the state to regulate corporations in the public interest. To bar a repetition of the gas industry abuses, he said he would seek a law to regulate all public utility corporations. On Election Day, the voters showed their gratitude to Hughes, but defeated every other Republican candidate on the state ticket. Progressivism had been launched in New York.

At first, it did not seem that the Democratic Party would benefit from the burgeoning spirit of reform. Like reformers before them, most progressives were instinctively hostile to political machines. It was the nature of machines to try to compromise the conflicts that existed in the political realm, which made them defenders of a status quo that encompassed great injustices. Everyone knew that Tammany Democrats in Albany were often guilty of cutting deals with Republicans that hurt the public interest. Tammany also received large campaign contributions from the Consolidated Gas Company, making it hard for people to believe that it could ever support meaningful reform of the gas industry. This skepticism was vindicated in the 1905 legislative session, when Tammany Democrats in the Senate joined Republicans in killing a bill that would have cut gas rates. Reformers targeted members of both parties for revenge. The Democratic Party could not succeed without Tammany, but in an era of reform Tammany appeared to be an insuperable obstacle to the party's success.

But the struggle between reformers and conservatives suddenly made politics a lot more interesting than it had been for many years. When Al Smith had arrived in Albany, the most important proposal in Governor Odell's annual message had concerned improvements to the state's canals. As important as canal improvements may have been to economic life, they could hardly compare in interest to the subject of utility regulation. In addition, the conflict in the Republican Party helped new, more liberal leaders to emerge. In October 1905 the death of Assembly Speaker Louis Nixon gave Republican reformers an opportunity to name their own man to lead the Assembly. The new Speaker, James W. Wadsworth, Jr., immediately began modernizing the rules of the Assembly, simplifying the legislative process that Al Smith and many others found so baffling.

It was Wadsworth who gave Smith his first break in the legislature. The men couldn't have been more different. Wadsworth came from one of the biggest landholding families in western New York, and he was the latest representative of a political dynasty. Nevertheless, they became friends, and Speaker Wadsworth was determined to help Smith. "Everybody in the Assembly knew that, potentially, he was the ablest Democrat from the City of New York," Wadsworth explained. Wadsworth violated protocol to appoint Smith to the Committee on Insurance, which was drafting legislation implementing the governor's recommendations for regulating the insurance industry. Smith was thrilled to be dealing with one of the hottest political subjects of the day and one that concerned many of his constituents. Not content merely to help frame the legislation that Hughes had requested, Smith would later introduce his own bill to provide safeguards against "pools, trusts, conspiracies or agreements to control fire insurance rates." By the end of the session, he believed that he had made a breakthrough. "I felt that I had made so much headway in that winter that I was eager for renomination," he said. The Citizens Union, a reform group that rated the performance of legislators, agreed. In 1905 the Union had dismissed Smith as "inconspicuous." In 1906 it called him "intelligent and active, somewhat about [sic] average of machine man."

Smith widened his activities during the 1907 session, when he was appointed to the Committee on Cities, a committee with direct impact on New York City affairs. By this time, he understood the keys to success for a member of the minority party. On the one hand, he poured on the charm to win the hearts of the Republicans. Beverly Robinson, a Republican from New York City, met Smith when he entered the Assembly and became chairman of the cities committee in 1907. Like the Assembly as a whole, the cities committee was dominated by Republicans. Ten of its thirteen members were Republicans and could easily have ignored the minority members if one of the three men had not been Al Smith. Robinson recalled, "We would have our executive sessions on Tuesday evening and on Thursday evening. Al would tell funny stories and entertain the Committee. If he'd been amusing enough, then just to keep him in good humor, we would report some little personal bill that he wanted—never anything with politics in it, that was out and he knew it—he knew too much to ask for it."

Yet Smith did more than clown. "[F]rom the very beginning Al Smith impressed me as having one of the greatest powers of clear statement of any man I ever listened to," Robinson said. "We might get into a long wrangle in the Committee involving all sorts of up-state, down-state politics and what not. After Al Smith had listened to us for about ten minutes he would break in and say, 'Now if youse'll let me, I'll [tell] you what it is all about.' In a few brief sentences he'd sketch the whole situation for us and then we'd go ahead and do business." Robinson learned that despite his charm, Al Smith had to be watched. As he became more skillful, he became more dangerous. Smith soon joined two other Democrats on Robinson's "black list." Every Monday, he would check the Legislative Index to see whether these men had introduced any bills over the weekend when nobody was looking. If they had, Robinson would alert the chairman of the relevant committee to bottle up the bill until it could be checked.

Smith was not just active behind the scenes. He was finally beginning to speak out in the Assembly itself. As a member of the cities committee, he was well informed on bills that would make changes in the New York City Charter, and he spoke up whenever these came to the floor. Because debates were not recorded, there is no complete record of what Smith said, but it seems certain that he would have strongly opposed the bill introduced that year creating a commission to write a new charter for New York. The Democrats did not oppose the idea of a new charter: everyone agreed that the existing document was badly out of date. But the legislation gave the Republican governor the power to appoint the members of the commission.

Smith also spoke out against the legislature's refusal to permit the people of New York City to play baseball on Sundays. At a time when Sunday was the only day off for most people, the ban on baseball was odious among city dwellers who longed to play and watch the game. Two bills were introduced by New York City Democrats in 1907 to change the law. Rallies were organized in support of the bills, including one in a Brooklyn theater that featured speeches by the borough president, controller, and district attorney. Many of the amateur baseball clubs were represented by their teams in uniform, including one that entered behind its own marching band. At a hearing in Albany the next day, the sponsors of the baseball bills argued that baseball was a moral and healthful activity. But they were followed by Protestant ministers from New York, Rochester, Buffalo, and Albany who spoke against Sunday baseball. The Catholic archbishop of New York sent a message in which he joined the Protestants in opposing it. Although Smith was not a leader in the campaign to legalize baseball on Sundays, he did speak out for it on the floor. It was better for boys to be at the ballpark than "be driven to places where they play 'Waltz Me Around Again, Willie,' " Smith said. The opposition of the Protestant clergy was decisive for the upstate Republicans.

Although the Assembly chamber increasingly rang with Smith's denunciations of the Republicans, after work he continued to pour on the charm. It was at about this time that Smith began inviting Republicans to a weekly dinner that he hosted at Keeler's Restaurant, an Albany institution famous for the freshness of its seafood and the elegance of its decor. During these bibulous meals, Smith established lifelong friendships with some of the leading members of the Republican Party. Smith's dinners at Keeler's may have also given rise to a personal trademark. Owner William Keeler later claimed that he had been the first to suggest that Smith put aside the black derby worn by most city men and wear a brown one to set himself apart. Smith reportedly told Keeler that he would have to buy it, and the restaurateur purchased one from a London hatmaker. Smith liked the message—that he was a city man with a difference—and the brown derby became his everyday hat.

The young legislator's growing confidence in Albany was mirrored by the increasing security of his position in his district. As long as he had Tom Foley's support, Smith had no serious concerns about his reelection. The downtown wards, which were composed of the city's poorest residents, were the strongest Democratic districts in the city. They remained Tammany's strong right arm even as the Irish and Germans who had formerly dominated there moved further north in Manhattan or into Brooklyn and were succeeded by the "new" immigrants from eastern and southern Europe. Smith worked hard to hold the support of the older groups and to earn the allegiance of the newcomers. Beverly Robinson remembered that Smith worked out of an office downtown. Robinson was amazed that the office could keep track of Smith as he traveled nearly ceaselessly from one event to the next.

I discovered that Al Smith had a regular evening mapped out. Every time he left his place somebody knew exactly where to go and where to reach him—knew his telephone number and everything else. I could always reach him at any hour of the day or night that I wanted. That was part of his job. How he stood it I don't know. He'd go to these political dinners and then a party afterwards and get home, God knows what hour in the morning.

Republicans could communicate by letter or through newspapers. For Democrats, there was no substitute for physical contact. Showing up, whether at a political dinner, a wake, or a bar mitzvah, was tangible proof that a legislator cared. (It was because he understood the importance of symbolism so well—and because the Italians in his district were becoming so numerous—that Smith would introduce a bill the next year establishing a state holiday in recognition of Columbus on October 12.) By the end of the 1907 legislative session, "I had so well established myself that renominations came practically as a matter of course," Smith said.

As Smith became more prominent, even some reformers began to praise the Tammany man. In 1907 the Citizens Union acknowledged Smith's "increased ability" and called him "one of the best Democratic representatives from New York." Laurence Veiller of the Charity Organization Society had been won over by Smith's role in the legislative investigation of the lower criminal courts in New York City. Smith was a member of the commission that recommended a complete overhaul of the lower court system. Everyone could see that the courts were overburdened, but the commission went beyond a mere expansion of the courts to change the way that the system operated. It recommended the creation of a night court for women that could deal with the problem of prostitution in a more systematic and humane manner. The commission also advocated a new court for domestic relations and changes that would offer probation to a greater number of offenders. In short, the politicians endorsed the reformers' goal of a criminal justice system that treated criminals like human beings. At the same time, they sought to curb the abuses of civil rights the commission had uncovered by sharply limiting the number of people who could be jailed for minor offenses and reducing the number of summonses issued by the courts by over 60 percent. But this was not the only pleasant surprise for Veiller and the other reformers, for once the commission had issued its report, the commissioners who were members of the legislature became the leaders in the fight for the changes and were instrumental in their enactment. "The Republican leaders said, 'If Al Page stands for this, it must be all right'; and the Tammany leaders said, 'If Tom Grady and Al Smith agree, why we will go along with them, sure.'" After the court reform had been approved, Veiller admitted he had been wrong to oppose the appointment of the Tammany men. "As it turned out, it was the best thing that could have happened," he said.

Even so, the reformers never forgot that Smith was a machine man. Their goal was to break the power of men like Boss Murphy and to return power to the people, and they knew that when the time came Smith would join with conservatives in the Republican Party to oppose them. The moment arrived in 1909, when Governor Hughes introduced a direct primary bill late in the legislative session. Reformers had long advocated the direct primary as the antidote to machine rule. They believed that the key to the political boss's power lay in his ability to choose the candidates for public office. Elected officials took orders from the boss because he had made them and he could unmake them just as quickly. Under a direct primary system, candidates for office were placed on the ballot by petition. Theoretically, they owed their election to no one but the people and would vote only as public interest dictated. The direct primary was not just a reform; it was the reform that would make all other reforms possible. Machine politicians could not stand idly by as the reformers passed a measure that would certainly undermine party discipline. This was something on which both Democrats and Republicans agreed. When the direct primary bill was introduced in March, its prospects were dim.

Hughes clearly had a problem in the Assembly. It was reported that Speaker Wadsworth was anxious to adjourn as quickly as possible so that Hughes would not have time to introduce his bill. Although the governor was able to submit the bill, he could count on the support of neither the Republicans nor the Democrats. In its coverage of the situation, the *New York Herald* announced the ascendancy of a new leader among the Assembly Democrats:

> [W]ithin the last week or two some of the New Yorkers and a few upstate men have been grumbling that the Speaker and a small clique, in which were Ray B. Smith, the Assembly clerk, "Al"

Smith, a Democrat from New York—no relative of the clerk's—
and one or two chairmen of important committees, absolutely
were dominating the Assembly. "Al" Smith, sometimes called the
"Bowery statesman," easily is the strong man in the Democratic
ranks in the Assembly, as he has been for three years, regardless of
the so-called majority leader.

The legislature adjourned without acting on Hughes's primary bill. The
Citizens Union reacted angrily to Smith's new role, and began to take
back the nice things it had said about him the year before. Smith's opposition to the primary bill was unforgivable. Smith "made one of the worst
records of the session, consistently voting against public interest on important issues and misusing his much increased influence," the Committee on Legislation concluded in its 1909 report.

Before the fight over the Hughes primary bill became serious, however, New York was rocked by new revelations of political corruption in
the Republican Party. Two Republican assemblymen were accused of
taking bribes, and in March 1910 the superintendent of insurance announced that he was extending an investigation of legislative corruption
that had already proved that the Republican lieutenant governor had received $150,000 in bribes.

These scandals completed the process of discrediting the conservatives who dominated the Republican Party—a process that had begun six
years earlier with the utility and insurance scandals. The reformers assembled a program to take control, which involved electing one of their
own to replace the Senate leader, removing the state chairman, and extending the investigation of corruption. But the conservatives remained
powerful, and they successfully fought off almost all of the reformers' ini-
tiatives. Governor Hughes, who had been fighting the party regulars since
1907, now despaired. Although there were calls throughout the state for
him to run for a third term, he was determined to leave politics. In January 1910 President Taft had asked him if he would like to be appointed to
the U.S. Supreme Court, and he had responded enthusiastically. On
April 25 Hughes announced that he was planning to resign. Both sides
recognized that the cause of reform had received a potentially lethal
blow.

But the battle over the direct primary wasn't finished. Although the bill that Hughes supported was defeated in both the Assembly and the Senate in May, the vote was close enough to encourage the governor to reach an accommodation with the Senate leader. Despite efforts by Republican conservatives, the compromise bill was approved and sent to the Assembly. Speaker Wadsworth remained resolute in his opposition to all primary legislation, however, and the Assembly rejected the Senate bill and adjourned. While the wrath of the reformers was directed primarily at the Republican majority, the Democrats did not escape chastisement. In the Senate, they had cooperated with the conservatives to try to block the compromise bill, and in the Assembly they had voted with their Republican colleagues to send the primary down to defeat. When Hughes called the legislature into special session to force reconsideration of the issue, Assembly Democrats were loud in their denunciations. Assemblyman James Oliver, also known as Paradise Park Jimmie, called the primary a plot against Tammany. Like personal registration and other election reforms, it was intended to reduce the legitimate vote of New York City. "They tell us that his bill is in the interest of pure elections," Oliver said. "Well, if that is the case, they want pure elections in only half of the State."

Al Smith was prominent in the debate on the last day of the special session. He gave the governor the back of his hand. "The present occupant of the Executive Chamber has never received the approval of the people of the city of New York," Smith said. Smith had come a long way from his early days in Albany. He had fully assimilated his role as a spokesman for the Democratic minority in Albany. Yet his accomplishments had won him no points among reformers. In its review of the 1910 session, the Citizens Union acknowledged that Smith was an "experienced and effective legislator." But he had "voted and worked against the public interest on important issues" and was an "opponent of primary and election reform." It called for his defeat. Far from opening a door to future advancement, success as a Tammany legislator seemed to bar Smith from entering the mainstream of New York politics.

# 4  ❃  DOING GOOD

On a late January day in 1911, Al Smith and Robert Wagner, the new leaders of the New York legislature, found themselves at the front door of a large house a few blocks from the Capitol in Albany. Franklin Delano Roosevelt, the new senator from Dutchess County, was paying a fortune for the place: the rent was more than three times the salary of a state legislator. Smith and Wagner had come to see Roosevelt about party business. Like them, he was a Democrat. But as they stood waiting for someone to answer the doorbell, they must have wondered what they could have in common with a Democrat who lived like a king. The door was opened by a butler. "Senator Wagner and Assemblyman Smith to see Senator Roosevelt," Wagner announced. The butler hesitated. "I know the Senator is expecting Senator Wagner," he explained. Smith laughed. "That's all right, I'll come along, too," he said. Years later, Smith and his family would recall with amusement the story of the butler who tried to block the entrance of the Assembly majority leader. But the social differences that separated the Tammany men from Roosevelt and the upstate Democrats were no laughing matter at the time. They had plunged the party into civil war.

Things had seemed so promising for the Democrats only a short time before. In the summer of 1910, Theodore Roosevelt had returned from an African safari and made a speech that was widely interpreted as an attack on the policies of his handpicked successor, William Howard Taft. Roosevelt's speech helped widen the growing rift between Republican liberals and conservatives, and the party had stumbled badly in the midterm elections in the fall, losing control of the U.S. House of Representatives for the first time in sixteen years. While the Republicans retained control of the U.S. Senate, which they had virtually owned for thirty years, the Democrats made progress in state and local elections across the country. They elected twenty-six governors, including Woodrow Wilson of New Jersey, who two years later would become only the second Democratic president since the Civil War. In New York, the Republicans were soundly beaten as the Democrats captured both houses of the legislature and elected their candidate for governor. The triumph was particularly sweet because most members of the U.S. Senate were still elected by the state legislatures, and the new legislature would have the opportunity to send a Democrat to Washington.

The 1910 elections were particularly good news for Tammany Hall. It drew its strength from the immigrants who had been pouring into New York City since the 1840s, and immigration hit its peak during the first decade of the twentieth century, when nearly one million immigrants arrived each year. Some 942,000 of them had settled in New York City since 1900, swelling the population to nearly five million. The 1910 elections cut the Republican delegation from New York City in half, sending five more Tammany men to the Senate and sixteen to the Assembly. As a result, Tammany could claim credit for winning twenty-one of the twenty-nine new Democratic seats. Even a determined foe like the *New York Times* agreed that Tammany had earned the right to lead the legislature. "It would be impracticable and unfair to try to ignore it," the *Times* said.

The Tammany leader, Charles Francis Murphy, however, knew just how difficult it was going to be for his organization to lead the Democratic Party. Murphy himself was a symbol of what was wrong with Tammany. He had risen to power in Tammany in the traditional way. Born in an East Side neighborhood that was also home to the massive and smelly natural gas tanks that lit the streets and homes of the city, Murphy rose from poverty to become a millionaire on the strength of his physical prowess, his shrewd business sense, and his political connections. He capitalized on his popularity as the leader of a local sports team to open a saloon. When this was successful, he opened two more. It was only then that he turned to politics and won election as an Assembly district leader.

But Murphy's style was diametrically opposed to that of earlier Tammany bosses. There was nothing crude or bombastic about him. He was clean-shaven, and his wardrobe consisted of immaculate business suits that he wore even on weekends. "His voice was the lowest and gentlest I have ever known a man to have," recalled Smith's daughter, Emily Smith Warner. Murphy was also reputed to be puritanical in his personal habits. "I would have just as soon thought of telling an off-color story to a lady as I would to Murphy," a Tammany colleague said. But Murphy's most distinguishing trait was his silence. In 1911 a reporter experienced the frustration of trying to drag answers from "Silent Charlie":

> "After the failure to-day of the first move for settlement of the Senatorial fight do you not regard the election of Mr. Sheehan as impossible?" the Tammany boss was asked. Mr. Murphy seemed to think deeply for a moment. "Repeat the question," he urged. When this was done the Tammany leader shook his head gravely and said: "I do not." "In the event of Mr. Sheehan's failure to withdraw and with the insurgents standing intact, when and how do you believe there will be a choice?" "I will not answer that tonight," said the Tammany chieftain.

Murphy was the shrewdest leader in Tammany's history. He came to power in 1902 as part of a triumvirate of men appointed to succeed Richard Croker. Tammany was near rock-bottom in terms of its influence, and the Progressive era was just getting under way. Murphy recognized that Tammany had to change to have any hope of remaining competitive. Soon after he shook off his partners in the triumvirate and became the sole Tammany leader in 1903, Murphy began distancing himself from previous Tammany bosses. He made it clear that he would not stand for what George Washington Plunkitt called "dishonest graft" — bribes received for protecting gamblers and prostitutes. Even William Travers Jerome, the Manhattan district attorney who had been a thorn in Tammany's side for many years, credited Murphy's good intentions.

Murphy understood that Tammany was not strong enough to really control the legislature. Although New York City was represented by eighty-seven assemblymen and senators, fewer than half of them were Tammany men. Despite the 1910 landslide, seventeen of the city's representatives were Republicans. Twenty-four of the seventy Democrats were from Brooklyn and were not directly under Murphy's control. If the Brooklyn boss differed with the Tammany chief, Tammany had a maximum of forty-one votes. "Kings [County], by combining with upstate Democrats, can sit on Tammany at any time," the *New York Times* reported. Most troubling of all, there was a small group of upstate Democrats who were openly hostile to the machine. Led by a wealthy manufacturer, Thomas Mott Osborne, the upstate Democrats had formed a Democratic League for the explicit purpose of checking the growth of Tammany's power. Members of the League who had been elected to the legislature were biding their time, waiting for Tammany's first misstep.

Even before the opening of the new legislature, Murphy made overtures to Osborne and other suspicious Democrats. In June 1910 he had agreed to the appointment of John A. Dix, a member of the Democratic League, as state party chairman. Later, at the state convention, where he controlled more than half of the delegates, he agreed to support for governor any candidate endorsed by the upstate men and remained good to his word when the man turned out to be Dix. Yet not even these concessions prepared Tammany's critics for Murphy's decision to choose a new Democratic leader in the Senate. In the weeks after the election, they had been moaning over the imminent promotion of Tammany's most veteran legislator, Senator Thomas Grady. His long tenure there coincided with the years when political corruption had been at its peak. Murphy agreed with the reformers that Grady had to go. When the Democrats met, they selected Robert F. Wagner as the new Senate leader. Wagner's family had emigrated to the United States from Germany when he was a boy, and he had worked his way through City College and law school. Although he had entered politics as a Tammany man, his record was clean. "The decision to throw over Senator Grady . . . is splendid," Franklin Roosevelt wrote in his diary. Wagner would be "fairly good," he added. "He has good intentions; the only obstacle is the pressure of his own machine."

Al Smith could only have felt some regret as he sat in the caucus that elected the new president of the Senate. Grady had taken Smith under his wing after his first disappointing years in Albany. But Smith knew that Wagner's promotion was good politics. Electing Wagner demonstrated the Democratic Party's commitment to making a record that would earn the confidence of the voters. Smith was elected the Assembly majority leader for the same reason. It would not be easy being Tammany's main point of contact with the upstate Democrats in the Assembly, but Smith knew what was expected and announced that his first act would be to call for the appointment of a committee to determine how the rules of the Assembly could be changed to shorten the long and expensive sessions of recent years. "The business of the House should be expedited and economy effected," Smith said. "The Democracy wants to make good."

Murphy had promoted Smith and Wagner because they were young men with clean records who would be able to work with Tammany's critics in the party. But when it came to his next big test, the choice of a new U.S. senator, he found himself unable to identify an acceptable compromise. The new senator from New York was going to be a very powerful figure. If Democratic strength continued to grow and a Democrat was elected president in 1912, the senator might control all of the federal patronage in the state, thereby gaining the power to determine which faction would rule the New York Democratic Party. Murphy did not like either of the leading candidates. Independent Democrats rallied around the candidacy of Edward Shepard, an attorney for the Pennsylvania Rail Road and a resident of Brooklyn. Murphy knew that even if Tammany supported Shepard, he owed his candidacy to Tammany's enemies and could be expected to side with them. But he hesitated before endorsing the other leading contender, William Sheehan. Sheehan had been the boss of the Democratic organization in Buffalo and was fully capable of using his position in the U.S. Senate to build up a machine of his own and kick Murphy out. But, lacking the votes to push through the nomination of any candidate he really liked, Murphy decided he had no choice but to back Sheehan.

Tammany's opponents were outraged when Murphy announced his endorsement on January 11, 1911. Upstate Democrats refused to accept a man who had been a relentless foe of their hero, Grover Cleveland, another Buffalo man. Independent Democrats in New York City were revolted by the prospect of a senator who had been the beneficiary of many corrupt deals. The *New York Times* blasted Murphy:

> For years men devoted to the principles of the Democratic Party have been driven to vote for Republican candidates because in so many States and cities coarse, tough, ignorant men have become

Democratic leaders, habitually inviting to their councils and raising to the offices only men more ignorant and less worthy than
themselves, while excluding brains and respectability from the
service of their party. . . . It is a monstrous travesty of politics that
Charles F. Murphy should have anything whatever to say about
the choice of a Senator.

What infuriated Tammany's critics most was that they seemed powerless
to stop the election of Sheehan. The senator would be chosen by a caucus of the Democratic members of the legislature, and Tammany's support gave Sheehan a majority of the votes. By party tradition, the vote of
the caucus bound all those participating to vote for the candidate who received a majority. The only way to defeat Sheehan would be to persuade
a significant minority of legislators to boycott the caucus and leave themselves free to vote for other candidates when the legislature met, depriving him of a majority. During the days leading up to the caucus, the
opposition to Sheehan continued to grow. When the Democrats finally
met on January 16, the caucus did endorse Sheehan, but a small group of
upstate legislators was missing when the vote was taken. "[T]he votes of
those who represent the people should not be smothered in the caucus,"
the rebels wrote in their manifesto. Tammany's critics were thrilled.
"Never in the history of Albany have 21 men threatened such total ruin of
machine plans. It is the most humanly interesting political fight in many
years," wrote Louis Howe, the Albany correspondent of the *New York Herald*. No legislative business was conducted for two and a half months.
"Gradually the struggle grew into one of the most relentless in the history
of the Legislature," wrote Roosevelt biographer Ernest K. Lindley. "For ten
weeks the small band of novices was subjected to every variety of pressure
and every stratagem known to some of the most resourceful politicians and
one of the most powerful political organizations the country has known."
    Howe saw the Sheehan fight in terms of the Progressive struggle
against bossism, but there was another way of looking at it. Murphy,
Smith, and Wagner believed that they were entitled to elect a senator
who would be responsive to the needs of urban Democrats, who made up
the overwhelming majority of party members. The refusal of a small
group of upstate men to accept their choice was a rejection of the democratic process. Like the electoral hurdles that denied New York City Dem-

ocrats a fair share of power at the state level, it deprived them of equal rights. In addition, the fact that Sheehan was a Catholic made many suspect that religious prejudice was playing a role. Although the story of the Sheehan fight has been told many times, it merits retelling from Tammany's point of view. It also reveals how Franklin D. Roosevelt's first political battle left him with a reputation as a bigoted elitist.

Roosevelt was the perfect spokesman for the rebels. Most of them were obscure members of the Assembly. Although the new state senator from Dutchess County was also unknown, the Roosevelt name instantly attracted attention. The reporters rushed to quote him after the insurgents had issued their statement with its oblique reference to efforts to dictate to the legislature by "someone outside the legislature." Roosevelt drove the point home. They were opposing the "boss rule system," he said. Roosevelt was good copy, and only days later the *New York Times* published a profile of him in its Sunday magazine. He was tall and handsome. "Those who looked closely at the lawmaker behind Desk 26 saw a young man with the finely chiseled features of a Roman patrician only with a ruddier glow of health on it. . . . [H]e could make a fortune on the stage and set the matinee girl's heart throbbing," it reported, almost breathlessly. He was a little too handsome for some tastes. A cousin recalled that she and her friends referred to Roosevelt as the "handkerchief box young man" because he resembled the pretty men whose faces adorned ladies' tissues boxes at the time. Roosevelt's aristocratic good looks were reinforced by a habit of tossing his head. "This, combined with his pince-nez and great height, gave him the appearance of looking down his nose at most people," recalled Frances Perkins, who was then a lobbyist in Albany.

Roosevelt's opposition to Tammany was a natural extension of his birthplace, religion, and class. If their fortune was not the biggest, the Roosevelts enjoyed the highest social status. Franklin Roosevelt grew up in the shadow of two of the oldest and "best" families in the country. The Roosevelts had emigrated to New York when it was still New Holland and had made their fortune selling Manhattan real estate and engaging in other trade. Sara Delano, Franklin's mother, believed her family was even more distinguished. They had also arrived during the colonial period and had grown rich in the China trade. (Their high social standing was not hurt by the fact that it was opium they had offered in trade for Chinese goods.)

The Roosevelts had every comfort. The family's Hyde Park estate, Springwood, included 110 acres that rose steeply from the Hudson to bluffs with a breathtaking view of the river. The manor house was not as spectacular as the neoclassical Vanderbilt mansion next door, but it had seventeen rooms and a full staff of servants. Close by lay James Roosevelt's stables, which he had built to accommodate the fine horses that were one of his passions. The rest of the land was divided between fields tended by tenant farmers and forest. There was also a townhouse in New York City and a summer house on Campobello Island in Maine, a sixty-foot yacht with crew, and a private railroad car. Finally, there were the long sojourns abroad in England and Germany, where the Roosevelts felt very much at home.

Roosevelt's election to the Senate had been a surprise. His district was primarily rural and traditionally Republican. But unlike Smith seven years earlier, Roosevelt found many friends waiting for him when he arrived in Albany. Franklin's father, James, had been a strong supporter of Grover Cleveland, so much so that when Cleveland was elected president, James visited him in the White House. He even took five-year-old Franklin with him on one trip. The new governor, John A. Dix, was a Cleveland man and an old friend of Roosevelt's father. Franklin and Eleanor paid a formal call on Dix on the day of his inauguration. Later in the day the governor telephoned to invite the young couple to the Executive Mansion for some informal dancing. "Accordingly, E.R. and I hurriedly dressed, drove up and had a delightful evening. It was almost a family party, only the military aides, two or three Albany girls and ourselves being there," Roosevelt reported. The next evening, the Roosevelts dined with the governor and some other of James Roosevelt's old friends.

But it was neither Franklin's looks nor his social connections that attracted attention: it was Theodore Roosevelt. The two were not close relations, although the connection had grown closer when Franklin married Theodore's niece, Eleanor. It didn't matter. The former president of the United States was one of the most beloved figures of his age, and he was never far from the thoughts of the New York Times reporter who interviewed Franklin for a January 22 profile. The reporter, W. A. Warn, wrote that Franklin did not seem much like his uncle. "It is safe to predict that the African jungle never will resound with the crack of Franklin D. Roosevelt's rifle." But there was a strong kinship. "[T]he Democratic Roosevelt . . . resemble[s] his more illustrious relative and

Republican namesake in a natural bent for bringing down big game." Franklin knew his part and played it to the hilt. He had arranged to meet Warn in the lobby of the Ten Eyck Hotel, which the insurgents used as their headquarters before moving meetings to the library of the Roosevelt home. "Shoot away quick. I must be back with my friends in about five minutes," he said. He wasted no time in declaring that he had Tammany in his sights. "There is nothing to gain by the Democratic Party through an alliance between Tammany Hall and the up-State Democrats until the character of the leadership in the Tammany organization has changed," Roosevelt said. "The control by Tammany Hall of the State Democracy will stand under present conditions as an insurmountable obstacle in the way of party success." Yet the Tammany boss was not unhappy. Murphy seemed almost as relieved as the insurgents when Sheehan failed to capture the senatorship. He sent Wagner to see Roosevelt and get a clarification of the motives of the insurgents. Were they mainly opposed to Sheehan and therefore willing to join Tammany in the search for a candidate who was mutually acceptable? Or was the insurgency a declaration of war against Tammany itself?

Smith and Wagner's report on their meeting with Roosevelt seems to have encouraged Murphy. He met with Roosevelt himself on January 30, two weeks after the caucus. Murphy showed no irritation with the young man, who was celebrating his twenty-ninth birthday. According to Roosevelt's later report, Murphy displayed "a delightful smile." "I know I can't make you change your mind unless you want to change it," Murphy said. "Is there any chance of you and the other 20 men coming around to vote for Sheehan?" Roosevelt said there was no chance: Sheehan was opposed by "a great many of our Democratic constituents" and was "too closely connected with the traction trust in New York City." Murphy pronounced himself satisfied that the opposition to Sheehan was "perfectly honest" and said he was ready to search for a compromise candidate. But Sheehan would have to be persuaded to withdraw before they could discuss alternatives. Murphy asked Roosevelt to meet with Sheehan and tell him that his cause was hopeless. Roosevelt agreed and invited Sheehan to dinner, where he tried to impress him with the impossibility of his position. Sheehan refused to quit, but it wasn't his stubbornness alone that prevented a resolution of the impasse for another two months. After Sheehan finally withdrew at the end of February, the insurgents appeared unwilling to consider any candidate who had a connection to Tammany, and Murphy changed his mind about the honesty of their motives. After two months of impasse, Murphy became convinced that religious bigotry lay behind their opposition.

The existence of anti-Catholic prejudice among upper-class Democrats was undeniable. Raymond Moley, a political scientist at Columbia University in the 1920s and later the organizer of Roosevelt's "Brain Trust," observed:

> Those who called themselves the better people of New York have always had mixed reasons for opposing Tammany. The reasons which they do not express are that Tammany suggests alien ancestry, religious affiliations antagonistic to those of most native Americans, and generally the "lower" and poorer element. The reasons expressed are the corruption, the misgovernment and the autocracy of the machine. These latter evils are not to be minimized. The former, however, are important and pervasive.

For James Roosevelt, Franklin's father, the influx of large numbers of poor immigrants into their party had been a disaster that was only partly compensated for by its rapid growth. At a time when Irish servants were common in the homes of the upper class, James refused to hire the people he called "Paddys." According to his brother, "Germans and Scandinavians [were] highly thought of; Irishmen rejected; blacks not considered." Prejudice in these homes was not the exception but the rule. Even Eleanor Roosevelt, who became an outspoken opponent of intolerance, was affected by anti-immigrant prejudice. When Franklin entered Columbia Law School, she wrote to inquire about his impressions. "I am anxious to hear about your first day and whether you found any old acquaintances or had only Jew Gentlemen to work with," she said. After Franklin entered the legislature, Eleanor became acquainted with Senator Thomas Grady, whom she found "very charming in spite of the fact that he likes his Irish liquor somewhat too well."

Franklin Roosevelt was smart enough to refrain from racial or religious slurs, but he didn't hide the contempt he felt for his colleagues in the legislature. In his *New York Times* profile, he said he was hoping for a revolution in politics led by young and ambitious men. Al Smith and

Robert Wagner were both, but they were not exactly the kind of men that Roosevelt was seeking. Roosevelt wanted a coup led by the young men like him. In an interview later in 1911, he made it very clear that he was not looking to the big cities but to the hinterland for his recruits:

> I might almost say that the political salvation of the country lies with the country men and boys. . . . The lives of your city people are artificial. . . . From just such [country men] who think and argue over national political matters comes the material that makes our best lawmakers and who in time will see to it that only the men that will serve the people wholeheartedly and unreservedly will be elected to office.

In celebrating the virtues of rural life, Roosevelt was echoing Thomas Jefferson, who had praised the farmer as the ideal citizen because of his independence and had expressed fear that the growth of cities would create an impoverished class that could be manipulated by men of wealth. Tammany was a symbol of everything that Jefferson had warned against.

While the insurgents insisted that they were attacking "the boss rule system," they were accused of anti-Catholic bigotry from the beginning. A reporter asked Roosevelt to reply to the charge on the day after the caucus. "This is absolutely untrue," he said. Five days later, bigotry became the issue again when he was forced to explain why anti-Catholic literature had been seen on his desk. The material had come in the mail, and he had dumped it in the wastebasket, he said. The sender obviously believed that religion was the underlying issue. So did some Catholics. Two weeks after the caucus, the bishop of Syracuse weighed in against the insurgents. "Why is the business of our legislature obstructed by the unseemly and unreasoning quarrel now going on about the election of the United States Senator?" the Rev. P. A. Ludden asked in a statement released to the newspapers. The answer was simple. "Bigotry and the old spirit of Knownothingism. Neither is yet dead and both are very much alive, although poorly and only transparently disguised," he said. Bishop Ludden was a man of extreme views. At one time or another he had condemned the Knights of Columbus, the mayor of Syracuse, millionaires, secret societies, public schools, Jews—even Santa Claus. But when he

talked about politics, the bishop expressed a sense of grievance that many
Catholics shared:

> I don't know exactly what the Tammany Democracy means in
> contradistinction to others of the State Democracy, but I do know
> that without the Democrats of the great city of New York the other
> Democrats of the State couldn't elect a single State official, great
> or little. The real meaning of the opposition led by the Osbornes
> and others against New York Democrats led by Murphy is . . .
> "You are an Irishman and that's agin you; you are a Catholic and
> that's agin you, and your name is Murphy."

Roosevelt was distressed when the insurgents met on January 26, the day
Ludden's remarks were published. "Gentlemen, this is a most uncalled
for and most unfortunate incident," he said.

At the end of March, Murphy shocked everyone by personally attacking the rebels. He insisted that it was not Tammany's endorsement of
Sheehan that had started the fight. It had begun before that. "[T]he party
was scarcely in power before a campaign of slander was begun against
those who were responsible for the victory," he said. He accused "two or
three" New York City newspapers of leading a crusade "to see that no
member of the regular Democracy could be elected to the Senatorship."
There were two reasons for the insurgency, Murphy said. One was very
obvious. The insurgents had been willing enough to participate in the
caucus before the Sheehan nomination. Why had they suddenly attacked
it? "Is it that Mr. Shepard and his friends only want to play when they are
sure that they are to win?" Murphy asked. "Their criticism of Tammany
Hall is beside the point. It is the old resort of the loser." But the second
reason was hidden beneath their rhetoric:

> No literary skill, no finished compliments to himself, no self-
> issued certificate of devotion to Democratic principles, no
> sophistry of any kind can conceal from the plain Democrats of the
> State the fact that in this fight Mr. Shepard is fighting with the
> minority to overthrow the rule of the majority and to defeat
> the party's nominee for some reason so un-American and un-
> Democratic that he does not dare even to avow it.

For Murphy and his supporters, only religious bigotry could explain behavior that was "so un-American and un-Democratic."

The insurgency collapsed two weeks later. After two and a half
months of deadlock, the legislators were restless: they were accustomed to
spending only three days a week in Albany during the legislative session,
but the necessity of being present for each of the votes on the senatorship
meant they had to stay in Albany all week. They were ready to bolt at a
moment's notice. On March 29, a fire in the Assembly chamber increased the pressure for adjournment to the breaking point. Faced with
the added burden of meeting in the crowded City Hall, even some of the
insurgents began to waver. They finally agreed to vote for a man who was
acceptable to Murphy when Smith and Wagner promised that there
would be no reprisals against them.

The insurgents had been outmaneuvered by Murphy. Sheehan was
gone, and Murphy had selected James O'Gorman, a Tammany man, for
the job. The rebels had been snookered, observed Chauncey Depew, the
outgoing senator. "The insurgents had said they would never take an
Irishman; that they would never take a Catholic, and that they would
never take a Tammany man. And they took one of the most popular and
active Irish Catholics in New York, a President of the Catholic Society
and a Grand Sachem of Tammany Hall." When the rebels entered Albany City Hall to elect O'Gorman, the Tammany men greeted them by
singing the Tammany fight song.

The election of O'Gorman was a hollow victory, however. What Murphy saw as a struggle for majority rights and religious equality, Tammany's
enemies portrayed as a battle to limit the power of an autocratic machine.
They were so successful that the New York controversy was credited with
hurrying the enactment of the amendment to the U.S. Constitution that
provided for the direct election of senators. Ten weeks of bad publicity
had confirmed the popular view of Murphy as a boss who was no different from Tweed and his successors.

Smith's first months of leadership had been a terrible disappointment.
For seven years he had been a member of the minority. This had bred a
deep resentment that surfaced even when he tried to pay the majority a
compliment. "I pick up ideas from the back country fellows," Smith said
during an interview early in his career. "They don't have a hell of a lot to
think about when they are at home and their thinking is generally pretty

straight and to the point." Smith's chauvinism was in part a response to the Republicans' abuse of power, though he almost immediately added that he didn't blame them for using power to "benefit their own communities in a legitimate way." The 1911 rebellion showed that upstate Democrats were just as unwilling as Republicans to work together with New York City Democrats. Smith tried hard to work out a compromise with the insurgent Democrats, even clarifying the rules of the caucus when not doing so would have meant an early victory for him. Nevertheless, Smith's support of Sheehan was criticized by the Citizens Union. While the group praised Smith for developing "considerable ability in floor leadership and real capacity for public service," it thought he showed "not the slightest evidence of independence." As long as reform and machine elements remained at odds, the Democratic Party in New York had no hope of providing the leadership that would earn the confidence of the voters and make it a real force in state politics. It would take a tragedy to force political change.

On March 25, 1911, four days before the fire in the chamber of the New York Assembly, a fire at the Triangle Shirtwaist Company took the lives of 146 workers in New York City. One hundred twenty-five of the 146 dead were girls and young women. They were immigrants— Italians, Russians, Hungarians, and Germans—most unable to speak English. Many of the women were the main support of their families, and their deaths left their survivors on the brink of economic disaster. But it was the drama of the fire itself that stuck in the minds of most people. It struck within minutes of the close of business at 4:45 p.m. on a Saturday. Many of the workers had already changed into street clothes and were about to leave when the fire broke out. Beginning on the eighth floor, it had spread rapidly, feeding on scraps of the thin lawn cloth used to make shirtwaists. As the room filled with smoke and flame, many employees made their way to the windows facing the street. With the fire catching at her clothes, a woman leaped. Soon others followed, jumping alone or in pairs, their arms wrapped around each other. Many spent long minutes watching before they were forced to jump. Twelve minutes passed before the final body fell. Sixty-two had plunged to their deaths.

The inability of the fire department to reach the victims with its ladders was a symbol of the inadequacy of the safety precautions. Although the Asch Building, which housed the Triangle company on its top three floors, was only ten stories high, the longest ladder in the New York Fire Department reached seven stories. Regulations required fire exits and a fire escape, but some of the exits were locked at the time of the fire. When they were accessible, the stairways were too narrow. The fire escape collapsed under the weight of too many women, throwing them to their deaths, some onto the iron spikes of a fence below. The fire hoses in the building didn't work. Safety nets had broken under the impact of the smallest victim. Some bodies struck so hard that they broke the pavement, falling into the basement of the building.

On Wednesday, April 5, no one worked in the factory sections of New York City. Several days before, hundreds of youths had distributed handbills in English, Yiddish, and Italian asking workers to "join in rendering a last tribute of sympathy and affection" to the victims of the Triangle disaster. There had already been several large protest meetings and demonstrations of outrage over the lack of adequate safety precautions that had led to the tragedy, but the April 5 march was the simplest and most eloquent demonstration. Under lowering skies, marchers gathered at two assembly points, downtown at Seward Park on the Lower East Side and uptown at the intersection of Fourth Avenue and Twenty-second Street. At 1:30 p.m. the downtown contingent stepped off, led by an empty hearse drawn by six white horses. On both sides of the hearse marched eight girls in mourning dresses, followed by the Triangle employees who had managed to escape and the relatives of those who had been killed. Marching north, they met the uptown contingent on its southern course at Washington Square, a block west of the Asch Building.

By the time the marchers reached Washington Square, their number had risen to between 80,000 and 120,000, and it had begun to rain. There were no speeches. Instead, the hearse headed up Fifth Avenue for the final leg of the march to Madison Square. The marchers wore buttons and carried banners that proclaimed "We Mourn Our Loss." A couple of muffled drums provided the only accompaniment. As the rain poured from clouds that obscured the tops of the surrounding buildings, observers were struck by the determination of the marchers. "I fear that pneumonia will claim more victims than the fire," a doctor standing near his ambulance told a *New York World* reporter. The reporter observed, "It seemed that three-fifths of those who plodded in the line were women, old, young girls of tender age. Most of them were bare-headed; not one in

50 carried an umbrella; the street mud oozed through their thin shoes, they marched on, silent, uncomplaining. More than 200,000 watched from the sidewalks."

The fire weighed heavily on the conscience of New Yorkers. In October 1909, the Triangle workers had gone out on strike, led by the fledgling International Ladies Garment Workers Union. Their strike surprised the city, which was unaccustomed to seeing immigrant Jewish and Italian women working together. It gave heart to other garment workers, and the strike spread to the entire industry. While many in the city were sympathetic, the power of government was turned against the strikers. The police took no action to stop professional strikebreakers, who used prostitutes and other agents provocateurs to start fights with picketing union members. Instead, they moved in to restore order, recording more than seven hundred arrests of union members. Nevertheless, three months after the strike began, the union scored a major victory, signing contracts with 354 employers. The employees of the Triangle were not among the beneficiaries, however. They returned to work without achieving their demands, including an agreement to keep the fire doors unlocked during working hours and to upgrade the fire escape.

Rose Schneiderman, an organizer for the Women's Trade Union League and a leader of the strike at the Triangle, measured the city's collective guilt at a protest meeting at Carnegie Hall on April 2. Schneiderman had been born into a poor family and had learned trade unionism in classes organized by the garment unions. She had listened as some of the city's leading citizens expounded on the guilt of greedy capitalists and indifferent public officials. She was the first person who could speak for the workers. As the small woman stood on the large stage, her fiery red hair held in a bun beneath her hat, she had difficulty overcoming her emotion. The audience strained to hear her.

We have tried you citizens: we are trying you now, and you have a couple of dollars for the sorrowing mothers and brothers and sisters by way of a charity gift. But every time the workers come out in the only way they know to protest against conditions which are unbearable the strong hand of the law is allowed to press down heavily upon us. . . . I can't talk fellowship to you who are gathered here. Too much blood has been spilled. I know from my experience that it is up to the working people to save themselves. The only way they can save themselves is by a strong working-class movement.

It was true that no one seemed to care about the workers' problems. Neither the Republicans, whose strength came from the rural regions upstate, nor the Democrats with their urban constituency advocated strengthening the power of government to control the conditions of factory workers. They were much more concerned about the fight for power than they were about the question of using the power of government to help workers. Even within the Democratic Party, the split between self-styled "progressives" like Roosevelt and "machine" men like Smith had little to do with differences over the role of government. Everyone agreed that government should not interfere in the relationship between the employer and his employees.

In January 1910 Frances Perkins, a thirty-year-old graduate of Mount Holyoke College, went to Albany as a lobbyist for the Consumers' League, charged with the responsibility of winning passage of a bill to limit the hours that women and children could work to fifty-four per week. As she was being shown around the Assembly chamber by a representative of the Citizens Union, she got her first sight of Al Smith, who sat reading while the politicians around him chatted. "That's what he does," the lobbyist explained. "He's reading the bills introduced last night." Another reformer, the representative of the City Club, called Smith over to meet Perkins. After she explained her mission, Smith gave her some advice. "Jackson's got your bill. It's still in committee and not moving very fast. Better ask for a hearing," he said.

Perkins succeeded in getting committee hearings in both the Assembly and the Senate. In the Assembly, she was able to make a full exposition of her case because Smith was a member of the committee and asked her many searching questions. In the Senate, though, the questioning was perfunctory. Although she had commitments from a majority of legislators in both houses, neither of the committees reported the bill. Perkins went to Smith for an explanation. "You're in favor of the bill. Can't you give me some assurance it will be voted on?" she asked. Smith hesitated. "Now, I'm going to tell you something. You have to be very careful. You mustn't repeat this. . . . The bill isn't going to be passed or reported this year." Shocked, Perkins reminded Smith that the Democratic Party had pledged itself to the measure at its last convention. "Yeah, but that don't mean anything," Smith replied. He explained:

> That was for the front. That sounded good because the Republicans didn't have any such thing. Your people agitated enough. Some of them got it introduced. The Democrats couldn't vote against it, and so they voted for it. Do you know who one of the big contributors to the Democratic fund is? It's the Huyler Candy Factory. They're great friends of Mr. Murphy's, and they live right down there near him.

Perkins couldn't believe it. She canceled a European trip to stay and fight for the bill, but Smith was right.

A year later, she returned to Albany as a member of the Committee of Safety, a group that was seeking the appointment of a blue-ribbon panel to recommend legislation that would prevent the recurrence of a tragedy like the Triangle fire. After talking to the state's leaders, some of the committee members may have concluded that Rose Schneiderman was right. Governor Dix, an upstate manufacturer, had referred them to Smith and Wagner, who tried to talk them into accepting a legislative investigation. Perkins trusted Smith. She had been told that he had been deeply moved when he talked about the tragedy to fellow legislators on the train back to Albany on the day after the fire. So she listened as he tried to persuade the committee to accept a legislative investigation: "These fellows in the Assembly are good men at heart. They don't want people to burn up in factories. They just don't know anything about how to prevent it, and they don't really believe that there is any hazard until you show them. And they'll be more impressed if it is shown them by their own commission and own members." Smith could point to the success of the commission to reform the lower courts as proof. In the end, the committee accepted a commission chaired by Wagner. Smith would be the vice-chairman.

When Smith spoke of the ignorance of working conditions among the members of the legislature, he was referring to upstate men, but the truth was that he and his urban colleagues did not know much more. They were certainly aware that people labored in appalling conditions in city sweatshops, but they did not have a thorough knowledge of conditions around the state. No one did. At a time when the state labor department did not even keep track of the number of factories, even reformers lacked the information they needed to form opinions on all of the problems that confronted factory workers. As an investigator for the commission, Perkins and the rest of the staff made sure the members of the commission saw everything. At a candy factory in Buffalo, Perkins watched as Smith climbed to a window that was marked as a fire escape. Crawling through pipes that blocked the window, he found that there was no ladder from the window to the ground. It was through experiences like these that Smith and Wagner "got a firsthand look at industrial and labor conditions, and from that look they never recovered," Perkins said.

Although the Triangle fire had focused attention on the issue of fire safety, the Factory Investigating Commission had received a broad mandate to investigate working conditions. At the same Buffalo candy factory, while other commission members occupied the attention of the factory manager, Smith slipped away to interview some of the workers. The manager had acknowledged that the hours were long—in the rush season, eleven or twelve hours a day, seven days a week—but he had stoutly denied that the factory employed children. The employees told Smith a different story: children without working papers were regularly employed, they said. At a rope factory in Auburn, Smith and Perkins watched an early-morning shift change. As women left the plant, they passed the men on their way in for the day shift. Some stopped to kiss their husbands. Smith was offended. "It's uncivilized," he told Perkins. They followed one of the women home and interviewed her. The woman, whose husband worked days, admitted that the arrangement was hard on her family. "It's almost impossible for the whole family to do things together," she said. But there was no alternative: wages were so low that she and her husband had to work long hours just to maintain themselves. Smith read the same desperation in the rapid work of the women shucking peas in a cannery that he visited on a surprise inspection at 4 a.m. Working beside them were a dozen children between the ages of five and twelve. A manager insisted that the children were not employed: their mothers had brought them because there was no one at home to care for them; the mothers had given them peas to keep them occupied.

Evidence piled up. The Factory Investigating Commission visited over 1,800 factories during the first year. The commission members held public hearings in New York City, Buffalo, Rochester, Syracuse, Utica, Schenectady, and Troy. At the twenty-two hearings held during the first year, they examined 222 witnesses. The work of the commission would continue for another four years. By the end, it had recommended over thirty new laws that strengthened the factory safety codes. One of the most important reforms was to place responsibility for the enforcement of these laws on the state government, eliminating the overlap in jurisdictions with local governments that had undermined the effectiveness of existing laws. The commission also pressed for laws to curtail child labor and to reduce the hours that women could be required to work.

The most controversial recommendation of the Factory Investigating Commission was to create a board to set minimum wages for women workers. The idea of a minimum wage was opposed not only by business but by many in the labor movement, including Samuel Gompers, the head of the American Federation of Labor. Gompers distrusted government almost as much as business and preferred to see wages set by collective bargaining. As a member of the Factory Investigating Commission, he balked at the proposal, but Smith was able to change his mind by persuading him to look at it as a health issue.

The Factory Investigating Commission is generally credited with having pioneered a new approach to the problems created by industrialization. In the future, government, which had been relegated to the sidelines in accordance with the doctrine of laissez-faire economics, would be expected to play an active role in protecting the health and safety of its citizens, even when this entailed limiting the rights of property owners. Some historians trace a direct line of descent from the reforms of the Factory Investigating Commission to the programs of the New Deal, which expanded the power of government beyond the regulation of industrial conditions and paved the way toward social security. Smith took the lead in defending this new approach. Sometimes he used biblical precedent to justify the new ways. When the canning industry attempted to win exemption from a law requiring it to give employees Sundays off, Smith had a one-sentence rejoinder: "There is a Commandment which says, 'Remember The Sabbath Day to Keep It Holy,' but I am unable to find any language in it that says 'except in the canneries.' "

By 1913 the Democrats seemed to have regained the ground they had lost after the Sheehan debacle. The 1912 elections had witnessed Democratic gains across the nation and the election of Woodrow Wilson, the first Democratic president in nearly a generation. In New York, the Democrats had regained control of the legislature, and a new Democratic governor, William Sulzer, had been elected. For Smith, things could hardly have gone better. Only seven years after he had told Tom Foley that he wanted to quit the legislature, he had been elected Speaker of the Assembly. Smith's daughter, Emily, remembered being present in the Assembly on the first day of the session. She was only eleven at the time and uncertain why the whole family was present. As she watched men walking up to her father to congratulate him, she began to understand. "[A]mong all the hundreds of people who were present, it was Father who was at the center of what was going on," she recalled. There was no ceremony to be observed. The Speaker did not take an oath of office. But with his mother, wife, and children looking on, Smith made the most of his first official act. "And how clearly I remember the loudness and sharpness of the sound when he raised the gavel and quickly brought it down, calling the Assembly to order," Emily said. It was a proud moment. Smith had achieved what he believed was "the peak of my political prominence."

The party was still divided between Tammany and its critics, however. Encouraged by Wilson's success in standing up to the political bosses during his term as governor of New Jersey, the party reformers were more determined than ever to wipe out the blight of "Murphyism." Within months of his inauguration, Governor Sulzer challenged Tammany, and the factions of the Democratic Party were once again at war.

Sulzer was a logical choice for governor. Although a member of Tammany, he had developed a liberal record during eighteen years representing the Lower East Side in Congress. Still, Murphy had misgivings when he endorsed Sulzer. Sulzer had been trying to win the Democratic nomination for governor for years, and both Croker and Murphy had refused to support him. They recognized in Sulzer a man whose ambition might lead him to turn against Tammany when it served his interests. There was also something disingenuous about the new governor, who liked to be called "Plain Bill" and presented himself as "a man of the people." Mr. Dooley, the fictional Irish bartender created by Finley Peter Dunne, called Sulzer "a man who has to blow his nose ivry time he thinks iv the trouble iv others." Al Smith found the governor crude. Sulzer chewed tobacco and, during a meeting with Smith and reformer Robert Binkerd, frequently used a spittoon next to his desk. "Al Smith was sitting right alongside of this spitton [*sic*] with his legs crossed," Binkerd recalled. "I think Sulzer shot at that spitton at least 20 times during our interview. Every time he did Al Smith would move his foot and look over at me as if to say, 'The ———!' " But Sulzer's greatest weakness was his vanity. It took a levelheaded man to steer the party at a time when it was so divided. Tammany's demands for recognition were met by cries of defiance by upstate Democrats and most New York City newspapers. Sulzer was besieged by reformers, who urged him to lead them in the fight against bossism and battered him when he seemed to be compromising with Tammany.

Three months after his inauguration, Sulzer declared war on Tammany. His weapon was a primary bill that was so extreme in form that it appeared to threaten the leadership in both parties. The Democrats had approved a limited form of the primary two years before. Under the compromise primary bill that had finally passed in 1911, only local candidates ran in primaries and the ballots displayed which men had the support of the local party committee. Statewide candidates were still chosen in conventions. One of the provisions that the Democrats had rejected was the elimination of the party emblem as a way of indicating which candidate was preferred by the party. In 1913 the reformers sought everything they had failed to get two years before. They wanted a primary that would extend to all elected offices and that would bar the party boss from indicating his preferences and prevent candidates from using party money to run their campaigns. They also demanded again that party emblems be barred from the ballot. For two and a half months, Governor Sulzer led the campaign for the primary. "He hopes that by using it he will be able to gain control of the Democratic Party in the State of New York," one of his supporters said.

Sometime in the spring, Boss Murphy decided that Sulzer had become such a threat that he would have to be removed from office. Smith tried to change his mind. He had never liked Sulzer and had not supported his nomination, but his impeachment would be viewed as a political act, one more example of Tammany's determination to use brute force to attain its ends. When Murphy refused to change his mind, Smith was forced to launch an investigation that revealed that the governor had been guilty of diverting campaign funds for his own use. When Sulzer was asked about it, he lied and made efforts to cover up his crime. As a result, he was impeached by the Assembly in August and brought to trial before the Senate and the members of the state's Court of Appeals. He was removed from office by a vote of forty-two to twelve with two abstentions. While Sulzer's impeachment was politically motivated, there was no question about the truth of the charges. Nine of the ten judges from the Court of Appeals voted to remove him, and the lone dissenter voted for him on a technicality.

Al Smith could only have felt terrible frustration at the end of the 1913 term. The legislative session should have been a triumph for Tammany. The Democrats had passed most of the remaining legislation recommended by the Factory Investigating Commission, as well as a workmen's compensation act. Tammany had helped give New York the most progressive labor laws in the country, but the impeachment of Sulzer allowed Tammany's enemies to portray the fight as another round in the battle of the people against the bosses. Sulzer's guilt or innocence was irrelevant in his removal, they charged. His crime was defiance of Murphy. "William Sulzer was impeached by Murphy's Assembly not for what he had done, but for what he refused to do," the World said. The first signs of danger for Tammany came in the September primaries upstate, where pro-Sulzer candidates defeated "organization" men in county after county. In Buffalo, the leaders who had allied themselves with Murphy saw their mayoral candidate and four of their assemblymen defeated by Democratic "progressives." The alliance with the Buffalo leaders was the cornerstone of Murphy's power over the New York State Democratic Party, and the defeat of the organization men there threatened to limit Tammany's influence to south of the Bronx county line. But Murphy had a much more serious worry. It seemed that he was about to lose control of New York City as well.

At home, Murphy confronted a strong fusion movement behind mayoral candidate John Purroy Mitchel, an independent Democrat. Making matters worse was Plain Bill Sulzer. Although he had been removed from office, Sulzer had escaped criminal charges and was running for the Assembly in the Sixth Assembly District. Sulzer had sworn that he would defeat the men who had removed him, and on November 1, he carried his fight into the heart of the Second Assembly District to attack Smith.

Standing on the steps of the Progressive Club within sight of the Downtown Democratic Club, Sulzer had considerable trouble getting his speech started. First, fire engines arrived on the scene, and Sulzer was forced to wait while the firemen looked for a fire. "My friends, this is a Tom Foley false alarm," Sulzer cried. When the fire engines finally left, Sulzer started again, only to be interrupted a second time as twenty-five large firecrackers were set off. Then a parade for Edward McCall, the Democratic candidate for mayor, tried to march through the crowd that had gathered on Madison Street. When Sulzer finally got the chance to speak, he blamed his opponents for the disruptions. "Al Smith and Tom Foley think they can break up this meeting, but they can't do it," he said. Soon a wagon with a McCall sign began to drive in circles through the crowd, but Sulzer pressed on. "I could not continue to be Governor because I would not do what Murphy wanted me to do. If I done [sic] what Murphy wanted me to do, Al Smith and Tom Foley would be patting me on the back and would be saying that I was the greatest Governor the state ever had. I would rather be right than be Governor." A few more large firecrackers exploded. "These bombs ain't scaring me," Sulzer insisted. He continued: "To be the people's man, I am content, and no boss will ever rule me, and before I get through, I will destroy bossism in the State. . . . Tammany Hall, in Murphy, is not a political organization. Tammany Hall is nothing but a gang that makes it their business to loot the treasury."

There were more interruptions, including a few eggs hurled at the speaker's platform, where there was some ducking. Later, the streetcars appeared to be running more frequently than normal, making it hard for Sulzer to be heard over the grinding of wheels and the clanging of bells. Nevertheless, he spoke for about forty minutes before going into the club and giving another speech. On the way out, he again encountered the crowd, which appeared even less friendly than before. When it looked like he was going to make another speech, some men began yelling insults. Sulzer changed his mind and began to leave. Catcalls and other rude remarks followed him as his car edged its way through the crowd. "Say Bill," a young boy yelled. "You are as welcome down here as a dose of the clap."

Sulzer was no coward, however, and he invaded Smith's turf again. Jonah Goldstein, a young man from the neighborhood who worked for

Smith in the legislature, remembered accompanying his boss to a meeting that Sulzer was addressing at the Madison House Settlement. It was Goldstein who had persuaded Smith to attend the meeting. Jonah had been participating in activities at the settlement house since he was a boy, and he believed that Smith should be present to give his side of the story. "I remember that we walked up to Madison Street and started to go up to the Madison House Settlement, and we could hear Sulzer's voice, 'and Murphy rules the world like a czar!' " Goldstein thought this was the first time Smith had ever visited a settlement house. At first this seems surprising. Settlement houses had first appeared in the city's poor neighborhoods in the 1890s, when middle-class reformers decided that the only way to become familiar with the causes of poverty was to live among the poor. The houses had since become major neighborhood institutions by offering educational and recreational activities. Most settlement workers, however, were hostile to political machines. Some, like Henry Moskowitz, the head of Madison House, had made opposition to Tammany a major element of their activities. As Smith ventured into Madison House for the first time, he must have felt that he was entering enemy territory.

The election results seemed to prove that there was no reason for a Tammany man to court support among reformers. Mitchel was elected mayor, and fusion candidates took control of the Board of Estimate, the Board of Aldermen, and most county and judicial offices. More than half of the incumbent Democratic assemblymen were defeated. Even Smith, who was used to winning by margins of three or four to one, was tested: his challenger doubled the vote of Smith's Republican opponent in 1912. (Smith still won 63 percent of the vote.) Murphy was philosophical about the worst defeat since he had become the Tammany leader. "There'll be another day," he said. But Smith predicted that the reformers would never accept the legitimacy of Tammany Hall. They "wanted to fix it so that no Tammany man could ever run for office," he said.

Although Smith was bitter, the defeat of the Democrats in 1913 would prove to be a blessing in disguise. Murphy had become a symbol of everything that was wrong with politics, and much of the good that his men in Albany had accomplished was obscured by the passionate hatred of "bossism" in all its manifestations. Recognizing this, Murphy announced after the election that he was removing himself from state politics and leaving the direction of the Democrats in the legislature to Martin Glynn, the Democratic lieutenant governor who had become governor following the impeachment of Sulzer. "Give the people everything they want," Murphy told Smith and Wagner and the other Tammany men in the legislature. Of course, Tammany's enemies were skeptical about the boss's "retirement" to the confines of the five boroughs. Yet before the end of the year, under the leadership of Governor Glynn, the Democrats proved that a real change had occurred. Glynn announced his support for a direct primary bill that was very similar to the one that had led to war between Tammany and Sulzer and called the legislature into special session to pass it. There could be no better test of Murphy's sincerity. For a moment, Tammany seemed to waver. Assembly Speaker Smith refused to commit himself at first. "Show me the bill and I'll tell you whether the boys will come back and pass it," he said. But they did pass it, along with other changes in the electoral laws long sought by the reformers. The Democrats also approved a sweeping workmen's compensation bill. Tammany's critics were stunned. The *New York Times* acknowledged that the legislature had passed "more constructive legislation in a week than other Legislatures have enacted in an entire session."

The Democrats did not find it easy to escape their reputation for being boss-dominated. The bad smell of the Sulzer impeachment continued to hang over them in 1914 as they sought to elect Glynn to his first full term. Despite his progressive record, Glynn was overwhelmed in a landslide that once again gave the Republicans substantial majorities in both houses of the legislature. The behavior of the new Republican legislature soon had many reformers longing for the days of Tammany domination. After more than four years of conflict, the liberals in the Republican Party had been defeated, and the conservatives believed they had won a mandate to undo every progressive measure that had been achieved by reformers in both parties. The new majority leader in the Senate, Elon Brown of Watertown, expressed the view of many conservatives in painting the 1914 election as a turning point: "We are at the end of an era—an era of vain and costly effort to substitute new forms of government for old. . . . The state and its people must be relieved of the vast and incalculable waste of capital and energy resulting from laws passed in the name of public welfare, but really for the benefit of classes at the expense of the whole people."

The Republicans also made it clear that their return to power would involve a significant increase in the conflict between upstate New York and New York City. In the 1915 legislative session, they imposed a direct tax on New York City that was soon producing more than 75 percent of the state's income. The tax might have been bearable if the residents of the city had seen any of the benefit of it. But instead of increasing state spending in the city, Brown threatened to cut the budget of the state health department, whose major operations were in New York and the other large cities. Meanwhile, the legislature increased expenditures to pave upstate roads.

But the new legislature's greatest sin in the eyes of the reformers was its attack on the legislation that had been passed in the wake of the Triangle fire. The Republicans created an industrial commission to supersede the newly created workmen's compensation commission and the labor department, which had been restructured along lines recommended by the Factory Investigating Commission. While the change was made in the name of "efficiency," the reformers who had struggled to shape these institutions feared that the purpose was really to undermine them. There was soon plenty of evidence of this, as bills were introduced to weaken the laws protecting workers. The governor himself called for an amendment to the workmen's compensation law that would give workers the option of accepting compensation offers made to them by their employers. Republicans also sought to lighten the burden of regulation on the owners of canning factories by giving women workers the option of working more than sixty hours per week. After this bill was passed, the protectors of the canneries went still further, introducing bills to extend from 10 p.m. to midnight the ending time for women and children workers and eliminating the ban on employing women and children on Sundays.

Smith and Wagner led the Democrats in defending the labor laws. "There never was a Legislature so completely owned by the private interests," Wagner said. But it was Smith who was the most withering critic of the Republicans. It had been nine years since he spoke his first words on the floor of the Assembly, and he had become a powerful debater. "Nobody has to put their hands to their ears to hear what he is saying," a reporter observed. "His powerful voice is at times almost sinister." Usually, there was nothing strident about his style. But Governor Charles Whitman's proposal for direct settlement of workmen's compensation claims

made his blood run cold. It gave the insurance companies for the employers the ability to pressure injured people into signing away their right
to fair compensation. When the Assembly passed the bill removing the
limit on the number of hours that women could work in the canneries,
Smith accused the Republicans of sacrificing women workers:

> This is the entering wedge, if you Republicans stay in power long
> enough you'll tear down the whole law that protects New York's
> most valuable asset, its womanhood. . . . Not only the people of
> this commonwealth, but the whole nation applauded our action
> in stopping canneries from working women 120 hours a week. . . .
> I had rather never see again in my life anything that comes out of
> a can if it has to be put up in the sweat and blood of the women of
> this state.

In the end, the reformers were able to limit the damage that the Republicans sought to inflict. Protest meetings in New York City and editorials attacking the legislature in the state's largest newspapers persuaded
the majority to back away from the most radical proposals. Public indignation was so great over the bill authorizing employers to work women
more than sixty hours per week that Governor Whitman held a public
hearing and then vetoed it. The reformers even managed to pass a bill in
1915 that extended the role of the state in protecting women. The so-
called widows' pension was proposed to Smith in 1913 by several prominent women who sought to end the practice of removing children from
mothers who were left destitute by the deaths of their husbands. The idea
of providing a state pension to the mother as a way of supporting her family immediately appealed to the Speaker, who might have been placed in
an orphanage himself had his widowed mother failed in her struggle. But
others were opposed. In the debate on the bill in 1915, Smith answered
those who believed that pensioning mothers exceeded the responsibility
of the state by pointing out that both parties had declared in favor of the
idea of conserving the state's natural resources. The widows' pension was
nothing more than "an act to conserve family life," Smith said.

> The State of New York, under the provisions of this act, reaches
> out its strong arm to the widow and her children and says to them,
> "We recognize in you a resource to the State and we propose to

take care of you, not as a matter of charity, but as a matter of government and public duty." What a different feeling that puts into the hearts of the mother and the children! What better citizens that policy must make!

Over the years, this rationale was used to extend public support to other classes of indigent mothers: to women whose husbands had abandoned them, to divorced women, and finally to unwed mothers.

But Smith never rested his argument solely on political grounds. In the same speech, he made it clear that aiding the destitute was a moral imperative:

> We have been slow to legislate along the direction that means thanksgiving to the poorest man recorded in history—to him who was born in the stable at Bethlehem. . . . by the adoption of this policy, we are sending up to Him a prayer of thanksgiving for the innumerable blessings that He has showered upon us, particularly in light of the words of the Savior Himself, who said: "Suffer little children to come unto me, and forbid them not, for of such is the kingdom of heaven."

The Republicans had no good answer to Smith's argument, and the bill was approved by both houses of the legislature and signed by the governor. But the passage of the widows' pension was not enough to save the reputation of the legislature. The World had been intensely hostile to Tammany Hall, but it proclaimed the 1915 legislature far worse. "The most corrupt legislature the state has had in a generation was less inimical to the common good than this legislature steeped in Bourbonism and consecrated to the almighty dollar," it said. As the Republicans became increasingly conservative, it was inevitable that the reformers would begin to notice the achievements of Democrats like Smith and Wagner. The 1915 New York State Constitutional Convention gave the two men another opportunity to demonstrate that even a Tammany man could be a reformer.

Smith knew that the constitutional convention would be an important opportunity for him to advance his political career. The 1915 legislative session was his last year as a member of the Assembly. Murphy had agreed that the time had come to reward him for his services to the party by electing him sheriff of New York County, a position that was rich in fees. What would come next wasn't clear. There was talk of Smith as a candidate for governor, but many believed the job was still beyond the reach of a Tammany man. Whatever was next, Smith was determined to be a standout at the convention.

On the surface, the 1915 convention recapitulated the divisions of the 1894 convention. Once again the delegates found themselves divided — between immigrants and natives, Catholics and Protestants, upstate New York and New York City. The Democratic delegates to the constitutional convention wanted to redistribute political power. Above all, they hoped to eliminate the apportionment provisions of the 1894 constitution that prevented urban Democrats from receiving their fair share of representation in the legislature. Unfortunately, representation at the convention was determined by the same unfair apportionment system that governed the legislature. There was never a chance that the Republican majority would agree to amendments that would reduce its power in Albany and New York City. But Smith and the other Democrats took every opportunity to press their grievances. After having already spoken at length on the injustice of the apportionment, Smith offered the Republicans an opportunity to shut him up: "I will stop talking about it today and forever if you will join the society that I have the honor of being the founder of, the Amalgamated Association for the Suppression of Political Fraud. Just plead guilty is the quickest way out of it. Why, there is no business reason, but we just want to keep control." But no one was willing to "come clean," and Smith kept talking.

In the continuing debate over home rule, Smith poured scorn on a Republican proposal that gave the legislature the right to nullify any changes in the fundamental structure of city government proposed by the city officials. The legislature was clearly unwilling to allow the people of New York to settle these important issues for themselves, Smith said.

> You want an appeal here from the decision of the elected representatives of the people on the decision on the simplest and the plainest home rule proposition I can think of [the drawing of aldermanic districts]. . . . Now President Schurman added considerable enlightenment to the whole subject when he picked up a

book and told us we would receive that kind of home rule in New York that Washington was satisfied to give to the Philippines, a half-civilized bunch of half-dressed men that we got by accident. . . .

The chairman of the Committee on Cities was Seth Low, who had earned the right to speak as a friend of the city. He asked Smith if he was aware that the cities of California had far less autonomy than New York's cities would enjoy under the proposed amendment. Smith shot back, "I would sooner be a lamp-post on Park Row than the Governor of California."

It fell to Smith to enunciate the change in philosophy that had led the Democratic Party to become the advocate of an activist state government. William Barnes, who had led the Republican conservatives for many years, had introduced a constitutional amendment that provided "the legislature shall not pass any bill granting hereafter to any class of individuals any privilege or immunity not granted equally to all members of the state." Although it was phrased in the language of equal rights, the Barnes amendment actually sought to abolish the factory laws that protected women and children and to forestall any other action by which the state might seek to limit the power of business. When it came to the floor for debate, George Wickersham, a liberal who led the Republican majority, gave Smith twenty minutes of the half hour that had been allotted to the majority. With the ten minutes he already owned, this gave Smith half an hour to explain why it was wrong to impose arbitrary limits on the power of government. The Barnes amendment expressed the view that "law in a democracy is the expression of some divine or eternal right," Smith said. In this view, government cannot exercise powers that are not expressly granted to it in the constitution. "I am unable to see it that way. . . . My idea of law and democracy is the expression of what is best, what fits the present day needs of society, what does the greatest good for the greatest number." It was this philosophy that led Smith to propose amendments that would forever ban manufacturing in tenement sweatshops and to create a board to set minimum wages for women and children. The convention rejected both proposals.

Smith made himself heard on other reform issues as well. The Democratic Party had committed itself to protecting the state's natural resources from commercial exploitation, and during the convention Smith supported an amendment to enlarge the power of the Conservation Commission to purchase and develop water sources capable of generating electricity. He also backed a short-ballot proposal, reducing the number of elective positions as a way of concentrating authority and increasing the accountability of public officials. With Wagner, he supported a proposal by Republican liberals to make the governor responsible for drafting the state budget, which was denounced by Republican conservatives who believed it would strengthen the executive branch at the expense of the legislature.

It was during the constitutional convention that Al Smith finally emerged from Tammany's shadow and established a reputation as a man who thought for himself. Smith knew how important the convention had been. As he later explained: "I am frank to say that the Convention of 1915 had afforded me a great opportunity. I got a lot out of it later on. And I never allowed my campaign managers to overlook anything that happened at its sessions." Although many of the liberal Republicans paid tribute to Smith's role in the constitutional convention, the most significant review of his performance came from Elihu Root, the elder statesman who had been present at the conventions in both 1894 and 1915. In 1880 Root had opposed the election of a Catholic as mayor of New York City because he feared that it would mean delivering government "to one sect to the exclusion of all others." Smith had erased this prejudice. "Al Smith knows more about the real needs of the State than do most of us," he said. On one of the final days of the convention, a Democratic delegate learned by telephone that Smith had received the nomination for sheriff and ran to the Assembly chamber to announce the news to the rest of the convention. Smith stood to acknowledge the applause of his colleagues. There seemed to be no limit to how high this Tammany man might rise.

# 5 ✳ RECONSTRUCTION

**D**ouglas Fairbanks and Charlie Chaplin stood beside the statue of George Washington on the landing of the Subtreasury building, surveying the noontime crowd that packed Wall Street. It was an October day in 1918, and the United States was halfway through its second year of war. Over a million American soldiers were abroad, but there was no shortage of men on Wall Street: a vast sea of men's hats tilted upward to watch the two actors sell war bonds. Americans were getting tired of war bond rallies. This was the fourth drive in eighteen months, and the contributions were lagging badly. So the fund-raisers were delighted when Fairbanks, Chaplin, and Mary Pickford agreed to tour the country. Fairbanks stopped the show at the bond rally by grabbing Chaplin by the seat of his pants, lifting him over his head, and holding him there with only one arm. Chaplin raised his hat.

The spectacular stunt was hardly noticed. The coverage in the *New York Times* the next day didn't discuss Fairbanks's magical lift or even mention the presence of Chaplin and Pickford. It was too full of lists. The names of loan subscribers were featured prominently to give them an added incentive for generosity. To foster competition, subscriptions were broken down by city, by industry, and by company. Taking up the most space were the daily lists generated at the front. On October 17, the day of the Wall Street rally, the *Times* published the names of 654 killed and wounded as well as the names of their next of kin. The number of casualties was mounting fast.

The Americans had been fighting for only eighteen months, and their losses were very small compared to the eight million men from European countries who had been killed since 1914, but the country's commitment to the war was complete. The economy had been converted from the production of consumer goods to the manufacture of the materials of war, which meant fewer luxuries for the civilian population and rationed food and fuels. During the winter, while residents of the Northeast suffered the worst weather on record, coal was diverted to the war industries to maintain production. The private sector had been virtually nationalized as the leaders of corporate America resigned their jobs and entered government service to develop and administer a bureaucracy capable of managing the economy. The disputes between industry and labor were adjourned as workers agreed to forgo wage increases in return for a minimal recognition of their right to bargain through their unions. Although most Americans were Republicans, they rallied behind Woodrow Wilson, a Democrat who promised that this was a fight not just for democracy but for world peace—a war to end all wars.

Nevertheless, Wilson and his advisers worried that many of the 13 million foreigners who had entered the country after 1900 would not support the war. There were also millions of American citizens of German ancestry who might feel divided in their loyalties. To meet this problem, the government established a Committee on Public Information to promote a desire to win the war. But propaganda was hardly necessary to build pressure for conformity at a time when America's sons were dying overseas. Hostility toward Germans and all things Germanic grew quickly. Sauerkraut was renamed "liberty cabbage," and prudent conductors dropped pieces by German composers from their concerts. There were many assaults on the property and persons of those who were judged disloyal. Teachers were fired for their personal beliefs, even when these entailed nothing more than sympathy for a beleaguered homeland or a philosophical commitment to pacifism.

Almost as quickly as it began, the war was over, and the country faced a new set of daunting problems as its soldiers returned home. The veterans expected to resume their civilian jobs, but the economy was still geared to making guns and tanks. Many prewar jobs no longer existed, and those that did were occupied by other people. Unemployment grew rapidly as men either looked for new jobs or were fired to make way for veterans. There were shortages of all kinds of consumer goods. Because civilian construction had been suspended, no new homes had been built for eighteen months. As people competed to buy the necessities of life, inflation appeared. The problem was compounded by wage demands from union workers who had not asked for raises during the war and were now feeling the pinch of higher prices. As if economic problems were not enough, the nation now faced the problem of race in a new way. African-Americans from the South had moved north in large numbers to fill labor shortages during the war, creating competition for the white working class. At the same time African-American soldiers were returning from the war, convinced that their contributions had earned them fair treatment from white America.

The United States in 1919 faced so many problems that an explosion was inevitable. The transition might have been smoother if the federal government had planned for peace in the same way that it had planned for war. But the minute the armistice was signed, the so-called "dollar-a-year" men began to leave their government jobs and return to their well-paid positions in corporate America. Government planning in peacetime was unthinkable in a country as deeply committed to the idea of free enterprise as the United States. Corporate leaders contributed to the instability. During the war they had reluctantly recognized unions in a number of industries as a step toward greater efficiency and in return for wage discipline. Now that the war was over, they had no intention of dealing with the unions. On the contrary, they were determined to do everything they could to restore the open shop. At this moment in 1918, when the conflicts that would plague the country were becoming clear but had not yet led to violence, the state of New York elected a new governor, Alfred E. Smith.

Like Fairbanks and Chaplin, Al Smith was selling war bonds in mid-October. On the day of the Wall Street rally, Smith joined financier Felix Warburg nearby in City Hall Park and sold over $200,000 in bonds. Smith had sold a lot of bonds since being elected president of the New York City Board of Aldermen in 1917. He had an extraordinary ability to make financial issues understandable to the average voter. "It is difficult to talk in figures, but from a comparison it might be useful," Smith told one audience. "The total cost of the administration of government from 1791 to 1917 was about what it cost us for one year of the war today." Clearly, the government needed funds badly, but it was not demanding support, Smith said. "All it asks is that you lend to the best of your ability on the best securities the world has ever known. Banking houses may crumble, commercial houses go into bankruptcy, but this Government will stand when all else is gone."

While Smith was not as big a celebrity as a movie star, his reputation was growing. When he retired from the legislature, the Citizens Union issued a statement praising his service and endorsing him for sheriff. This outraged some reformers, but they could not get anyone to listen to their protests. What could you do when Smith had the support of such a bitterly anti-Tammany paper as the *New York Times*, which called him "a man of quite unusual ability for that office"? Many of the reformers saw in Smith a hope that the machine might yet transcend its evil ways and become a true instrument of popular government. Some Tammany men saw him the same way. "The proposed nomination of Alfred E. Smith for Sheriff is most commendable," Magistrate Joseph E. Corrigan said. "It is a proclamation to the young men of New York that the profession of politics as practiced by Mr. Smith, aggressively but always kindly, shrewdly but always honorably, is a good one for a clever man with clean ideals."

At first, Smith enjoyed being sheriff. He was happy to be working in New York City full-time and providing for his family better than ever before. The sheriff received $50,000 in fees as well as a $12,000 salary, making the job one of Tammany's richest patronage plums. Smith's official duties were light, and much of his time was occupied by attending dinners that were given in his honor by each of the districts of the sheriff's jury. Smith excelled at entertaining with stories, jokes, and songs on these occasions. One evening, "His address was a succession of epigrams and humorous stories and the crowd went from one spasm of laughter into another," reporter Martin Green remembered. But when he met Green a few days later, Smith said that he was dissatisfied with his speech. "You were never funnier," Green assured him. "It was too damned funny," Smith explained. "I am in danger of being classed as a humorist. If I keep on making these funny speeches people will begin to think I can't do anything else." He told Green he intended to change. "Al Smith is going to turn over a new leaf," he said.

Several months later, Green was present when Smith presented his new face to the world. His audience that night in February 1917 was still another sheriff's jury panel dinner attended by "bankers, lawyers, editors, statesmen, professors, leaders in various movements and Tammany district leaders and captains," who expected the usual comedy and good fellowship from Sheriff Smith. Cocktails preceded the dinner, which was served with highballs and wine. So the crowd was primed to laugh when Smith got up to speak. Instead, they heard Smith make a patriotic address. The country was only months away from entering World War I, and Smith discussed the prospect of war with a knowledge of national and international affairs that surprised many, Green said. Yet there was nothing dry in his delivery.

> Ten minutes after Al Smith began to talk the great banquet room was absolutely still except for the sound of his voice. And no other sound, save occasional applause, disturbed that stillness until he closed. His hearers sat spellbound—the word is right. At the doors were massed groups of waiters, cooks and other help, listening breathlessly.

Later Green asked Smith how he had acquired the extensive vocabulary that he had displayed in his speech. "What are your favorite books?" he asked. Smith was frank. "I never read books," he said. "I don't have time to read. . . . I'm a good listener, and I have a good memory."

Smith obviously intended his speech to serve as a reminder that he was qualified for high elective office, but it was not immediately clear what that office would be. Robert Wagner had also established an outstanding record in Albany, and there was a lot of contradictory speculation over what the future held for the two men: one report had Boss Murphy grooming Wagner for governor; another article had Smith succeeding Murphy as boss; a third projected him as Manhattan borough president. Much of the speculation concerned the upcoming mayoral campaign. In 1915 the people of New York had elected a reform administration headed by John Purroy Mitchel, but Mayor Mitchel had antagonized so many groups with his abrasive personality that a Democratic victory in 1917 was almost certain. Both Smith and Wagner were mentioned as possible candidates for mayor. Wagner was said to be Murphy's choice, although Smith was said to be more popular with the Tammany rank and file.

In the end, it was all idle gossip. Boss Murphy depended on the sup-

port of the Brooklyn Democratic organization headed by John F. Mc-
Cooey and had agreed that the Democratic candidate for mayor in 1917
would be a resident of Brooklyn. In August a committee of 170 prominent Democrats, including Smith and Wagner, announced that they
would support an obscure Brooklyn magistrate, John F. Hylan, for mayor.
Hylan had been working as a motorman on the elevated trains and attending law school when he was befriended by McCooey. After receiving
several minor judicial appointments, he was appointed a magistrate in
1914. By this time, Hylan had become active in several Brooklyn groups,
including the Allied Boards of Trade, the Taxpayers Association, and the
Municipal Ownership League. His commitment to municipal ownership
attracted the support of William Randolph Hearst and won Hylan the
nomination. Although many of Smith's admirers were disappointed that
he was not nominated for mayor, Smith himself was pleased to receive
the nomination for president of the Board of Aldermen, which was second only to the mayor in terms of influence in city government. On election day, the Democrats swept the reformers from office by a margin of
almost two to one.

Smith soon learned, however, that being second in command is a difficult job when your leader is a fool. Whatever sterling qualities Hylan
may have possessed, intelligence was not one of them. He quickly alien-
ated the newspapermen who covered City Hall by announcing that he
would only give interviews to reporters from the *Journal* and the *American*, the two Hearst dailies. While Smith privately agreed with the reporters who complained to him, he initially tried to protect Hylan. Both
Smith and Hylan were members of the Board of Estimate, which controlled the city budget and was thus far more powerful than the Board of
Aldermen. Not long after the election, the Board of Estimate was listening to engineers debate whether a bridge or a tunnel was the best way to
move cars and trucks between Manhattan and New Jersey. Feeling
slighted by what he perceived as a lack of deference shown him by these
professional men, the new mayor attempted to assert himself. "This tunnel, now, is it your plan to build it by the open cut or by the bore
method?" he asked. As the engineers tried to figure out what the mayor
was talking about, two reporters slipped from the room to report this latest
gaffe. Smith stopped them. "Say, have a heart," he implored. "The Mayor
wasn't thinking when he pulled that! A tunnel built under a river by open

cut; you'd have to hire fish to build it! If you print anything about that he'll be the laugh of the town. Can't you forget it?" Although aching to retaliate against the mayor for his unfair treatment, the reporters were too fond of Smith to deny him.

Events were moving in a direction that promised Smith an early release from his unpleasant chore of cleaning up after the mayor. A gubernatorial election was only seven months away, and many of Smith's supporters believed he was the man for the job. Calls for his candidacy had begun on the night of the Democratic triumph in 1917, when workers at Democratic headquarters gave three cheers for Al Smith as the next governor of New York. These sentiments weren't confined to the rank and file. In April, Edwin S. Harris, the state party chairman, declared Smith the obvious choice for governor. "In my judgment, the one man whose knowledge of State affairs, whose sympathies with the people have always been the keenest, whose courage is unsurpassed and whose ability to think clearly and act quickly and forcefully is unequaled among public men, is the present President of the Board of Aldermen," he said. Harris, however, did not believe that Smith could win the nomination. It had been only seven years since the party ruptured over the nomination of Blue-Eyed Billy Sheehan for the U.S. Senate, and the upstate Democrats remained deeply suspicious of Tammany. It seemed impossible that they would ever support a Tammany man.

Not only was Smith a Tammany man, he was a Catholic. While no one was willing to talk about it publicly, there was no question that some upstate Protestants would refuse to vote for a Catholic. This had been shown as recently as the 1914 elections, when Martin Glynn, the man who had become governor following the impeachment and removal of William Sulzer, sought election to a full term. Although Catholic, Glynn was from upstate and thus did not suffer the taint of Tammany. In addition, he had compiled a creditable record during his year in office. He even succeeded in winning Tammany's support for a direct primary bill. As the fall elections approached, however, literature began to appear upstate that claimed that Glynn's religion was influencing his conduct as governor and accused him of favoring the use of public funds to support parochial schools. Glynn denied these charges publicly but was defeated by nearly 122,000 votes. The Democratic candidate for the U.S. Senate was also defeated, but ran 60,000 votes ahead of Glynn, which the New York Times credited to the fact that he was a Protestant.

In the spring of 1918, however, the candidacy that upstate Democrats feared the most was that of William Randolph Hearst. Hearst had run for governor before. In 1906 he had amazed political observers by joining forces with Boss Murphy, whose machine he had incessantly assailed, and challenging Governor Hughes. At the time, upstate Democrats had attacked Hearst as an irresponsible "radical" who used his newspapers to whip up class warfare. He had made himself even more unpopular by indulging his hatred for England to the point that he seemed to be pro-German. In some places in the country, Hearst newspapers were burned in demonstrations against their alleged disloyalty. In an effort to head off a disastrous Hearst candidacy in 1918, upstate leaders sought the advice of Charles F. Murphy.

Murphy played a subtle game. He told the upstate leaders that he would not support Hearst and was willing to accept any candidate they were willing to back. Yet the possibility that Murphy might still endorse the newspaper publisher meant that the upstate leaders could not choose an outright Tammany foe like William Church Osborn, who had been a leader of the 1911 revolt. In fact, Murphy had a candidate. In May he told the Democratic leaders of Troy and Binghamton that he favored Al Smith for the job but insisted that he was leaving the decision up to the upstate leaders. If the upstate Democrats had been able to agree, they might have been able to force Murphy to live up to his promise, but they were badly divided. Like the party chairman, most party leaders recognized Smith's ability. "Mr. Smith is the best representative of the worst element in the Democratic Party in this state," Samuel Seabury, a longtime Tammany foe, acknowledged. When a poll of upstate leaders showed significant support for Smith, he became an easy choice. During the Democratic convention, even Seabury, who had voted against Smith on principle, later changed his vote to make the nomination unanimous.

Smith was ecstatic at having captured the nomination. "Al Smith seemed as pleased as a boy with a new top," a reporter noted. He was also humbled. "No man owes more to this country than I do," Smith said. "No man has been more benefitted by the free institutions of this state than I have." But Smith was realistic about his chances of actually defeating Governor Whitman. No Democrat had beaten his Republican opponent in a two-man race in nearly thirty years, and there was no prospect of a third-party candidate to split the Republican vote this time. In addition, Governor Whitman had an air of invincibility. He was running for his third term and had beaten his last opponent by 163,000 votes. Add to these problems Smith's religion and Tammany connection and the obstacles seemed practically insurmountable. "Only a miracle, it was thought, could elect him," Joseph M. Proskauer, one of his key advisers, would write many years later.

Nevertheless, Smith's nomination filled the Democrats with hope. The party had been crippled by the conflict between Tammany and its opponents, but Smith was a man with friends on both sides. As the state campaign approached, the growing excitement of the Democrats was palpable. The *New York Times* had been restrained in its response to Smith's nomination in July. Only three weeks later, however, it declared itself fully on board the Smith bandwagon:

> He knows this city. He knows this state. The lasting antinomy of the two would be ended, at least for a time, if he should become Governor. He knows how to make budgets; and the fact that he is a brilliant and exceptional offshoot of Tammany Hall is not an offset to his positive qualifications for the office. He began his political career in the only way it was natural and possible for him to begin it. He has grown in a way Tammany has not. He has fitted himself to be Governor. He understands the business.

The support of such an inveterate opponent of Tammany was important, but Smith needed more than the independent Democrats to win. He would have to get the votes of liberal Republicans. Many of them had left their party in 1912 to support Theodore Roosevelt and the Progressive Party. Although they had returned to their party, they continued to be dissatisfied with its conservative, upstate leadership.

As a result, Smith's campaign organization was divided into three parts. The "official" campaign was led by an upstate Democrat, Will Kelley. Murphy and his Tammany machine went to work with new passion to bring in a record vote from New York City's working class, and Abram I. Elkus organized an Independent Citizens Committee for Alfred E. Smith. Elkus himself was no independent. The son of Eastern European Jews who had settled on the Lower East Side, he became a lawyer and joined Tammany in the 1890s. Appointed ambassador to Turkey in 1917, Elkus was more prominent than most Tammany men. He was also a friend of Smith's: both men were members of the Seymour Club, and

Elkus had served as the counsel for the Factory Investigating Commission. He seemed like the logical choice to organize a committee of leading citizens for Smith.

Like other campaign committees, the Independent Citizens Committee for Alfred E. Smith was hardly more than a letterhead organization that existed for the purpose of associating the candidate's name with a list of prominent supporters. Smith's list included its share of important businessmen and lawyers. Yet it was very different from the lists of the past. Almost a third of the vice-chairmen announced on October 17 were women. This might have been nothing more than a gesture, a bow to the ladies who had been enfranchised by New York voters the year before and would be voting for the first time in the fall elections. But many of the women vice-chairmen had acquired their prominence as reformers: Harriot Stanton Blatch was a suffragist like her mother, Elizabeth Cady Stanton; Mary L. Chamberlain was a social worker who had been on the staff of the Factory Investigating Commission; Mary Simkovitch had founded Greenwich House, a settlement on Jones Street. The committee was also unique in featuring a large number of well-known German Jews, including Proskauer, who was Elkus's partner, attorney Samuel Untermyer, and Jesse Isidore Straus, whose family owned the city's biggest department stores. Many of the committee members had never voted for a Tammany candidate in their lives. Some had played prominent roles in the municipal reform movement that had helped elect John Purroy Mitchel and had cast their ballots against the machine as recently as a year before.

Many of the members of Smith's coalition were strangers to each other. Smith himself had little understanding of the college-educated women who were supporting him. He had a very traditional view of women. Like most Americans, he believed that a woman's place was in the home, rearing future citizens. He had scoffed at those who demanded the vote for women. Both the Republican and Democratic parties opposed woman suffrage until 1912. Even then, they came out in favor of a referendum on a state constitutional amendment giving women the vote largely because they were confident that it would be defeated, which it was in 1915. Yet Smith possessed more appeal for women than most politicians. He had worked closely with Frances Perkins and other women experts on the problems of industrial labor, and he was a strong advocate of using government to protect women and children.

Belle Lindner Moskowitz was one of the women reformers who supported Smith and later became one of his key political advisers. Moskowitz's parents were Jews who had emigrated from East Prussia soon after the Civil War. After living briefly on the Lower East Side, they moved to the Bronx, where Belle was born in 1877. Her father was a watchmaker who ran his own store, and she grew up in modest circumstances. Although she briefly considered becoming a teacher, Belle had grander dreams. She left college after a year to study drama and, like Smith, became an expert at dramatic readings. Where star turns led to politics for Smith, however, there were no obvious outlets for Belle's dramatic talents. She worked for several years at a settlement house on the Lower East Side, and then quit to marry and have children. But even when she was home with her young children, she worked as a freelance writer. She became involved with reform through the Council of Jewish Women. As an unpaid member of its Committee of Amusements, she fought the problem of prostitution by seeking legislation to license the city's dance halls, revealing in the process a prodigious capacity for organization and publicity. After her first husband's death, she supported her two young children by working as a grievance clerk at the Dress and Waist Manufacturers Association.

By the time she met Al Smith, Belle was a seasoned political operative. She had joined the Progressive Party in 1912 and served as a ward leader and delegate to the state convention. The next year she worked actively to support the fusion movement that elected Mayor Mitchel. In 1914 she married Henry Moskowitz, a man who was as passionately interested in politics as she. Moskowitz, the former head of Madison House, had run for Congress on the Progressive Party ticket and been appointed to a paying job in the Mitchel administration. Nevertheless, Henry and Belle had become admirers of Al Smith and voted for him when he ran for sheriff in 1915. When Elkus invited Belle Moskowitz to serve as a vice-chair of the Independent Citizens Committee for Alfred E. Smith, she jumped at the chance.

Belle Moskowitz was not the kind of person to lend only her name to a cause. Shortly after the announcement of the citizens' committee, she proposed the creation of a women's division to Frances Perkins, who was working with Elkus. Elkus and Proskauer approved the idea and put Moskowitz in charge. Not long after, she was summoned to her first personal meeting with the candidate. Smith and his advisers were worried about how women would respond to his opposition to Prohibition. For many years, women had played a prominent role in pressing for a ban on the sale of alcoholic drinks. Under the leadership of the Anti-Saloon League, Prohibitionists had made steady progress, using local option laws to dry up one town after another. By 1915 Prohibition was one of the hottest political issues in western New York, and the Anti-Saloon League campaigned hard for the next two years to win over the larger cities in the state's interior. In April 1918 the Prohibitionists had won referendums in half of them. As he sat with his advisers, Smith asked Moskowitz what he could do to win the votes of women who supported Prohibition. She urged him not to try to duck the issue but to explain his opposition plainly.

Moskowitz organized three meetings for Smith but told him about only two of them ahead of time. The first two speeches before groups of women went off without a hitch. For the most part, Smith gave the same kind of speech he had been giving to mixed audiences, although in one address he did caution the women not to trust too much in Governor Whitman's commitment to temperance. Smith quoted an upstate Prohibitionist who claimed "more rum was consumed in the Executive Mansion in the last four years than in the 20 years preceding." The only tense moment came when Moskowitz told Smith that she had booked him at a meeting of the Women's University Club. This was a very different kind of meeting than the other two. In addition to the Women's University Club, there would be members present from the Colony, Cosmopolitan, and Women's City clubs. Smith had never addressed so many educated women at once and was uncertain about the right approach. At first he was inclined just to shake hands and let Robert Wagner, a college graduate, address his intellectual peers. But Moskowitz told him that this was a mistake. She produced a list of topics that would interest his audience, including steps to improve public health, the fight to protect women from unsafe working conditions, and his position on woman suffrage. Soon after he began his speech, Smith realized that Moskowitz had been right. In a matter of months, she would be working for him full-time.

The New York women who voted for the first time in the 1918 elections were probably pretty disappointed by the gubernatorial campaign. Because of the war, it lasted only a couple of weeks and featured only a handful of major speeches by Smith and Governor Whitman. Moreover, the incumbent was a particularly uninspiring candidate. From the beginning, there had been those in his own party who had raised questions about his character. Theodore Roosevelt had called him a liar in 1914. In the 1918 Republican primary, his opponent, the state attorney general, had accused him of using the state payroll to create a political machine that would help him win the presidency. The governor might have counteracted this cynicism by presenting a program during his campaign. Instead, in his first address in late October, he made it clear that he hoped to win reelection by running against Tammany Hall:

> The only question to be submitted to the voters is, shall the power that has managed to get its grasp on the city, that has been termed an "organized appetite," reach above the limits of the city and gather in the whole state? . . . Tammany has had three Governors of the State in four years. There was Dix who was refused renomination, Sulzer who was impeached, and Glynn who was repudiated by the people and the man who was leader of the assembly during this time now asks the city to forget it all and put Tammany back into power because Tammany Hall has been removed to Syracuse. It didn't move the candidate with it, either.

In later speeches, Whitman sought to embellish this theme by accusing Smith of appointing men with checkered pasts to public posts at Tammany's behest.

Smith defended his party's recent record in Albany. The Democrats had supported the constitutional amendments providing for direct election of candidates to the U.S. Senate and a federal income tax and placed on the law books some of the most progressive labor legislation in the country. Whitman refused to be drawn into a debate by his challenger and ignored Smith's attacks on his administration. He appears to have known little about Smith. Early in the campaign, he made the mistake of challenging his opponent to identify what parts of the state budget he would cut. The former chair of the Assembly Ways and Means Committee replied with chapter and verse. Later, he asked what Smith had ever done to help labor in the state.

Whitman's biggest mistake, however, may have been to portray Smith as a Tammany hack. In one speech he claimed that Smith had never worked for a living. Smith jumped at the chance to prove otherwise. "The

Governor says I never earned a dollar laboring with my hands," Smith said.

> He is wrong again. When he was an Amherst College student, I was working in the Fulton Fish Market at the hardest labor that any man could do. I started before sunrise and worked until dark night. I know labor's needs. I have lived and worked all my life among men and women who labor for their bread and I will continue to live among them when I am the Governor of this State and when I come home to New York they can meet me and find me in my old neighborhood and talk to me. They won't have to break through hundreds of pounds of gold lace in the St. Regis Hotel to make known their troubles.

What Whitman failed to understand but Smith understood well was that many potential voters were inspired by the rise of a man from the Lower East Side to candidate for governor. In one of his final speeches of the campaign, Smith accused Whitman of opposing him because he was ill-born:

> In the closing hours of the campaign his sole reply seems to be that I am unfit for the office of governor because I was born in a tenement house on the East Side. That is true. In fact, it is one of the few things he has said which are true. I not only admit it, but I glory in it. That is one of the things about America that put the spirit, the courage and the vigor into the youth of this country to so great a degree that the American army, the hope of civilization, has challenged the admiration of the world. One of the great benefits of America is the equal opportunity that comes to all men, however low and humble may be their beginnings, to raise themselves by their own efforts to the highest place in the gift of the people, and it is the embodiment of that spirit of America which permits a man born in a tenement house, if he be worthy, to become the Governor of the State of New York.

Inadvertently, Whitman had played to one of Smith's greatest strengths — his appeal as a man of the people.

On Election Day, the voters of New York City went to the polls in unprecedented numbers, and Smith astonished the experts by running more than 250,000 votes ahead of Whitman there. The heavy Irish Catholic vote for Smith was no surprise, but he also did extremely well with Germans and scored impressive gains among the newest immigrant groups, Eastern European Jews, Italians, and Poles. Smith did well with immigrant American groups in cities across the state. At Smith headquarters in the Biltmore Hotel, people started celebrating early. At a party sponsored by the citizens' committee, many of Smith's supporters began slapping him on the back and calling him "Governor" before midnight. Soon the upstate vote began to come in, reminding the crowd that their man had always been the underdog. By 3 a.m. it was clear that there would be no declaration of victory anytime soon, and Smith sent his mother home to bed. Two hours later he was trailing by 1,500 votes. What concerned Smith and his advisers most was that the count of the upstate vote had slowed to a crawl. It was a common Republican tactic to withhold some votes until the size of the city vote could be definitely established, at which time enough phony votes were added so that their candidate could win. Unable to reach party workers in these districts by telephone, Smith and a party of his advisers, including Robert Wagner and State Senator James J. Walker, boarded the Empire State Express at 8:30 a.m. and headed for Democratic headquarters in Syracuse.

Soon after their arrival, Smith and his entourage determined that all was well. Dividing the disputed upstate districts among themselves, they called local party officials to find out what was going on. Smith was relieved to learn that they had the job in hand. He called one Democratic commissioner of elections, whose job it was to guard against fraud at the polls, and was surprised to find him at home eating dinner. The commissioner told Smith not to worry: his wife was sitting on the ballot boxes until he got back. The next morning, Smith returned to New York, where he found his suite of rooms at the Biltmore crowded with anxious friends. Before addressing them, he took Katie aside. The day before he had missed her fortieth birthday. But as Smith began to address his supporters, the look on her face made it clear that she had been given the present she wanted most. With over 2.1 million votes cast, Smith had won the governorship by 15,000.

During the campaign, Smith had made a speech in Albany, promising to return as "the Governor, Mrs. Smith, the five small Smiths and the dog." On December 30, 1918, Smith's forty-fifth birthday, his promise was fulfilled as the Smiths left Oliver Street for Albany. Actually, the Smith children were not so small—Alfred was almost 18, Emily, 17, Catherine, 14, Arthur, 11, and Walter, 9—and the dog was an enormous Great Dane named Caesar. But they certainly shook things up. The governor of New York had been a remote figure who ruled Albany society from within the walls of the Executive Mansion. Governor Whitman was standing before the fireplace in the entrance hall of the mansion when the Smiths arrived. As he walked forward to greet them, a uniformed military aide walked by his side. This was not the Smiths' style—something that was made plain only a few moments later. Alfred, whom Smith called "young Al," had not been in the car that carried his family from the train station. Caesar had needed a walk. Since the mansion was not far from the station, the boy and dog arrived as Smith and Whitman were exchanging pleasantries. Seeing his master, Caesar broke free and leaped up on Smith. Surprised, Whitman and his aide stepped backward. "Don't be frightened, Governor," Smith said, holding the dog by his collar. "It's only the Tammany tiger come to take possession of the Executive Mansion."

The arrival of the Smith family at the Executive Mansion represented nothing less than a social revolution in the politics of New York State. As she surveyed the mansion for the first time, Emily Smith marveled at the change in her family's circumstances. "To me, it was a palace," she said. Until 1915, the seven Smiths had lived on two floors of a house with only one bathroom. Compared to the conditions in the tenements that surrounded them, these were luxurious accommodations. It was true that they were cramped, and the children had shared bedrooms. After Smith became sheriff, he could afford to rent the third floor, build a two-room addition, and install a second bathroom. The Smiths were living quite comfortably when they closed the house on Oliver Street and left for Albany. But the Executive Mansion was another world. On the ground floor there was a library, a dining room that could seat thirty-two, a breakfast room, a morning room, a music room, and a drawing room. When the children rushed upstairs to claim one of the nine bedrooms, they were shocked to discover that each room had its own bathroom and a button to summon one of the fifteen members of the domestic staff. "I had never rung bells before to get anything done for me," Emily said. "It took some time to grow accustomed to the idea, and then a little more time to learn not to overdo it."

It took the social elite of Albany some time to accept the situation as well. Its first chance to observe the new governor came the next night at the inaugural ball. The ball was actually a charitable event that was held every year on New Year's Eve and doubled as an inaugural event during election years. This had never caused problems before because the incoming governor was usually an upstate man of the same class as those who attended the ball. In 1918, however, Albany's social elite found themselves rubbing shoulders with hundreds of Smith's neighbors in rented suits who had come to town for the inauguration the next day. Mrs. William Bayard Van Rensselaer attended the ball as usual. The newcomers included Mr. and Mrs. James Colombo, Jimmy Kelly, Solly Bernstein, Michael Kuku, and Dr. Paul Sarrubbi. The boss of Tammany Hall himself, Charles Francis Murphy, attended, escorting his wife and Miss Mabel Murphy, his daughter. This was a precedent that could only have boggled the minds of Albany society watchers.

The next day, January 1, 1919, Al Smith took the oath of office in the chamber of the New York Assembly, the institution that had been his university. He was intensely aware of how different he was from the governors of the past. On one occasion, he would decline an invitation to dinner from one of Albany's aristocratic families. When his refusal caused comment, he was forced to explain. "I have met all the members of that family socially a number of times," he said. "This is the first time they have invited me to their home. Governor Al Smith may be different from Assemblyman Al Smith to them—but not to me." On the day of his inauguration, Smith was determined to prove himself worthy. In his memoirs, he recalled, "I was eager to demonstrate that no mistake had been made by the people of the state of New York when they entrusted their government to a man who had come up from the lowest rung of the ladder to the highest position within their gift." Smith was determined "to make good for the state of New York."

Few governors had entered office under more inauspicious circumstances. Immigration had almost doubled the population of New York State in less than thirty years. The annual cost of government had risen from $14 million to nearly $100 million, and income had not kept pace with expenses. The state was heavily dependent on property taxes, which

were already so high that they could not be raised. It collected a third of
its income from liquor licenses, which were declining in number as the
Prohibition movement upstate dried up county after county, and the state
would lose all revenue from liquor only a few months later when national
Prohibition was enacted. The end of the war made Smith's position even
worse. Taking office only seven weeks after the signing of the armistice,
Smith confronted the problems created by the rapid conversion of the
war economy. Unemployment grew rapidly as companies laid off many of
the nine million workers employed in war work, and the country's corporations were more determined than ever to resist the unions' demands for
collective bargaining, provoking 3,600 strikes during 1919.

But Smith was an optimist who looked at the transition from war to
peace as an opportunity for change. During the campaign he had criticized Governor Whitman for failing to outline plans for making New
York a "gateway of opportunity" for the returning veterans. "If democracy
is worth spilling the best blood of America for in foreign lands, why can't
we have it at home?" he asked. In his first message to the state legislature,
Smith outlined how he hoped to bring this about. There were many
problems that required attention: a new approach to taxation; a reduction
in the cost of producing and distributing food, fuel, and other necessities;
employment; education; the position of women in industry. Smith announced that to analyze and propose solutions for these problems he
would appoint a Reconstruction Commission consisting of many of the
same leading citizens who had volunteered their help to the government
during the war. If he was not ready yet to announce a detailed program
on these issues, Smith was clear about one thing. "We must enact more
stringent and more universal laws for the protection of the health, comfort, welfare and efficiency of our people," he said. Smith recommended
the creation of a Minimum Wage Commission to fix a living wage for
women and children on an industry-by-industry basis. He wanted another
commission to investigate the high cost of milk, "a public menace" that
threatened the health of hundreds of thousands of poor people, particularly children. He advocated a system of health and maternity insurance
and the extension of workmen's compensation to cover occupational dis-
eases. He called for the construction of new hospitals to reduce the over-
crowding in the state's asylums and proposed reforms that would make
rehabilitation the goal of the prison system.

Smith's first message to the legislature was greeted with skepticism by the *New York Times*. The new governor seemed to be speaking out of two sides of his mouth, it said. On the one hand, he acknowledged the heavy burden of taxation and spoke about the importance of reducing it. Yet he had proposed at least three new commissions. Smith's proposals faced a much bigger problem than the state's limited resources. The Republican Party controlled both houses of the legislature and was likely to oppose most of them. Under the circumstances, "a sort of unreality makes itself felt in [Smith's] first message," the *Times* concluded.

No one knew better than Smith the problems that the legislature could create for a governor, particularly a Democrat. Smith had used his message to propose several measures that were intended to right the imbalance of power that existed in the state as a result of its undemocratic apportionment provision. Smith said he would seek either a law or a constitutional amendment granting home rule to cities. More immediately, Smith called on the legislature to forgo its right to ratify the federal Prohibition amendment in favor of a referendum that would give all the people of the state the right to decide the issue. On this occasion, Smith did not openly accuse the legislature of being unrepresentative of the people of the state as a whole. But it was obvious to everyone that if the legislature decided the issue, it would reflect the view of the rural areas of the state where support for Prohibition was strong.

The earliest criticism of Smith came not from Republicans, however, but from independent Democrats who worried that he would not show enough independence from Tammany Hall. Their fears were soon allayed. Murphy had told Smith soon after his election that he would do everything he could to help him make a good record. It was as important to Tammany as it was to Smith. One way of helping Smith was by not insisting that he hire men with Tammany connections for the top positions in his administration. While the machine Democrats would take their share of the lower jobs in the administration, Smith was to be free to hire the best people for the top jobs. As Smith announced his appointments during the first weeks of January, even the irascible *New York Times* could not hide its pleasure.

One of Smith's surprising choices was his appointment of Frances Perkins to the State Industrial Commission. Perkins was directly related to anti-Tammany forces through her marriage to Paul E. Wilson, who had been Mayor Mitchel's secretary. She was a reformer who currently served as chairman of the legislative committee of the Consumers' League and secretary to both the Committee on Safety and the Maternity Center Association. Once confirmed by the State Senate, Perkins would be the first woman to serve on the Industrial Commission. While some Democrats reportedly complained to Smith that Perkins was not a member of their party, most of the opposition came from representatives of the state's manufacturers who feared that Perkins would favor the interests of industrial workers. During a committee hearing, one Republican accused her of being a professional agitator: "It has been said here that Miss Perkins represents the women in industry. She does not represent women, nor does she represent anything but agitation. To such an extent did she regard her name synonymous with agitation that she did not dare to change it when she got married for fear that she would sink into oblivion."

Smith refused to withdraw Perkins's name and threatened a "hard fight" if the Senate continued to withhold its approval. When her appointment was finally confirmed, he lost no time in putting her to work, sending her to Rome, New York, to mediate a strike between the management and workers at the Rome Brass and Copper Company. Company officials were shocked. "They seemed to imply by their attitude the belief that any such undertaking was entirely outside the province of a woman," Smith recalled. After Perkins helped settle the strike, company officials praised both Perkins and her boss.

Soon after the election, Belle Moskowitz told Perkins that the end of the war offered an opportunity to promote planning for the future, and the two drew up a plan for a commission that would address the state's problems. Smith liked the idea of creating an advisory group that would include leaders in every major field of endeavor and every political persuasion. Smith charged the commission with finding a solution to the state's housing emergency, identifying new sources of taxation to relieve the inequities of the current system, lowering the high cost of food, and promoting employment and public health.

The Reconstruction Commission would enhance Smith's reputation as a statesman with a vision of the future. In the early months of 1919, however, it was the man and his family who emerged most clearly. It was his new neighbors in Albany who got to know him first. The Smiths had always encouraged their children to bring their friends home. In an article in the *Woman's Home Companion*, Katie explained that this allowed them to keep an eye on them and to know who their friends were. But the only way this would work was to make it fun to be home:

> Home, to them, has always meant "good times." It has meant a welcome to their friends; the door is ever open to the boys and girls my boys and girls like. Home has meant simplicity and laughter and good-natured teasing, impromptu children's parties, after-dinner "sings" in which my husband and myself join, putting on the phonograph records and pushing back the rugs whenever the youngsters want to dance, lengthening the luncheon or dinner table to include any child guest.

One evening not long after the Smiths' arrival, a mother came to the front door of the mansion looking for her daughter. The governor himself came to the door and escorted the woman to the dining room where the family was having dinner. She found her daughter sitting next to Smith's vacated chair. The woman apologized for the interruption. "I have seen several Governors' families come and go," she explained. "When she told me that one of your daughters had invited her over . . . well, I just had to come over and see for myself."

The Smith children dominated life at the Executive Mansion. No conference was too important to get in the way of Saturday evening baths or good-night kisses. The children's tastes shaped the physical appearance of the mansion itself as the tennis courts were ripped out to make way for the ponies and other animals that the Smiths had longed to keep on the crowded Lower East Side. The Smith stable soon became a zoo filled with animals contributed by people from around the state. Consequently, it was a sensation but not entirely a surprise when the governor showed up in downtown Albany one day driving a pony cart.

Smith certainly knew that the honeymoon he enjoyed in his first weeks in Albany would not last. The Republican leaders of the legislature were not about to let their personal affection for Al Smith obstruct their political goals. While many of them were happy for their friend, Smith's leadership aroused their deepest fears, and they fully expected to defeat his program and recapture the governorship. In March 1919 the Republicans refused to appropriate funds for the Reconstruction Commission.

They claimed that the commission was a "super-legislature" that would assume the initiative for lawmaking in New York, reducing its elected bodies to rubber stamps. Over the next four weeks the Assembly also refused to consider Smith's proposals for a minimum wage commission, workers' health insurance, an eight-hour day for women and children, and the extension of workmen's compensation. Unfortunately for Smith, the Republicans were supported by a rapid change in public opinion. A fear of Communism was beginning to sweep the nation. Smith and his advisers had seen the transition from war to peace as an opportunity for reform. Events over the summer and fall revealed that it could also be a time for profound reaction.

The American people were tired. After the delirious celebrations of the end of the war, the dawn of the new year had been an anticlimax, and the crowd in Times Square on New Year's Eve was noticeably smaller than usual. New Yorkers did manage to summon some enthusiasm when President Wilson arrived in the city in early March. In introducing the president, Governor Smith praised Wilson for his idealism:

He told the mothers of our country that they were giving up their youth not only that the world might be made safe for democracy, but that there would never be another war. To the fulfillment of that promise he has dedicated himself with all his heart, and all his soul and all his strength, and all his great ability and the rank and file of the American people are standing squarely and solidly behind him.

Yet the tide had begun to turn against the president. His call for a Democratic Congress to support his policies had been rejected by the voters, and the Republicans now controlled both the House and the Senate. Earlier in the day, Senate Republicans had announced their opposition to the draft covenant of the League of Nations. Now Wilson was on his way back to Europe to finish negotiating the peace treaty with allies who rejected his notion of a just peace for Germany. As the president stood up to speak, the crowd jumped to its feet and waved handkerchiefs and the band played "Over There." He smiled and nodded to the music, waiting for his chance to begin. "I accept the intimation of the air just played," Wilson said. "I will not come back 'till it's over over there."

But the country was far less interested in what was happening in Europe than in signs of European radicalism in the United States. Most Americans disliked the radicals and their opposition to the capitalist system, but they had rarely seemed a serious threat. Although the Industrial Workers of the World (IWW) advocated class warfare through the use of strikes, most radicals were dedicated to gaining power through peaceful means. Socialists served in the legislatures of twelve states and held more than one thousand offices in municipal government in 1914. But the success of the Bolsheviks in Russia threw a new light on American radicalism. Enthralled Americans were soon organizing their own Communist Party. In February 1919 conservatives were alarmed when labor leaders in Seattle announced a general strike in support of shipyard workers. General strikes were unknown in the United States, and the Seattle strike was denounced in newspapers across the country as an attempt at a radical coup d'état. The strike was abandoned only a few days after it started, but the fear of radicalism continued to grow.

At first Smith dismissed the growing pressure for the government to do something about the radicals, but he didn't deny their existence or that they could pose a threat. There was a strong Socialist Party vote in New York City, and it threatened the Democrats more than anyone else. Anarchists were potentially more dangerous because they rejected the political process and sought to overturn the capitalist order through strikes. Their noisy New York City demonstrations ultimately led the legislature to ban the display of the red flag as an incitement to violent revolution. Smith signed the bill into law, but he was convinced that the large Socialist vote and the noisy anarchist demonstrations were both protests against poor living conditions that would disappear when government helped eliminate the underlying problems. He noted that the Republicans in the State Senate had created a special committee to investigate the threat of Bolshevism, while Republicans in the Assembly were blocking his social welfare proposals. "What I am afraid of is that by the action of the Assembly the Government may be creating something to investigate," Smith said. But the fear of radical terrorists was not entirely unfounded.

Two weeks after Smith's speech to the National Democratic Club, someone mailed a bomb to Seattle mayor Ole Hanson, who had helped defeat the general strike. The bomb was defective, but the next day a second bomb exploded in the hands of a maid in the house of a former U.S.

senator in Atlanta. Reading a newspaper account of these attacks, a postal worker in New York City remembered recently setting aside sixteen similar packages for insufficient postage and called the police. Eighteen more were intercepted elsewhere. May Day, 1919, produced riots in a number of American cities that lent credence to the fears of conservatives, even though most of the violence was caused by members of patriotic groups who demonstrated their commitment to the Constitution by attacking people who disagreed with them. Nevertheless, the riots were taken as still another sign that something was seriously wrong in the country.

The hysterical search for Communist infiltrators that would eventually be called the Red Scare began in earnest on the evening of June 2, 1919, when eight bombs exploded outside the homes of prominent men, including the mayor of Cleveland and judges in New York City, Boston, and Pittsburgh. A night watchman was killed in New York, but the only other casualty was an Italian anarchist who stumbled trying to plant his bomb outside the Washington home of A. Mitchell Palmer, the new U.S. attorney general. Only an anarchist pamphlet threatening further bloodshed survived the blast. The June bombings convinced many that the United States must be ruthless if it was going to meet the threat of Communist revolution. A Montana senator introduced a bill making it a crime to advocate violent revolution. Palmer appointed a new chief of the Justice Department's Bureau of Investigation to take charge of the search for the bombers and created a new assistant attorney general to help. Congress gave the federal Red hunters $500 million to speed their work.

The biggest beneficiary of the June bombings was the Lusk committee, which had been appointed by the New York legislature in March to investigate the threat of Bolshevism. Although not scheduled to begin its work until July, the committee recognized that its moment had arrived and met for the first time on June 12 in New York's City Hall. Meanwhile, only a few blocks away, Justice Department agents and members of the state police were raiding the offices of the Russian Soviet Bureau in the World Tower Building. The head of the office was served with a subpoena and escorted to City Hall, where he was questioned by the committee. The Lusk raid made front-page headlines in newspapers across the country and was followed two weeks later by raids on the headquarters of the IWW and the Left Wing Socialists as well as a socialist academy, the Rand School. Though it found no evidence of any crimes, the committee insisted that it could prove that one hundred trade unions were controlled by radicals and that the Rand School was working with the Russians to bolshevize American labor. The committee also accused the school of planning to radicalize African-Americans by paying orators to arouse fury over acts of racial injustice and by subsidizing radical newspapers targeting the black community. Charging that the Rand School was the headquarters of the American Bolshevik movement, the Lusk committee filed suit to revoke its charter.

The Lusk committee's success in stirring fear of revolution put Smith on the defensive. It was no longer enough to suggest that wise legislation could diminish the danger of radicalism. The governor was expected to take action to protect public safety, and Smith did what was expected of him. Two days after the bombings, he traveled to New York City to discuss the situation with the state attorney general. Under the terms of a law passed by the legislature in 1917, the governor and attorney general were given the power to order measures to protect public peace. Attorney General Charles D. Newton, however, was a Republican and the chief counsel of the Lusk committee. He had no interest in cooperating with Smith and allowing him to steal the spotlight. So he left town before Smith arrived. Smith met with the head of the Justice Department's Bureau of Investigation at his suite in the Biltmore Hotel instead. He also began to take a hard line toward radicals in his public comments. In a speech at Cornell University's commencement exercises, Smith talked about the importance of education as an antidote to radicalism, but he acknowledged that education might not be enough:

> There are two things that can be done with these ultra-radicals, but we would like to educate them and show them what the United States really means. But we may have to suppress them, and that will be the work of the State in which it will not hesitate.

Following the second round of raids by the Lusk committee, Smith authorized a special session of the State Supreme Court to determine whether any charges should be brought based on the information seized. The crusade against radicalism, however, was not the only challenge that Smith was forced to meet in the summer of 1919. A far more serious threat began to emerge.

# 6 ❊ THE VOCATION OF
# POLITICS

A month after Smith's inauguration, on January 28, 1919, the great German sociologist Max Weber walked to the front of a meager lecture hall in Munich to deliver an address on the nature of leadership in the modern world. It was a timely topic in the aftermath of a war in which millions had died for reasons that had come to seem vague if not meaningless. It had an especially sharp point in Germany, where revolution had raged in many of the principal cities since November. But it was hardly less urgent in the United States, which had been hit with a wave of strikes that convinced many Americans that they, too, faced the prospect of an imminent revolution. In his lecture on "The Vocation of Politics," Weber hoped to identify the qualities that political leaders would need to meet the problems confronting democratic countries.

Weber was not optimistic. He believed that the greatest threat to freedom came not from the power of organized capital or the revolutionary masses but from the relentless advance of bureaucracy. As society grew more complex under capitalism, the power of the bureaucrats had increased to the point where elected politicians had little chance of realizing goals that were based on moral values. Instead of being an arena for debating values, politics had become a mechanism for dividing society's wealth based on the strength of its competing interest groups—a boring and sordid affair.

Weber saw only one chance of escaping the iron grip of bureaucracy. Only a leader with charismatic authority was capable of leading a popular

movement strong enough to effect significant changes in the direction of
the state. Today, the word "charisma" is applied to film stars as often as to
politicians. Weber drew his concept of charisma from religion, and the
devotion of the followers to a charismatic leader was similar to the passion
that acolytes feel for their messiah. After the rise of Adolf Hitler, Weber
would be criticized for extolling charisma. Weber's charismatic leader
was no totalitarian, however. His leader required passion, responsibility,
and perspective. He must strongly advocate some cause, but he must also
care enough about it not to sacrifice its interests for his own advancement. For this reason he must have an objectivity that enables him to
judge the political situation accurately.

Ultimately, Weber's pessimism grew from his conviction that charismatic leadership was rare. It seemed practically impossible to combine
the necessary characteristics. "For . . . how can warm passion and a cool
sense of proportion be forged together in the one and the same soul?" he
asked. If this wasn't difficult enough, the leader must be capable of bearing terrible adversity:

> Politics is a strong and slow boring of hard boards. It takes both
> passion and perspective. Certainly all historical experience con-
> firms the truth—that man would not have attained the possible
> unless time and again he had reached out for the impossible. But
> to do that a man must be a leader, and not only a leader but a hero
> as well, in a very sober sense of the word. . . . Only he has the call-
> ing for politics who is sure that he shall not crumble when the
> world from his point of view is too stupid or too base for what he
> wants to offer. Only he who in the face of all this can say "In spite
> of all!" has the calling for politics.

In the summer of 1919, it was an open question whether Al Smith
had what it takes to be a two-term governor, much less a great political
leader. He was charming, of course. The coming of the Smiths to Albany
had been a delicious change of pace. But the legislature had crushed his
political program, confident that its power would endure long after this
accidental governor had been forgotten. Events seemed to be bearing out
this prediction, for Smith was being pounded mercilessly by the Hearst
press, and its criticisms were targeting the working-class voters who were

the core of Smith's support. As Smith silently absorbed the Hearst attacks, no one could have predicted that he would emerge as a truly charismatic leader who would transform the government of New York State. He would not just survive Hearst's assaults, he would eliminate the publisher as a significant factor in state and national politics.

There was no question who was more powerful at the start of the summer. Had Hearst decided to bear a grudge against Al Smith for helping eliminate him as a candidate for governor in 1918, he could have defeated him easily. Smith's victory had depended on a record turnout by the city's working class, and while Tammany could claim a lot of the credit, Smith could not have won without the support of the *American* and the *Journal*. For over twenty years, these newspapers had made a strong appeal for working-class readers, competing with Joseph Pulitzer's *World* to be the voice of the city's laboring man. By imitating the innovations introduced by Pulitzer, including large headlines, bigger type, and more illustrations and comics, Hearst's *American* was selling 800,000 copies per day only a year after he bought it. Hearst introduced colored comics pages, gave extensive coverage to the most sensational crimes, and exploited prurient appeal whenever possible. Hearst's papers also championed the economic interests of the working class by attacking business monopolies. On the national level, Hearst called for legal action to break up the Standard Oil Company and demanded the nationalization of the railroads. In New York, he challenged the companies that exploited workers through their monopolies on the city's ice, natural gas, electricity, and transit. It was largely due to his efforts that New Yorkers paid 20 percent less for gas than the monopolists once demanded. Hearst's denunciation of the country's corporations was so strident that many business leaders feared him as a dangerous radical.

It was the presidency, not a revolution, that was Hearst's goal. He had already made two serious bids for the Democratic presidential nomination. A man who worshiped great leaders and had a painting of Napoleon hanging above his desk, Hearst was not easily discouraged. Although his opposition to America's entry into the war had made him anathema to many Americans, he continued to believe that the presidency would be his. His media empire was continuing to grow, and his position in New York had been strengthened by the election of Mayor Hylan in 1917. Hylan became a virtual mouthpiece for Hearst during his two terms as mayor, and his control of the city's patronage gave Hearst almost as much power over city affairs as Boss Murphy. It was not crazy to think that with his strong New York City base, Hearst might yet attain the governorship and the Democratic presidential nomination.

Political observers were not particularly surprised when Hearst's New York papers began to criticize Smith in April 1919 over an appointment to the New York Supreme Court. Smith had ignored Hearst's choice and appointed an attorney who had once worked for the New York Central Railroad. The next day, the Hearst newspapers attacked the appointment, calling the new judge "a tool of the interests." Reporters asked Hearst if he wasn't really angry about the rejection of his request. He replied, "I have been particularly careful never to ask any appointment or any other political favor of Governor Smith, for I have never been quite convinced of the sincerity of his profession of progressive principles. He has always been too close to Tammany, and too close to certain public service corporations to make him an ideal public official from my point of view." Over the next week, the Hearst papers began picking at the governor's record, criticizing his appointment of a county judge upstate, a speech to the wealthy members of the Metropolitan Club, and his purported role in the removal of the head of the Prison Commission. A week later, Mayor Hylan joined in the criticism by protesting Smith's decision to approve a wage increase for the state's teachers. If these attacks were mild, it was only because it took Hearst's men some time to find truly scurrilous things to print. Three weeks after the opening salvo, the Hearst papers printed a story in which the Rev. O. R. Miller, state superintendent of the New York Civic League, charged that when Smith was Speaker of the Assembly he had used bribery to secure the removal of Governor Sulzer. But the charge didn't stick. Unable to produce any witnesses, the Hearst reporters began searching for a new angle. They finally found what they had been looking for in the issue of milk.

There were few things as important to the people of New York City as a steady supply of cheap milk. Milk was an important source of nourishment for the city's children, and working-class families were particularly dependent on it. Yet, because it was produced by farmers who lived upstate and was consumed in the cities, it was also a highly contentious political issue. The farmers had created a powerful Dairymen's League to ensure that they got the best possible price for their product, and the

League had used its influence with upstate legislators to protect their monopoly by granting them an exemption from the state antitrust laws. The only state agency with any power over the milk producers was the Department of Farms and Markets, and upstate legislators had removed it from the reach of the executive branch by providing that its personnel would be appointed by the Council on Farms and Markets, a body that was answerable to the legislature, not the governor.

In the absence of effective state regulation, not only was milk more expensive than it should have been in New York City, but also supplies were subject to disruption. Soon after Smith took office, a dispute between producers and distributors cut off the city's milk supply. Smith helped arbitrate an agreement that got the milk flowing again, but the underlying problem persisted. He created a commission representing the interests of producers, distributors, and the public to make recommendations for improving the situation. But only the legislature could repeal the antitrust exemption. Smith later ordered an investigation of the Department of Farms and Markets that revealed close ties between Commissioner Eugene H. Porter and the Dairymen's League. Smith demanded that the Council on Farms and Markets fire Porter, but he was ignored. He was in an impossible situation: although the public believed that he had the responsibility to act, he lacked power to do anything. With his hands tied behind his back, Smith was a perfect target for Hearst's attacks.

Hearst's reporters began to scour Smith's record in an effort to paint him as a tool of the "Milk Trust." There wasn't much to find. They tried to make something of Smith's appointment of members of the Dairymen's League to the commission investigating the milk situation. They discovered an attorney who had worked for the League acting as an adviser to a committee surveying prison conditions. They accused the state of allowing the League to pressure independent producers through the New York Central Railroad. These news stories were accompanied by almost daily editorials that painted Smith as someone who had sold out the poor. The *Journal* claimed that Smith "does nothing while thousands of babies are suffering—many of them are dying—from lack of sufficient food in order that the Milk Trust may fatten its pocketbook." He was responsible for "the multiplication of the little mounds in the graveyards and the added death dollars in the Milk Trust's treasury." But the most damning part of the Hearst attack was not words but pictures. His car-

toonists were famous for their ability to paint corporate leaders and political bosses as enemies of the people. Smith's prominent nose and heavy
accent made him an easy target. The *American* presented him as the hero
of a series of cartoons titled "Trusteroodle Film Co. Presents" that depicted him as the lackey of the transit and milk trusts. In one, Smith is
drawn as Hamlet, holding up the skull of the public and declaiming,
"Alas, poor New Yorik I'm too busy to help him just now." The *Journal's*
cartoonists didn't even try to be witty. A typical cartoon showed two ema-
ciated infants with empty bottles wailing, "Save us from the milk profiteers," while over the Executive Chamber hung a sign, "Nobody home."

Smith later said that he had ignored the attack at first, believing that
"it was so stupid and silly that nobody else would pay any attention to it."
Many of Smith's early biographers believed a story that he decided to
fight back after hearing that his mother, while ill, had cried out in delir-
ium that her son had not killed any babies. Smith does not refer to such
an incident, and his daughter, Emily, later denied that it occurred. In his
autobiography Smith says he made the decision to challenge Hearst after
realizing that the charges were beginning to hurt him politically. "[T]his
foolish attack was making some impression on the minds of people, who
from the nature of things, would naturally be friendly to me," he explains.
Smith also hoped he could help defeat Hearst's latest political initiative,
the nomination of a slate of candidates for municipal judge to challenge
Tammany's nominees.

Smith's attack on Hearst was carefully planned. His first criticism of
the publisher was made in a speech to three thousand members of the
Women's Democratic League. He explained to his audience that Hearst
was angry with him because he had not shown the proper degree of subservience. Hearst had accused him of being disloyal to the working class
from which he came, but Hearst's own loyalty was open to question,
Smith said. "Just this time a year ago every small municipality in a radius
of fifty miles from where we are sitting was burning his newspapers in
public squares because they had in their minds that he was not loyal to
this country. I have been loyal; I have lived among my people, and they
have respect for me and confidence in me. He has been loyal to nobody,
not even his own." The women jumped to their feet, applauding the first
sign of Smith's break with Hearst. Then Smith challenged Hearst to a debate. The publisher would receive half of the tickets for his supporters.

"He can ask me any question he likes about my public or about my private life, if he will let me do the same," Smith said. Within days, a citizens committee was formed to sponsor the debate and announced that it had rented Carnegie Hall for the night of October 29.

The biggest showman since Barnum had been upstaged by Smith's challenge. When Hearst and his newspapers failed to respond, it was Smith's turn to needle the publisher: "It is a particularly easy thing for an unscrupulous newspaper man to hide behind the green shade of a lamp and put his foul, dirty pen into the slimy ink that would destroy the character of other men. But it is a hard thing for that type of man to come out into the open and that is the reason why his filthy sheets are strangely quiet about my challenge to meet him." Hearst waited until two days before the Carnegie Hall debate to announce that he had no intention of participating. In a letter to the sponsoring committee, Hearst explained that it was not his job to debate:

> I do not have to meet him, as I am not running for office, and I certainly do not want to meet him for the pleasure of association, as I find no satisfaction in the company of crooked politicians. Neither have I time or inclination to debate with every public plunderer or faithless public servant whom my papers have exposed, for the reason that every pilloried rascal in every city where my papers are published always tries to divert attention from the real issue of his political crookedness by making some sort of blatherskite onslaught upon me.

Hearst's pose as a journalist who was above the political fray was laughable. His unwillingness to debate the governor only encouraged the belief that Smith was about to wipe him from the political map.

Smith's first biographers would portray his Carnegie Hall speech as a furious, even heavy-handed, assault on his absent opponent. One of his most sensitive chroniclers, Henry Pringle, wrote, "All that was savage in him and all that was crude were close to the surface. . . . Then his words came in a gushing stream, a torrent so mad that grammar and phrasing and niceties of syntax were swept away." There was nothing phony about the passion that Smith felt that night as he faced the packed tiers of the country's most elegant concert hall. But he was too practiced a performer to allow it to overwhelm him. His job was a difficult one, for he was not speaking only to the well-wishers who packed the hall. He could count on their ovations ahead of time. He was seeking nothing less than to demolish Hearst's claim to speak for the working class and to establish his own leadership. This meant he must convincingly disprove the charges that the Hearst papers had made against him. He would also have to reveal the selfishness that made it impossible for Hearst to cooperate with other politicians in improving the lives of the people he said he cared about. Knowing that this would be the most important speech that he had ever given, Smith acted like a surgeon using a sharp blade to excise a malignant tumor.

He opened his speech by asking for "absolute silence and attention." "I feel that I am here tonight upon a mission as important, not only to myself but to this city, to this State and to this country, as I could possibly perform," he explained.

> Of course I am alone. I don't know whether the chairman or the committee expected that I would be alone, but I knew that I would and I felt that I would, because I know the man to whom I issued the challenge, and I know that he has not got a drop of good, clean, pure red blood in his whole body. And I know the color of his liver, and it is whiter, if that could be than the driven snow.

He poked fun at Hearst, blaming his poor grasp of New York affairs on his being "in Palm Beach all winter and in California all summer."

Smith began to get serious when he mentioned the full-page ad that had appeared in the *American* that morning. It displayed a picture of Smith with cartoons of a workingman on one side and a mother and her children on the other. Fingers pointed at the cartoons under a headline that read "Answer These People, Governor Smith." "I want to say to this audience that I was anxious to bring him on this platform so that he could answer to these people," Smith said. He then began to build his case against Hearst. "In order to show the motive of this attack upon me I propose to take this audience by the hand and walk them through my administration since the first of January up to tonight." He showed them how his rejection of several of Hearst's requests had led to the first critical editorial and then a final break over the failure of Hearst's candidate to receive an appointment to the Supreme Court, and how the Hearst writers had struggled to find an issue before they finally hit on milk. He then turned to a detailed rebuttal of the charges that he had acted in the interest of a Milk Trust, clarifying each of the important misrepresentations.

But Smith's speech was more than a masterly defense of his own record. Having proved that he had been falsely accused, Smith attacked Hearst at his weakest point—his selfishness.

I cannot think of a more contemptible man—my power of imagination fails me to bring into my mind's eye a more despicable man than the man that exploits the poor. Any man that leads you to believe that your lot in life is not all right, any man that conjures up for you a fancied grievance against your government or against the man at the head of it, to help himself, is breeding the seeds of an anarchy and a dissatisfaction more disastrous to the welfare of the community than any other teaching that I can think of, because, at least, the wildest anarchist, the most extreme Socialist, the wildest radical that you can think of, may at least be sincere in his own heart.

Had Hearst been on the platform that night he would surely have protested that he was not interested merely in fomenting discontent; that he supported a well-defined program whose implementation would benefit the poor. But Smith anticipated this objection. The problem with the Hearst newspapers was not that they criticized politicians but that they had discredited all political leaders and undermined faith in the democratic process. They were claiming that Hearst was the only man capable of providing solutions, Smith charged.

Smith reminded his audience that they were living through troubled times. Only that morning, he had been called out of bed an hour early by "striking and rioting and murder" that had taken place in a city upstate. Nevertheless, he professed his confidence that these troubles would pass. "I am one of the men that have supreme confidence in the good sense, in the hard common sense and in the good judgment of the American people to be able to weather any kind of storm. Labor unrest will cure itself. We will attend to all of our internal problems." But the Hearst papers were obstructing the task of reconstruction. Because of their attacks, "I cannot be expected to have the influence I ought to have in this State at this time," he explained. Smith then drew back for the final blow. "What could there possibly be about me that I should be assailed in this reckless manner by this man?" he asked.

I have more reason probably than any man I will meet tonight to have a strong love and a strong devotion for this country, for this State, for this city. Look at what I have received at its hands: I left school and went to work before I was 15 years of age. I worked hard, night and day; I worked honestly and conscientiously at every job that I was ever put at, until I went to the Governor's chair in Albany. What can it be? It has got to be jealousy, it has got to be hatred, or it has to be something that nobody understands, that makes me come down here, into the city of New York, before this audience, and urge them to organize in this city to stay the danger that comes from these papers, to the end that the health, the welfare, and the comfort of this people, of the people of this State, may be promoted, and we may get rid of this pestilence that walks in the darkness.

As Smith left the stage of Carnegie Hall, the crowd cheered and waved little American flags. A new leader had emerged.

Like Hearst, Smith was critical of existing institutions, but there was a crucial distinction between them. Hearst's papers offered their working-class readers a stark world in which capitalists and workers were locked in battle. Smith rejected theories of class conflict. He believed that all the problems faced by the American people could be worked out within the framework of democratic institutions. His optimism about effecting change through the political system gave him enormous appeal. It encouraged workers to believe that he was a man who was sincerely committed to helping them, while middle-class voters responded enthusiastically to his promise that the changes that he was advocating could be made without advancing the interests of one group over another—that they would serve the interest of all. Weber had said that unless a politician was willing to reach for the impossible, he could not expect to achieve anything meaningful. Smith's courage in attacking Hearst convinced many that he was a leader who could do great things.

Smith's emergence at this moment seemed almost providential, for the country appeared to be coming apart at the seams. Labor unrest had been growing all year. The first strike was staged by the very conservative members of the Boston Police Department, who had been driven to distraction by the unwillingness of the police commissioner to bargain with their union representatives. They left their posts on September 9. Two weeks later, the same intransigence by the chairman of the U.S. Steel Corporation, Judge Elbert H. Gary, and other leaders of the steel industry sent 375,000 steel workers into the streets, where they were soon joined by nearly 400,000 miners, all striking for the right to collective bargaining. There was little public sympathy for the Boston police strike, which made a national hero of Governor Calvin Coolidge. In more normal times, the public might have supported the steel workers and miners. These were not normal times, however, and the owners played expertly on the fears of Bolshevism that had been awakened earlier in the year. Most of the nation's newspapers had no trouble portraying even the Boston police strike as an insurrectionary movement.

Al Smith's reaction to the strikes that were occurring all over New York was very different from that of the mostly Republican chief executives in other states. He was a strong supporter of the right to collective bargaining and had run for office with backing from the American Federation of Labor. His platform in 1918 had included a plank calling for the abolition of the state police, which Republican governors had used along with the state militia to help break strikes. Smith did send the state police into Beacon when the mayor claimed that local officials couldn't cope with the riotous behavior of striking hat makers, but he pulled them out again when the police chief contradicted the mayor. His clear preference for settling strikes was to persuade both parties to accept state mediation. When the mayor of Rome asked Smith to send the state police to calm the crisis created by a strike against the Rome Brass and Copper Company, he made their arrival contingent on the willingness of the manufacturer to meet with Frances Perkins, who helped broker a deal that included a raise, a shorter workday, and eventual recognition of the union. In September Smith formalized his approach by creating a Reconstruction Labor Board, which helped avert strikes by public utility workers in Buffalo and garment workers and truckers in New York City.

On several occasions, Smith intervened personally in an effort to settle strikes. He wasn't always successful, but on the evening of Sunday, November 2, 1919, he proved in dramatic fashion that he could back up the claims of leadership that he had made only a few days before at Carnegie Hall. New York City was once again facing the prospect of a milk famine. This time the threat came not from the producers or distributors but from the nine thousand members of the Teamsters Union who drove the city's milk wagons. The men who gathered in a hall in upper Manhattan were in a rebellious mood. Although the milk companies were willing to submit the dispute to arbitration and the union leaders urged their members to agree, they were expected to vote to strike beginning at midnight. In desperation, union leaders called Smith, who had just returned to his hotel in midtown after a Sunday visit with his mother in Brooklyn. Leaving his dinner on the table, Smith rushed uptown. The governor was not recognized when he first arrived at the hall and began elbowing his way through the waiting men. When the truckers realized that the small man pushing his way forward was the governor, they began to cheer. Smith knew these men: they looked like his neighbors in the Fourth Ward, and he was sure that they desired not Bolshevik revolution but a living wage and decent working conditions. When he finally reached the stage, Smith told the men that he "wanted to be right to the laboring man." It was for this reason that he urged the drivers to listen to their leaders and accept arbitration:

> I contend there is no disorder—social, political or labor—so great that it cannot be settled. Now, you men can settle your troubles. You have the ability and the intelligence to do it in an orderly, peaceful manner, if you will follow your leaders. If you will follow your leaders, I will go with them. I'll put all my strength into it to see that you get an absolutely fair, square deal, both personally and as Governor.

The motion authorizing the strike was defeated.

But Americans were more scared than ever by the threat of revolution. In October the U.S. Senate had unanimously adopted a resolution directing Attorney General A. Mitchell Palmer to explain why the federal government was not being more vigorous in deporting foreigners who advocated the overthrow of the government. Soon after, Justice Department agents raided the New York City headquarters of the Union of Russian

Workers, an organization of four thousand "atheists, communists and an-archists" who believed in the violent overthrow of all institutions of gov-ernment and the confiscation of all wealth. The government also invaded branch offices in ten cities and arrested a total of 250 aliens, who were put aboard a ship and deported to Finland in late December. On Janu-ary 2, 1920, more than four thousand alleged radicals were arrested in thirty-three major cities and twenty-three states. Nearly every local Com-munist group in the country was targeted, and the entire Communist leadership ended up in jail. Deportation proceedings were initiated against foreign-born radicals, while American citizens were turned over to local authorities for prosecution under state conspiracy laws. After two or three days, the government was forced to release eight hundred who had been picked up for no other crime than being in the wrong place at the wrong time. Even the Communists were guilty of nothing more than ad-vocating revolution, which was not a crime. The attorney general insisted that criminal acts were not necessary. "Each and every adherent of this movement is a potential murderer or a potential thief," Palmer said. He continued: "Out of the sly and crafty eyes of many of them leap cupidity, cruelty, insanity, and crimes; from their lopsided faces, sloping brows, and misshapen features may be recognized the unmistakable criminal type." The overwhelming majority of Americans shared the attorney general's conviction that the most important thing was halting the advance of "Red radicalism."

As Al Smith prepared to deliver his second annual message to the New York legislature on January 7, he couldn't ignore the Red Scare. From the beginning, he had been skeptical of the motives that led to the creation of New York's own Red-hunting Lusk committee. He was dismayed by the ready identification of the foreign-born with radicalism. (The Lusk com-mittee even prepared a map of New York City that showed that the radical parties and their journals were overwhelmingly located in immigrant neighborhoods, particularly those occupied by Russian Jews.) He knew that public school teachers in New York City who were socialists or Com-munists were being fired because they could not set "a patriotic example." Smith was also feeling pressure to act, though, and did not want to appear indifferent to the threat of radicalism. On the day after the first Palmer raid in November 1919, the Lusk committee launched its own raid, using 700 policemen to invade seventy-three radical centers and make 500 arrests. Federal agents had arrested another 400 only a few days earlier to nearly universal acclaim. How could Smith express his concern without running afoul of public opinion?

The governor began his address by challenging some common assumptions. "Much of the dissatisfaction spoken of and written about has been largely exaggerated," he said. After an initial sharp recession, the economy had rebounded and employment was rising. "Work is plentiful, and the general condition of prosperity among our people is shown by bank balances and savings bank deposits," Smith said. "We seem to have emerged from a war of arms to a war of ideas," he said. But he had complete faith in the ability of "the American ideal triumphantly to resist Bolshevism." He pointed out that those who were exaggerating the threat of Bolshevism and radicalism were actually making the problem worse. "These are at present receiving an unnecessary amount of advertising, on which they thrive," he said. "During the war, in the interest of national unity and for our common defense against our enemy, every sane American relinquished some freedom," Smith continued. But the war was over. "[W]e should return to a normal state of mind, and keep our balance, and an even keel." The country must again be ruled democratically.

Smith had used the first five minutes of his speech to raise a significant question about the reality of the Communist threat without directly challenging those who were making a political issue out of it. But there was something else about the Red Scare that made him go further. He was no defender of radicalism. "The anarchist, the violent revolutionist, the underminer of our institutions should receive no mercy at our hands. He does not belong here." But the attack on Communism was becoming an assault on all Americans of immigrant birth. Smith acknowledged that many immigrants were discontented and therefore an obvious target for radicals. But this only underlined the importance of a "constructive" Americanization program. "We must immunize them against the infection, by approaching the problem in a spirit of sanity, a thorough and sympathetic understanding and a fearless and courageous meeting of their needs," he said.

Smith had hardly left the Assembly chamber at the conclusion of his speech before Thaddeus Sweet, the Speaker of the Assembly, demonstrated the extremism that he had been warning against. In virtually his first act in the new session, the Speaker summoned to the well of the chamber all five Socialist members of the Assembly. The sergeant at arms stood guard as Sweet denounced them as disloyal Americans and claimed, "It is therefore quite evident that you, elected to public office, in spite of your oath of office are bound to act subject to instruction received from an executive committee which may be made up in whole or in part of aliens or alien enemies owing allegiance to governments or organizations whose interests may be immediately opposed to the best interests of the United States." Citing a provision of the state constitution that gave the Assembly the right to judge the qualifications of its members, Sweet then moved to suspend the Socialists until the Judiciary Committee could decide whether they should be expelled. The Socialists were allowed to return to their seats and to vote on the motion, which was carried 140 to 6.

The Assembly's suspension of the Socialists was an outrageous abuse of its power. As Smith would later explain, the power to judge the qualifications of its members had been given to the Assembly to permit it to bar men who may have committed a criminal act since the time of their election. It certainly was not intended to provide a way to deny office to people whose political views were offensive. Ironically, those who were expelled were members of the Socialist Party's right wing, who believed that power should be sought through the ballot box, not the gun.

Smith decided to fight the suspension of the Socialists soon after he learned about it. When he informed the Democratic leaders in the legislature of his intention, they tried to change his mind. Many feared he was handing the Republicans an issue that could be used again them. But Smith refused to be dissuaded and issued his statement at a political dinner in the Waldorf-Astoria that was attended by the leaders of both parties: "Although I am unalterably opposed to the fundamental principles of the Socialist Party, it is inconceivable that a minority, duly constituted and legally organized, should be deprived of its right to expression so long as it has honestly, by lawful methods of education and propaganda, succeeded in securing representation, unless the chosen representatives are unfit as individuals." If the Assembly had evidence that the Socialist members were trying to overthrow the government "by processes subversive of law and order," they should have presented it to the legislature and put them on trial. "Meanwhile, presumably innocent until proven guilty, they should have been allowed to retain their seats," Smith said. Sweet found Smith at the dinner and protested that he had not been told of the statement in advance. Smith was unrepentant. Over the next five months, his defense of constitutional rights would lead him into repeated conflict with the legislature.

During the conflict that began with the suspension of the Socialist assemblymen in January 1920 and ended with Smith's veto of six bills known as the "Lusk laws" in May, it was far from clear whether the public would come to agree with the governor about the importance of protecting minority rights. Smith was not alone in his position. Former governor Charles Evans Hughes and Senator William Borah of Idaho also denounced the suspension. There were few legal decisions to cite in support of their position, however. Although the First Amendment to the U.S. Constitution guaranteed the right to freedom of speech, this right had not been well defined by Congress or the courts. During the war, the public had strongly supported legislation that punished speech that might interfere with the war effort, and the postmaster general banned antiwar magazines from the mail. The U.S. Supreme Court had approved the government's right to suppress dissent. Socialist Eugene Debs was sent to prison for saying, "The master class has had all to gain and nothing to lose, while the subject class has had nothing to gain and all to lose—especially their lives." Even the great jurist Oliver Wendell Holmes, Jr., joined in upholding Debs's imprisonment. It wasn't until November 1919 that Holmes changed his mind about the importance of protecting speech. In a dissenting opinion that would later become one of the pillars of First Amendment law, he urged that speech be protected from censorship unless it posed a clear and present danger to the government.

In April 1920 the legislature expelled the Socialists and approved six bills that were intended to bar Socialists from participating in future elections and to limit the ability of radicals to propagate their views in both public and private schools. The Lusk laws gave the state extremely broad powers to curb dissent, including the power to revoke the license of any teacher who was not "loyal to the institutions of the United States and of the State of New York" and to close any private school whose instruction was "detrimental to the public interest." As a Democrat, Smith was philosophically committed to protecting individual rights and curbing the arbitrary exercise of power by the state. As a former legislator, he could only have been appalled at legislation that was so badly drafted that it would lead to years of litigation. He was instinctively opposed to the reactionary Republicans who had led the fight for these laws. He also had another reason for vetoing the Lusk laws.

With the exception of two years, Smith had been in the minority throughout his legislative career, and he believed that protecting minority rights was essential to the preservation of political freedom. In 1918 Smith was serving as the president of the Board of Aldermen when Socialist aldermen were elected for the first time. He promised the Socialists fair play: "I have a keen understanding of the relationship to the body of the minority and the minor minority—meaning the Socialist members. The people rule negatively as well as affirmatively, and a good, healthy, vigorous minority is the necessary check on great power." For Smith, there was nothing theoretical about the importance of free speech. He was gifted with a pair of leather lungs, and he used them frequently to denounce the injustices visited on his constituents by an indifferent majority. At times, they were the only thing preventing the people of New York City from being ignored altogether.

In explaining his position to the public, Smith was careful to make his arguments as clear and simple as possible. He told the Young Men's Bible Class of the Fifth Avenue Baptist Church that not all radicals were committed to the violent overthrow of government. The five Socialist assemblymen were "all right" because they were attempting to achieve their goal through peaceful means, he said. Later, when the Lusk laws were sent to him for signature, Smith made sure that his veto messages would be understandable to the man in the street. Smith's friend and legal adviser Joseph Proskauer prepared his most important legal memorandums. Smith told Proskauer he wanted the Lusk memos to be something special. Would he include "some highbrow college stuff"? Proskauer sent him messages that quoted Benjamin Franklin, Thomas Jefferson, and Alexis de Tocqueville. When the messages appeared, the Tocqueville quote was missing. Moskowitz later called Proskauer to tell him that the governor had instructed her to relay his explanation for the quote's absence word for word (because it contained an obscenity, she apologized in advance): "Tell Joe I'm supposed to know Benjamin Franklin. I'm supposed to know Thomas Jefferson. But if I had ever used that quotation from that French ——, everyone would know that Al Smith never wrote that message."

Smith had taken out the quote from Jefferson, too, but he had gotten what he wanted from Proskauer. Despite his caution, he was not willing to rest his vetoes on practical considerations, and Proskauer's memos provided an eloquent explanation of the importance of free speech in a democracy. The real sin of the teacher-licensing bill was that it undermined the First Amendment rights of teachers:

It deprives teachers of their right to freedom of thought; it limits the teaching staff of the public schools to those only who lack the courage or the mind to exercise their legal right to just criticism of existing institutions. The bill confers upon the Commissioner of Education a power of interference with freedom of opinion which strikes at the foundations of democratic education.

In words that echoed Justice Holmes, Smith said the Assembly was wrong to believe that it could protect truth by licensing schools on ideological grounds. "The clash of conflicting opinions, from which progress arises more than from any other source, would be abolished by law, tolerance and intellectual freedom destroyed, and an intellectual autocracy imposed upon the people," he explained. Since it was the clash of opinions that produced truth, it was essential that government protect the freedom of everyone to have their say, no matter how they might offend the majority: "Law, in a democracy, means the protection of the rights and liberties of the minority. Their rights, when properly exercised, and their liberties, when not abused, should be safeguarded. It is a confession of the weakness of our own faith in the righteousness of our cause when we attempt to suppress by law those who do not agree with us." Like Hearst, the Assembly had shown that it had little faith in the democratic system. "[T]he safety of this government and its institutions rests upon the reasoned and devoted loyalty of its people," Smith said. "It does not need for its defense a system of intellectual tyranny which, in the endeavor to choke error by force, must of necessity crush truth as well."

Smith's fight for freedom of speech was one aspect of his effort to make government in New York more democratic. At the beginning of January 1920, Smith had reintroduced all of the legislation that the legislature had killed the previous year—the bills providing for minimum wages and an eight-hour day for women and children, the expansion of workmen's compensation, and the provision of health and maternity insurance for factory workers. He also included a bill authorizing the state to develop and operate power-generating plants on its waterways, and, later in the year, a bill to provide loans to builders in an effort to end a worsening housing crisis. But the most contentious issue in the 1920 session was Smith's program of government reorganization, which consisted of constitutional amendments for consolidating the state administration, creating an executive budget, and extending the governor's term of office from two to four years. Smith also wanted the governor elected in non-presidential years so that the campaigns would be focused on state issues. Smith's reorganization program has been justly celebrated for modernizing the government of New York State, but the goal of these reforms has not always been fully understood. While they created a more efficient government, their main purpose was to shift power away from a legislature that represented only the interest of upstate voters and vest it in the governor, an official who was elected by all the people of the state. In the absence of a democratic reapportionment, reorganization was designed to help democratize state government. The Republicans in the legislature recognized that and prepared to do everything they could to defeat it.

The idea of reorganizing state government in New York was nothing new. For many years, critics had argued that the state's administrative organization had "nothing in common experience of human reason to commend it." When New York instituted an income tax in 1919 to help recoup the tax revenue lost as a result of Prohibition, politicians of both parties promised to take yet another look at the issue. Smith's Reconstruction Commission picked up where the 1915 constitutional convention left off. Under the direction of Robert Moses, a thirty-year-old reformer recruited by Belle Moskowitz, the Committee on Retrenchment issued its plan for reorganization in October 1919. The committee's focus on "retrenchment" reflected the prevailing concern with cutting the cost of government. The committee proposed to reduce the number of boards and commissions by transferring their functions to eighteen administrative departments headed by appointees of the governor. The governor was given the power to propose a budget that the legislature could not increase except for clearly stated reasons. Together with the extension of the governor's term, these changes were designed to make the governor a real force in state affairs.

The people of New York wrongly believed that the governor was a powerful official. "Everybody writes to me about everything in this State," Smith said. It was really the legislature that ruled through its control of the nearly two hundred boards and commissions that administered the real business of the state. The legislature had created most of these agencies itself, and it maintained its control by appointing the department heads and controlling their appropriations. The governor's power was further circumscribed because many of the key administrators either were directly elected or were holdovers from a previous administration, which meant that they were often members of the other party. All the important policy decisions were made by lower-ranking officials who often didn't even bother to consult the governor. For example, the Tunnel Commission, appointed by the legislature to oversee the construction of the first tunnel between New York City and New Jersey, had recently decided to reject a $2 million design by George W. Goethals, the engineer who built the Panama Canal, in favor of another plan that could cost as much as $25 million. "All I can do now is to shut down and see what the legislature wants to do about it," Smith said. The governor could deliver a special message outlining his views, but the commission was not required to listen. It was not even required to provide him with information. As New York prepared to build one of its most important public works since the Erie Canal, its chief executive officer was an outsider. The solution was simple: give the governor the power that everyone thinks he already has. "Now, whom do the people of the state look to?" Smith asked. "They look to the Governor."

The governor's weakness was clearest when it came to preparing the state's budget. The budget was intended to establish the spending priorities for the coming year, and everyone agreed in theory that it should be prepared by the state's chief executive officer, the official with the broadest view of its needs. In fact, it was the chairmen of the Assembly Ways and Means Committee and the Senate Finance Committee who decided where the money would be spent, often negotiating directly with the heads of the administrative departments. This not only undercut the governor's control of the executive branch, it frustrated his efforts to set priorities for the state's spending. Because the legislature was Republican, it also led to the systematic underfunding of state activities in urban areas. The constitutional amendment creating the executive budget gave the

THE VOCATION OF POLITICS

governor real budgetary authority by preventing the legislature from increasing any item in the budget. The legislative role in the budget process was approving or disapproving the governor's budget. It could also reduce or eliminate any proposed appropriation.

In his drive to win approval for reorganization, Smith often stressed how much money it would save. It was obvious that the existence of ten engineering departments and seven tax collection agencies was wasteful. While it was true that many of the members of the state's 187 commissions and boards were volunteers, Smith pointed out that the state paid the salaries of their administrative staffs. Nor were salaries the only expense. State employees were constantly on the move. "I would say today that probably the State of New York is the best single customer that New York Central Railroad has," Smith said. "If they live downstate there is occasion for them to travel north in the summer, and if they live upstate they invariably have to come to New York week-ends during the winter."

Yet Smith made it clear that the purpose of reorganization was not to reduce the cost of government but to make it possible for the state to do a better job of fulfilling its responsibilities. "The real fact is, that the State is not paying enough money for the service it is receiving," he told the City Club of New York in his first major address on reorganization. At the time Smith was waiting for a report on the condition of the state hospitals for the insane, but he knew enough to predict that "it is not going to make for pleasant reading." Because the state could afford to pay only $7 per week for attendants, the facilities were badly understaffed.

> Over here in Ward's Island one 19-year-old girl is attempting—is only attempting—to take care of 25 insane women of the violent kind; and when Dr. Biggs and Dr. Bailey called there last week and asked her if she did not have quite a job on her hands, she said, "Well if you got a look at me once in a while you would think I had," and she rolled up the sleeve of her dress and her arm was all torn where a number of them had made an attack upon her.

At some facilities, there was one nurse for forty patients. Because there was no one to take them outside, many patients were forced to remain in their stifling rooms during July and August. Smith believed that the budget for the state hospitals had to be increased at least 30 percent. The state's prisons had also been neglected, and the roads were falling apart under the weight of larger trucks. "We must banish from our minds the idea of cutting down the expense of the State," Smith concluded.

Political tact prevented Smith from saying that the chief benefit of the reorganization program was that it would help counter the domination of state government by upstate voters. Yet this was clearly the implication of many of his speeches. It came closest to the surface in his remarks about the Council on Farms and Markets, which had consistently refused to take any action to control the milk industry. He could not openly charge that it was the legislature's subservience to agricultural interests that led it to remove milk from any kind of effective government regulation. Such charges would have turned reorganization into a partisan issue and killed any chance for its passage.

The Republicans couldn't speak frankly either. They could not say that they opposed the reorganization program because it threatened their control of state government. Instead, they accused Smith of trying to make himself a king. The Republican lieutenant governor, Seymour Lowman, made this accusation in a debate before the Women's City Club. Smith rose with a big smile on his face. "Meet the King, the King of Oliver Street," he replied. But jokes were not going to make the charge disappear. From the beginning, Smith and his advisers knew that this would be the main point of attack for the opponents of reorganization. The usual response was that reorganization made the governor no more powerful than the mayor of New York or the president of the United States, both of whom served four-year terms and appointed their chief administrative officers. This answer did not satisfy the Republicans.

Another way of countering legislative opposition was by enlisting the help of Republicans outside the legislature. Men like Elihu Root and Henry L. Stimson, who had seen long service in the federal government, deplored the wastefulness of New York government. They had been the ones who introduced reorganization at the constitutional convention. Recognizing that the so-called federal Republicans were potential allies, Smith disclaimed any partisan motive in reorganization and insisted that he was willing to share the credit with the legislature: "I am well supplied with good cigars. I will bring them all over to the Capitol and sit down and talk it all out and let us get some place, but above all things, everybody that can do it, ought to make their best possible attempt to crush out the idea that nothing should be done for fear that it may revert to the credit of any individual. That is too small and it does not go." To push re-organization, Smith created a Citizens Committee on Reorganization in the State Government that soon included Stimson, former governor Charles Evans Hughes, and even Frederick C. Tanner, a former chair-man of the New York Republican Party. Although a heavily amended ver-sion of the consolidation amendment was finally approved, the rest of the reorganization program failed. Even the victory of the consolidation amendment was not final, since the next legislature would have to ap-prove it again before it would be put before the voters. In addition, the Republicans refused to give serious consideration to Smith's labor or wa-ter power bills, and they remained buried in committee.

Smith was scathing in his assessment of the 1920 legislative session. "The utter disregard by the members of the majority for what meant progress and welfare constitutes a formidable challenge to democratic representative government," Smith said in a statement released after the legislature had adjourned. He accused the Republicans of using the party caucus to prevent a debate of measures that had no partisan implications and related only to the health and welfare of New Yorkers. "The welfare bills were not defeated; they were smothered," he charged. The Republi-cans had at least been consistent. They had followed a policy of nega-tivism from beginning to end:

> The entire program of reconstruction not only met defeat, but nothing was suggested in its place. Measures of sane and enlight-ened progress were met by a policy of repression. What there was of leadership was political and calculated only to serve the ends of selfishness. The great forum for public discussion was darkened, and the decisions that meant so much to the people of this State were made in a side room behind closed doors.

But the Republicans had accomplished one thing that Smith failed to mention. They had helped turn a first-term governor into a national figure.

Smith would have played a prominent role in national politics during 1920 even if he had not become a leading liberal. Because he was gover-nor of the nation's most populous state, it was inevitable that his name would arise as his party sought a successor to Woodrow Wilson. There was never a real chance that Smith would win the nomination at the

Democratic convention in San Francisco in July. But Tammany was eager to block William Gibbs McAdoo, the secretary of the Treasury, who had made himself anathema by his strong support for Prohibition. Working with Democratic leaders in Indiana and Illinois, Boss Murphy decided that the best strategy was to postpone a commitment to any of the contenders until after the first ballot. Until then, the New York delegation would support the candidacy of its favorite son, Al Smith.

Smith basked in the attention he received on his arrival in San Francisco. His greatest thrill came when Bourke Cockran gave the speech nominating him for president. As a student of great orators, Smith had idolized Cockran in his youth. Emigrating to New York from Ireland at the age of seventeen, Cockran had become a successful lawyer on the strength of his unmatched eloquence and was elected to Congress. He was also strongly independent and had opposed at various times almost every major leader of the Democratic Party, including Cleveland, Bryan, Croker, and Murphy. It wasn't until late 1919 that he and Murphy had reconciled at a dinner that Smith arranged in a private dining room of the Waldorf-Astoria. According to Smith, Cockran was as excited at the prospect of the nominating speech as he was. "I am about to achieve the joy of my life," Cockran said. "For as long back as I can remember, at national conventions I have been fanning the wind either against somebody or against something. At last I have the opportunity to be for somebody." Smith wasn't supposed to be in the convention hall during Cockran's speech, but he hid in a place where he could listen:

> I nominate here today a man whose career savors more of a page from a romance than a mere biographical narrative, a man who, starting in the very humblest condition, has risen in the comparatively short space of 16 years to the second highest public office in this country; a man who has risen from a peddler's wagon to the Governor's chair of the greatest state in the Union, and who in the whole course of that progress has never lost a friend he had gained in his youth.

Cockran compared Smith to Woodrow Wilson, a hero "to whom the world looks up, whom few men expected to parallel or to approach. Grand, peculiar, his is the isolation of eminence, which he will occupy to the end of time." This was not Al Smith's kind of greatness:

No, Al Smith is no way different from us. We love him because he is like us and one of us, because he embodies in the highest degree the qualities which are best amongst us, and he is eminently qualified to lead us, not far off, but close beside us, touching us shoulder to shoulder.

"He threw his whole heart into that speech for me," Smith said.

If Cockran's speech was remarkable, the demonstration that followed it was extraordinary. It was "a demonstration that will stand out in the history of such events," the reporter for the *New York Times* wrote. "Men who have visited every national convention of the party for generations said that they had never witnessed a demonstration so whole-hearted, sincere and stirring." H. L. Mencken, who covered the convention, was more cynical. The delegates were drunk on "Jim Rolph's Bourbon," he insisted. "[I]n 10 minutes Al was forgotten." But Mencken did not deny that something unusual had happened as soon as Cockran finished his speech. The delegates were cheering louder than they had at any point in the convention and waving American flags as four giant searchlights roamed the crowded convention floor. At first, the band began playing "Tammany," but it quickly turned to a different song, "The Sidewalks of New York." As the crowd recognized the tune, "[a] murmur of appreciation ran through the hall, and by the time the band got to the second stanza someone in the gallery began to sing," Mencken reported. "The effect of that singing, as the old-time reporters used to say, was electrical. In 10 seconds a hundred other voices had joined in, and in a minute the whole audience was bellowing the familiar words." Everyone knew at least the chorus:

> East Side, West Side,
> All around the town,
> The tots sang "Ring-a-rosie,"
> "London Bridge is falling down,"
> Boys and girls together,
> Me and Mamie O'Rorke,
> Tripped the light fantastic,
> On the Sidewalks of New York.

A man and woman began waltzing. "They were joined quickly by others. . . . [T]he convention was in recess, and a ball was in progress," Mencken said. The band played "Little Annie Rooney," "The Bowery," "A Bicycle Built for Two," and "Maggie Murphy's Home." "By the end of the first half hour the only persons who were not dancing were a few antisocial Hardshell Baptists from Mississippi and a one-legged war veteran from Ohio."

It is possible to make too much of the Smith demonstration. One reporter claimed that "it converted a man who until a short time ago was not looked upon as an important cog in the Tammany machine into a figure of national importance." Smith himself downplayed the importance of the moment. "I had accomplished comparatively little in the governor's office that would give me national prominence," he said. "I always believed that most of the credit for the San Francisco demonstration was due to Bourke Cockran." But it is notable that the songs that moved the delegates to sing and dance were songs about urban life. A growing number of those participating in Democratic conventions had been born in cities, and songs from the 1890s like "The Sidewalks of New York" readily kindled their nostalgia. In addition, many of the delegates were Irish Catholics who could not fail to see the honor paid to Smith as recognition that immigrant Americans were rising rapidly. Ironically, Smith's status as a political star was confirmed when he was defeated for reelection.

The handwriting had been on the wall for the Democratic Party since 1918. In the elections that year, President Wilson had pleaded for the return of a Democratic Congress that would support the League of Nations. But the Republicans had captured control of both the Senate and the House, killing any hope of ratifying Wilson's peace treaty without significant changes. The Republicans were particularly insistent on the removal of Article X of the Covenant of the League of Nations, which committed member nations to help defend each other against external aggression. Wilson lost whatever chance remained when he suffered a stroke in September 1919 during a tour intended to build public support. The president's illness further undermined his party's chances of winning the 1920 elections by depriving it of strong leadership over the next year. By the time the polls opened, the odds against Democratic nominee James M. Cox were very steep.

Smith's chances for a second term as governor were considerably better, but he still faced a difficult campaign. The Republicans had chosen a very conservative but able candidate to oppose him. Nathan L. Miller was a lawyer from Syracuse who had once served as the general counsel of the United States Steel Company. Miller charged Smith with being a big spender but otherwise attempted to focus attention on national issues, where the Republicans appeared to have an edge. "The thing I intend to do in this campaign, first of all, is to fight for the election of Harding and Coolidge," Miller explained. What could be more important to the people of New York than Article X? he asked. "[T]he welfare of every man and woman in this commonwealth is, first of all, dependent upon retaining in our own hands the decision of the question as to whether Americans boys shall be sent across the water to fight," he said. The issue of establishing a minimum wage board was "a bagatelle" compared to the "great national issues." Smith was forced to make what hay he could from his opponent's evasiveness. He told a crowd of ten thousand at Madison Square Garden that he had assumed office in 1919 with a burning desire to prove that a Tammany man could be a good governor:

> And I want to say to you tonight in all sincerity that I did make good, for if I did not Judge Miller would not be talking about the St. Lawrence River. He would not be talking about the appropriations in Washington. He would not be talking about Article X. I would be the article. I would be the whole covenant.

Two days later, over one million New Yorkers agreed with him.

Al Smith achieved a political miracle on Election Day: he was almost reelected while the Republican Party was rolling up the biggest landslide in American history to that point. Harding received almost twice as many votes as Cox and carried every state outside the South. In New York City, he trounced Tammany, carrying all but one Assembly district, including even Boss Murphy's "gas house" district. But the faces in Tammany Hall on election night were not downcast. Smith and Miller ran neck and neck through most of the night, dividing over 2.5 million votes. It was only with the arrival of the final returns from upstate that it became clear that Smith had lost—but by fewer than 75,000 votes. Political observers were astonished by the result. In some respects Smith had improved on his performance two years before. He had not only carried New York City with nearly twice as many votes as Miller, but he had run better in upstate cities, which gave him nearly 100,000 additional votes. It was clear to everyone that only the Harding landslide could have denied Smith a second term. "Governor Smith, defeated, has achieved an extraordinary personal and political triumph," the *New York Times* observed. William Church Osborn, the upstate Democrat and old foe of Tammany, telegraphed his congratulations. "Even in defeat you came nearer to swimming up Niagara Falls than any man I have ever seen," he said. Tributes like these, which arrived daily, made it considerably easier for Smith and his family to accept defeat. On the eve of his departure from Albany, Smith joked about all the nice things that had been said about him since Election Day. At a banquet in his honor, Smith had been introduced by former governor Martin Glynn, who observed that Smith was a bigger man in defeat than when he arrived a victor in 1919. "After Governor Glynn's speech, I very seriously think of canceling my room at the hotel and going back to the mansion to live," Smith said.

# 7 ❋ THE KLAN RIDES AGAIN

After two years in Albany, it wasn't easy for the Smith children to return to the small brick house at 25 Oliver Street. Nineteen-year-old Emily had to return to sharing her room with sixteen-year-old Catherine, and possession of the bathroom was contested with Arthur, thirteen, and Walter, eleven. Even with young Al away at college, the house seemed cramped. This was only part of a larger adjustment for the children. Al Smith had run for political office fifteen times without suffering a defeat. His children were used to the idea that he was invincible, and his loss confronted them with new problems. On election night, Arthur and Walter, who had been left behind in Albany, put through a call to their parents at Democratic headquarters in New York. Finally reaching Emily, they asked the question that was uppermost in their minds. "Do we have to go to school tomorrow?" Arthur asked. "They'll all kid us about Pop getting licked." Emily knew how they felt. Without consulting her parents, she granted the boys permission to nurse their wounds in private.

The biggest shock, however, was their father's decision to leave public life. While many of his supporters assumed that he would seek the governorship again two years later, Smith was convinced that the time had come to begin a new career and had accepted the chairmanship of the United States Trucking Company, a new company that already controlled nearly 80 percent of the trucking business in Manhattan. "It was definitely fixed in my mind that my political career, so far as public office holding was concerned, had come to an end," Smith wrote in his memoir, *Up to Now*. It is not hard to understand why he had come to this decision. Smith had just turned forty-seven, and his children were growing quickly. During his career in the Assembly, he had been away in Albany for long stretches. Even when he was home, his time was devoted to the endless round of christenings, baptisms, weddings, wakes, and other affairs of his district that kept him away from home most evenings. Whenever he could, he had brought his family with him. They were in Albany during the 1915 constitutional convention, where young Al was a volunteer messenger. Katie, young Al, and Emily had also joined him at the 1920 Democratic convention in San Francisco. He had even less time for the family during his governorship. Smith was so pressed that he and Katie started playing cards before going to bed as a way of spending time together and to help him relax. Even the children welcomed the return to private life. "Our whole family had accepted Father's retirement from politics as an actuality," Emily recalled. "Now, at least, he was free to spend Sundays and most evenings at home."

Smith also needed to make money. During his twelve years in the legislature, he had never made more than $1,500 per year. He had received more than $100,000 during his two years as sheriff, but then he had been elected president of the Board of Aldermen, and his salary as governor was $10,000. While this was a lot of money to most families living on the Lower East Side, Smith wanted to save a significant sum to help his sons establish themselves in business. There was also his future and Katie's to look after. These were all reasons to quit elective office while he was still young enough to start a new career. While many friends remained skeptical about Smith's decision, it had not been hard to convince himself that his future lay in business.

Smith enjoyed both his salary of $50,000 and the work of consolidating the interests of the small, mostly Irish companies that dominated the hauling trade. U.S. Trucking had acquired more than 2,000 trucks and 2,500 horses from firms like Monahan's Express, Healy & Callahan, and Daniel & Kennedy, and it was Smith's job to make sure that the new company made a profit. Smith also accepted appointment to the National Board of Indian Commissioners and the new Port Authority of New York and New Jersey. It seemed for a time that Smith could make money and remain politically active at the same time. He even traveled to Albany to testify in favor of the government consolidation amendment that had passed in 1920 and would have to be repassed before it would be put before the voters. The Republicans lost no time in driving home the limits of his new position. "They enjoyed heckling me as a private citizen appearing before them without the power of the governorship," he said. Nevertheless, he continued to insist that he would not run for governor again in 1922. "I am going to stay in the trucking business," he said.

Smith changed his mind only when it appeared that the man with the best chance of gaining the Democratic nomination was Hearst. After helping reelect his protégé Mayor Hylan the year before, Hearst had once again set in motion a campaign whose purpose was to "draft" him at the state convention. As in 1918, the threat of a Hearst candidacy galvanized his opponents, and 150 upstate leaders met in Syracuse in July to demonstrate their determination to stop the demagogic publisher. Franklin D. Roosevelt did not attend the meeting. He had been stricken by polio the previous summer and was still far too ill to make a public appearance. His letter urging Smith's nomination, however, was read to the Democratic leaders. Although they took no official action, it was clear that once again upstate Democrats would issue the call for Smith's nomination. A month later, Roosevelt wrote Smith directly, urging him to accept his party's nomination, and Smith consented.

With the support of both upstate Democrats and Tammany, Smith's nomination was assured. But the state convention was not without its moments of drama. If the governorship was not available, the ever pliable Hearst was willing to run for U.S. senator. Moreover, he seemed to have a good chance to secure the nomination. Murphy's commitment to Smith was so strong that he had been willing to risk the possibility of alienating Hearst. But the senatorship seemed a small price to pay for party peace, and the newspapers reported that Murphy wanted to put him on the ticket. Although Smith was confined to his hotel room throughout the convention by pain in his legs, he told the various emissaries from Hearst and Murphy that if the publisher was nominated, he would not run for governor. Newspaper reporters portrayed an embattled Smith, holed up in his hotel bunker, turning back wave after wave of pressure. It seemed as if Smith had no friends left in the Democratic Party until Tom Foley stuck his head into the room with one word of advice— "Stick." Not long afterward, Murphy withdrew his support for Hearst. Considering Murphy's skill at orchestrating the circumstances that seemed to force him to take certain actions, it is certainly possible that the whole thing had been a show to forestall Hearst's anger. In any case, Smith emerged from the convention with an enhanced reputation for independence.

At the very moment when he was demonstrating his freedom from Tammany dictation, Smith had entered into an arrangement with a wealthy lawyer that would have raised serious questions about his independence if it had been revealed publicly at the time. Although he had agreed to run for governor, Smith remained deeply concerned about the financial security of his family. Soon after his nomination, he discussed his concerns with Thomas L. Chadbourne, a Wall Street lawyer who was also a major contributor to the Democratic Party. According to Chadbourne's autobiography, the lawyer agreed to subsidize Smith's personal expenses and gave him $85,000 in cash during 1923 and 1924. In 1924 Chadbourne also gave Smith an option to buy two thousand shares of stock in the Brooklyn-Manhattan Transit Company and one thousand shares of the County Trust Company. Chadbourne continued to assist Smith during his final two terms as governor, giving him an additional $58,000. When Smith exercised the BMT and County Trust options, earning a profit of $250,000, the subsidy was worth almost $400,000, Chadbourne said. Chadbourne insisted that he gave the money to Smith to make it possible for an important public servant to continue to serve. There were no strings attached. He was so concerned about honoring his commitment to Smith that he added a provision to his will in 1925, bequeathing him $100,000.

Chadbourne later grew disenchanted with Smith over what he perceived as his failure to support a two-cent increase in the nickel subway fare. Although the increase would have significantly increased the value of Chadbourne's substantial holdings in the BMT, Chadbourne said he did not expect the increase as a quid pro quo for his payments to Smith. In fact, the governor did not possess the power to increase the fare. Smith did express support for the fare increase, but Chadbourne believed he should have done more. It was an example of the "Irish Tammany sense of gratitude," Chadbourne claimed. He also charged Smith with deceiving him about his real intentions while continuing to take his money. "Smith was determined not to be frank with me," Chadbourne wrote in his memoir. "I suppose he thought that if he were he would lose his meal ticket because that is just what I had been to him for years." Chadbourne's subsidy was not revealed during Smith's lifetime, but his friendships with wealthy men would become an issue in the 1930s.

In 1922, however, Smith appeared practically invincible. The early returns from upstate showed him doing far better than he had two years before. He was leading in every city except Elmira and would eventually carry even Syracuse, the hometown of Governor Miller. Although rural voters gave Miller the edge, it was not large enough to overcome the New York City vote, which astonished even the professional politicians. The Democratic vote "south of the Bronx County line" had been growing strongly, giving Smith a plurality of 260,000 in 1918 and nearly 320,000 in 1920. Two years later his winning margin had grown by 45 percent to 464,000. The record city vote enabled Smith to amass a statewide plurality of more than 375,000, one of the highest in state history. It also swept into office the full slate of Democratic candidates for statewide office. "That was certainly a magnificent Tuesday," Franklin Roosevelt wrote Smith the next day. Smith agreed that it was "a great victory." It had even made his mother change her mind. "My Mother was opposed to me running any more for public office from the standpoint of my own health, but when she saw the returns on Election Night she forgot all about everything else," he said. Smith's victory was so impressive that political observers began talking about his prospects for the 1924 Democratic presidential nomination. Although the Republicans remained in control of Congress, the party's performance in the election had been so disappointing that some Republican leaders in Washington considered it unlikely that President Harding would be renominated. Al Smith had been lucky throughout his career, and now it seemed that fate had positioned him to bid for the highest office in the land.

But the obstacles that lay between Smith and the White House were daunting. American society had been deeply polarized for many decades. The growth of industry had created great disparities in wealth, not only between classes but between regions of the country and between rural and urban areas of the same region. Industrialization and immigration had introduced a new element of ethnic diversity. A new culture was being born as radio and motion pictures made it possible to address a mass audience; the theory of evolution challenged fundamentalist Christian theology, and new ideas on the role of women threatened the traditional family.

There was no more important symbol of the polarization of American society than Prohibition. Historians have provided many, often conflicting explanations for the movement that began in the early nineteenth century and finally ended the sale of alcohol in the United States on January 1, 1920. Some have seen it as an attempt to deal with the serious problem of alcohol abuse; others as a stage in the development of the women's movement; and still others as a sincere but naive attempt to solve complex social problems by purifying the hearts of men. At least some of those who supported Prohibition were nativists who believed that immigrant Americans should be forced to abide by a standard of morality that they clearly were unwilling to recognize on their own. From the beginning of the great immigration wave that began in the 1840s, Protestants had believed that Irish and German immigrants were far too fond of liquor. In their view, the rising tide of immigration contributed to an increase in alcoholism, destitution, and dependence. At a time when many of the immigrant political leaders were also saloon keepers, attacking alcohol was also a way of striking a blow at the emerging political machines.

The issue of liquor had divided the Democratic and Republican parties for many years. Many of those who joined the new Republican Party in the late 1850s were former members of the Know-Nothing party, which had hoped to exclude immigrants from citizenship for twenty-one years. Democratic leaders in the North never let their German and Irish constituents forget this—or that the Republicans supported laws that would curtail their personal freedom. Later, many Democrats, particularly in the South, became strong advocates of Prohibition. The formation of the Anti-Saloon League in 1893 gave the Prohibitionists a vehicle for seeking support from politicians in both parties. But in New York and other states with large immigrant populations, support for Prohibition remained confined to the Republican Party.

The fight for Prohibition was bitterly contested in New York. It was a significant feature of the political struggle throughout Smith's years in the legislature, when the Anti-Saloon League was a power in state politics. Once the legislature had granted small towns the right to ban the sale of alcohol, Democrats and Republicans fought over whether the right of "local option" should be extended to cities and counties. They fought over the sale of alcohol on Sundays and over creating alcohol-free zones around churches and schools. By 1908 the Prohibitionists had succeeded in drying up four hundred upstate towns. But Democrats never believed that the League represented a majority, even upstate. The legislature took up ratification of the Eighteenth Amendment in 1919. The amendment was quickly approved by the Assembly, where upstate power was greatest. In the Senate, however, the Prohibitionists were unable to persuade several prominent Republicans, including the majority leader, Henry M. Walters of Syracuse. It was only after the drys used the party caucus to silence the dissidents that the measure was finally ratified.

Smith was outraged by the legislature's action. In his first message to the legislature as governor, he had urged the Republicans to let the voters of New York decide the question in a referendum. "Are the people of the State prepared to forfeit any part of their police power?" Smith had asked in his inaugural address. "Are they reconciled to the policy of incorporating in the Federal Constitution a rigid restriction upon their personal liberty?" The legislature's refusal to let the people vote was blatantly undemocratic, Smith charged.

> The Republican majority in the Legislature, by the aid of a party caucus, have succeeded in ratifying, by strict party vote, the pending amendment to the Federal Constitution providing for prohibition. . . . As the Governor of the State I can only take my place in the great army of our citizens who have faith in the fundamental democratic principle that the majority should rule, and I deplore the fact that we have been denied a right so fair that it does not admit of argument except from those who are unwilling to listen.

Smith rarely lost an opportunity to urge changes in the Prohibition law. The next year, he called on the legislature to rescind its ratification. When it was finally clear that the Eighteenth Amendment was the law of the land, Smith took a new tack. While granting that many of the criticisms of the saloon were just, Smith insisted that the American people had never supported a total ban on alcoholic drinks. The amendment referred to "intoxicating" drinks, which clearly meant hard liquor. But the extreme drys had pushed through Congress the Volstead Act, a bill that defined intoxicating drink as any containing more than one-half of 1 percent alcohol and therefore banned beer and wine. Henceforth he would support modification of the Volstead Act to legalize the consumption of "non-intoxicating" drinks with alcoholic content of less than 2.75 percent. In 1922, modification of the Volstead Act was one of the planks of the Democratic platform on which Smith was returned to office, and in his annual address in January 1923 he unexpectedly urged the legislature to send a message to Congress expressing New York's support for modification. Repeating his belief that the legislature had approved Prohibition in defiance of a majority of the people of the state, he also urged a new constitutional amendment that would require popular ratification of all future amendments.

There was more than politics—or even thirst—involved in the opposition to sumptuary legislation like Prohibition. Many Americans resented laws that prevented them from engaging in activities that were not harmful to others. Such laws were particularly irksome because they were an attempt to enforce religious views that were not shared by everyone. An anonymous Catholic complained in 1876 that what he did on a Sunday was no business of his Protestant neighbor. "[M]ay not my daughter play the piano on Sunday on account of his tender conscience?" he asked. Such restrictions seemed to be at odds with the Constitution's guarantee of personal freedom, including freedom of religion. The Sunday laws made criminals of Catholics and Jews who engaged in activities that were legal every other day of the week. It was a mark of their second-class status.

There were two ways to fight back against prejudice, and Al Smith advocated both. One was to lead a blameless life, he told the Friendly Sons of St. Patrick in 1923.

> We are watched a little more than anybody else. We have to be just a little bit better than the other fellow, and we have to be constantly on the watch that we do our full duty as citizens and on every recurring anniversary we should review our pledges of good and worthy citizenship. Let us do everything we can to keep Irish names off the calendars of the police courts and divorce courts. Let us do everything we can to pledge obedience to the Church and to the State. Let us live our lives in such a way as to do full justice to our neighbor, and let every one of our business transactions be above suspicion, because in that way we can turn back to

its source the foul breath of prejudice that for years has been directed against us.

The other way was to strike back against sumptuary legislation when he had the opportunity. When, several months after it ratified Prohibition, the legislature sent Smith a bill that allowed local communities to vote on whether they wanted to allow baseball to be played on Sundays, he signed it with alacrity. "I am of the firm opinion that those members of a community who oppose all recreation on Sunday . . . have no right, in law or morals . . . to impose those views on the majority who disagree with them," Smith said. Sumptuary laws, including Prohibition, were an obstacle to the enjoyment of equal rights and therefore an obstacle to the growth of democracy.

Of course, there was more to Smith's opposition to Prohibition than principle. If anyone in the country was unclear as to his views on the desirability of a mug of beer, they were reminded early in 1923 when a reporter published a remark that Smith intended to be off the record. It was a warm day in early spring, and Smith had been reminiscing during his afternoon conference with the legislative reporters. "Wouldn't you like to have your foot on the rail and blow the foam off some suds?" he asked. The remark outraged Prohibitionists. As New York's chief executive officer, it was his duty to uphold enforcement of Prohibition, and they were particularly incensed by his favorable reference to the evil saloon. Smith was forced to issue a retraction. He had been speaking "facetiously" of the bar rail, he said, adding, "I have enough common sense and experience of life to understand that the saloon is and ought to be a defunct institution in this country."

Even Smith had to think long and hard a few months later when the legislature presented him with a bill repealing the state version of the Volstead Act. Repealing the state enforcement act, which was known as the Mullan-Gage law, raised serious political problems for a politician who aspired to the highest elective office in the country. The state had passed the Mullan-Gage law to assist in the enforcement of an amendment to the U.S. Constitution. The Prohibitionists argued that New York did not have the right to repeal it and that if it did it would amount to the nullification of the Eighteenth Amendment. They knew that Prohibition would be a dead letter without state enforcement, because the federal government did not have the resources to interdict the importation of alcoholic beverages. President Harding himself appeared to take this view in mid-May when he replied to a letter from a Newburgh, New York, publicist, who wanted him to suspend Smith and the members of the New York legislature if the Mullan-Gage repeal was signed into law. "Every State official who voted for this bill is subject to the law of treason, having taken the oath to sustain the Constitution of the United States," Dr. Wesley Walt wrote. In reply, the president demurred from promising specific action against New York's elected officials, though he did agree with the main points of Walt's letter. He conjured a picture of the great conflict that would ensue "if any of the States shall decline to assume their part of the responsibility of maintaining the Constitution." In an editorial the next day, the *New York Times* accused Harding of intervening in New York politics in an effort to bolster his sagging reelection prospects and dismissed the specter of an impending constitutional crisis. "The State has a perfect right to forbear the exercise of its concurrent power," it said. Yet the question of how the state could repeal its enforcement act without effectively nullifying the Constitution bothered a lot of people, not all of whom were militant drys.

At the same time, the pressure on Smith to sign the Mullan-Gage repeal was enormous. Clearly, there were many in New York, particularly in New York City, who hoped the repeal would do exactly what the Prohibitionists feared it would do. The saloon keepers who had been put out of business or were now operating speakeasies wanted to operate openly. The people who were pushing for repeal had pressed Tammany for support, and now that victory was at hand they were using Tammany to pressure the governor.

On June 1, 1923, the day after a public hearing in the Assembly chamber, Smith signed the bill repealing the Mullan-Gage law and released a memo to the legislature explaining his decision. At four thousand words, Smith's message was unusually long for a legislative memo, indicating both the importance that the public attached to this bill and the difficulty that Smith had in justifying his action. He could not be forthright in expressing his feelings that Prohibition was a terrible mistake and that the Mullan-Gage repeal was the first step toward reversing it. His oath of office required him to uphold the U.S. Constitution. He could not justify his action as an expression of his personal opinion. As a result, he was forced to find other arguments: he cited a danger of double jeopardy under state and federal enforcement acts and claimed that it was important to the federal system to insist upon the right of states not to pass separate enforcement acts. Smith even insisted that federal enforcement would be more efficient. Henry F. Pringle, an early biographer of Smith, would later describe the memo as "composed of equal parts of bunk, sincerity and specious reasoning."

Editorial reaction to the Mullan-Gage repeal was mixed. The *Boston Herald* said that Smith had hurt his prospects for the 1924 presidential nomination because "the South . . . has long been just as solid for prohibition as for Democracy." Yet Southern newspapers were not unanimous in their view. While the *Memphis Commercial Appeal* saw the repeal as reflecting "a determination to set aside national law and to flout national sentiment," the *Richmond Times-Dispatch* praised it as a victory for states' rights. But the Southern press may not have been a good barometer of the attitude of Democratic drys. A week after Smith signed the repeal, William Jennings Bryan dispelled whatever uncertainty there may have been over the position of rural Democrats. In an article published in the *New York Times*, he virtually read Smith out of the party.

It is not surprising that reporters asked Bryan for his comments on the Mullan-Gage repeal. Although Bryan had not always been a supporter of Prohibition, he had made himself the most prominent Democratic advocate in the years after 1916. As soon as the House approved the Eighteenth Amendment in December 1917, Bryan had walked onto the floor to accept the congratulations of Democratic representatives. "Generations yet unborn will rise up to call you blessed," the Anti-Saloon League told him. Bryan drove on toward total victory, opposing efforts to exempt beer and wine from the provisions of the federal enforcement act. Consequently, the repeal of Mullan-Gage was nothing short of a personal insult. But Bryan professed to be little concerned by it. Prohibition had the support of the overwhelming majority of the people, he said. Its only opponents were distillers and brewers who made money from the suffering of others. He predicted that Smith would soon feel the retribution of an aroused populace, particularly its women, "the women whose husbands wasted at the saloon the money that belonged to the family." "Governor Smith has simply dishonored his office and disgraced himself: he cannot lead the nation back to wallow in the mire," Bryan said. He concluded by

giving Smith some political advice. He didn't know whether the New
York governor harbored presidential ambitions, he said. But "if so he
ought to read a familiar passage in Shakespeare and find out what his
friends will say when they dig up his remains: 'Alas, poor Yorick! I knew
him well.' "

Smith responded to the Great Commoner with obvious relish. In his
memo on the Mullan-Gage law, he had been forced to justify his apparent refusal to enforce a constitutional amendment. By praising Prohibition, Bryan gave Smith a chance to set forth his real views. The repeal
had nothing to do with being for or against Prohibition, Smith insisted.
The Eighteenth Amendment was not a political issue but the law of the
land. Where politics had intruded was in the drafting of the Volstead Act:

> Mr. Bryan knows, as well as I do, that the Volstead act is a dishon-
> est and hypocritical interpretation of the Eighteenth Amendment.
> He knows as well as I do that fanatical "drys" in control of Con-
> gress wrote that law to accomplish their narrow and bigoted pur-
> pose and not to give honest expression to a constitutional
> argument. If Mr. Bryan's reasoning is to be followed to its logical
> conclusion three-quarters of one per cent of alcohol in a beverage
> intoxicates. Nobody with an ounce of brains believes that. That
> much alcohol might well be discovered on a lump of sugar.

Most Americans were neither fanatical drys nor fanatical wets, but people
who want "a possible and constructive solution of this question on a common sense basis," Smith said. The New York legislature had reflected the
view of these people when it voted by large margins to urge modification
of the Volstead definition to legalize the sale of beer and wine, Smith
said. Finally, Smith denied Bryan's suggestion that he had aspirations to
the presidency. "Unlike himself, I am not a candidate," he said. "When I
have been in the past, I have usually been selected by the people, but in
Mr. Bryan's case, a wise and discriminating electorate usually takes care
to see that Mr. Bryan stays at home."

Smith did not speak with complete candor about his presidential ambitions. Starting in July 1923 Boss Murphy worked hard to convince
other Democratic leaders, particularly Thomas Taggart of Indiana and
George E. Brennan of Illinois, that Smith was a viable candidate. One of

his strategies was to press the party to adopt a plank calling for the modification of the Volstead Act. Had he succeeded, Smith, the party's most
outspoken supporter of this change, would inevitably have benefited. At
first, Smith's chances seemed slim. Industrialist Henry Ford and former
secretary of the Treasury William Gibbs McAdoo were considered the
most likely Democratic presidential nominees throughout most of 1923.
Ford, a self-made man from the Midwest who scorned ostentation and
Wall Street, had a strong appeal in rural areas, where his anti-Catholic
and anti-Semitic views were well known and approved. But the always
unpredictable Ford endorsed Coolidge in December. It seemed that the
relieved Democrats were about to close ranks around McAdoo.

McAdoo was an attractive candidate. Raised in a small town in Georgia, he had practiced law in Tennessee before moving to New York City
in 1892. Ten years later he became president of a corporation that constructed the first tunnels between Manhattan and New Jersey. He was an
active supporter of Woodrow Wilson and became first his secretary of the
Treasury and then his son-in-law, marrying Eleanor Wilson at the White
House in 1914. McAdoo became one of the president's closest advisers.
When the United States entered World War I, he ran the nation's railroads. McAdoo also possessed a reputation for liberalism, and his close
cooperation with the railroad unions during the war had gained him the
support of organized labor. In addition, it had been his job as secretary of
the Treasury to implement the Federal Reserve Act, whose goal had been
to curb the power of J. P. Morgan and other Eastern financiers. The 1920
Democratic presidential nomination would probably have been
McAdoo's for the asking if his father-in-law hadn't entertained hopes of
renomination. To avoid alienating Wilson, McAdoo did nothing to seek
the nomination and still received over 30 percent of the votes on the delegates' first ballot. Sixty years old in 1924, he was now determined to capture what had so nearly been his four years earlier. "I am going to make
the best of it, and do the job . . . even if it takes my life," he told his
daughter.

McAdoo's candidacy suffered from serious weaknesses, however. Despite his long residence in New York, he was essentially a Southerner in
outlook. A Presbyterian, he had been raised to admire a puritanical respectability that seemed narrow and extreme outside of small towns. He
parted his hair in the middle and wore the old-fashioned collars whose

stiffness encouraged men to keep their chins high. It didn't help that McAdoo was so fond of quoting homilies that an unkind Eastern press came to characterize them as "McAdooleisms." But his most substantive difference with the Eastern wing of his party was over Tammany and Prohibition. Like many Democrats, he had a traditional loathing for Boss Tweed's machine that did not subside when Tammany began supporting reform. Even if he had acknowledged that Tammany had changed, McAdoo was a dry who could never have worked easily with a political organization that was committed to the modification of the Volstead Act. In 1922 he had moved his family out of New York and established a residence in Los Angeles, which not only seemed a more promising political base but also measured the social and cultural distance that separated him from the people of New York City.

Nevertheless, McAdoo appeared virtually unstoppable in January 1924. Ford's decision not to run for president had given him new momentum, and political observers were predicting that he had enough strength to defeat the effort by Murphy and his allies to block him. Just as McAdoo's supporters began to congratulate themselves on defeating the machinations of the Tammany boss and his friends, however, they were hit by a crisis that convinced many of them that McAdoo must withdraw. A committee of the U.S. Senate had been investigating the unusually generous terms under which Secretary of the Interior Albert Fall had leased U.S. oil reserves to wealthy oilman Edward L. Doheny during the Harding administration. At a hearing on January 24, Doheny admitted that he had made a $100,000 loan to Fall shortly before the leases had been signed. The country was shocked by this evidence of corruption at the highest levels of the federal government. Most of the evidence uncovered in the Teapot Dome scandal would concern the misdeeds of Republicans, but Doheny didn't discriminate. A week after his initial revelation, he testified that he had paid large retainers to four members of the Wilson cabinet. McAdoo had received $250,000, he said.

The impact of the Doheny disclosures completely changed the outlook of the race for the Democratic presidential nomination. Later, Doheny would acknowledge that McAdoo had received only $50,000 during two years that he had served as a special counsel to Doheny's oil company. Thomas Walsh, the chief investigator, issued a statement that absolved McAdoo from any involvement in the scandal. Nevertheless, most of McAdoo's advisers believed that his candidacy had received a fatal blow and advised him to withdraw. After all, $50,000 was still a lot of money, and McAdoo had little chance of escaping the suspicion that the money had been paid to buy influence. His advisers even handed him the draft of a statement withdrawing from the race. But McAdoo refused to quit. Twice he had been within an arm's length of the nomination, and he was not ready to believe that his political career was suddenly over. Instead, he engineered a meeting of supporters from around the nation who expressed undiminished enthusiasm for his candidacy. Remaining out of sight throughout the meeting, he emerged as soon as the resolution urging him to stay in the race had been adopted. "You command me to accept the leadership. I accept your command," he told the three hundred cheering delegates.

But few people were fooled by McAdoo's theatrics. The Doheny disclosures had stripped his candidacy of its air of inevitability and created an opportunity for any candidate who could demonstrate national appeal. Murphy continued to believe that he had both the candidate and the issue: Al Smith could become a national leader based on his advocacy of changes in the Volstead Act. Smith had appeared on the national stage only a few months before when President Coolidge had called a conference of the nation's governors to discuss ways to improve Prohibition enforcement. The politicians arrived in Washington armed with excuses for weak enforcement. Smith's were better than most. "[I]n New York we are next to the sea, and open to all the possibilities of smuggling by rum-runners and by incoming ships in general," Smith said. But with Coolidge himself in attendance, Smith reiterated his proposal that Congress modify the Volstead Act by raising the permissible percentage of alcohol, allowing states to authorize the sale of beer and wine or to ban it depending on the desires of their people.

Murphy and Smith saw this proposal as a compromise between the wet and dry wings of the party. Despite the claims of the "radical" drys, it was not a proposal for repeal of the Eighteenth Amendment. They knew that there were many wets who would not be satisfied by modification of the Volstead Act. While the brewers would be happy, it left the distillers out in the cold. As men who saw no harm in a stiff drink, Murphy and Smith were sacrificing their own personal feelings. They advocated modification because they believed it had a reasonable chance of success. In addition, it allowed Smith to call for enforcement of Prohibition without appearing hypocritical. Two days after McAdoo's Chicago rally, Smith convened a conference of law enforcement officials in Albany to discuss ways to coordinate federal, state, and city efforts to enforce Prohibition. "The so-called Volstead Act . . . is just as sacred as any other law in this country," Smith insisted. These were strange words coming from a man who had effectively gutted state enforcement eight months earlier, but they were understandable in the context of an increasingly serious bid for the presidency.

In the spring of 1924, Al Smith was still a longshot to win the Democratic nomination. McAdoo remained the candidate of the drys, and the wets were ready to support either Senator Oscar Underwood of Alabama or John W. Davis of West Virginia, a former solicitor general and ambassador to Great Britain. Both men advocated modification of the Volstead Act, and neither had recently signed legislation that could be read as repealing Prohibition in their states. But Murphy continued to nurse Smith's candidacy in the belief that his man possessed advantages not enjoyed by his rivals. One was that the Democratic convention was to be held in New York City for the first time in over fifty years, and he clearly hoped that the delegates might be favorably influenced by Smith's many friends. Murphy was also counting on Smith's enormous personal appeal. In early April Smith had won the Wisconsin primary, even though his name had been entered without his permission and there had been no official campaign. "It's strange that I should get this support in a State where I never have been," Smith said. When he was erroneously informed that his name was on the ballot in the Iowa primary, he could not suppress a smile. "What, have they entered my name there, too?" he asked.

The formal announcement of Smith's candidacy occurred at the Democratic state convention in Albany. The two thousand delegates had little interest in anything else. During a keynote address that focused on questions of policy, they listened quietly until the speaker announced that New York had a candidate for president and asked the crowd to identify him. "Al Smith!" they cried, jumping to their feet and cheering wildly. Later, the convention adopted a resolution that came as close to instructing the New York delegation to vote for him as was legal in a state where that decision was supposed to lie with Democratic voters acting through the primary. Eleanor Roosevelt introduced the resolution and following its adoption was delegated to bring Smith to the stage. As the crowd was waiting, some delegates in the back of the auditorium began singing "The Sidewalks of New York." By the time Smith appeared on the stage, the band had taken up the song and more than one thousand men and women were singing the refrain. When the music and cheering were finally over, Smith briefly discussed the recently concluded legislative session, in which the Republicans had once again killed most of his legislation. He then thanked the delegates for their resolution. "If I were to tell you that I haven't heard anything on this particular subject for the last year, you wouldn't believe it because it wouldn't be true," he said. He also acknowledged a desire to be president. "The man who would not have an ambition for that office would have a dead heart," he explained. But Smith insisted that he would not neglect his duties as governor by actively campaigning for the nomination. He concluded with a promise: "If my nomination is brought about and it results in a triumph for the party, you can say to every delegate that you meet at the convention in New York City that I promised you in the capital city of this State, before God Almighty himself that neither they nor you will ever have any cause to regret the confidence they or you see fit to repose in me." Smith was confident and so were his friends. Boss Murphy stood smiling as the members of the Tammany delegation cheered wildly around him.

The last thing anyone expected was that Murphy would not be present at Madison Square Garden in June working to ensure the nomination of his protégé. The boss was sixty-four years old and in good health. Ten days after the state convention, on the evening of April 24, he felt unwell and went to bed early. He awoke in pain a couple of hours later and sent for a doctor, but he collapsed and died before help could arrive. The cause of death was listed as "acute indigestion." Smith was stunned. "The Governor was affected visibly when he learned of the death of the Tammany chieftain, and his eyes were filled with tears," the *New York Times* reported. He broke down twice when he met later with newspaper reporters. "It's awful," he said, brushing his eyes with his handkerchief. "No one had a better friend and no man could have had such a friend as he was to me." He collected himself enough to make a fuller statement:

I am so deeply grieved at the news of the sudden death of Charles F. Murphy that it is most difficult for me to gather my thoughts together. I am suffering the loss of a close personal friend of many years standing—not a fair-weather friend, but a friend in need; possessed of the qualities that endeared him to every man privileged to call him a friend. He was a noble, clean, wholesome, right-living man, and growing up as he did from the sidewalks of New York to a position of power and influence, he made of his life a lesson and example to the youth of this country.

Some of Murphy's political opponents refused to join with those who now praised the fallen boss. In its obituary, the New York Times reminded readers that Murphy had made himself wealthy through his manipulation of city contracts. "[W]ith what good public cause did Mr. Murphy ever identify himself?" the Times asked. "What monuments has he left?" Other New Yorkers recognized that Murphy had contributed to making New York a better place. "The New York City Democratic organization has lost probably the strongest and wisest leader it has had in generations," Franklin Roosevelt, a former foe, observed. The day after Murphy's death, Smith returned to New York City to attend his funeral. As he climbed the steps of Murphy's house to pay his respects, tears streamed down his face. The governor himself was the best symbol of Murphy's accomplishments.

Murphy would have been the first to observe that there was no time for mourning. The Democratic convention was scheduled to open on June 24, which gave Smith and his supporters just two months to regroup and win the nomination. Business was interrupted again, however, when Smith's mother developed pneumonia. Catherine Smith had suffered two previous bouts of pneumonia from which she had never fully recovered, and her son had noticed during his weekly visits to her that her health was gradually failing. When he learned of her new illness, Smith rushed to Brooklyn, but Catherine rallied, and Smith returned to Albany to wrap up his legislative work. She seemed so improved when he saw her next that he left town for a short golfing vacation at a resort on the New Jersey shore. When Catherine suddenly grew worse, Smith flagged down a train in an effort to reach her, but she died while he was on his way home. A nephew greeted him at Grand Central with the news. A front-page story in the New York Times the next day reported Catherine's death and recalled her struggle to save her family in the face of desperate poverty. On the day of the funeral, three thousand people crowded the streets around the Church of the Assumption near her home. Her mass was read by a cardinal and attended by all of the state's political leaders. "It was the first real sorrow I had ever suffered," Smith said later.

When Smith was finally able to focus on his candidacy, he discovered that the political situation was deteriorating rapidly. As the national convention approached, the Democrats were becoming polarized over a proposal to formally condemn the Ku Klux Klan. The *New York World* had reported the emergence of a Klan revival in September 1921. The founder, William J. Simmons, was an unsuccessful minister from Alabama who made a living as an organizer of fraternal lodges. He had long dreamed of creating a new fraternal organization based on the hooded order that had risen in the South to defend white supremacy following the Civil War. He saw his chance in the fall of 1915 with the opening of D. W. Griffith's motion picture *The Birth of a Nation*, which portrayed the order as heroic defenders of hearth and home. The Klan grew slowly at first. Its commitment to 100 percent Americanism and the supremacy of the Caucasian race did not distinguish it much from other fraternal associations in the South. During World War I it was only one of many patriotic organizations that kept watch for alien enemies and domestic radicals. In 1919 its membership consisted of several thousand Southern men.

But the Klan had vast potential. Most of the 18 million immigrants who had entered the United States between 1890 and 1914 were from Southern, Central, and Eastern Europe. Many Americans believed the "new" immigrants were inferior to the "old" immigrants, who had come mainly from Northern and Western Europe. They were abetted in their fears by social scientists, who claimed to have scientific proof that the new immigrants were not only poor and uneducated but racially inferior. "The intellectual superiority of our Nordic group over the Alpine, Mediterranean and Negro groups has been demonstrated," claimed Carl C. Brigham, a psychology professor, citing data from the newly invented IQ test. The fear that the country would be undermined by amalgamation with inferior white races abroad played a role in finally ending the "open door" immigration policy in 1921. Eastern colleges and universities adopted quotas to restrict the entry of Jewish students. (Columbia University cut Jewish admissions almost in half.) Real estate contracts in residential neighborhoods began to carry clauses barring the sale of houses to Jews. Help-wanted ads often indicated that only gentiles were sought or that Protestants were preferred. One analysis of employment in the 1920s found that Jews were barred from 90 percent of the jobs available in New York, Italians from 80 percent, and Catholics from 75 percent.

The Klan prospered by exploiting the deep anxiety that many Americans felt over the presence of so many foreigners in their midst. The original Klan had accepted all white men, but the new Klan wanted only Protestants. One of the first steps in starting a new chapter of the Klan was to approach a Protestant minister and offer him a free membership. Hundreds of ministers served as the Kludd, or chaplain, of their local chapter (Klavern). Sometimes the Klan announced its presence in a town by showing up in their hooded robes during services and marching to the front of the church to hand the minister a contribution. Even when the minister was hostile, the Klan saw itself as the enforcing arm of the Protestant church. Its job was to uphold the moral order that was preached on Sunday by punishing adulterers, bootleggers, gamblers, and Sabbath breakers. The Klan attempted to intimidate its foes with burning crosses, night-riding visits, and acts of violence. But its main appeal was to the desire for solidarity in the face of the enemy. All Klansmen were encouraged to practice Klannishness by patronizing the businesses of other Klansmen and boycotting those run by Catholics and Jews. Through such measures, they were told, the Klan would thrive, becoming a force capable of checking a Catholic plot to seize control of the United States and destroy the Protestant religion. In talks to fellow Klansmen, Simmons would start by pulling a gun from each pocket and laying them on the table. "Now let the Niggers, Catholics, Jews, and all others who disdain my imperial wizardry, come on," he said.

The Klan's success exceeded even Simmons's fondest dreams. By the time of the *World* exposé, the Klan had 100,000 members and was growing with phenomenal speed. A year and a half later, its nearly one million members had helped elect governors in Georgia, Alabama, California, and Oregon; sent a member of the Klan, Earl Mayfield of Texas, to the U.S. Senate; and almost managed to unseat Senator James Reed of Missouri. It was estimated that seventy-five members of the House of Representatives had received the support of the Klan. At first confined primarily to the South and Southwest, the Klan was soon opening chapters everywhere. By 1924 there were almost as many Klansmen in Ohio, Indiana, and Illinois as there were in the South and Southwest combined. Nor was the Klan confined to rural areas and small towns. Much of its strength resided in cities where Protestants who had recently migrated from rural areas found themselves living in close proximity to foreign immigrants and their children, most of whom were Catholics or Jews. On a percentage basis, "Indianapolis, Dayton, Portland, Youngstown, Denver, and Dallas were the hooded capitals of the nation." In Ohio, Akron, Dayton, Cincinnati, Columbus, and Youngstown each boasted more than 15,000 Klansmen.

The issue of the Klan was uppermost in the minds of many of the delegates who gathered in New York City for the Democratic convention in June. Delegates from the North and East were looking forward to striking at least a symbolic blow against the Klan by voting for a resolution condemning the group by name. Delegates from the South and West were just as adamantly opposed to such an act. Above all, they were determined to prevent a statement that they viewed as suicidal to Democratic prospects in the South. The explosiveness of the situation became apparent during Alabama delegate Forney Johnston's speech nominating Senator Oscar Underwood of Alabama, the sponsor of the anti-Klan resolution. Johnston informed the delegates that in 1856 the Democratic platform had condemned the Know-Nothing party, "a quasi-secret order based on the same objective and affording precedent for a similar movement which has intruded into the two main parties today." Loud applause met the claim that modern Know-Nothings were trying to gain secret control of the Democratic and Republican parties. But Johnston had still not mentioned the Klan by name. Then he read the text of Underwood's proposed platform plank, condemning "as un-American and un-Democratic political action by secret or quasi-secret organizations . . . for the purpose of proscribing the political rights and privileges of citizens of the United States." Even before Johnston had spoken the words "Ku Klux Klan," the Alabama and New York delegations were pouring into the aisles, where they were soon joined by the delegates from the New England states, Maryland, New Jersey, Ohio, Illinois, Minnesota, and Wisconsin. "Come on, stand up, you Kleagles," marching delegates yelled at the eighteen McAdoo delegations that remained seated. The fight over the Klan had just begun.

None of the other nominating speeches addressed the Klan issue directly. In nominating McAdoo, former California senator James D. Phelan could not avoid it altogether. Phelan, a Catholic himself, defended McAdoo from the charge of religious bigotry. While the speech nominating Smith said even less, the religious issue was its critical subtext. To deliver it, Smith turned to Franklin Roosevelt. It was Smith's close friend and adviser Joseph M. Proskauer who first suggested Roosevelt's name. "For God's sake, why?" Smith had asked. "Because you're a Bowery mick and he's a Protestant patrician and he'd take some of the curse off you," Proskauer replied.

Roosevelt was delighted to be nominating Smith. Roosevelt's life had changed dramatically in the four years since he had been chosen as the Democratic nominee for vice president. Then, he had been the dashing young aristocrat from the Hudson Valley. From the waist up he was still that man, but his pants hid withered limbs that were no longer able to support him. He perpetuated the illusion of walking by locking his braces in place and using his shoulders to pivot his weight from one leg to the other, leaning heavily on the arm of his sixteen-year-old son, James, who provided his forward momentum. At an early age, Roosevelt had announced his intention of following the path of Theodore Roosevelt to the presidency. To do so, he had to dispel doubts about his health. He had to make his way across the dais unassisted and stand at the podium through his thirty-minute speech. In the library of his home on East Sixty-fifth Street, he measured out the fifteen feet and practiced his walk over and over again.

As if the fear of falling down in front of 12,000 people were not enough, Roosevelt hated the speech that Proskauer had written for him. It was too poetic, he complained to the judge. The delegates weren't going to get the reference to the lines in Wordsworth's poem:

> This is the Happy Warrior; this is he
> Whom every man in arms should wish to be.

Roosevelt had written his own speech, but Proskauer rejected it. Finally, they had called in Herbert Bayard Swope, the managing editor of the *World*, to decide which was the better speech. Although he was not told who had written which speech, Swope thought it was obvious. "Joe, this is the goddamnest, rottenest speech I've ever read," he said, tossing Roo-

sevelt's speech on the floor. Then, he read Proskauer's. "This is the greatest speech since Bragg nominated Cleveland," he said. But Roosevelt
was still unconvinced. Finally, Proskauer gave him an ultimatum. "Frank
. . . I have just enough authority from the Governor to tell you that
you'll either make that speech or none at all," he said. Roosevelt surrendered. "Oh, I'll make the goddamned speech and it'll be a flop!" he
replied.

Frances Perkins would later recall that everyone in Madison Square
Garden appeared to be holding their breath as Roosevelt used his
crutches to slowly traverse the distance to the speaker's rostrum. Because
he was leaning so heavily on the crutches, he was unable to use his regular trick of distracting attention by talking and laughing with Jimmy as he
made his painful progress. His head was down, and sweat was pouring
from his face. When he finally reached the podium, Roosevelt looked up
and beamed a triumphant smile. The delegates leaped to their feet and
cheered and applauded for three minutes. After three years of illness, the
thrill of being at center stage again invigorated Roosevelt, and his voice
betrayed none of the strain his body was experiencing as his rich tenor
brought Proskauer's words to life. He began by rejecting the suggestion of
some that Smith's supporters would attempt to stampede the convention
by "emotional appeals." This was unnecessary for a man with Smith's
record, Roosevelt said. Over the opposition of a Republican legislature,
he had inaugurated a program of government reform that had become a
model for other states. Through his leadership, Roosevelt said, Smith had
inspired faith not only in himself but in government. "This faith in him
and in his fundamental rugged honesty, this knowledge of his intuitive
ability to go down to the heart of any problem, to offer solutions understood by and for the ultimate good of the average man and woman—
these are the reasons why this man above all others will bring order out of
chaos in the national capital." In 1920 the Republicans had played on the
disillusion of the postwar period to achieve victory. But the American
people are fundamentally idealists, and they will rally again. "They await
the opportunity to support a man who will return America to the fold of
decency and ideals from which she has strayed," Roosevelt said.

This our candidate will do. His is the quality of militant leadership. He has the ability to campaign and to campaign in the highest and finest sense. He has the rare power to express the great

fundamental truths and ideals in homely language carrying conviction to the multitude. He has the power to strike at error and wrongdoing that make his adversaries quail before him. He has a personality that carries to every hearer not only the sincerity but the righteousness of what he says. He is the "Happy Warrior" of the political battlefield.

At the very moment that Roosevelt spoke the words he had feared, the sun, which had been obscured by clouds, suddenly began to shine through the skylights in the Garden, flooding the dais with light.

Roosevelt then delivered a solemn invocation of equal rights: "I ask your judgment. I ask you to render it in the spirit of devotion to the principles of our party, in the faith that all citizens are equal before the law, in the conviction that the solid Democracy of this nation will stand without fear and without hesitation loyally behind the nominee of this Democratic Convention." For delegates who were gearing up for a fight over the role of the Ku Klux Klan in the party, the meaning of these words was unmistakable. Roosevelt was calling on his fellow Protestants to put aside their dislike for the Catholic church and to consider Smith as nothing more than a fellow Democrat. Roosevelt's final words were delivered over a wave of swelling emotion:

If you will render your verdict in that sacred mood, it can only be for the nomination of the man whom I present to you—the one above all others who has demonstrated his power, his ability to govern; this leader whose whole career gives convincing proof of his power to lead; this warrior whose record shows him invincible in defense of right and in attack on wrong; this man, beloved by all, trusted by all, respected by all; this man who all admit can bring us an overwhelming victory this year—this man of destiny whom our State proudly dedicates to the nation—our own Alfred E. Smith.

At first it was hard to recognize the noise that greeted Roosevelt's conclusion as anything human. Actually, much of it was artificial. In the visitors' gallery, Smith partisans had hooked fire sirens to cases of dry-cell batteries, and these blared for the first thirty minutes of an hour-long demon-

stration. Outside, confetti was dumped from the windows of the surrounding buildings, and the crowd of five thousand people who had been
listening to Roosevelt's speech in the park sang and snake-danced in the
street.

These were the last happy moments of the convention. Even as Roosevelt spoke, a fight was under way in the platform committee over the
"religious freedom" plank. On Saturday morning, the committee chairman appeared before the convention to beg for more time to settle the
dispute, and the convention adjourned until 3 p.m. The committee was
torn between those who wanted to condemn the Klan and those who believed such a step would be divisive. At last the committee approved a
plank that condemned religious bigotry without mentioning the Klan.
There was tension in the air when the convention finally began debating
the issue at 8:30 that night. Every seat in the Garden was filled, and the
overwhelming majority of the crowd supported a plank explicitly denouncing the Klan. William Pattangall, a gubernatorial candidate from
Maine, made their case. He read from a Ku Klux Klan ad that asked, "Are
you a Protestant? Are you white? Are you native born?" Pattangall was all
three, but he had a question for the Klan. "I wonder if its leaders, when
questionnaires were being prepared in 1917 to send to the youth of America—" Pattangall was interrupted by loud applause. "—I wonder, I wonder if when Senator Owen patriotically voted for a draft law as a member
of the United States Senate he or anybody else suggested that we should
only draft to defend our Country the boys who were white, Protestant and
Native born." A roar went up at the end of Pattangall's speech that surpassed even the noise that greeted Roosevelt's nomination of Smith.
There were no fire sirens this time. It was the sound of thousands of human voices that had at last found an opportunity to express their opposition to the Klan.

But as thousands screamed, hundreds of McAdoo delegates burned
with resentment. Many doubted the sincerity of those condemning the
Klan. Now they were convinced that it was nothing but a cynical attempt
to exploit religious differences in the interest of Al Smith. McAdoo's advisers believed that the vote on the anti-Klan plank would be a critical test
of strength with their foe, and during two hours of balloting they exerted
every pound of pressure they could to ensure its defeat. The balloting was
prolonged by the necessity for polling many of the delegations on the

floor. As the recording secretary called the name of each delegate, the floor of the convention was in a perpetual uproar: delegates cheered and booed as each vote was announced, called each other names, and sometimes came to blows. Only the arrival of a thousand beefy Irish cops prevented the gallery spectators from joining the fistfights on the floor. When the vote was finally completed, the anti-Klan plank was defeated by one vote, 542 3/20 to 541 3/20. (In many state delegations, the number of delegates exceeded the number of votes the state was entitled to cast, so they split the votes, permitting each member to cast a fraction.)

The fight over the Klan poisoned the atmosphere surrounding the balloting for the presidential nominee. Neither side was happy. Supporters of the anti-Klan plank knew that they would have won if not for the operation of the unit rule, which some states used to require all members of the delegation to vote the way the majority wanted. The McAdoo managers were also upset. Despite their candidate's strenuous efforts to avoid a position on the anti-Klan plank, McAdoo was now widely identified as the Klan candidate for president, making it impossible for him to capture the urban delegates that he needed to win. Both sides had said things that could not be taken back. Even Will Rogers found it hard to laugh. "Saturday will always remain burned in my memory as long as I live as being the day when I heard the most religion preached, and the least practiced, of any day in the world's history," he said.

The vote had a strong effect on Smith too. A late and reluctant supporter of the anti-Klan plank, Smith found himself swept up in the emotion generated by the platform fight on Saturday. In his head, he knew that splitting the party along religious lines could only hurt his prospects as a candidate by hardening the attitudes of many Protestants. Yet, as he followed developments from the top floor of the Manhattan Club across the street from Madison Square Garden, Smith became convinced that the forces of bigotry were already hard at work to defeat him. He knew that hundreds of copies of *Fellowship Forum*, an anti-Catholic newspaper, had been distributed to the McAdoo delegates. *Fellowship Forum* was the unofficial organ of the Ku Klux Klan, but Smith knew that the Klan was not the only group fomenting religious bigotry. The Anti-Saloon League was a major presence at the convention, spending large sums to pressure delegates with telegrams from back home. Wayne Wheeler, the League's general counsel, told Smith that the League had only one objective—the defeat of Al Smith. In Smith's mind, there was little difference between the Klan and the Prohibitionist forces at the convention. Both appealed to a segment of the party that was deeply bigoted. When Senator Robert L. Owen of Oklahoma suggested to Smith that both sides were playing the religion card, Smith disagreed.

> It certainly was not introduced by the New York delegation, because on that delegation there are men of all religions and men of no religion. I could probably secure their votes for you in the convention and there would be no question asked about your religion. The same would apply to a great many more of the Eastern States. How many votes can you get for me, Senator, in the Oklahoma delegation? You know, and I know, that you cannot secure one vote for me from your state, and you know why.

Smith spoke so confidently about the Oklahoma delegation because several days earlier the governor of the state himself had told him about the prevalence of religious bigotry there. "I am the Democratic governor of that state and I had all I could do to get on this delegation myself because I married a Catholic woman," he said.

In his autobiography, Smith wrote that he realized that he could not win soon after Roosevelt's nominating speech. The first ballot confirmed that the Democrats would be deadlocked along the same lines that had been revealed in the Klan fight. Almost all of the 431 delegates who voted for McAdoo on the first ballot had voted not to name the Klan, and all but one of the 241 who supported Smith had voted for the minority plank. The stalemate would last for ten days. Despite his lead, McAdoo was far short of the required two-thirds vote that he needed to win. He was stymied not just by Smith but by the candidacies of several "favorite sons" who hoped that a deadlocked convention might miraculously turn to them for salvation. Ballot followed fruitless ballot. Whenever it seemed that McAdoo might be poised to break through, a delegation that he was counting on would shift back into the column of another candidate. At no point did he obtain even a majority of the votes. Nevertheless, McAdoo clung stubbornly to the belief that the next ballot would produce a change and vowed to fight on to victory. By the end of the fourth day of balloting, the Democratic Party had set a record for the longest political convention. The city had already taken down the decorations on Fifth Avenue, and only the man who held the food concession at Madison Square Garden was happy. A week later, on the 103d ballot, the Democrats finally nominated John W. Davis, a West Virginia native who was a prominent New York attorney.

Smith denied any bitterness over the outcome during a brief speech to the delegates. "If I were to tell anybody that I was disappointed, it would not be true," he said. "I have gotten as far in the public life of this country and of this State as I ever expected to get, and even further." On the contrary, he was full of gratitude, he said. "I have a heart that is just breaking out with gratitude for the men and the women and even the children . . . that have been interested in me during the progress as well as the beginning of this National Convention," he said. "I shall not forget them." In conclusion, Smith complimented his fellow Democrats on their choice of a candidate. "You have made a wonderful nomination," he said, and he promised to work hard for Davis: "I shall take off my coat and vest, and so will everybody who follows me in the party in this State and do what we can to improve conditions in the United States of America by the election of the ticket that is going to come from this convention." Despite the loud applause that greeted Smith's closing remarks, there were a lot of complaints about his speech. Even some Smith partisans said that their candidate had taken the wrong tack. Although his short speech was not without humor, he came before the convention determined to vindicate his city, his state, and himself. He had listed his achievements, pouring salt on the wounds that he should have been binding. He had not acted like a national figure. "Al's not yet ready for the White House," said one supporter.

Smith was angrier than he was willing to admit, perhaps even to himself. His pride had been stung. The McAdoo delegates had been disrespectful. They had criticized the biggest Democratic city in the country and failed to show appreciation for the achievements of the state's Democratic administration. They had also refused to allow the party to take a principled position opposing religious bigotry. Smith was still angry a few hours later when Democratic leaders met in the dining room of the Manhattan Club to choose a vice presidential candidate. Smith recommended Governor Silzer of New Jersey, but most of the leaders wanted a

Westerner to balance the ticket. When Josephus Daniels of North Carolina suggested William Jennings Bryan's brother Charles, the governor of Nebraska, Smith immediately objected. William Jennings Bryan's militant Prohibitionist views, his opposition to the anti-Klan plank, and his advocacy of McAdoo had made him a symbol of intolerance. Many voters in the Northeast would refuse to support the ticket if his brother was on it. But the majority, including George Brennan, the Chicago boss, believed that Bryan's selection would appeal to McAdoo supporters, who were bitter over the failure of their candidate and unhappy over the selection of Davis, a New Yorker with ties to the monied interests on Wall Street. In addition, the choice gave the Great Commoner a reason to support the ticket. This part at least was true. When the leaders' choice was announced, Bryan did an immediate about-face and loudly proclaimed his support for Davis. "If monkeys had votes, Mr. Bryan would be a champion of evolution," observed one reporter.

On his return to Albany, Smith expressed a desire to return to private life. "There must come a time when I must settle down to the serious business of laying aside something for a rainy day," he told a crowd of 15,000 that met him at the train station. But Davis had already told him that it was essential to the national ticket for him to seek a third term, something no governor had done successfully since 1836. Smith told Davis about his money concerns. He also observed that he had been unable to help Cox in 1920. Smith had run nearly a million votes ahead of the national ticket then, and there was a good chance that it would happen again, particularly with Bryan as the vice presidential candidate. Still angry, Smith said he wanted to make sure his supporters weren't accused of "cutting" the national ticket by voting for him and against Bryan.

Despite his misgivings, Smith agreed to run for reelection. As his anger cooled he realized that the Democratic convention had enhanced his chances of winning the presidential nomination. His opposition to the Klan had made him a hero to Catholic and Jewish voters who were anxious to support someone like themselves for national office. If this hadn't been clear before, it was obvious in October when Smith visited Boston for the first time to make a speech on behalf of the national ticket. Fifteen thousand people crammed Mechanics Hall, the city's largest building, to hear him; another 15,000 listened to loudspeakers in a drizzle outside. Senator David I. Walsh of Massachusetts and Mayor James M. Curley of

Boston spoke before Smith, and both excoriated the Klan. When Smith rose to speak, he was greeted with a huge ovation. Clearly moved, Smith repeatedly expressed his gratitude for the support of the Massachusetts delegation during the Democratic convention. Nevertheless, most of his speech was devoted to criticizing Republican policies, and it was only toward the end of his speech that he mentioned the Klan. While he chided the Republicans for not denouncing the Klan, Smith himself seemed to downplay the threat: "I don't take the Ku Klux Klan very seriously. I look upon it as something we have got to go through with every now and then. Thirty or 35 years ago we had the American Protective Association. The stage comedians in New York did more to break that thing up than any other agency. They just laughed it out." But Smith made his attitude toward the Klan's beliefs very clear. "That thing can't live in this country," he shouted, banging the podium with his fist. The crowd rose and cheered. "The Catholic can stand it, so can the Jew and the Negro, but the United States of America can never stand it," he said.

A month later Smith was elected to a third term with a plurality of over 100,000, while Davis and Bryan lost New York by more than 850,000. The Republican vote was so heavy that Smith was the only Democrat to win statewide office and both houses of the legislature went Republican. But Smith showed no signs of disappointment during his inaugural address in the Assembly chamber. "This is the sixteenth time that I have taken the oath of allegiance to the state in this room," he observed. "I have a deep and abiding affection for the assembly chamber. It has been my high school and my college; in fact, the very foundation of everything that I have attained was laid here." As he reflected on his success, the anger and resentment of the Democratic convention finally dissolved. Had people really opposed him because he was a Catholic or was it that they didn't really know him? Smith knew he would be a candidate for president again in 1928. As always when faced with questions about his ability, the boy from the Lower East Side redoubled his effort. In four years, the whole world would know what he could do, and he would do it despite monolithic opposition by the New York Republican Party.

# 8 ✳ PROTESTANT TRIUMPH

Sometime after 1 a.m. on January 15, 1925, Al Smith was awakened by a knock on the door of his bedroom in the Executive Mansion in Albany. A father of five gets used to rising in the middle of the night, but it had been some time since Smith had had to answer the call of one of his children. He had turned fifty-one a few weeks earlier. Now unexpected calls usually brought bad news about someone he loved. He had already suffered the deaths of his mother and Boss Murphy. Now a third member of the elder generation was sick. Tom Foley had developed chills while meeting with Smith at the Downtown Tammany Club the previous Saturday. While Smith was able to talk him into leaving work early, the seventy-three-year-old Foley was afraid of hospitals and refused to seek medical attention for several days. Finally, Smith brought the state commissioner of health, Dr. Matthias Nicoll, to see him. "I'm all right," the district leader told the commissioner. "I just got a pain under my shoulder." Nevertheless, Foley allowed himself to be taken to the hospital. So Smith was prepared for the worst when he was called to the telephone in the middle of the night. "As soon as the knock came on my door, I knew what it was," he said.

At the time of Murphy's death, the *New York Times* had refused to adopt the conciliatory tone used by Franklin Roosevelt and others who had once opposed the boss. But it ran the news of Foley's death on the front page with a picture. Its obituary noted that while Foley was one of the last of the "old-time" Tammany leaders, he was also exceptional. Where George Washington Plunkitt, the former district leader, had confirmed that he was working for his pocket every day like other men, Foley had never been interested in money. "Money never meant anything to me in all this life or I'd had [sic] this room full of it," he once testified. Instead, the hundreds of thousands of dollars that flowed through his hands had been distributed to the needy, a generosity that was repaid with such intense loyalty that the Second Assembly District was the only district in New York City to resist the Harding landslide. Foley was motivated by his desire to serve his neighbors and by his faith in democracy. Al Smith got to run for the Assembly because Foley believed the incumbent had lost interest in the welfare of his neighbors. Foley encouraged his protégé to have faith in the judgment of the common man. Smith remembered, "He used to say: 'When anybody comes to see you about anything, tell them the truth. They won't like it at the time you tell it to them but six months afterward they will be your friends because they will find it out. It may take some time, but they'll be your friends after that when they find out you didn't deceive them.' " From the perspective of a more cynical age, Foley's faith in the average voter and in the power of honest leadership may seem naive. But it was only because Smith shared Foley's confidence in democracy that he had the courage to attempt to transform the government of New York State.

If Smith had not been such a firm believer in democracy, he could never have accomplished so much against great odds. The Assembly was never under Democratic control during Smith's governorship. There was a Democratic majority in the Senate during 1923 and 1924, but clinging tightly to the coattails of their presidential candidate, Calvin Coolidge, the New York Republicans recaptured the Senate in 1924 and held it for the remainder of Smith's governorship. Smith was able to counteract the Republican advantage by proposing programs that earned wide public support. In 1925 he reintroduced his reorganization program and a bill reducing the workweek for women and children from fifty-four to forty-eight hours. He also proposed legislation that took the first steps toward a dramatic expansion of the state park system. Unwilling to allow Smith to portray them as heartless reactionaries, the Republicans approved a "compromise" bill on limiting working hours as well as a parks bill that would have allowed Smith's plan to go forward only if they could exercise veto power over site selection. This would have enabled them to block the centerpiece of the park plan—the development of Jones Beach and other parks on Republican Long Island, which were intended to provide summertime relief to the masses sweltering in New York City.

When the legislature attempted to block Smith, he appealed to the public for support. He vetoed both the working hours and the parks bills, accusing the legislature of trying to fool the public and saddling the Republicans with responsibility for the failure to make progress on these issues. The legislature often made it easy for Smith by being almost perversely obstructionist. They even fought his proposal for an income tax cut. This was the second tax cut that Smith had recommended, and in both cases the Republicans instinctively recoiled from a measure that they feared would increase the governor's popularity. They had reluctantly agreed to the first cut and thus shared at least some of the credit with Smith, but the second cut was more than they could stand. The Republicans were so desperate to prove that the $13 million surplus anticipated by Smith did not exist that they worked into the small hours of the morning anticipating every possible forthcoming expense they could imagine, including $2.5 million for settling a lawsuit against the state that had not even gone to trial. In the end, it was all in vain. Smith announced he would take his case to the people using radio. "At that time I had little experience in talking through a microphone, but I felt I must get the story to the people quickly and intelligibly," Smith recalled. So General Electric wired the governor's office for the first time, and Smith gave a dramatic speech shortly before midnight on one of the last days of the 1925 legislative session. A "wagonload of mail . . . came up Capitol Hill the next day and saturated the post office," Smith said. The Republicans bowed to the inevitable and approved the tax cut. Interviewed at the circus soon after, Smith was asked to compare the action under the big top to the recently concluded legislative session. "There is no comparison," he insisted. "The animals are very intelligent."

Though it wasn't easy, Smith succeeded in significantly expanding government efforts to improve the lives of workers. In 1927 he finally won his battle to make it illegal to work women and children more than eight hours per day and forty-eight hours per week. His most important contribution to social welfare, however, was his successful advocacy of increased government spending. During Smith's years in the legislature, the state had operated under a pay-as-you-go approach to capital spending that required that all long-term improvements like the construction of buildings must be paid for out of the state's operating budget. The budget, in turn, was limited by the state's tax revenue, and there was rarely enough left over for building the facilities required by a growing population. Smith argued that the capital budget should be separated from the operating budget and funded by the sale of bonds, which would shift to later generations some of the costs of improvements from which they would receive the benefit. He led the fight for five bond issues that were approved in referendums and significantly increased the state's indebtedness: $45 million for bonuses to World War I veterans; $50 million for the construction of new state hospitals and psychiatric facilities; $15 million for the development of the state park system; $300 million for the elimination of dangerous intersections where trains crossed roads; and $100 million for a ten-year public works program.

The Smith administration would have been remembered for the new park system alone. With the exception of the forest preserves in the Adirondacks and Catskills, New York's parks had been few and far between in 1920. By the time Smith left office, the system would grow to include seventy parks with over 125,000 acres, including 9,700 acres on Long Island, where some of the world's best beaches now belonged to even the poorest people living in the worst housing in New York City. Smith was also responsible for giving the state a major role in paying teacher salaries in local schools. Education spending increased 500 percent during the Smith years and accounted for almost half of the budget in 1928.

But the greatest achievement of Smith's governorship was the passage of the reorganization program. The process of amending the state constitution was laborious, requiring that amendments be passed not once but twice by the legislature before they were referred to the people for a final vote. The consolidation amendment wasn't approved by the voters until 1925. In 1926 the legislature finally endorsed the executive budget and passed it again the next year, when it was overwhelmingly approved by the voters. Although the rural districts of the state would rule the Assembly for the next generation, Smith had largely succeeded in redistributing power.

By 1927 Smith had established such a habit of winning that he appeared practically unbeatable—both in the legislature and at the polls. In 1925 he had taken on Hearst again by throwing his support to Jimmy

Walker in the Democratic mayoral primary. The quick-witted Walker had made short work of Mayor Hylan, winning more than 60 percent of the vote and beating him even in Brooklyn, his home borough. Two months later, Walker was elected mayor and all three of Smith's constitutional amendments received voter approval. The *New York Times* was ecstatic: "Alfred E. Smith today is the most powerful leader the Democratic Party has ever had in the greatest State of the Union. Not only is his leadership over his own party in the State undisputed, but the election has shown that he has a tremendous following among Republicans." He won reelection in 1926 with a plurality of 257,000 votes, becoming only the second governor in state history to serve four terms. The next year, New Yorkers gave another sign of the unmatched political mastery of their governor. There were eight constitutional amendments on the ballot that year, including a Republican proposal to create a four-year gubernatorial term. Smith had been the one to propose the four-year term in the first place, but the Republican proposal was unsatisfactory to him because the governor would have continued to be elected during presidential elections, and national issues would continue to overshadow state concerns. Smith endorsed all the other amendments but called for the defeat of the four-year term. The voters followed Smith down the line, defeating only the amendment he had marked for extinction.

Smith's record was so strong that it filled Walter Lippmann with dread. Lippman was not opposed to Smith. On the contrary, as the chief editorial writer for the *New York World*, he had provided strong support for the governor and his policies. But in December 1925 he expressed the fear that Smith's presidential candidacy would aggravate the deep conflict between two different kinds of Americans. On one side there were Smith's supporters. "He holds these crowds as no man can hold them," Lippmann observed.

> He holds them without the promise of a millennium, without a radical program, without appeal to their hatreds, without bribes and doles and circuses. How does he do it? . . . The answer, I think, is that they feel he has become the incarnation of their own hope and pride; he is the man who has gone, as they would like but do not quite dare to go, out into the great world to lift from them the secret sense of inferiority.

On the other side were Smith's opponents, the "older American stocks in the South and the West and in the East, too." Their opposition "is inspired by the feeling that the clamorous life of the city should not be acknowledged as the American ideal," Lippmann said.

> That, at bottom, is the opposition to Al Smith and not the nonsense about setting up the Pope in the East Wing of the White House. The Ku Kluxers may talk about the Pope to the lunatic fringe, but the main mass of the opposition is governed by an instinct that to accept Al Smith is to certify and sanctify a way of life that does not belong to the America they love.

As Lippmann sensed the approach of this irrepressible conflict, he had stopped celebrating Smith's successes. "His victories have ceased to be victories merely; they are premonitions," he said. "These victories, which prove his mettle and increase his stature, cast long shadows ahead of him. They have come to portend a tragic conflict in which he seems destined to be the central figure."

Neither Smith nor his advisers could be convinced of the truth of this gloomy prediction. On the contrary, they saw a country that was finally beginning to come to its senses. The best example was the obvious decline of the Ku Klux Klan. In 1924 the Klan had been near the peak of its influence, winning important election victories in Indiana, Colorado, Oklahoma, Kansas, and Kentucky, but an improving economic climate, revulsion against Klan violence, and internal dissension combined to undermine the Hooded Empire. The Klan's weakness began to be apparent in the 1925 elections, which saw the election of a Catholic as state treasurer in Virginia and the defeat of Klan mayoral candidates in Detroit and Buffalo.

The 1926 elections produced more hopeful signs. Since the passage of the Eighteenth Amendment, its critics had contended that the approval process had been undemocratic. In 1926 referenda on a variety of issues related to liquor control finally enabled them to argue that most people opposed Prohibition, or at least favored the amendment of the Volstead Act to permit the sale of beer and wine. Voters in New York, Illinois, Wisconsin, and Nevada demanded a change. In New York the majority was over one million, and while the vote in the other states was smaller, it was decisive in many cities, ranging from three to one in Chicago to five to one in some Wisconsin towns. Downstate Illinois was hardly less emphatic than Chicago, voting two to one for reform. Even their victory in Colorado was troubling for the drys. In a state that had en-acted Prohibition even before the passage of the Eighteenth Amendment and was considered one of the driest in the country, the amendment call-ing for the repeal of the state enforcement act had come uncomfortably close to passing.

These developments certainly enhanced Smith's prospects of captur-ing the Democratic presidential nomination. But Smith's biggest advan-tage was the absence of any strong opponent. McAdoo had established a formidable national organization in 1924, but his identification with the Klan in the minds of many Democrats made him an impossible choice. Even many of his own supporters blamed him for the disastrous stalemate at Madison Square Garden, and his advisers told him he did not have a chance in 1928. There were some who believed that Senator Thomas J. Walsh of Montana might be able to challenge the New Yorker. Walsh had established a national reputation as the prosecutor of the Teapot Dome scandal and was also a supporter of Prohibition. Because Walsh was dry, his candidacy depended on receiving support from Democrats in the South and West. But Walsh was also a Catholic, and few Democratic leaders in these sections believed that they could rally their forces behind even a dry Catholic. The South was also cool to Senator James A. Reed of Missouri, the only significant threat to Smith following Walsh's with-drawal. As a result, when Smith announced his candidacy, his nomina-tion was a foregone conclusion. It wasn't even necessary for him to campaign in the handful of states that held presidential primaries during 1928. On the eve of the Democratic convention, Smith had received the pledges of over 700 of the 1,100 delegates. His campaign managers had spent only $153,000.

The biggest question during the pre-convention period was not whether Smith would be the Democratic nominee but whether his reli-gion would doom his candidacy. Smith would be the first Catholic to run for president on a major party ticket. A few weeks after his reelection in 1926, the *Charlotte Observer* reviewed the various efforts being under-taken by Southerners to prevent Smith's nomination. Based on this evi-dence, the *New York Times* concluded that Smith's religion was the main reason that Southerners, particularly Methodists and Baptists, opposed him. Most political observers believed that it would be a mistake for Smith to answer the charge of disloyalty that was being leveled against Catholics because it would only give increased attention to the religious issue and help revive the Klan.

The political equation changed in March 1927 when Ellery Sedgwick, the editor of the *Atlantic Monthly*, sent Franklin Roosevelt an advance copy of an "open letter" to Smith by Charles C. Marshall, which Sedgwick intended to publish in the April issue. Marshall, a Protestant lawyer, gave the loyalty issue a new respectability by citing a wide array of papal encyclicals and other official statements of the church that suggested that on issues where religious duty conflicted with a Catholic's allegiance to his country, he must put his religion first. Both Roosevelt and Belle Moskowitz believed that Smith would have to reply, but Smith at first refused. "I'm not going to answer the damn thing," he told Joseph Proskauer. Even if he wanted to respond, he did not think he knew enough about Catholic history and theology to do it: "Joe, to tell you the truth, I've read it; but I don't know what the words mean. I've been a devout Catholic all my life and I never heard of these bulls and encyclicals and books that he writes about. They have nothing to do with being a Catholic; I just don't know how to answer such a thing." At Smith's request, Proskauer agreed to draft a response. As an adviser, Proskauer enlisted Father Francis P. Duffy, the priest whose loyalty had been well established during his wartime service as chaplain of the highly decorated Irish-American regiment, the "Fighting Sixty-ninth."

Smith's letter to Marshall was highly effective. Although written by Proskauer and guided by Duffy, it captured Smith's voice convincingly. From its first words, readers could sense an outrage that was barely restrained by the necessity of making a point-by-point rebuttal of Marshall's alleged "facts." "[Y]ou 'impute' to American Catholics views which, if held by them, would leave open to question the loyalty and devotion to this country and its Constitution of more than 20 million American Catholic citizens," Smith began. "These convictions are held neither by me nor by any other American Catholic, as far as I know." As a religious minority, American Catholics had benefited directly from the separation of church and state, and Smith cited numerous statements by the leaders of the American church that demonstrated their gratitude for it. The

Marshall letter had failed to specify many issues on which a Catholic president would differ from a Protestant. He did raise the possibility that a Catholic president would undermine public education and support the Catholic church in foreign affairs, perhaps intervening to overthrow revolutionary governments like the one in Mexico that had recently expropriated religious property and persecuted priests and nuns. Smith had already demonstrated his support for public education, however, and he proclaimed his opposition to intervention in the internal affairs of other countries. In conclusion, he underlined his personal philosophy:

> I recognize no power in the institutions of my Church to interfere with the operations of the Constitution of the United States or the enforcement of the law of the land. I believe in absolute freedom of conscience for all men and in equality of all churches, all sects, and all beliefs before the laws as a matter of right and not as a matter of favor. I believe in the absolute separation of Church and State and in the strict enforcement of the provisions of the Constitution that Congress shall make no law respecting an establishment of religion or prohibiting the free exercise thereof.

The publication of Smith's reply was a major news story throughout the country. Anticipation had been mounting ever since the release of the Marshall letter, which by itself had nearly doubled sales of the *Atlantic*. Most of the major daily newspapers in the country were planning to carry at least some of Smith's reply. There was so much interest in what Smith would say that a *Boston Post* reporter visited the *Atlantic*'s offices and absconded with an uncorrected proof of the article. (The *Atlantic* was forced to hire trucks and rush the magazines to New York to keep from being scooped.)

Smith's answer was not immediately embraced by other politicians. It is a measure of the sensitivity of the religious issue that when a summary of the letter reached Washington on April 17, many prominent Democrats were unwilling to comment. Most refused to say anything until they had read the complete statement. Only Senator Walsh made a public comment, calling it "good plain Americanism." Several days later, it was clear that Smith's reply had everyone talking. Senator Robert F. Wagner of New York got an earful during a trip upstate. "Even on the train coming up here from New York, people who did not know me from Adam discussed it," he said. "I trust the question is now beyond the stage of a serious issue—that the Governor's letter will forever remove religious rancor from political affairs."

As the weeks passed, it appeared that the religious issue would subside. Only Senator J. Thomas Heflin of Alabama openly challenged Smith's fitness to serve on religious grounds. He was outspoken in his anti-Catholicism and frequently attacked the Catholic church during speeches in the Senate. As Smith's nomination appeared increasingly likely, Heflin stepped up his attacks until the leader of the Senate Democrats, Joseph Robinson of Arkansas, finally challenged him in January 1928. When the other Senate Democrats supported Robinson in a caucus the next day, some saw the vote as a turning point in the battle against religious prejudice. There appeared to be a strong reaction against Heflin in the South. "The revulsion of feeling against Heflin was the most important and most widespread I have ever observed in more than 30 years of newspaper experience in the South," Julian Harris, a *New York Times* reporter, observed. Harris believed that Smith had actually gained strength in the South because of Heflin's attacks. "Even newspapers which do not favor him as the nominee admit that the reaction from Heflinism has brought about this result," he said.

Four years later, Michael Williams, the editor of the Catholic weekly *Commonweal*, would look back on the Senate's repudiation of Heflin with considerable skepticism. The resolution endorsing Robinson's leadership contained no condemnation of religious bigotry. It didn't even criticize Heflin, who made his next anti-Catholic speech in the Senate the same day and without objection. "Politicians had once more blown hot and blown cold while striving to look as if not blowing at all," another political commentator observed. It is also doubtful that the South's embarrassment over Heflin's remarks translated into real support for Smith. In the absence of a legitimate contender to Smith, party leaders in the South were bending to political reality because they feared that a concerted effort to deny him the nomination might permanently alienate Catholic Democrats. But Lippmann's was a minority view. Many contemporary observers shared Julian Harris's belief that the South was beginning to accept Smith. Even Michael Williams was fooled. In April 1928, after touring the country, he pronounced religious bigotry "practically dead." "I believe the battle is over and done with," he said.

Before the Democratic convention could meet, however, the Smith family had one major piece of business to get out of the way. On June 8, with the convention only three weeks away, Catherine Smith was scheduled to marry Francis Quillinan, a lawyer in the U.S. attorney general's office. Though Francis was a Republican, Smith confidently predicted that he would be converted to the Democratic faith, which he was. Al and Katie were relieved that another of their children had made a good match. They had been shocked four years earlier when Alfred had eloped with Bertha Gott, a woman he had met at the New York State Fair only four weeks before. Katie had nearly fainted when she was told. Smith attempted to laugh off the episode as a grand romantic adventure, but he, too, must have been deeply disappointed. Smith could not understand a four-week courtship as anything other than a surrender to lust. Alfred may have been trying to send a different message, however. It was obvious to anyone who knew the Smiths well that the governor doted on his daughter Emily, who took a deep interest in politics. Emily was eager from an early age to understand her father's business and to give him her opinion of what he should be doing. He often teased her about it. Young Al's elopement may well have been both an act of defiance and a cry for attention from a father who seemed to have too little time for him. A few months after Alfred's, the Smiths received one more matrimonial shock from their children when seventeen-year-old Arthur belatedly announced that he had also eloped.

Emily's engagement to Major John A. Warner, the head of the state police, was more in keeping with the Smiths' expectations. Even this relationship had its complications, because Warner was both a Republican and a Protestant, but the biggest problem was solved when he agreed to convert to Catholicism. Emily's wedding in 1926 included over 1,500 guests. "It was the biggest crowd since *Ben Hur*," Smith joked. The happy couple received so many gifts that they threatened to buckle the floor of the room where they were stored in the Executive Mansion. There were seventy-two dozen plates, enough to "throw at each other for 25 years and still have enough left over to serve a seven-course dinner to a lot of people," her father said. Catherine's wedding was even bigger. The marriage was performed by Patrick Cardinal Hayes of New York, whose scarlet vestments "gave an aspect of majesty to the scene," according to the *New York Times*. They also drew attention to the prominent role of the Catholic church in Smith's life and to Smith's prominence in his church. Not every young couple starts their life together by receiving an apostolic blessing from the pope.

There had been something almost reckless about Catherine's wedding. The presence of the cardinal would have been unobjectionable if the wedding hadn't been only three weeks before the Democratic convention, but there were some Southern Democrats who would see it as a deliberate provocation on Smith's part, a way of defying their legitimate concerns over the role of the Catholic church under a Smith administration. One of Smith's campaign managers, George Van Namee, was reported to be frantic over the possibility of a hostile Protestant reaction. "He is weeping because Al's youngest daughter is to be married . . . at Albany and insists on having the Cardinal himself," Louis Howe reported to Franklin Roosevelt. "I hope the young couple won't have to kiss the Cardinal's toe as part of the ceremony."

Smith went ahead with the ceremony knowing that it would be offensive to some, and was applauded by those who believed it was another example of Smith's honesty. But others noted that since becoming the undisputed leader of the New York Democrats in 1926, Smith had grown increasingly unwilling to listen to advice. Journalist Henry Pringle observed that Smith "is more inclined to impatience and is less tolerant when associates disagree with him." Jonah Goldstein could attest to this fact. An old friend, Goldstein had attempted to pass along some constructive criticism from David Sarnoff, the head of the Radio Corporation of America. "I was in a position to try and help him to get somebody to show him how to get the most out of a microphone, but those around him were doing what he always said, yessing him, and in that particular instance he fell prey to them," Goldstein recalled. Smith believed he was ready for whatever the campaign might bring. He had almost always had confidence in his abilities. Now, he felt certain they were going to help elect him president.

There was practically no disharmony at the Democratic convention in Houston at the end of June. Smith's nomination was a foregone conclusion, and it had already been decided that a Southerner, Senator Joseph Robinson of Arkansas, the man who had finally confronted Heflin, would be Smith's running mate. During the opening session Robinson provided one of the few moments of excitement by claiming that Thomas Jefferson would have been a Smith supporter. "Jefferson gloried in the Virginia statute of religious freedom," Robinson told the crowd of 20,000 gathered in Sam Houston Hall. "He rejoiced in the provision of the Constitution that declares no religious test shall ever be required as a qualification for office or trust in the United States." Although Robinson had provided no context for his remarks, which were not included in the written version, the delegates sprang to their feet and were soon marching in the first demonstration of the convention. Later, the crowd got another thrill when Franklin Roosevelt made the nominating speech for Smith. "I offer one who has the will to win—who not only deserves success but commands it," Roosevelt concluded. "Victory is his habit, the happy warrior, Alfred E. Smith." As in Madison Square Garden four years before, a cacophony of noise filled the hall, drowning out the orchestra. Only one fire siren was heard this time, for George W. Olvany, the Tammany leader, responded to complaints of overzealousness at the last convention by forbidding his troops to use noisemakers.

Smith was in Albany when his name was placed in nomination, although almost all of his family and friends were in Houston. Custom barred a nominee from being present at the convention during the nominating speeches and the balloting; even after the candidate had been chosen, he did not customarily make an address. At the Executive Mansion Smith tried to follow his routine as much as possible. The next day he went to his office, although somewhat later than usual because the excitement of the previous night had kept him awake until 4 a.m. He also accepted the gift of a two-month-old puppy, the tenth to join his menagerie. He called the newcomer "Houston." Smith dined with guests and later led them outside to visit his private zoo, where he fed bananas to four monkeys and spoke to the other animals, including an elk. He told his guests that he had spent a week teaching a six-month-old fawn to eat out of his hand. Yet Smith's thoughts were never far from the impending vote on his nomination. He was wearing a ten-gallon cowboy hat when he strode into the study of the Executive Mansion to listen to the balloting on the radio with his daughter Emily and a small group of friends, including Belle Moskowitz and Robert Moses. "A delegate from Texas on the dead run," he said, saluting his friends with the hat, a recent gift from Tom Mix, the movie cowboy. Smith sat down and lit a cigar.

In the days leading up to the convention, Smith was picking up delegates so quickly that a first-ballot victory had begun to appear possible.

But the platform had to be approved before the balloting could begin. Sitting next to a huge radio with his Great Dane, Jefferson, at his feet, Smith kept his visitors amused with comments on the proceedings. The tension increased when the balloting finally got under way, with almost everyone in the room following along on a paper tally. At the end of the first roll call, Smith was only a few votes short of the nomination when the Ohio delegation announced that it was shifting its forty-five votes to him. "There it is," cried William A. Humphrey, one of Smith's golfing partners, rushing forward to shake the candidate's hand. "Thanks, Chief," Smith replied, using Humphrey's nickname. "I guess they have done it." He embraced Emily and shook hands with his friends while a small crowd of well-wishers cheered on the front lawn. As he posed for the newspaper and newsreel photographers, Smith could hear them singing "The Sidewalks of New York." Stepping outside to address the crowd, the Democratic nominee was surrounded by reporters. "My nomination on the first ballot fills me with joy and satisfaction that I know is shared by my family and friends," Smith said. "My heart is where my palate should be."

The excitement grew over the next six weeks as Albany prepared to host the ceremony held to formally notify the candidate of his nomination and to give him a stage for his first campaign speech. A crowd of over 100,000 was expected, and the prediction seemed accurate in the days immediately preceding the August 22 ceremony. Trains, cars, and ferries disgorged thousands of Democrats onto the streets of the state capital, where every public building had been hung with bunting. There wasn't a hotel room available anywhere. A platform extended from the landing of the steps of the capitol building, and loudspeakers were placed in every tree in Capitol Park. On the day before the ceremony, Smith himself tested the sound system. The newsreel cameramen were also rehearsing, along with technicians from WGY, one of the first television stations. They were hoping to use the occasion to demonstrate that TV cameras could be used to transmit outdoor events. When the cameramen and newspaper photographers asked Smith to pose for them, he readily complied, taking over the direction himself. " 'Move the arm,' he shouted, swinging out his right arm. 'Move it again. And over here toward the little fellow at the end.' " A crowd of four hundred tourists laughed and applauded. All the rehearsal was in vain, however, because it rained steadily the next day, forcing the evening ceremony indoors into the Assembly chamber, the biggest room in the city. Even crammed full, it held only two thousand people. Another ten thousand listened outside under umbrellas, including Franklin Roosevelt, who chose not to force his wheelchair into the dense throng of people inside. His wife, Eleanor, sat with him. A national radio audience of millions was also present, listening on what the newspapers claimed was the largest network of stations ever assembled for a speech.

The crowd greeted Smith rapturously when he finally appeared shortly before 7:30 p.m. He wasn't wearing the tuxedo that presidential candidates normally favored for the occasion. "That old-fashioned statesman stuff doesn't convince anyone nowadays," he said. Dressed in a double-breasted gray suit and a bow tie, he waved back at the people. In a short speech, Senator Key Pittman of Nevada, the chairman of the notification committee, announced Smith's nomination for president. The candidate stepped to the rostrum amid a new roar from the crowd. He began by expressing his gratitude to the remarkable country where a poor boy could become president. "The greatest privilege that can come to any man is to give himself to a nation which has reared him and raised him from obscurity to be a contender for the highest office in the gift of its people," he said. But this didn't mean the country couldn't be improved, he said. "Government should be constructive, not destructive; progressive, not reactionary. I am entirely unwilling to accept the old order of things as the best unless and until I become convinced that it cannot be made better."

Smith believed that his activist political philosophy was in tune with the principles of the Democratic Party as they had been expressed by Jefferson, Cleveland, and Wilson. He quoted Wilson: "First, the people as the source and their interests and desires as the test of laws and institutions. Second, individual liberty as the objective of all law." Republicans like Theodore Roosevelt and Robert M. La Follette had also endorsed this expansive view of the role of government, but the modern Republican Party was dominated by reactionaries, Smith charged—men who believed "that an elect class should be the special object of the government's concern" and who made "the concern of the government, not people, but material things." He knew them well: "I have fought this spirit in my own State. I have had to fight it and beat it, in order to place upon the statute books every one of the progressive, humane laws for whose enactment I assumed responsibility in my legislative and executive career. I shall know how to fight it in the nation." Smith dismissed the reactionary's favorite complaint. "It is a fallacy that there is inconsistency between progressive measures protecting the rights of the people, including the poor and the weak, and a just regard for the rights of legitimate business," he said.

The nominee promised government intervention to curb the overproduction that had driven agricultural prices lower throughout the 1920s. He would appoint a commission of experts that would begin working on a plan as soon as the election was over and present it by the time Congress convened in January. He would also fund programs to relieve unemployment and to "strive to accomplish a national well-being resting upon the prosperity of the individual men and women who constitute the nation." He endorsed federal involvement in a program of flood control that would prevent the recurring devastation of the Mississippi Valley, and he promised to expand the federal government's role in developing water power. He also pledged to "greatly" extend the national park system and increase federal aid for social welfare programs:

> I shall continue my sympathetic interest in the advancement of progressive legislation for the protection and advancement of working men and women. Promotion of proper care of maternity, infancy and childhood and the encouragement of those scientific activities of the National Government which advance the safeguards of public health, are so fundamental as to need no expression from me other than my record as legislator and as Governor.

Al Smith intended to be one of the most activist presidents in American history.

Unfortunately for Smith, the Republicans had not nominated a reactionary. Herbert Hoover could legitimately claim a record as a progressive. His training as a mining engineer was considered an asset by those who believed that reform involved the application of scientific principles to the problems of the age. After spending twenty years working on mining projects around the world, Hoover entered public service during World War I and played a conspicuous role as the director of America's relief efforts in ravaged and starving Europe. In 1921 Calvin Coolidge appointed him secretary of commerce, at which post he actively promoted the idea that government could play an important role in the economy by conducting research on business problems and then encouraging businessmen to solve them by entering into voluntary agreements through trade associations and other nongovernmental agencies. Actually, as time would prove, Hoover was far more conservative than Smith. Although Republican Party regulars were suspicious of him, he was completely orthodox in his view that government should never force business to do something that it doesn't want to do. For Hoover, the genius of the American system lay in its commitment to individualism, and any deviation from that principle risked a rapid and irreversible descent into socialism.

Even in 1928 it was apparent to many that Smith was the liberal candidate. The philosopher John Dewey saw him as the candidate most committed to helping people:

> Mr. Smith's record as Governor is proof of the fact that a humane and sympathetic spirit will at least color the treatment [of fundamental issues] as far as his influence can extend. Administrator for administrator, he is at least the equal of Mr. Hoover, and his extraordinary administrative abilities are as much controlled by a human sense of his fellow-beings as Mr. Hoover's are by a hard efficiency which works out to strengthen the position of just [those] economic interests that most need weakening instead of strengthening.

At first, George N. Peek, a Republican farm leader, was unwilling to accept assurances of Smith's humaneness. He had been fighting for the McNary-Haugen bill, which required government to intervene to control farm surpluses. When Smith committed himself to the principle of federal intervention, Peek went to work for the Democratic ticket. Senator George Norris, Republican of Nebraska, who had led the campaign for public development of water power on federal lands, was another skeptic who questioned Smith's commitment to government operation of the power facilities at Muscle Shoals, Alabama, and Boulder Dam in Nevada. After Smith convinced him that he favored public operation at both the state and federal levels, Norris broke with his party and endorsed Smith.

Still, it wasn't easy to make voters appreciate the importance of reform when the nation's economy had been growing strongly for seven years. While the benefits of that growth were unevenly spread and many of the nation's farmers were suffering, most people thought that the good times would continue and that those who had not yet fully realized the American dream would eventually do so. It was during the 1928 campaign that the Republicans made the promise of an automobile in every backyard and "a chicken in every pot," which became infamous following the stock market crash a year later. An important part of the Republican campaign was to persuade voters that the election of a Democratic president threatened prosperity. For more than a generation, Republican politicians had been warning that the economic policies of the Democrats were unsound. They tied America's success to the protective tariff and warned that Democratic calls to lower tariff rates would lead to a flood of cheap manufactured goods from abroad that would produce unemployment and depression. They also reminded voters that the Democratic Party was the home of men like William Jennings Bryan, who advocated monetary inflation and other unsound measures that could undermine business confidence and bring the whole edifice of prosperity crashing down.

In an effort to disarm these attacks, Smith and his advisers supported a modification of the party's traditional opposition to the protective tariff and promised that rates would be cut only after careful investigation of the affected industry. They also began looking for a leading businessman to serve as campaign chairman. When Smith's first choice, Owen Young, the chairman of General Electric, declined the honor, his advisers favored Senator Peter Gerry of Rhode Island, who was both wealthy and Protestant. Smith's second choice was John Raskob, whose climb to wealth and fame in business was almost as dramatic as Smith's political rise. The son of second-generation immigrants (his father's family was from Alsace in Germany; his mother's from Ireland), Raskob had grown up in Lockport, a town on the Erie Canal in western New York, where his father was a cigar maker. He was a business school graduate working as a stenographer at $5 per week when Pierre du Pont, the president of a Lorain, Ohio, streetcar company, hired him as a secretary. In 1902 Pierre and two of his cousins took control of the family firm, E. I. du Pont de Nemours, and transformed it into a modern corporation that controlled two-thirds of the black powder and dynamite production in the United

States when war broke out in Europe in 1914. World War I would have made Raskob and the du Ponts very rich all by itself, but Raskob's acumen helped them take control of a fledgling automobile company, General Motors. By 1928 their investment was worth $800 million, and Raskob had emerged as a financier whose views were widely sought not only by professional investors but by popular magazines like *Ladies' Home Journal*, which published an interview with him two months before the stock market crash under the headline "Everybody Ought to Be Rich."

Raskob had serious weaknesses as a candidate for Democratic Party chairman, however. Prior to meeting Smith in 1925, he had taken little serious interest in politics. He had voted for both Democrats and Republicans for president. Most people assumed he was Republican, and it was on that assumption that he had been admitted as a member to the Union League Club. But the more serious problems were his Catholicism and his wetness. Raskob had given so generously to the church, including a $500,000 gift to the diocese of Wilmington, that he had been knighted by the pope. He had also invested heavily in the repeal of Prohibition through his support of the Association Against the Prohibition Amendment. In short, Raskob was a political novice whose leadership could only underline those aspects of Smith's record that hurt him most in the South and West. Both Belle Moskowitz and Joseph Proskauer tried to talk Smith out of his decision.

Smith believed that Raskob's lack of experience was not significant because he intended to make the important decisions himself, but the objection to Raskob's background was harder to dismiss, and he wavered momentarily. His decision was made more difficult by the outcry over the telegram that he had sent to the Democratic convention on the morning after his nomination. The telegram pledged support for the party platform but reaffirmed his commitment to seek a modification of the Volstead Act. Some dry Democrats accused Smith of undercutting the platform's promise that the party would enforce Prohibition. Methodist Episcopal bishop James G. Cannon, Jr., of Virginia, and the Rev. Arthur J. Barton, a leader of the Southern Baptist Convention, announced that they would hold a convention of dry Democrats within weeks to lay plans "for the defeat of the wet Tammany candidate for President." But Smith set aside the political consequences of selecting a Catholic wet in order to repay Raskob's generous support of his campaigns. "It's the only thing Raskob has ever asked of me, and I've got to give it to him," Smith told Belle Moskowitz. His choice of Raskob turned out to be the least of Smith's problems. Soon after Smith's acceptance speech in August, his campaign became mired in controversy over his personal morality.

Smith's Tammany Hall connection made his morality suspect in a large part of the country. Tammany had been synonymous with corruption since the days of Boss Tweed, and it was only logical to assume that a man who had risen to prominence as a member of the machine must be corrupt. Smith's presumed support for vice soon became the grist for gossip. Two weeks after his nomination, the *New York Times* took note of the existence of a "whispering campaign" against the Democratic candidate. "[T]here is no doubt that gossiping tongues have been enlisted for the Republican cause, and are whispering all kinds of insinuations and slanders against Governor Smith to their neighbors, by them to be passed on," it charged in an editorial. But at least one Republican who believed that Smith had done Tammany dirty work felt no need for furtiveness. In mid-July, William Allen White, a well-known Republican editor from Kansas, claimed that a study of Smith's legislative record showed that he had voted ten times to block any restriction on the sale of alcohol; four times against restrictions on prostitution and gambling in saloons; four times in favor of removing a zoning restriction that barred saloons from areas around churches and schools; and three times in favor of laws sponsored by organized gambling. While praising Smith as "a man of unusual intelligence, splendid courage and rare political wisdom," White insisted that his election would subject the nation to Tammany rule. "Tammany is Tammany and Smith is its prophet," White said. "The whole Puritan civilization which has built a sturdy, orderly nation is threatened by Smith."

Smith charged that his legislative record had been distorted: "Let's take the worst thing. 'Four times in the Legislature Smith voted against stopping gambling and prostitution in connection with saloons.' What kind of a statement is that for a sane person to make? Was there ever any law in this State to let gambling and prostitution go on in a saloon? Was it ever necessary to adopt a bill to stop it?" When White refused to withdraw his charges and issued a report that documented Smith's record on these bills, Smith explained his vote on each piece of legislation. In the end, all White had succeeded in doing was proving that there were differences between Democrats and Republicans on the issue of Prohibition. He later dropped the prostitution and gambling charges, and in effect surrendered the moral high ground to Smith. "No one in all of the 25 years of my public life has ever dared to make the vile suggestions which emanated from Mr. White," Smith said. On the antiprostitution bill, Smith made it clear that White's charges affected not only the candidate but his family. "On this bill and this single bill alone, William Allen White would have my wife, my children and my friends believe that in my long public career, I was a friend of public prostitution," he said. "I denounce as unfair, unmanly and un-American this slanderous attack upon me and my record," he concluded. Smith's appeal to America's highest values had worked well for him in 1919 when he denounced Hearst's slanders. It was reasonable to believe it would work again.

Rumors that Al Smith was an alcoholic were also spreading. It was no secret that he had enjoyed a drink in the years before Prohibition, and that he had not stopped drinking on January 1, 1920. Many supporters of Prohibition believed that alcohol was so addictive that anybody who drank was an alcoholic, so they were easily persuaded that Smith was not just a drinker but a drunk. The alcoholic rumor was so pervasive that Robinson addressed it directly during his first campaign speech. Speaking to a group of Dallas Democrats on Labor Day, Robinson found the crowd undemonstrative until he put aside his prepared remarks and addressed the whispering campaign against Smith. "The statement has been made that he is a drunkard. There is not one word of truth in it," Robinson thundered, drawing cheers at last. A few days later, the Smith campaign made a concerted effort to answer the charge. They had received a report from a man in Parkersburg, West Virginia, that a local woman was spreading the rumor that Smith had been drunk when he appeared at the State Fair in Syracuse. The woman claimed that a friend in Syracuse had said that the governor was so intoxicated that he had to be helped to his feet by the people sitting on either side of him.

Smith was hurt by the questioning of his personal morality, but the underground attacks on his wife were even more painful. Katie Smith had lost much of her youthful attractiveness by 1928. After the birth of five children, she had gained weight, and she possessed a prominent double chin that made her look even heavier. As a result, the pictures of her at the time make her look matronly, and she could appear conceited when her great pride in her husband and children showed in her face. But Katie was the same woman who fell in love with an impecunious clerk and married him despite her parents' objections. The most important thing in her life besides her husband were her children. She explained in a 1925 interview:

> It never occurred to me and I know it never occurred to my husband that there was anything in the world which we wanted more than our children. . . . My children have always interested me. Spending the evening with them has given me greater pleasure than a theatre or restaurant could offer. My youngest boy, Walter—my "baby," although he is 12 now—is a whole vaudeville show!

Throughout their childhoods, the Smith children had spent Sunday evenings at home with their parents and usually some family friends. The entertainment almost always featured singing, with Katie providing accompaniment on the piano. "I have spent one of those gay joyous evenings with the Smith children," a reporter for the *Woman's Home Companion* wrote in 1928. "The Smiths at home are a darn good show!"

Smith's meteoric rise posed problems for Katie Smith. Although she had more of an education than her husband, she did not understand politics. Like most women of her day and almost all the women of her class, she did not attend college and was not much of a reader. Like Al, however, she had worked hard to meet her responsibilities. During the legislative years, she had traveled to Albany when her husband was scheduled to make a major speech. Later, as the governor's wife, she and Emily went to the Senate weekly to listen to the debate and gain an understanding of the political process. Katie also learned to meet the social demands on the governor's wife, which included hosting formal dinners and weekly teas. She traveled to Europe. She even tried to improve the decor of the Executive Mansion, which many believed to be an impossible task. Whether on Oliver Street or in Albany, though, Katie Smith considered her first job to be taking care of her husband and children. With her husband away from home so frequently, it was she who decided where the children would go to school. When the Smiths returned from Albany in 1921, Katie enrolled both girls in a convent school in the

Bronx and sent Arthur and Walter to a boarding school uptown. When she noticed that Al was lonely, she changed course, bringing the younger boys home to live. The family called Katie "the Chairman."

As a result, Smith was deeply wounded when he heard people saying that Katie was not qualified to be the first lady. In its editorial announcing the existence of a whispering campaign, the *Times* noted a recent speech by Senator Frederick H. Gillett of Massachusetts. In a recent address to a women's Republican club, Gillett had praised Mrs. Hoover's qualifications as first lady, adding, "I cannot say very much of Mrs. Smith, but if the contest were between Mrs. Hoover and Mrs. Smith . . ." Gillett did not finish his sentence, leaving his audience with the clear impression that Katie was not qualified. Mrs. Florence T. Griswold, the Republican national committeewoman for Texas, was more direct. Addressing a meeting of the Women's Christian Temperance Union in Houston, she asked, "Can you imagine Mrs. Smith in the White House? Can you imagine an aristocratic foreign Ambassador saying to her, 'What a charming gown,' and the reply, 'You said a "mouthfull!" ' " According to a newspaper report, "shrieks of laughter and applause" greeted this slighting of Katie. Katie was said to be guilty of the sin of so many newly rich women—wearing too much jewelry. Her "weakness" was for bracelets, according to a writer in the *Outlook*. Smith expressed some of the outrage he felt at Katie's treatment when a photographer asked her to remove some of her jewelry. "Leave Katie alone!" he shouted.

Even if Smith had been able to set aside all the personal abuse, he would still have confronted the problem of religion. There were still many in the United States who believed that excluding a Catholic from the White House was fully in line with the nation's highest ideals. It was the religious issue that distinguished the whispering campaign against Smith from others that had been conducted against a presidential candidate. Anonymous attacks on Smith's faith were part of the campaign from the very beginning. Expressions of concern about the danger of electing a Catholic president emanated from the highest levels of many Protestant denominations. Church leaders could not be as frank as they wished. After all, the Declaration of Independence upheld at least the equality of all citizens. It was far easier to oppose Smith for his Prohibition stand. Still, many did put their religious objections on the record. The Rev. George W. McDaniel, the president of the Southern Baptist Convention, had expressed the views of four million Baptists in 1926 when he condemned Smith for kissing a cardinal's ring. The Methodists had also expressed their alarm publicly. "Governor Smith has a constitutional right to run for President, even though a Catholic. This we confess," said the *Wesleyan Christian Advocate* soon after Smith's nomination. "And we have a constitutional right to vote against him because he is a Catholic." Three of the five bishops of the Southern Methodist Episcopal Church announced their opposition to Smith. While they insisted that they were motivated primarily by their support for Prohibition, the *Christian Register* of Boston declared that Prohibition was "not more than one-half the real reason for their determination. The other half is religion."

"Shall we have a man in the White House who acknowledges allegiance to the Autocrat on the Tiber, who hates democracy, public schools, Protestant parsonages, individual right, and everything that is essential to independence?" Dr. Charles L. Fry asked a large gathering of Lutherans in New York. At about the same time, the Associated Press reported that the Rev. Albert C. Dieffenbach, a prominent Unitarian, had said during a conference on religion and politics that no Catholic should be elected president. Dieffenbach denied making the statement but defended the right of voters to weigh a person's religious views in deciding whom to vote for. "To call them intolerant for doing so is itself a species of intolerance," Dieffenbach said.

Since many Protestant leaders were at best equivocal about the prospect of a Catholic president, it is not surprising that their followers provided a ready market for the flood of anti-Catholic propaganda that was soon sweeping the country. By mid-July Democratic leaders were expressing astonishment at the appearance all over the country of newspapers, pamphlets, and handbills attacking Smith's candidacy because of his religion, the *New York Times* reported. Because much of this literature was issued anonymously, "a large corps of headquarters workers and some investigators in the field" were devoting their time to tracking down the authors so that their charges could be refuted. Much of the anti-Catholic propaganda came from well-established newspapers like the *Rail Splitter* and *Fellowship Forum*. William Lloyd Clark, the editor of the *Rail Splitter*, had been fighting the Catholic church since the 1890s, when the nativist American Protective Association was at its peak. The *Fellowship Forum* had prospered as a result of the rapid growth of the Ku Klux Klan in the early 1920s; although its audience had waned with the decline of the Klan, the paper still reported a circulation of 360,000 in October 1928. Obviously, there could have been no greater gift to editors like Clark than the nomination of a Catholic for president. After years of warning against Catholic plots to take over the United States, the danger was now clearly at hand. "It is time for heroic action, for sacrifice and service," roared Clark. "Only a mighty campaign of education will whip the Smith-whiskey-Papal gang and save America." According to Clark, the first step in the campaign was ordering the July issue of the *Rail Splitter*. Other anti-Catholic papers also cranked up production in these boom times. In *The Shadow of the Pope*, a study of anti-Catholicism in the 1920s, Michael Williams estimated that as many as one hundred anti-Catholic newspapers were publishing three to five million copies each week.

The nomination of Smith was also a godsend for hundreds of anti-Catholic lecturers who traveled the country. The National Catholic Bureau of Information, which kept track of the lecturers, evangelists, preachers, and editors whose principal business was to attack the Catholic church, counted more than 550 between 1912 and 1928. These men and women, many of whom falsely claimed to be ex-priests and ex-nuns, were often itinerants who made a living by lecturing about the dangers of Catholicism wherever they could, often delivering their lessons outdoors—in parks or on the steps of rural courthouses. The anti-Catholic lecturers spread written propaganda wherever they went. Their lectures were often advertised on posters or in locally produced handbills. "To Murder Protestants! And Destroy American Government! Is The Oath Binding Roman Catholics," warned the advertising for Mrs. Ed C. Alumbaugh, the "Protestant's Joan of Arc." In addition, the lecturers often sold pamphlets that revived the old charges that priests and nuns had sexual relations, that children entrusted to the care of the Catholic church were sexually abused, and that the children born of illicit sexual unions were murdered at birth.

One anti-Catholic flier contained an anonymous "Obituray" (*sic*) for the Democratic Party, listing the cause of death as "an over-dose of Tammany and Romanism." ("No flowers, as the grave will be decorated with fruit jars and whiskey bottles.") Another handbill, titled "10 Reasons Why Al Smith Should Not Be Elected," consisted of statements attacking the separation of church and state that it claimed had been made by Catholic leaders. (" 'We must take part in the elections, move in a solid mass in every state against the party pledged to sustain the integrity of the public schools,' —Cardinal McCloskey"; " 'I would as soon administer sacrament to a dog as to Catholics who send their children to public schools,' — Father Walker.") There was also a pamphlet with a bogus prediction by Abraham Lincoln warning of religious strife ahead. ("I see a very dark cloud on our horizon, and that cloud is coming from Rome.") Cartoons showed priests demanding control of public institutions, including one who offers Uncle Sam a crucifix and says, "Here, Sam, just slip this over your neck and 'we' can rule the universe." Others recalled the elaborate anti-Catholic cartoons that Thomas Nast drew in the nineteenth century, including a *Fellowship Forum* drawing featuring the head of the pope and octopus arms labeled "Insolence," "Rascality," "Deceit," "Tyranny," "Treachery," "Bigotry," "Intolerance," and "Greed." One arm is wrapped around the neck of the figure of Columbia; another around a public schoolroom where a nun teaches her students with a map that shows Rome and Ireland at the center of the world. The mottos "Erin Go Unum," and "E Pluribus Bragh" are scrolled along the bottom.

The Democrats had taken at face value Herbert Hoover's assertion in his acceptance speech on August 11 that "by blood and conviction I stand for religious tolerance both in act and in spirit." As a Quaker, Hoover was the member of a sect that had been harshly persecuted and remained suspicious in the eyes of many Americans because of its opposition to violence even in defense of one's country (Hoover dissociated himself from this belief). Three weeks later, Hubert Work, the chairman of the Republican National Committee, promised "a clean fight." But as the tide of anti-Catholic propaganda rose, the Democrats found it increasingly difficult to believe that the Republican Party was not directly involved in the effort to stir up religious feeling against Smith. Activity appeared to be originating from the ranks of disgruntled Democrats. But many Democratic workers in the South believed that the Republicans were financing the so-called Hoover Democrats. After the conclusion of the campaign, a Democratic worker in Oklahoma explained how it worked in his state:

> The Republican Headquarters was the parlor affair, the real place
> of activity was across the street in the so-called Hoover-Democrat

Alfred Emanuel Smith, Al Smith's father, stands behind one of his many friends on South Street in the heart of New York City's Fourth Ward. His truck is in the background.

(*Museum of the City of New York*)

Already a well-known amateur actor, Smith (center) poses with friends in front of a painted backdrop of the ocean. During the day he was a laborer. (*Museum of the City of New York*)

Katie Dunn disappointed her upwardly mobile parents when she fell in love with a poor boy, Al Smith. "If Al had gone on being a clerk, it would have been all right with me," Katie said.

(*Museum of the City of New York*)

Smith had escaped the rigors of manual labor and was working as a supervisor in the office of the commissioner of jurors when he and Katie posed around 1902 with their children, Alfred III and Emily.

(*Museum of the City of New York*)

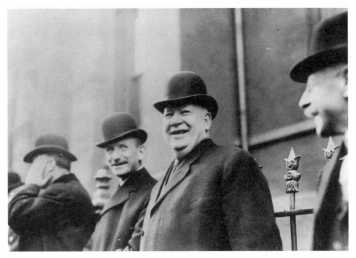

When he took over the leadership of the Second Assembly District in 1901, saloon keeper Thomas F. (Big Tom) Foley (third from left) promised to choose candidates for public office based on their ability, not their wealth. Three years later, he sent Al Smith to the New York Assembly. (*Museum of the City of New York*)

"Silent Charlie" Murphy was able to preserve the power of Tammany Hall during the height of the Progressive attack on machine politics by promoting men like Al Smith and Robert F. Wagner. (*Museum of the City of New York*)

Smith never lost his taste for acting. Here, dressed as Annie Oakley, he poses with "Buffalo Bill" in a skit performed around the time of the 1908 Democratic National Convention. (*Museum of the City of New York*)

Catherine Mulvehill Smith, Al's mother, had opposed giving women the vote, but that didn't stop her from voting for the first time in 1918 when her son was a candidate for governor.

(*Museum of the City of New York*)

The Democratic candidate for governor in 1918 poses with his family. Smith is flanked by his sons Arthur and Walter. Behind them are Alfred, Katie, his mother, his daughter Catherine, his sister Mary Glynn, and his daughter Emily. (Little girl is unidentified.)

(*Museum of the City of New York*)

*"No principle is better established in the laws of nations, as well as in common reason, than that one nation is not to be the interpreter of the constitution of another. Each nation must adjust the form and operations of its own government."*—JAMES MADISON

# Answer These People, Governor Smith

## They Would Like to Know Why You Are Helping the Milk Trust and Traction Trust and Doing Nothing for Them.

GOVERNOR SMITH, your audience in Carnegie Hall amounts to very little.

It will be composed partly of Tammany henchmen who will probably vote for you under the Boss's orders, if by any chance you should ever be nominated for another office.

It will be composed partly of Milk Trust representatives, who want twenty-cent milk, and representatives of the Traction Trust, who want ten-cent carfares, and representatives of other big financial interests, who will use you while you are in office and throw you over when you are out of office regardless of what you may say to-night or any other time, regardful only of their own pocket and their precious privilege of plundering the public.

The audience which really amounts to something, which is of determining importance to you and to Boss Murphy and to Boss Murphy's hand-picked candidates, will not go to Carnegie Hall at all.

But they will go to the polls in a week, and they will go to the polls again in a year.

Speak to that tremendous audience—tremendous in numbers, tremendous in power.

Speak to these plain, straightforward, typical, honorable American citizens.

Speak to the men and women who put you in office to represent them and whom you have failed to represent.

You say you have come to New York to "explain."

Explain to them.

Explain to this woman, typified on this page.

Explain why you cannot do anything for her or her children.

Explain why your "hands are tied."

Explain why you appoint representatives of the Milk Trust to important positions, and then when they are exposed and you are compelled to remove them, you appoint them to still more important positions.

Explain why you receive confidential letters from food profiteers and then pass these letters along with a note recommending that something be done to "temper the wind" to these poor profiteering "shorn lambs."

Explain to this woman why she has to pay extortionate prices for milk—a necessity of life for her children—or if she cannot pay these extortionate prices, why her babes have to go without milk, to the injury of their health and the impairment of their future strength and usefulness.

And then, when you are done explaining to these women citizens, turn and explain to this workingman how it is that, although you were elected on a public ownership platform and issued a public pledge in favor of government ownership and municipal ownership, you have never done anything to help bring about proper municipal ownership and operation of the outrageously incompetent and inadequate privately owned traction lines of New York City.

Explain why you appoint a commissioner and pay him out of the public purse and send him down to New York City to speak and work in the interests of the Traction Trust and against the interests of the people who pay him his salary and pay you your salary.

Explain why you favor ten-cent fares and believe that the people who voted for you and elected you should pay twice as much as they have ever paid in the history of traction in New York City; when other cities, like San Francisco, which have public ownership of their street car lines, carry passengers for the same five-cent fare as formerly; pay the employees of the road higher wages; give clean, comfortable and sufficient accommodation, lay by a surplus, and pay a handsome profit to the city.

And if your commissioner fails to represent you and your sentiments, as he certainly fails to represent the people and their sentiments, why do you not remove him?

For surely the people will remove him, and you along with him, whenever they have an opportunity to express at the polls their resentment of their betrayal.

Speak to this great audience, Governor Smith, and tell them why you have thrown to the winds their good will, their faith in you, your opportunities for honest service and great reward.

Tell them what it is that you consider more important than their favor, more important than the love and gratitude of the people, which most honest men consider the highest of all rewards.

The Hearst newspapers in New York attempted to destroy Smith by blaming him for the high cost of milk in New York City. This full-page article from the *New York American* ran on October 29, 1919, the day Smith attacked Hearst from the stage of Carnegie Hall.
(*New York Public Library*)

A portrait of Katie and Al Smith taken around the time of the 1928 campaign. Because of his demanding jobs, they had to make special arrangements to spend time together. Every night they played a game of cards before retiring. (*Museum of the City of New York*)

In official pictures Smith often appears grim. Normally he smiled easily. (*Museum of the City of New York*)

Poor boys who made good, John J. Raskob and Al Smith each rose close to the pinnacle of his profession. They were closely associated in the years after 1928. (*Hagley Museum*)

During one of his campaign trips in 1928, Smith found an unexpected crowd of 25,000 waiting for him in Witchita, Kansas, and made an unscheduled speech. (*Museum of the City of New York*)

Al and Katie during a Western campaign tour in 1928. He sought the farm vote by promising to use the power of the federal government to help raise agricultural prices. (*Museum of the City of New York*)

Smith had an unusually close relationship with the press. He is shown here at one of the press conferences he held daily during the 1928 presidential campaign. (*Museum of the City of New York*)

The leaders of the Tammany Society observe the laying of the cornerstone for the new Tammany Hall on Union Square in 1929. From left: Willis Holly, New York Mayor James J. Walker, grand sachem John R. Voorhis, and Al Smith. (*Museum of the City of New York*)

At the beginning of their careers, it didn't seem possible that Franklin Roosevelt and Al Smith could ever become friends, but they did. (*Museum of the City of New York*)

Following the dedication ceremonies on May 1, 1931, Smith shows Governor Roosevelt the view from the observation deck of the new Empire State Building. With the economy plunging, the building was soon being called the Empty State Building. (*Museum of the City of New York*)

Smith and Roosevelt give concrete evidence of their reconciliation following the 1932 Democratic National Convention by appearing together on the stage of the Brooklyn Academy of Music. (*Corbis*)

Wearing white tie and tails, Smith broke with the New Deal on January 25, 1936, in a speech delivered at an American Liberty League dinner in Washington, D.C. (*Corbis*)

The Smith clan gathered to celebrate Al's seventieth birthday in December 1943. Army Captain Alfred E. Smith III (known as young Al) stands behind and to the left of his father. Five months later Katie died unexpectedly, throwing Smith into a depression from which he never recovered. He died in October 1944. (*Museum of the City of New York*)

Young Al and old Al pose in Smith's office at the Empire State Building in 1943. Although scandal touched the life of Smith's oldest son on several occasions, the two remained close. (*Museum of the City of New York*)

Headquarters, a combination of Ku Klux and ultra-protestants with four times the clerical force and activity of the Republican Headquarters, and every item of expense paid by the Republican Headquarters, numerous paid speakers, big and little, constantly speaking all over the state with the most horrid stories of what the Pope would do to the people of this country. The Republican State Headquarters financed, managed and directed this activity.

A Senate investigation of contributions during the 1928 campaign subsequently documented links between the Republicans and the anti-Smith Democrats. Among other things, it revealed that Methodist Episcopal bishop James Cannon, Jr., who headed the anti-Smith Democrats, received $65,000 from E. C. Jameson, a man who gave $172,000 to the Republicans in 1928.

For six weeks, Hoover made no public statement condemning the growing anti-Catholic crusade. He explained in a private memorandum to the press in late September that condemnation of bigotry would only cause it to spread. He also insisted that he was being victimized by a whispering campaign that was far worse than the one against Smith. An unspoken reason for Hoover's failure to speak out may have been a conviction that by acknowledging that bigotry was a significant problem he would be handing Smith an issue that he could use to rally support. This was something that worried the Republican *New York Herald Tribune*: "First they will try to arouse public indignation and then to turn the indignation against the Republican ticket in an effort to duplicate the 1884 reaction to the 'Rum, Romanism, and Rebellion' cry that is credited with having defeated James G. Blaine." Whatever the explanation, Hoover dealt with the religious issue only when he had no choice. When a Republican national committeewoman was caught writing an anti-Catholic letter, Hoover condemned it. "Whether this letter is authentic or a forgery it does violence to every instinct I possess. I resent and repudiate it," he said. But the committeewoman was not fired and neither was the Republican chairman in Alabama, who admitted disseminating 200,000 copies of an anti-Catholic pamphlet that he had written. The Alabaman was so unabashed by his reprimand that he continued to insist that the Catholic church was "a very live and vital issue" in the campaign.

As Smith prepared for his first campaign trip in early September, the extent of Republican involvement seemed to become clear. On September 7, an official of the Coolidge administration appeared before 2,500 members of the Ohio conference of the Methodist Episcopal Church and urged them to use their church to help defeat Smith. There was no reference to the Catholic church in the address delivered by Mabel Walker Willebrandt, an assistant attorney general who was involved in the enforcement of the Prohibition laws. Willebrandt attacked Smith for signing the repeal of New York's Prohibition enforcement law and paving the way for flagrant violation of the Volstead Act, particularly in New York City. The Republican officials who arranged for Willebrandt's appearance and reviewed her planned speech saw no problem in a Republican official criticizing Smith's position on Prohibition before a gathering of dry church leaders, but the political climate had changed dramatically as a result of the anti-Catholic campaign. The Ohio conference of the Methodist Episcopal Church had demonstrated the polarizing effect of Smith's candidacy earlier in the day when it considered a resolution declaring its support for Hoover based on his endorsement of Prohibition. Although it may have been the first time that a Methodist body had ever been asked to endorse a political candidate, the delegates did not hesitate when the vote was called, leaping to their feet and cheering to signal their approval. In her speech, Willebrandt spurred the Methodists on:

> There are 2,000 pastors here. You have in your churches more than 600,000 members of the Methodist Church in Ohio alone. That is enough to swing the election. The 600,000 friends have friends in other States. Write to them. Every day and every ounce of your energy are needed to rouse the friends of prohibition to register and vote.

Given that the Methodists had already endorsed Hoover, Willebrandt seemed to bestow Republican approval for sectarianism. At a time of extreme polarization between Catholics and Protestants, it sounded to many like a declaration of a holy war.

Although a report of Willebrandt's speech was carried on the front page of the New York Times, Smith did not respond to it immediately. His aides were already hard at work attempting to answer the arguments advanced in anti-Catholic literature. The day that Willebrandt's speech was reported, New York Secretary of State Robert Moses released a report showing that Smith had not favored Catholics in making appointments. When a reporter asked Smith about Willebrandt's speech, he said he had not read it.

"She said you were Tammany-reared and a nullifier," the reporter said.

"I've heard that before," said the Governor.

"And she urged the ministers to speak against you from their pulpits," another reporter advised him.

"That's the first time I knew they needed an invitation," the Governor came back.

The *New York Times* called Willebrandt's speech "outrageous." In an editorial citing the fistfights that had broken out when anti-Smith Democrats in Texas attempted to walk out of a party convention, the paper warned that "dark, fierce currents are sweeping toward the Presidential election." The *Times* urged the Republicans to take a strong stand against intolerance. But it would be Smith, not Hoover, who would address the religious issue publicly. He was already working on a reply to Mrs. Willebrandt.

He decided to prepare an address on the religious issue before he left New York in mid-September for a two-week tour of the West. Herbert H. Lehman, the finance director of the Democratic National Committee and a member of Smith's inner circle, recalled that all of his advisers agreed on the necessity of the speech. "We all felt that it was very important that he carry the fight in regard to the Ku Klux Klan and the religious issue right into enemy territory," Lehman said. "The only question was where he was going to do it." The time Smith spent rehearsing the address in the days before his departure reflected its importance. Lehman was looking forward to a powerful attack on religious bigotry. Later, Herbert Hoover would argue that the speech on intolerance that Smith delivered in Oklahoma City on September 20 only made things worse, but Smith believed that he had no choice. He knew the speech had no chance of silencing, much less converting, the bigots, but he hoped it would enable him to put questions about the religious issue behind him. The Oklahoma City speech gave Smith his best chance of political and personal vindication.

Al Smith's train arrived in Oklahoma City on the morning of September 20, a day after the candidate had given his first major address of the campaign in Omaha, Nebraska. The train consisted of eleven cars, including three sleeping cars for reporters, newsreel cameramen, and photographers. "It will look like a circus coming into town," the candidate joked. Smith, his wife, and his daughter Emily occupied the *St. Nicholas*, the private car of Smith's good friend William F. Kenny, the millionaire contractor. The Smiths were asleep when their train crossed the Oklahoma border, so they missed the sight of a burning cross that had been erected for their benefit in a field near the tracks. It could not have surprised Smith when newspapermen told him about it the next day. The Ku Klux Klan had been a powerful force in the state, and many of the state's Democrats were hostile to Smith, including former senator Robert L. Owen, who had announced his defection to Herbert Hoover shortly before Smith's arrival. Nevertheless, a crowd of over 70,000 was waiting for the candidate when his train pulled into Oklahoma City. They cheered as Smith and his party got into a twenty-car motorcade for a brief tour of the downtown district. With a fresh cigar in his mouth, Smith waved his brown derby. A horseman in cowboy regalia headed the parade. Once they had arrived at their hotel, the Smiths emerged on a balcony overlooking the street, where they were met with "a storm of applause," according to one reporter.

But some of Smith's party noticed that not everyone was happy to see the New Yorker. Joseph Proskauer recalled that on their arrival, "as we stepped down from the cars we were confronted by groups of thin-lipped, evil-looking, sneering men, and we heard rumors of violence." The tension grew during the day as Smith told local Democrats about the subject of his speech. Some tried to talk him out of it. Even Belle Moskowitz, listening to the speech on the radio in New York, almost immediately began to have second thoughts. Over ten thousand people had gathered in the Oklahoma City Coliseum to hear Smith. How would they react to an attack on religious intolerance? Would they feel insulted? Might they riot? The primitive radio transmission of the event made it impossible to tell anything except that the crowd was roaring, and Moskowitz would remain panic-stricken until she was able to talk to Smith at his hotel later. Years later, Lehman, who had also listened to the speech on the radio, would remember Smith facing a hostile audience in Oklahoma City.

In fact, the opposite was the case. As Smith stepped on the stage, the audience jumped to their feet with "a thunder of applause" that lasted for a full minute. Standing at center stage, Smith saluted the crowd with his outstretched brown derby as the band played "Tammany." "The audience was always with the Governor," the *New York Times* reporter observed. He wasted no time in telling them the subject of his speech.

> In this campaign an effort has been made to distract the attention of the electorate . . . and to fasten it on malicious and un-American propaganda. . . . I know what lies behind all this and I shall tell you. I specifically refer to the question of my religion. I, as the candidate of the Democratic Party, owe it to the people of this country to discuss frankly and openly with them this attempt of Senator Owen and the forces behind him to inject bigotry, hatred, intolerance and un-American sectarian division into a campaign which should be an intelligent debate of the important issues which confront the American people.

Smith charged that the anti-Catholic campaign was in direct conflict with the founding principles of American life. "It is contrary to the spirit, not only of the Declaration of Independence, but of the Constitution itself. During all our national life we have prided ourselves throughout the world on the declaration of the fundamental American truth that all men are created equal." Smith noted that those who were behind the anti-Catholic campaign considered themselves 100 percent American—"yet totally ignorant of the history and tradition of this country and its institutions and, in the name of Americanism, they breathe into the hearts and soul of their members hatred of millions of their fellow countrymen."

> Nothing could be so out of line with the spirit of America. Nothing could be so foreign to the teachings of Jefferson. Nothing could be so contradictory of our whole history. Nothing could be so false to the teaching of our Divine Lord Himself. The world knows no greater mockery than the use of the blazing cross, the cross upon which Christ died, as a symbol to install into the hearts of men a hatred of their brethren, while Christ preached and died for the love and brotherhood of man.

As Smith spoke, he looked directly at the audience, never glancing at the prepared text before him. "Again and again they interrupted him with applause," the *Times* reporter noted. Smith was frequently forced to raise his arm to quiet the crowd.

The candidate charged Republicans with supporting the anti-Catholic campaign. "There is abundant reason for believing that Republicans high in the councils of the party have countenanced a large part of this form of campaign, if they have not actually promoted it," he said. "A sin of omission is sometimes as grievous as a sin of commission." He pointed out that no Republican spokesman had come forward to disown Willebrandt's speech to the Ohio Methodists. "What would the effect be . . . if a prominent official of the government of the state of New York under me suggested to a gathering of the pastors of my church that they do for me what Mrs. Willebrandt suggests be done for Hoover?" Smith asked. It is wrong to use religion to win votes for any candidate, Smith said, adding that perhaps "the meanest thing" he had seen in the propaganda used against him was a phony appeal to Catholics on his behalf. "It is false in its every line," Smith said.

> I here emphatically declare that I do not wish any member of my faith in any part of the United States to vote for me on any religious grounds. I want them to vote for me only when in their hearts and consciences they become convinced that my election will promote the best interests of our country. By the same token, I cannot refrain from saying that any person who votes against me simply because of my religion is not, to my way of thinking, a good citizen.

Smith found it inconceivable that anyone could accuse him of threatening the separation of church and state. His own political rise had been made possible by the religious freedom guaranteed by that separation: "I attack those who seek to undermine it, not only because I am a good Christian, but because I am a good American and a product of America and of American institutions. Everything I am, and everything I hope to be, I owe to those institutions."

As the campaign train sped toward Denver, where the next speech was scheduled, Smith knew that his Oklahoma City address had not put an end to the religious issue. On the contrary, he had attacked the Americanism of those who opposed him on religious grounds, perhaps increasing their bitterness toward him. But if he had not banished the religious issue, he had given a national audience an example of his willingness to speak plainly about issues that other politicians refused to address. As the Oklahoma City audience had demonstrated, many people were thrilled by his attack on bigotry and were rallying to his support. Election officials around the country were reporting dramatic increases in registration for the November vote, including a remarkable surge in the nation's big cities that many assumed would benefit Smith. In Denver, Smith received the biggest welcome of his trip. He led a caravan of automobiles through more than a mile of streets where people overflowed the curbs, leaving only a narrow lane for the cars. "Doesn't this look like the sidewalks of New York?" a Denverite yelled. Smith was encouraged. "I have been agreeably surprised by the receptions I have been getting," he acknowledged. "Naturally, the enthusiasm of the crowds and the size of the gatherings have been very pleasing and very hopeful."

Smith was also reassured by the support he was receiving from many Protestant leaders. They were as shocked as anyone by the recrudescence of bigotry among their coreligionists. One of the most prominent Protestants to speak out was Dr. Nicholas Murray Butler, the president of Columbia University. "The foundations of America are under attack," he said. "A vast army of straight-thinking, fine feeling, broad-minded, liberal men and women should spring to their defense in a way that will make their complete and permanent defense both quick and secure." Similar statements were made by Dr. S. Parkes Cadman, the president of the Federal Council of the Churches of Christ, and by Methodist Episcopal bishops Warren A. Candler and Collins Denny, who were appalled that three of their fellow bishops were campaigning against Smith. Dr. Henry Van Dyke, a Princeton religion professor, tried to lead by example. Van Dyke recalled being assailed by another professor who asked, "Would you vote for a Catholic as President?" "His look of contempt was unmistakable, and I was tempted to answer, 'Even if there were no other reason, beloved brother, it might lead me to vote for a good Catholic just to shake your self-complacent Phariseeism, and maintain America's honest faith in real religious liberty.'" Like Van Dyke, many Protestants were deeply concerned that the bigotry unleashed during the campaign would permanently damage the country by undermining its philosophical commitment to equal rights. They got into countless arguments with colleagues, family, and friends, and when it came time to vote many abandoned their lifelong allegiance to the Republican Party to uphold the freedom of religion.

Smith was also making inroads among African-Americans, who then normally voted Republican. Many had been disillusioned by the party's failure to do more for them. In addition, many African-Americans admired Smith's fight against the Ku Klux Klan during the 1924 Democratic convention and believed that his triumph over bigotry would assist their own fight for equality. The leading African-American newspaper, the *Chicago Defender*, explained:

> Since it is immaterial to the Negro worker which party gets into office, it would be striking a severe blow at intolerance, prejudice, and bigotry if Negroes should help send this Catholic gentleman to the White House. Whatever sins may be charged against the Catholics, it cannot be said that in this country they have aligned themselves with the Negro baiters and lynchers.

Smith told Walter White of the National Association for the Advancement of Colored People that he was ready to issue a statement declaring his unwillingness to be dominated "by an anti-Negro South." The statement would show "that the old Democratic Party, ruled entirely by the South is on its way out, and that we Northern Democrats have a totally different approach to the Negro." White's colleague, the great African-American scholar W. E. B. Du Bois, told him not to get his hopes up. As Du Bois suspected, Smith changed his mind after some of his advisers convinced him that his statement would cost him the South and any hope of winning the presidency. Nevertheless, the African-American elite abandoned the Republican Party in 1928, and most black newspapers either supported Smith or remained neutral.

Meanwhile, Smith was desperately searching for some way to shatter the aura of invincibility that surrounded his opponent. He longed to trade rhetorical blows with Hoover, but the Republicans were determined to avoid this at all costs. As the front-runner, Hoover believed he had nothing to gain from direct exchanges with his opponent. Moreover, he had never campaigned for an elective office before, and public speaking was not one of his strengths. Consequently, while Smith would make seventeen major addresses, Hoover delivered only seven and never mentioned Smith by name. When the Republicans felt they had to reply to something that Smith had said, it was not Hoover but other leading members of the party who responded, leading Jimmy Walker to joke that the Republican candidate had been represented "by counsel" during the campaign. In speech after speech, Smith pounded the Republican Party and Hoover personally in an effort to provoke a response.

Even without the drama of direct exchanges with Hoover, Smith was creating enormous excitement wherever he went. Frances Perkins was amazed by the passion of the 200,000 people who greeted Smith in St. Louis:

> The behavior of the crowds was a surprise. I recognized their liking him, but they cried. Tears rolled down the cheeks of many people. I saw people rush out, so that the Secret Service men who were supposed to be guiding him couldn't cope with the crowds. Men and women would rush up and try to touch the automobile. I remember saying to somebody—Eppes Hawes, I guess—"My God, they're trying to touch the hem of his garment."

A crowd of over five thousand people jammed Union Station in Chicago to welcome him. Smith was beginning to feel that his campaign was at last gaining momentum when Hoover finally attacked. Two weeks before the election, in a speech to 22,000 people at Madison Square Garden, Hoover denounced Smith's proposals on farm relief, water power, and Prohibition as a form of "State socialism." "[W]e are confronted with a huge program of government in business," Hoover charged. "It would impair the very basis of liberty and freedom." Smith could not have been happier. Conservative Republicans had been accusing him of supporting socialist policies for almost twenty years. In the process, they had proved only that they were opposed to constructive change. Smith leaped at the chance to identify Hoover with his party's conservative wing.

There could hardly have been a more dramatic setting for Smith's next attack on Hoover than Boston. Massachusetts had always voted Republican in presidential campaigns, but as the train carrying Smith approached Springfield, where 20,000 people were waiting, it was immediately apparent that change was in the air. Another 15,000 greeted Smith at Worcester. In Boston, police efforts to hold back the thousands who had gathered at South Station collapsed. The Smith party was instantly engulfed by shouting people trying to shake the candidate's hand or at least touch his coat. Katie Smith was separated from her husband by the crowd twice and had to be rescued by Senator David I. Walsh. The Boston crowd, estimated at between 200,000 and 400,000, far outstripped the largest crowds that Smith had seen. Enthusiasts rolled over police lines and swamped the automobiles in the parade, creating such a frenzy that some were injured and had to be carried from the scene. That night Smith stepped out on the stage of the Boston Arena to give his answer to Hoover. Fourteen thousand sprang from their seats and yelled themselves hoarse as Smith raised his arm in greeting. They cheered for eight minutes and stopped only long enough to sing "The Sidewalks of New York." Once the song was over, the crowd began cheering again and refused to stop for another four minutes. The ovation momentarily overwhelmed Smith, and his eyes filled with tears.

As the candidate began to speak, however, he quickly gained control of himself and his audience. He noted that at the beginning of the campaign Hoover had promised, "We shall use words to convey our meaning, not to hide it." But Hoover had refused to state clearly his position on the role of government in the development of water power until his Madison Square Garden speech, Smith charged. Then, "the cat got out of the bag and . . . he told the progressive members of his own party, as well as the Democrats of the country, that their proposals, would 'cause us to turn to State socialism.'" Hoover had also promised a farm relief program, but the Madison Square Garden speech revealed that he had no intention of using government to help the farmer, because that, too, was a form of state socialism. It was an absurd claim that Smith took delight in burlesquing by identifying all the Republican "Socialists" who had voted for the McNary-Haugen bill. Smith explained that there was nothing new about Hoover's tactic. "The cry of Socialism has been patented by the powerful interests that desire to put a damper on progressive legislation," Smith said. What was new was that the Republican candidate had revealed that he belonged to the reactionary wing of his party. He had made the differences between the two candidates crystal clear:

As far as all these problems are concerned, I have certainly used words to convey my meaning and I have not attempted to conceal it, and it made no difference in what part of the country I was talking. To refer to the remedies for all these evils as State Socialism is not constructive statesmanship, it is not leadership; and leadership is what this country is hungry for today. . . . The solution of these problems along sane, sensible, progressive lines can only come from the restoration of the Democratic Party to power under a leadership that I promise will be active, alert, forward-looking and successful.

Having condemned Hoover as both a reactionary and a hypocrite, Smith entered the last two weeks of the campaign in high gear.

The Democrats were openly exultant in the wake of Smith's Boston address. They believed that Hoover's Madison Square Garden speech had been a turning point. "I think you will see a tremendous change in sentiment," John Raskob told a reporter the day after the Boston speech. Smith believed the enthusiasm of the crowds he was encountering was also significant. "It looks like there is something in the air. It cannot be that these people cheer the way they do and then vote the other way." To make the most of this excitement, the Democrats announced that Smith would wrap up his campaign with a whirlwind tour of Eastern cities, making five speeches in eight days.

The Eastern tour was everything its planners had hoped. Philadelphia was controlled by a Republican machine and had long been considered a lost cause by the Democrats. No presidential candidate had visited it since William Jennings Bryan in 1896. But the crowds that greeted Smith along his parade route were so large and enthusiastic that Democrats began to believe reports that the local machine had been broken. Baltimore residents had not witnessed so much cheering, flag waving, and downpours of confetti since Armistice Day. When Smith appeared on stage that evening, the audience of 14,000 delivered an eighteen-minute ovation during which they jumped on and off their chairs and threw hats and paper into the air. On Smith's drive through northern New Jersey to a speech in Newark, large crowds frequently broke through police lines, surging around Smith's caravan and bringing it to a halt. The salute included firecrackers, rockets, and red and green flares that sent up a cloud of smoke along the fifteen-mile parade route.

The final Smith parade was held in Manhattan four days before the election. Although the day was dark and wet with mist and intermittent rain, a crowd estimated at a million and a half cheered Smith with the same ardor they had cheered Lindbergh in 1927. As the candidate made his way up Broadway, people blew on any noisemaker they could lay their hands on and drummed on parked cars. At one place, construction workers high above the street beat their hammers on the girders of the skyscraper they were building. The noise was so terrible that the horses of the mounted police jumped and reared in fear. Many children wore brown derbies they had made with wrapping paper. At one intersection, the children of St. James School, Smith's alma mater, stood holding paper liberty bells and wearing hats that were red, white, and blue. "Wonderful, wonderful!" Smith reported at the end of the parade an hour and a half later. "Little old New York showed her affection for me once more." Smith received another overwhelming demonstration when he appeared at Madison Square Garden the next day. As many as 30,000 people surrounded the Garden, many hoping that they could get a seat in the balcony, which was open to the public. "A subway crush during rush hour was as nothing compared to it," a reporter wrote. Even after the balconies had been filled and ticket holders had been seated, thousands stood in the rain hoping to catch a glimpse of the candidate. He finally arrived in a big red Fire Department car behind an escort of a dozen motorcycle policemen. The crowd clanged cowbells, blew horns, and shouted deliriously.

When the candidate entered the Garden shortly before 10 p.m., the 25,000 people inside had already been cheering for almost two hours as speaker after speaker addressed them. Nevertheless, as word spread that Smith had entered the building, the cheering began again, growing so loud that the speaker at the podium gave up the effort to make himself heard. Smith soon appeared at the front of the stage and stood regarding the pandemonium of confetti and waving flags with the ease of a man standing in his own living room. John W. Davis, the 1924 Democratic candidate, stepped forward and put his hand on Smith's shoulder. Franklin Roosevelt, the candidate for governor, also came forward to welcome Smith along with other members of the state ticket. Then Smith spotted Senator Pat Harrison of Mississippi in the audience and pulled him onto the stage. First Mayor Walker, then Smith himself, tried to quiet the crowd. The speech was being broadcast, and the hour of radio time set aside for it was rapidly waning. When Smith was finally able to start his speech, he had lost fifteen minutes of "air time." After sixteen speeches, however, Smith had honed his message to where he could deliver it easily in the remaining time: the Republicans had refused to allow their candidate to enter into a real debate on the issues; the claim that the Republican Party was responsible for the country's prosperity was a "smokescreen" that obscured the fact that many groups were not better off; Hoover was a conservative; only government intervention could solve the agricultural problem and preserve the public's right to benefit from the development of water power; the states must be allowed to determine their own liquor policies; the Republican Party had exploited religious bigotry for political gain. The biggest sin of the Republican Party was complacency, Smith charged. Knowing that it was the majority party, it had mounted a cautious campaign that offered no concrete solutions to the country's problems for fear of alienating anyone. This would be its undoing. Another twenty-minute ovation followed the conclusion of Smith's speech, and there was more cheering as Smith emerged from the Garden and got in his car. As the car pulled away, the crowd broke through police lines and ran after him, cheering and waving.

Smith's prediction of victory was expected, but many political commentators, while skeptical about Smith's chances for victory, nevertheless agreed with him that the race appeared to be a lot closer at the end than at the beginning. "It has been many years since party leaders have admitted at this stage of a national campaign that such a long list of States could be considered doubtful," a reporter for the *New York Times* said in late October. One of the reasons was that Smith had succeeded in putting the whispering campaign behind him and putting the Republicans on the defensive. "He is an extraordinary man. He has made an extraordinary campaign," Frank R. Kent, a political reporter for the *Baltimore Sun*, commented two days before the election. Kent believed that it would take a political miracle to elect Smith. By Kent's count, he could be elected only if he received the electoral votes of every doubtful state, while Hoover could lose all but one and still be elected. But Kent was not willing to discount the possibility of a miracle. It was not implausible that normally Republican farmers would vote for the man whose plan offered a concrete promise of relief. It was also undeniable that many Republicans were supporting Smith because of his promise to fight for changes in the Prohibition laws. In addition, the "solid South" had voted Democratic since 1880. It was inconceivable to many that there were enough bigots and dry extremists to change that.

As Al Smith stepped out of the Biltmore Hotel on his way to vote shortly after noon on Election Day, he felt confident of victory. Cheering and blaring car horns accompanied Smith and his wife as they walked to a polling place located in a nearby stationery store. Once again, a crowd broke through police lines and engulfed the candidate, who shook hands until the police were able to extricate him. Mrs. Smith received a bouquet of flowers from a small welcoming party of Democratic officials. "The hands are kind of swollen after all the handshaking," Smith said, removing his gloves and coat. "This is a lot of work for one vote," he joked. "Alfred E. Smith," the clerk at a table announced. "Over twenty-one!" the candidate responded. Later in the day, as Frances Perkins later recalled, "I remember his saying . . . 'I know politics and I know political crowds. I know political loyalties. I have never seen anything like this. This must mean something. I've run for election before and this is not just [an] ordinary election . . . This can't mean anything else.' " Belle Moskowitz was also convinced that Smith was about to be elected. When Perkins expressed her belief that Smith would be beaten, Moskowitz rejected her pessimism. "She said, 'You're absolutely wrong, Frances. You're absolutely wrong! It's all right. We have intimate reports that we're all right. The Governor feels absolutely sure.' " A long night of vote counting was expected, but no one publicly expressed any doubt that Smith was going to be elected president.

The moment of truth arrived with brutal swiftness. Smith received some scattered returns back at his apartment in the Biltmore, including a report of an increased Democratic vote in the small town of New Ashford, Massachusetts, and a telegram from a North Carolina newspaper indicating that Smith had carried the home ward of a Democratic senator who had not supported him. At 9 p.m. he traveled to the Seventy-first Regiment Armory, where three hundred Tammany leaders had gathered to follow the returns being broadcast on the radio, and settled into a seat in the second row of the chairs that had been set up there. By then Smith's daughter Emily, who was listening to the returns at Democratic headquarters in the General Motors Building, had begun to hear disturbing reports from the South. She called Herbert B. Swope, the executive editor of the *World* and a strong Smith supporter, to get an explanation:

> "Herbert," I replied when he had answered, "this is Emily. Tell me, is it possible that these reports we are getting from down South are right? That Virginia and North Carolina and Florida are going Republican? It isn't possible. It simply cannot be." He paused before he replied. "I'm sorry, Emily," he said in effect, though the language he used was more sulphurous than anything I can print, "but there's no mistake. That's what is happening. But there is something else that bothers me even more. "What?" I demanded. "New York State," he replied, adding a few very sturdy epithets. "Your father is going to lose that, too."

Less than a half hour after Smith's arrival at the Armory, a radio broadcaster reported that New York appeared to have given its vote to Hoover. "The Governor's ruddy face never moved a muscle," the *New York World* reported. "Only he looked tired and spent, with haggard lines in his forehead and cheeks. He had stopped chewing his cigar." Soon after, he rose to leave. As he moved toward the door, the Tammany men shook his hand and congratulated him on his campaign. "You put up a good fight," they told him.

Smith was driven back to his apartment at the Biltmore, where Katie and the rest of his family and some friends were waiting. Election Day had coincided with Katie's birthday, and Smith had ordered a cake to celebrate. He asked his family to join him in the bedroom, where he planned to give them the bad news that they had already heard. Emily was so stunned that she could not remember later what her father said or how she and her siblings had responded. But she did remember her mother's words. "It's God's will," Katie said with tears in her eyes. "It's all for the best." Katie reminded everyone of the threats on Smith's life that had been made during the campaign. At least they would not have to worry about his safety anymore. "But aside from all that, we'll see more of you now," she said. Smith then led his family back into the living room, where they joined their friends and shared Katie's cake. Soon after, a little past midnight, he sent Hoover a telegram congratulating him on his victory.

"Nothing embarrasses me," Smith had once told Perkins. But it seemed to many that he had been embarrassed. He had lost in a landslide: Hoover polled a record 21 million votes, defeating him by more than six million; Hoover's margin was even larger in the electoral vote, 444 to 88. The loss to Hoover of four states in the formerly "solid South" seemed to surprise Smith. The defection of New York was a stunning blow. "Losing his own state was more than he could stand," Lippmann observed. Tammany had not only failed to deliver a record majority in New York City, it had not even been able to produce the majorities it had in the past. There were rumors that some Tammany district leaders had sabotaged Smith to settle old scores or teach him a lesson. Someone was quoted as saying, "Well, we're rid of that high hat." Smith himself appears to have discounted the charge. Long after the election, he sought to understand why groups that had supported him for governor deserted him when he ran for president. The shock of discovering that some of his own supporters didn't believe he was qualified to be president showed on his face election night. Perkins remembered, "I'll never forget how very strange he looked—so unlike himself. He had that kind of glassy eye that I never saw on him before . . . Usually no matter what it was he had to go through with he looked human and at ease. He was always at ease." Smith shared his bewilderment with Perkins: "Al looked hurt that night and he said to me, 'I never could believe it. I never could believe it. You saw them crowds in St. Louis, didn't you?' He remembered that I was there. I said, 'Yes.' He said, 'It was just the same everywhere. . . . After the way they felt how could you believe they wouldn't vote that way?' "

The next day, after thirty-four years in politics and twenty-two years in public office, Smith announced his retirement from politics. "I will never lose my interest in public affairs, that is a sure thing. But as far as running for office again is concerned—that's finished," he said. Asked what he planned for the future, he responded, "I don't know. I'm not going to talk about that now. I must think about that."

In the weeks following the election, many journalists attempted to explain Herbert Hoover's landslide victory, but there was little agreement over its causes. "No single State, no single cause, is chargeable with the defeat of Governor Smith," a New York Times editorial concluded the day after the election. Although more bitter than the Times, the World agreed that the answer was unknowable:

No one can say today, probably no one will ever be able to say, how many votes were cast for Mr. Hoover to preserve "prosperity," how many were cast to preserve Prohibition, how many were cast to preserve the unwritten law that the President must be a Protestant, how many were cast against the unconventionality of Governor Smith's demeanor, how many were cast against Oliver Street and Tammany Hall.

Historians have argued ever since about the relative importance of the many factors that influenced voter behavior in 1928. Most have concluded that no Democrat could have won at a time when the Republican Party was riding a tide of prosperity. The Republicans had simply maintained their dominance: Smith lost by six million votes; Davis and Cox had each lost by seven million. But something new had happened in 1928: the turnout had grown by 7.5 million, a 26 percent increase over 1924. What issue explains this tremendous increase in voter interest?

Those historians who have attempted to dissect the thinking of the 1928 electorate have had a hard time agreeing on what issue was most important. The first study, published by William F. Ogburn and Nell Snow Talbot a year after the election, asserted that attitudes toward Prohibition were almost three times more important than the religious background of the voter in determining the choice of candidate; religion was the next-strongest influence. A generation later, Ruth Silva concluded that the only significant factor was the voter's nativity—whether he was an immigrant or born in America was significant, while religion, Prohibition, and urban or rural residence were insignificant factors. In 1979 Allan J. Lichtman published the most comprehensive survey of the 1928 electorate yet; it was based on data for all 2,058 counties outside the Confederate South (as opposed to Ogburn and Talbot's 173-county sample and Silva's thirty-eight-state survey). Lichtman concluded that the religious issue was by far the most important influence on voting.

Many of Smith's partisans did not understand how there could be any debate about the primacy of the religious issue. While the *New York Times* saw the election shattering "the miserable tradition that a Catholic must not be named for President," others were more pessimistic in their interpretation of its significance. "My, oh my, how they fear the way we talk to the God of all of us," wrote one Catholic. "Well, I'd like to know a

good place to move to. How would Paris do? Or perhaps some spot in Ireland." Catholics were not alone in believing that Smith had been beaten
because of his religion. "The greatest element involved in the landslide
was religion," Senator George W. Norris thought. Herbert Lehman held
the same belief years after the event.

Smith's opinion of the major reason for his defeat was not made
known to the public at that time. Instead, Charles Michelson of the
*World* reported: "Governor Al Smith's philosophy of his defeat is that
again it has been demonstrated that the American people do not vote for
a candidate but against one. He attributes his defeat first to prosperity,
second to Prohibition and only third to bigotry." In private, Smith re-
versed the order in which Michelson listed the causes. Shortly after the
election he spoke with Perkins: "He said finally, 'Well, I'll tell you, I don't
think we can allege the reason anywhere, or put the reason at any of these
things. To tell you the truth, Commissioner, the time hasn't come when
a man can say his beads in the White House.' " While bitter about the
prejudice that he felt had denied him the presidency, Smith did not express his views out of fear of exacerbating religious tensions. This was not
his fear alone. "The religious issue has done damage," Senator Norris
said several days after the election. "It has sown the seeds of hatred, prejudice and jealousy and they will grow and bear fruit long after the present
generation has passed away."

# 9 ❋ THE GATEWAY
# OF OPPORTUNITY

The light was already beginning to fade as Al and Katie Smith left the Biltmore Hotel to walk the short distance to Grand Central Terminal, where a train waited to carry them back to Albany. Although they were accompanied by two patrolmen, no one recognized the couple as they walked through the hotel lobby. It was only when they reached their private car that some station employees began to applaud. "It's all right, Al," one shouted. "We're all with you yet." "All right, thank you," Smith said. Two days after the election, he could still feel the shock of his defeat. But not all the election news had been bad. Although Smith had been defeated decisively, his 15 million votes had more than doubled the 1924 Democratic total. When the election returns were still coming in, it had appeared that he might receive more votes than Harding and Coolidge had. "There is one thing that the figures indicate and that is that no man in the country except one got more votes for the Presidency than I did," Smith told reporters on the day after the election. "Who was that man?" a reporter asked. Smith laughed. "Herbert Hoover," he replied. The final count would reveal that Smith had not beaten Harding or Coolidge, but it would show something almost as remarkable. For the first time, a Democrat had received a majority of the votes cast in the nation's fourteen biggest cities. Smith had carried not only New York but Boston (by over 100,000 votes), Cleveland, St. Louis, San Francisco, and Newark.

The excitement that Smith had inspired showed no sign of waning as his train pulled into the Albany station. Ten thousand people were waiting. "He paused and seemed almost to quiver," a reporter said. "His hand automatically stole to his hat." "We are with you, Al," people shouted as they surged around him. A week later, Smith announced that he had no intention of abandoning his followers. He had decided to deliver a radio speech out of a concern that the bitterness aroused by the religious issue would continue to haunt the country. He reaffirmed his belief that the Republican Party had not done enough to discourage religious attacks. "[N]o political party can afford to accept the support of forces for which it refuses to accept responsibility," he said. But he urged his Catholic supporters to put the campaign behind them. "It will not do to let bitterness, rancor and indignation over the result blind us to the one outstanding fact, that above everything else we are Americans." The important thing was to look to the future. The Democratic Party must build on the new sources of strength it had discovered in the campaign by continuing to fight for its principles, Smith said. He promised to help.

> Thousands of letters and telegrams have come to me since Election Day, asking that I not lose interest in the future welfare of the Democratic Party. Let me take this modern means of making reply to them by making the definite statement that I do not regard the defeat of the Democratic Party at this election as impairing in the slightest degree the soundness of the principles for which it stands. I am just as anxious to see them succeed as I was when the party honored me with the nomination, and with all the vigor that I can command I will not only stand for them, but I will battle for them.

In defeat, Al Smith still sounded like the Happy Warrior.

But defeat would inevitably bring changes in Smith's life. It was widely assumed that he would return to the business world, where he had enjoyed success after his defeat in 1920. Although the Republicans had often accused him of being antibusiness, he had never disliked businessmen as a class. There were reactionary businessmen, but there were also businessmen who were outstanding progressives. Some knowingly exploited their workers. Yet during the Factory Investigating Commission's research, Smith discovered that many manufacturers were simply ignorant of the working conditions in their own establishments and were quick to respond once they knew about them. He believed that a majority ultimately supported the reforms proposed by the commission. Most of the opposition to these reforms had come not from businessmen but from the representatives of rural areas whose constituents did not want to pay for government programs that helped urban workers. Businessmen were actually vital allies in the struggle to modernize state government.

Smith also believed that business provided the opportunity that allowed the newcomer to rise. One of his oldest acquaintances was William F. Kenny, a contractor whose work for the Consolidated Edison Company founded a fortune that finally amounted to $100 million. Like Kenny, many of Smith's business friends were second- or third-generation Irish-Americans. The president of the U.S. Trucking Company was James J. Riordan, a poor boy who was on his way to becoming a millionaire. William H. Todd and Michael Meehan made their fortunes in shipbuilding and stock speculation, respectively. John Raskob had started his career as a stenographer. In 1915 Smith, who was then sheriff of New York County, addressed a banquet for newsboys. Smith told the boys that he had been a newsboy himself and urged them not to be discouraged: "The flag stands for equal opportunity. It left open the gateway of opportunity irrespective of race, creed or color, so that the most humble in the land may rise to greater things. . . . Help one another and keep doing your work, and when you go ahead others will follow you." "The gateway of opportunity" was a metaphor that Smith would use throughout his career to explain the importance of America to the immigrant. With his executive experience and unrivaled political connections, he had every reason to believe he would succeed in the same way as so many of his friends.

There was a great deal of public speculation about which business Smith would choose. He turned down an offer to return to the U.S. Trucking Company. He also rejected a job selling real estate at a salary of $50,000. The press speculated that much more prestigious jobs were in the works for Smith. There was a persistent rumor that Smith was to become the chairman of a new Wall Street bank. "I read about that bank job with a great deal of interest," he commented. It was predicted that he would become the head of a movie studio after a number of studios had been reorganized in a merger. As in several other stories, Raskob was said to be a figure in the deal. "It's all news to me," Raskob said. "Every day they have the Governor and myself entering some new industry. The movies were certain to be reached sooner or later." There was even a report that Smith would take a front office job with the New York Giants baseball team, which was owned by the Mara family, strong Smith supporters. After two months of being asked about every rumor, Smith finally put his foot down: "And let me tell you this, too, when you get these reports that I am going to take all kinds of jobs; that I'm going to be a baseball player on the Giants; why I wish you wouldn't come running up here to ask me about them because you'll know there's nothing to these dope stories. When I get ready, I'll let you know what job I'm going to take." It would be another eight months before Smith's new job would be announced. In the meantime, he took a vacation in Florida and began work on a memoir, *Up to Now*.

On his return from Florida, Smith entered business in a small way. James Riordan had long anticipated the day when Smith would become associated with the County Trust Company, which he had founded in 1926, and Smith was elected a director in January 1929. He also became the director of the Consolidated Indemnity and Insurance Company, which had been organized by a former schoolmate, John F. Gilchrist. The directors of both the County Trust and Consolidated Indemnity were largely Irish-Americans known to Smith. "This meeting seems to me like a reunion of the East Side boys," Smith said during the first meeting of the Consolidated Indemnity directors. Smith accepted a more prominent directorship when he became a member of the board of the Metropolitan Life Insurance Company. Social welfare groups also clamored for his aid, and he was soon named a director of the Beekman Hospital and the Henry Street Settlement; he was also elected the honorary president of the Child Welfare Committee.

In distinct contrast to his attitude when he left office in 1921, Smith was not overly concerned about finding a new job. Then, he had leaped into harness, starting work at the U.S. Trucking Company almost on the day he returned to New York. By 1929, however, Smith's financial position had improved dramatically because of the generosity of wealthy friends and a roaring stock market that was swelling portfolios. His biggest benefactor had been Thomas Chadbourne, the lawyer who had been giving him money since 1923. In addition, John Raskob had bought stock on Smith's behalf in a special account opened with his broker. This was not unusual for Raskob. He had a number of special accounts that he had opened on behalf of influential politicians like Mayor Jimmy Walker, a Democrat, and U.S. Assistant Attorney General William J. Donovan, a Republican. Raskob's practice was to invest on behalf of his friends. Then, when these investments paid off, as they almost always did at the time, he would sell the stock and send a check representing the profit. Presumably, had the stocks lost value, Raskob would have taken the loss. They were nothing less than gifts to his politician friends. If Smith was not Raskob's only friend, he does appear to have been his favorite. On January 18, he told Smith that he had sold the stock in his special account and was transferring the balance, $139,000, to Smith's personal account.

Had Raskob's "gifts" been made public, they would clearly have raised ethical issues and could have prompted an investigation of whether he was violating the laws against bribing public officials. Indeed, Raskob may have been trying to avoid such a problem by turning Smith's account over to him only after he had left office. It appears that Smith did not consider this arrangement to be improper. He hadn't seen anything wrong with accepting money from Chadbourne while he was still governor. In both cases, Smith appears to have believed that accepting money was okay because nothing was being asked in return. (Chadbourne's memoir indicates that he defined the notion of obligation differently from Smith.) He apparently had the same kind of relationship with financier Bernard M. Baruch, who purchased 2,500 shares of Pennsylvania Rail Road stock on Smith's behalf.

Like many of their fellow countrymen, the Smiths had never been more flush than they were in 1929. They not only had money in the bank and the market, they received a $10,000 advance from the Viking Publishing Company for the rights to Smith's autobiography and another $55,000 from the *Saturday Evening Post* for the right to print excerpts. As a result, the Smiths could now afford to live anywhere in Manhattan they chose. Moving back to Oliver Street seemed out of the question. Although still legally residents there, they had been living at the Executive Mansion for the last six years and staying at an apartment in the Biltmore Hotel whenever they came to New York. "[A]fter living in a mansion for six years, I couldn't see First Avenue so well, so I went over to Fifth Avenue," Smith explained later. They moved into the penthouse of a new apartment building at 51 Fifth Avenue and began looking for a summer home in the Kensington and Great Neck areas of Long Island, where rents were between $2,500 and $3,000 per month. Not long afterward, they moved uptown to 820 Fifth Avenue, taking a whole floor of a building at the corner of Sixty-third Street that had a commanding view of Central Park. Their new rent was $10,000 per year, which was Smith's entire salary the previous year. But they wanted a place that was big enough for the whole family to visit and thought they could afford it.

After four terms, it wasn't easy to stop thinking like the governor, and Smith remained deeply interested in state politics. The separation was made even more difficult because one of the reforms that he considered most critical to his reorganization of state government, the executive budget, would not be implemented until after he left office. It was still possible that the Republicans would attempt to sabotage it, and Smith was watching for trouble. Things would have been worse if he had been succeeded by a Republican, but one of the few bright spots in the election had been the narrow victory won by the Democratic candidate for governor, Franklin Roosevelt. Smith would have felt an obligation to help any Democrat, and he had special reasons for believing that Roosevelt would need more help than most.

Although Smith had personally asked Roosevelt to run for governor and professed delight when he reluctantly agreed, the truth was that Roosevelt was not his first or even his second choice. Smith preferred Owen Young, the head of the General Electric Company, who fulfilled the important requirements of being progressive enough to continue the policies that Smith had inaugurated while also possessing the kind of prestige among businessmen that would win Republican votes. When Young declined to run, Smith turned to Herbert Lehman, a banker who had worked hard on Smith's campaigns. Lehman, however, was unknown outside New York City. In addition, he would be the first Jewish candidate for governor of New York, and party leaders believed that the prominence of the religious issue in the national campaign made it inadvisable to roil the waters further with another minority candidate. In August 1928, James A. Farley, who was Smith's commissioner of sports, traveled to Albany with George W. Olvany, the Tammany leader, and other New York City politicians to discuss possible nominees with Smith. Farley recalled that as names were being discussed, "I presented Roosevelt's. Smith threw it out on the theory that it was a mistake to attempt to nominate a man in his physical condition. He stressed the great amount of work attached to the Governorship and said Roosevelt could not be expected to do it." Roosevelt was still undergoing treatment in an effort to restore his paralyzed legs, and his health was a legitimate concern.

But Smith was not just worried by Roosevelt's health. He was more frank with Perkins and his adviser Bernard Shientag than he had been with Farley. "Impossible—the man hasn't got any brains. He couldn't possibly be Governor of New York," Smith said. If he had been challenged, Smith would have insisted that this was not a snap judgment. After all, he had met Roosevelt seventeen years earlier, when Franklin was a twenty-nine-year-old freshman state senator from rural Dutchess County. For the next six years Roosevelt waged a quixotic battle against Tammany Hall, although the Democratic organization in New York City represented an overwhelming majority of the state's Democrats. Roosevelt's fight continued long after Tammany men like Smith and Robert Wagner had become leaders in the fight for factory safety, workmen's compensation, a minimum wage, and the fifty-four-hour workweek. As Roosevelt himself acknowledged many years later, "I was an awfully mean cuss."

As a young assemblyman, Al Smith had prided himself on his ability to make friends with anyone. But Roosevelt was not just another rural legislator. Even someone like Frances Perkins, who was born in the same class as Roosevelt, found him aloof and insufferable:

> I have a vivid picture of him operating on the floor of the Senate: tall and slender, very active and alert, moving around the floor, going in and out of committee rooms, rarely talking with the members, who more or less avoided him. . . . I can see "that Roosevelt" now, standing back of the brass rail with two or three Democratic senators arguing with him to be "reasonable," as they called it, about something; his small mouth pursed up and slightly open, his nostrils distended, his head in the air, and his cool, remote voice saying, "No, no, I won't hear of it."

Roosevelt was so intent on demonstrating his superiority to his colleagues that at one point he rejected a small appropriation earmarked for his own district because he had not been apprised of the necessity for it. Timothy Sullivan, a Tammany leader, was disgusted. "Frank, you ought to have your head examined," he said. Sullivan later gave Frances Perkins his opinion of the young senator: "Awful arrogant fellow, that Roosevelt."

But in the eyes of Tammany men, the greatest sin was not arrogance but political ineptitude, and on at least two occasions during his early career Roosevelt committed errors that made the political pros laugh. In 1911 he lost his fight to prevent Murphy's choice from going to the U.S. Senate. But Roosevelt had been unrepentant. "C. F. Murphy and his kind must like the noxious weed, be plucked out root and branch," he told a Buffalo audience soon after the collapse of the Sheehan revolt. Three years later, Roosevelt opposed the Tammany candidate for U.S. senator in the Democratic primary. His only real hope lay in the chance that Murphy would choose a weak candidate. Instead, the Tammany boss selected James W. Gerard, the ambassador to Germany, who insisted that he could not leave his job to campaign at this moment: war had broken out in Europe. Roosevelt suffered the worst political defeat in his life. He was outpolled three to one and carried only a third of the state's sixty-six counties. His only consolation was that he won a bare majority of upstate counties, although some of these had as few as three hundred Democrats. "[T]here was a tendency to laugh at Roosevelt a little for that performance about the Senatorship," Joseph Proskauer recalled.

Roosevelt finally bowed to the inevitable and made peace with Tammany in 1917, but both sides continued to harbor doubts. In a conversation with Woodrow Wilson the next year, Roosevelt agreed with the president that Smith was well qualified to run for governor but told him that his religion would hurt him upstate. Later, Roosevelt supported Smith's opponent in the Democratic primary. Murphy also appeared to bear a grudge. When Roosevelt's name came up as a possible vice presidential candidate in 1920, the boss initially objected. Nevertheless, the 1920 Democratic convention was an important turning point in the relationship between Al Smith and Franklin Roosevelt. Smith asked Roosevelt to make a speech seconding his nomination. Roosevelt happily agreed to make his first appearance at a national convention. When he reached the podium, he was effusive in his praise of Smith: "I love him as a friend, look up to him as a man, and am with him as a Democrat. If you could come back to the Empire State and learn to know and love him, you would nominate him. The Democracy of New York is united behind our Governor." Roosevelt enjoyed the increased recognition that came to him as a speaker at the convention, but he also appreciated the opportunity to improve his relationship with Tammany.

Smith also saw the advantage in an alliance with Roosevelt. Roosevelt's support helped draw a line between the old Tammany of Tweed and Croker and the "new" Tammany that now provided solid support for reform. This was so important to Smith's political ambitions that he may have taken the initiative in improving relations between Murphy and Roosevelt. There is evidence that he urged Murphy not to oppose the selection of Roosevelt as the candidate for vice president. Smith also seconded Roosevelt's nomination. The governor did not exaggerate the warmth of their relationship. He confined himself to making jokes at the expense of the Republican Party. (Picking up the Republican platform was like "picking up a fish in cold weather," he said.) But his endorsement of Roosevelt was an important step toward the unification of New York Democrats.

Yet even after Smith and Roosevelt had become allies, it didn't seem possible that they would ever become friends. Roosevelt was resentful of Smith's success. He believed that had it not been for America's entry into the war he would have been the Democratic nominee for governor in 1918. He would later tell people that, following his 1917 reconciliation with Tammany, Boss Murphy had sent an emissary to him promising his support for the nomination. He also believed he had Wilson's support. But Roosevelt was assistant secretary of the Navy when the United States entered World War I and could not have resigned his post to run for political office without being charged with traitorous ambition by the Republicans. Thus, Roosevelt had been forced to stand by while Smith was elected. As Smith rapidly grew to be one of the most popular and accomplished governors in New York history, Roosevelt must have felt himself sinking deeper and deeper into his rival's shadow.

The 1928 campaign provided new fuel for Roosevelt's resentment. After nominating Smith for the second time and again acting as his floor manager, Roosevelt was hoping to play a leading role in the campaign. Instead, he was put in charge of raising funds from businessmen. Later, he would reveal anger over his treatment by Smith and his advisers: "I was treated by Raskob and Mrs. Moskowitz all the time I was there in July, August and the first part of September as though I was one of those pieces of window dressing that had to be borne with because of a certain political value in non-New York City areas." Roosevelt quit going to the campaign office in July, turning over his responsibilities to Louis Howe and two secretaries who knew how to forge his signature on fund-raising appeals.

Smith's feelings toward Roosevelt were not much warmer. Like the rest of his party, he had been moved by the spectacle of Roosevelt's Happy Warrior speech in 1924, but he could not escape his initial perception of Roosevelt as a rich man who was merely playing at politics. The squire of Hyde Park had only held elective office twice for a total of three years, and during that time he had helped divide the party, spoiling its first opportunity in a generation to act as the majority. His appointment as assistant secretary of the Navy and nomination for vice president both seemed largely honorific, nods toward his unrivaled social connections and the power of his name. Smith had only recently had reason to reprove Roosevelt, whom he had appointed chairman of the Taconic Parks Commission. Roosevelt had complained bitterly when his commission did not receive the funds he had requested. Smith sent Roosevelt a long letter in reply that was probably drafted by Robert Moses, the governor's point man on parks. The reply ended with some unsolicited advice that probably made Roosevelt's resentments burn more hotly:

> [D]on't be so sure about things that you have not the personal handling of yourself. I have lived, ate and slept with this park question for three and one-half years. I know all about it. . . . When I told you at the Hotel Biltmore that the legislative leaders would not stand for these appropriations, I was telling you what I knew to be a fact and you were only guessing at it.

The conflict only strengthened Smith's belief that Roosevelt lacked any real understanding of politics.

Despite their differences, the two men were in perfect agreement about the necessity of nominating someone else for governor in 1928. Although his wife and doctors had abandoned hope that he would ever walk again, Roosevelt clung to a belief that continuing rehabilitation at the resort he had built in Warm Springs, Georgia, would one day put him on his feet again. Running for governor would interfere with his quest for full restoration of his health. Roosevelt and Louis Howe, his political torchbearer, also had a political motive for wanting someone else to run. The next Democratic candidate for governor would face a difficult race. Any Democrat except Smith would have a hard time, and losing a race for governor was not how they envisioned the beginning of Roosevelt's comeback.

By mid-September 1928, Smith had become convinced that there was no good alternative to Roosevelt. Shortly before leaving for his Western campaign tour, he instructed Edward J. Flynn, the Democratic leader from the Bronx, to try to persuade Roosevelt to run. Roosevelt rejected Flynn's overtures, citing not only his health but his responsibility for raising funds for the Warm Springs Foundation, which had been set up to develop the property in Warm Springs, Georgia, where Roosevelt and other polio victims were receiving physical therapy. Roosevelt told Smith the same thing when the governor called him from Milwaukee. Smith did not press Roosevelt hard on this occasion. "Okay, you're the doctor," he said. But he changed his mind several days later at the New York Democratic convention. Following a conference of Democratic leaders, Smith called Roosevelt again. He put Lehman on the telephone to tell Roosevelt that he was willing to run for lieutenant governor and to relieve him from administrative duties during the first months of the legislative session so that he could go to Warm Springs for treatment. Then Raskob got on the phone to assure Roosevelt that he would loan the Warm Springs Foundation whatever it needed. Finally, Smith got back on the line and told Roosevelt that he was asking him to run as a personal favor. Roosevelt agreed.

Roosevelt campaigned on a platform of 100 percent loyalty to Al Smith and his program. "The policies of the state as administered by Governor Smith are excellent now," Roosevelt declared. "I may not be able to improve on them." For many, Roosevelt's apparent lack of new ideas was not important. He was hailed as a leader in the fight for religious tolerance. The *New York World* wrote, "He has been in the front line of the battle for toleration, striking the hardest blows and leaving the cleanest and least painful wounds. Franklin D. Roosevelt more than any man in this nation today has shown in what spirit the defense of the American spirit should be conducted." Roosevelt had demonstrated that a wealthy Protestant could be a loyal supporter of the leader of immigrant America.

Almost as soon as the election was over, however, it appeared that the wartime friendship of Smith and Roosevelt would break down under the strains of peace. The two men had very different perceptions of their future relationship. Smith had assured New Yorkers that Roosevelt was healthy enough to assume the rigors of being governor. "[A] Governor does not have to be an acrobat. We do not elect him for his ability to do a double back flip or a handspring," he said. Of course, the deal that had been engineered to persuade Roosevelt to run was based on the assumption that he could not be a full-time governor. Smith also had no idea that Roosevelt was planning to run for president. This had always been his goal, and now that he had attained the governorship the White House seemed within his grasp. Had Smith known of Roosevelt's ambition, he would probably have laughed at his temerity, but at least he would have understood why Roosevelt began his governorship by rejecting his help.

Nettled by persistent reports that Smith would be the power behind the throne in his administration, Roosevelt's first priority was to establish his own record of accomplishments as governor. The *New York Times* quoted "unnamed sources" to the effect that "Mr. Roosevelt intended to be his own Governor and to assume active direction of his administration." Unfortunately, the next day it was reported that Smith had rented a suite of rooms with the intention of staying in Albany after the inauguration. It was reported that Smith wanted to be available to help Roosevelt, particularly with the budget. His unnamed "friends" denied that he wanted to exercise an undue influence on Roosevelt: "All talk that Mr. Smith is harboring aspirations to continue wielding influence as 'the power behind the throne' is discounted by his friends. . . . The Governor has made it known that he will always be willing to aid Mr. Roosevelt but this will mark the extent of his concern with developments at the state Capitol." Smith was forced to cancel his reservation, but he continued to expect that he would play an important role in the new administration.

On the eve of the inauguration, Smith made both public and private offers of assistance. When Roosevelt came to dinner at the Executive Mansion, Smith greeted him in the presence of reporters: "Well, I'll tell you Frank, I've taken the oath so many times that I feel I'm practically in the competitive civil service. But you know that it will take only about five minutes to get me on the telephone and any time you want my help just give me a ring." Privately, he suggested that Roosevelt hire Moskowitz and Moses. "I recommended that he have [Moskowitz] right there in his own office," he told Frances Perkins. "She can see people. She can arrange things. She can keep in touch with me, tell me what's going on. I can tell her what ought to be done." Roosevelt was probably appalled, but he told Smith he would think about it, encouraging his belief they would be working closely together.

Still assuming that Roosevelt would be spending the first months of the legislative session in Warm Springs, Smith made plans to be the governor's point man while he was away. "I told him I'd come up every week if he wanted me to," Smith told Perkins. "I could be there Monday and Tuesday. Those are the big legislative days. I could see people for him. I could deal with them. I could talk with the Republicans and Democrats. I could help him with a lot of things." Perkins was shocked by the role that Smith had imagined for himself. She tried to reason with him, but Smith insisted that Roosevelt wanted him to play a big role. "Of course . . . I'll be here a lot. Frank wants me to help him."

Smith was disappointed when Roosevelt decided not to hire either Moskowitz or Moses. The failure to reappoint Moses was not much of a surprise. He was aware that the two men had come into conflict in the past, and he was mollified by Roosevelt's choice of his friend Edward J. Flynn, the Bronx boss, to replace Moses as secretary of state. The rejection of Moskowitz was another matter. Roosevelt insisted that he needed a male secretary, Guernsey Cross, because he had to have someone strong to assist him in moving around. But Cross was not politically savvy enough to act as Smith's liaison with the Roosevelt administration. "I can't tell Guernsey Cross things," he complained to Perkins. "Guernsey Cross don't know anything." For his part, Roosevelt was plainly irritated by Smith's repeated offers of assistance. Several weeks after his inauguration, he told Perkins that Smith was calling him on the telephone every day or two and offering to return to the capital for consultations. After Smith and Roosevelt became political opponents, many people would trace the origin of their conflict to these first few weeks of Roosevelt's governorship. Historians have tended to adopt this view, suggesting that their relationship continued to deteriorate until a break became inevitable. They have overlooked that just as tempers were fraying, help appeared in the unlikely form of the New York Republican Party. The decision by Republicans in the legislature to attack the executive budget instantly united Smith and Roosevelt in a battle against a common enemy.

A compromise had cleared the way for the passage of the constitutional amendment establishing the executive budget in 1926. Under the original proposal, the power to initiate appropriations lay entirely with the governor, leaving the legislature with a veto over spending of which it disapproved. After controlling the budget process for so many years, however, the Republicans had been unwilling to forgo entirely the right to propose spending items. Smith finally agreed to allow the legislature to introduce appropriations, as long as they were offered as separate bills that were subject to the governor's veto. At the time, Robert Moses and others warned Smith that this gave the legislature the opportunity to sabotage the executive budget by deleting the governor's specific proposals and introducing bills providing lump sums that could only be divided with the approval of the chairmen of the legislative finance committees. Smith did not doubt that the Republicans were capable of such a subterfuge, but he believed the courts would reject such a move as inconsistent with the clear intent of the executive budget.

As Moses had predicted, when the first executive budget was introduced in 1929, the Republicans attempted to reassert their authority by striking out the governor's appropriations and substituting lump sums that could not be allocated without their approval. It was clear in the public mind that this was less a dispute between Roosevelt and the Republicans than a continuation of the conflict between Smith and his old foes. Smith's role in the fight was clearly revealed when the legislature sent the appropriation bills to the governor. Roosevelt had initially favored a conciliatory approach, accepting the bills and letting the courts decide the issue. Smith persuaded him that his legal position would be stronger if he vetoed the bills. Although the initial court decision went against the governor, the state's highest court ruled unanimously in his favor.

Even had there been no occasion for Smith and Roosevelt to make common cause, it is doubtful that their disagreements would have multiplied. The correspondence between the two men indicates that both were determined to maintain friendly relations. Roosevelt's letters to Smith routinely closed with an invitation to visit him. In March, Smith took him up on his offer, wandering into the governor's office during a press conference being held by Roosevelt and Lieutenant Governor Lehman:

"Hello, Frank," the former governor said as he was ushered in. . . .
"Whom do you represent," asked Lt. Gov. Lehman smiling.

"The Legislative Correspondents' Association; I'm a member. . . ."

"Well, Al, you are a member of a very belligerent crowd then," put in Gov. Roosevelt. "They are always looking for a fight. You have trained them wrong."

"You have got to get your publicity. . . . There wouldn't be much to write about without a battle."

Smith went on to explain the value of publicity, describing how publication of the fact that he was seen in his shirt and suspenders on a hot day had prompted many of his admirers to send him suspenders. "And as long as you can't see their colors, they are all right," Smith explained. The newspapermen then resumed their questioning of the governor. Smith "listened in silence but with a look of satisfaction as his successor was compelled to do the answering to questions." The next night, he and Mrs. Smith had dinner at the Executive Mansion with the Roosevelts.

Undoubtedly, one of the factors contributing to the tension between Smith and Roosevelt was Smith's lack of a full-time job to absorb his energies. Finally, on August 29, 1929, in a news conference held in his suite in the Biltmore Hotel, Smith announced that he had become the chairman of a corporation headed by John Raskob and Pierre du Pont that would build the world's tallest building on Fifth Avenue between Thirty-third and Thirty-fourth Streets, the Empire State Building. The breathtaking dimensions of the proposed skyscraper made it a fitting symbol of the mood of the country in the summer of 1929. Following eight years of economic growth, most Americans believed they had finally escaped the dreary cycle of boom and bust and were now embarked on a journey toward unlimited wealth. The 1,250-foot tower was to be the embodiment of Raskob's philosophy that in America the builders are the reapers and that, freed from the constraints of conservative finance, any man with daring who was willing to work hard would become successful. Smith, a symbol of what hard work could achieve, was a natural to head his project. His involvement made the construction of the building practically a public monument. For his part, Smith seemed glad to be using his talents fully again. In September he told a reporter, "I'm working hard now and hope to accomplish something if they let me alone."

Only a month later, however, New York Stock Exchange crashed.

The first major break occurred on the morning of October 24, "Black Thursday," when more than 12 million shares changed hands as stockholders frantically sold at any price they could get. The drop was so dramatic that it drew a crowd of men to the steps of the Subtreasury building, where they stood staring at the Stock Exchange across the street, their voices creating a low roar that prompted a call for more police. The day did not end badly, however, because a group of banks led by J. P. Morgan stepped in to support the market. The terror really began on the following Monday, when the market once again began to fall and the bankers, concluding they could no longer afford to prop up prices, stepped aside and let it. Blue-chip stocks plunged. By the middle of November, thousands of men and women all over the country had lost everything because they had purchased stock using other stocks as collateral. When the value of the underlying stocks fell, people were unable to come up with the money to pay their margin loans and their stocks were sold. The small investors were the first to go bankrupt, but the crash soon began to affect even the wealthy. Al Smith's friend Jim Riordan was one of them.

Like the Empire State Building, the County Trust Company of New York was the brainchild of an immigrant American who hungered to make his mark on the business world. Launched with a relatively modest capital of $1 million, the County Trust was an Irish-American bank whose board of directors was made up almost exclusively of contractors and other small businessmen. Operating on Eighth Avenue near Fourteenth Street, it aimed to serve the beef and poultry dealers in nearby Gansevoort Market. Despite its humble origins, the County Trust Company's political contacts helped it grow.

The bank was a success from the day it opened its doors and Al Smith made the first deposit. Its stock was selling at twice its face value of $100 from the beginning. As deposits grew from $1.4 million to $35 million in its first three years of operation, the bank's earnings quadrupled from $10 to $41 per share. Riordan added considerably to the wealth he had begun acquiring as president of U.S. Trucking Company by founding several real estate companies, which went on to acquire extensive holdings in the Greenwich Village area. By the fall of 1929, the bull market had driven his large stock portfolio to dizzying heights. His County Trust Company stock was selling at between $500 and $1,000 per share. Riordan was also a respected member of the community. He served as president of the Market and Business Men's Association of Greenwich and Chelsea Districts, and, like Smith, was a director of the Consolidated Indemnity and Insurance Company and the Beekman Street Hospital. As a tribute to his friend, Riordan bought the house on Oliver Street where the Smith family had lived during Smith's career as a state legislator.

The stock market collapse abruptly ended the rise of James Riordan. The stock of County Trust had risen in value as a result of a spectacular increase in earnings, but the crash threatened to destroy the bank. Worried depositors were rushing to withdraw their savings at any sign of a bank's weakness, and Riordan was afraid that his bank's falling share price might have this effect. As the stock fell to $400 per share, he made a desperate attempt to persuade large stockholders in the bank not to sell their holdings. One director, Howard Cullman, even agreed to buy an additional two hundred shares in an effort to stabilize the stock, but it continued to slide. All of Riordan's stocks were declining. As if things weren't bad enough, it was Riordan's duty as president of the bank to call loans that were outstanding to cover the losses on the bank's stock portfolio. Many of these note holders were friends who were facing financial ruin.

On November 8, Riordan removed a pistol from one of the teller's cages at the bank and went home early. A teller reported seeing him take the gun, and bank officials warned Smith of the danger to his friend. Smith and William F. Kenny rushed to his home, but were told that he had not returned from work. They left but were summoned again after Riordan's son-in-law discovered the body. The banker had slipped home and shot himself unseen and unheard by his staff. According to the teaching of the Catholic church, suicide was a mortal sin. Riordan's son-in-law was so shocked that he hid the gun from the medical examiner. Before addressing the question of how to persuade the church to permit a funeral mass for Riordan, however, Smith, Kenny, and Raskob were faced with the problem of how to prevent the run on County Trust that would surely occur the next day if Riordan's suicide was revealed to the public.

The three men agreed they would have to cover up the death until the bank had closed the following day, which was Saturday. The delay would give them time to undertake an audit of the bank's condition and convene a meeting of the directors to appoint a replacement for Riordan in an attempt to prevent a run on the bank on Monday. The first task was to get the medical examiner to delay reporting the death to the police. The examiner agreed, later telling reporters that Smith had asked him for the delay. (Smith denied it.) It wasn't until the Sunday morning papers were on the street that the public read front-page stories of Riordan's demise. By that time, Raskob, who had been named temporary chairman of the bank, had released an audit that demonstrated that County Trust was in excellent financial shape, a finding that was lent credence by an audit conducted by state bank examiners. Not convinced that the audits in themselves were enough to prevent a run, the directors also arranged for prompt delivery of a Federal Reserve shipment of cash to the bank. The arrival of the funds was documented in newspaper pictures that were inserted in the Sunday editions by friendly editors. Finally, Raskob announced that wealthy friends of Riordan's had agreed to make up any deficit the bank might experience as a result of withdrawals upon its reopening. The rescue worked: on Monday, County Trust opened its doors on time; when they closed again, deposits had actually increased as a result of the intervention of Riordan's friends. A week later, the *New York Times* praised Smith for saving the County Trust:

> He acted with great boldness. He took chances which most men would have regarded as desperate. Had he failed, we know, and he knows, what would have been said of him. But in the crisis he forgot everything except the opportunity to spend all his energy, even at personal risk, to save an imperiled bank and prevent a blow to trust in our financial system which would have been struck by its failure.

But there was no saving the financial system. Even as the Empire State Building began its miraculous rise on Fifth Avenue, the country was entering the Great Depression.

The construction of the Empire State Building captured the public imagination. Before 1929, people thought the 793-foot Woolworth Building or the 927-foot Bank of Manhattan building the largest edifices of which man was capable. Even the 1,046-foot Chrysler Building, completed in 1930, could not rival public interest in the Empire State Building, which would stand 1,250 feet over Fifth Avenue. In fact, the height of the newest skyscraper was determined by public relations concerns.

Walter Chrysler had surprised his competitors by increasing the height of his building with a spire that was secretly constructed and elevated through the dome at the last minute. The spire threatened the predominance of the Empire State Building. Then Raskob hit on the idea of topping his building with a two-hundred-foot mast to moor dirigibles. The mast was a failure as a transportation terminal, but it was a public relations triumph. The building would now qualify as the eighth wonder of the world.

The Empire State Building enjoyed other advantages over its rivals. It rose on the site formerly occupied by the Waldorf-Astoria Hotel, an elegant establishment located in the heart of a neighborhood of mansions, the winter homes of the New York aristocracy. In the Empire State Building, the public saw an old order that revolved around four hundred elite families giving way before the demands of a business civilization that distributed its rewards according to a man's accomplishments. (Smith was fond of noting that the Waldorf-Astoria was a victim of the advance of a business civilization: its luxurious appointments were worth little compared to the rent the site could command. What could be more democratic?) The decision to locate the building on Thirty-fourth Street instead of farther uptown, where most new commercial buildings were located, was a bold statement of the promoters' belief that the business district was moving south. The location also gave the building mastery of the Manhattan skyline. Finally, the building benefited from having as its president one of the most colorful and well-loved public figures of the age.

Smith made sure that the construction of the Empire State Building fulfilled expectations that its rise would be breathtaking. The day after Smith announced plans for the building in August 1929, a truck drove up the steps of the Waldorf-Astoria Hotel, which had been closed since May, entered the lobby, then roared down Peacock Alley past gold mirrors and velvet drapes. On October 1, Smith and Raskob traveled to the top of the building to remove the topmost stone in its cornice, and demolition began. The speed of the project would set records. Seven hundred men followed Smith and Raskob into the building; over the next three months, using welding torches, crowbars, and cranes, they demolished the hotel, hauling the debris away to barges. Even before demolition was complete, excavation for the new foundation began. In March 1930 the workers were ready to begin constructing the steel frame. Demonstrating his flair for publicity, Smith delayed the setting of the first piers until March 17, St. Patrick's Day.

The erection of the superstructure of the Empire State Building in six months awed even the most jaded New Yorker. Each steel beam, arriving in a steady flow from the mills in Pittsburgh, was poured, shipped, and riveted into place in the framework in only eighty hours. As the ironworkers were pushing upward, stonemasons were attaching the walls at the rate of one floor per day. In all, 3,400 men were at work at the peak of construction, taking their meals in place to avoid the time lost in traveling up and down the structure. Lewis W. Hine immortalized the ironworkers in photographs that showed them calmly working at historic altitudes. A year after demolition had begun, the steel work was done— twelve days ahead of schedule. Six months later, in April 1931, the completion of the building was announced, and opening ceremonies were set for May 1. The building's contractor called it "probably the greatest attainment in metropolitan construction in our time."

Meanwhile, the relationship between Smith and Roosevelt was growing closer. Any remaining doubts that Smith may have had about his successor's political skill disappeared in early 1930 when Roosevelt executed a stunning political coup that achieved one of Smith's long-sought goals for New York. For several weeks before the convening of the legislature, the Republican leaders met in an effort to find a way of laying the waterpower issue to rest. Their new state chairman, W. Kingsland Macy, wanted to clear the party of the charge of being in the pay of the utility interests, who had always been heavy contributors to the party in return for its steadfast opposition to public development of waterpower. In a meeting with Roosevelt, however, the Republicans failed to gain the concessions they were seeking, and the legislature opened without an agreement. The Republicans attempted to sidetrack the issue by agreeing to the creation of a waterpower commission to study both the private and public alternatives for developing waterpower plants on the St. Lawrence River, but announced that the Republicans had finally accepted the principle of public development. Although they had done nothing of the sort, they would only have justified their reactionary reputation by complaining, so they kept silent. Roosevelt wrote Smith to announce victory in the eleven-year struggle: "You will be happy to know that the Republican legislative leaders have introduced and come out in favor of an electric power bill which seems to accept the great basic principle for which you and I have fought so long."

The newspapers endorsed Roosevelt's view of what the Republicans had done. "We are interpreting the outcome as a complete triumph for the things you have been fighting for," Walter Lippmann of the World told Roosevelt. Smith was overjoyed: "Hearty congratulations on your victory. It was a long battle and you should get great personal satisfaction from the outcome. All hands in the party rejoice with you and send best wishes." Recognizing that the waterpower commission could still bring back a report adverse to public ownership, Roosevelt and Smith worked closely together to ensure the selection of the right men.

As the political alliance between Smith and Roosevelt grew stronger, their social ties also became closer. Soon after the waterpower victory, Roosevelt wrote Smith that he had recently been mistaken for the former governor: "By the way, did I tell you that it is high time for you to return to Albany? A few weeks ago when my graddaughter was here, your granddaughter came to the house to spend the afternoon and five minutes after I had joined the party Mary was calling me 'Ganpa.' I felt highly honored and have certainly cut you out." Smith displayed no fear of being upstaged. He replied, "Letter received. I will be up in Albany when I return. . . . I will be glad to see you and will take that little girl away." Smith's feelings were clearly revealed at the conclusion of a nostalgic visit to Albany while Roosevelt was in Warm Springs. "I spent considerable time in Albany and I missed you very much," he wrote. He also accepted Roosevelt's invitation to meet him in Albany when he returned. "There are a number of things I want to talk to you about with respect to the fall campaign," Smith said.

Democratic prospects looked excellent in 1930 because of the sudden economic downturn. The stock market recovery that began after the crash lost momentum in April; the market then declined inexorably until the spring of 1932. Over 1,300 banks would fail before the end of 1930, and unemployment was becoming a serious problem. In New York City there were already widespread reports of distress by March. Six months later the bread lines at St. Vincent's Hospital had grown to include over 1,500 men, and the police department was receiving over five hundred requests for aid every day. Throughout the country there were signs that the voters were preparing to punish the Republicans for failing to keep their promise to make prosperity perpetual. Smith told Raskob that he had received more than one hundred requests for speeches. But he turned almost all of them down because of his heavy commitment to the state campaign. Besides placing Roosevelt in nomination for another term as governor, he planned to make six speeches around New York.

Smith's nominating speech would have melted the heart of any candidate. His greatest praise was for Roosevelt's waterpower victory.

> [I]f there is a man in the State of New York that takes great plea-sure and great satisfaction in congratulating Franklin Roosevelt for the beginning of the settlement of the [waterpower] question, it is myself, because I was unable to do it. . . . No man worked harder in the Governor's office during all my experience in Albany than did Franklin D. Roosevelt. . . . And I go a step further and say that in all my experience no man has accomplished more in two years than Franklin D. Roosevelt and that in the face of a bitter and at times personal hostility. . . .

He concluded with a meditation on the qualities that made Roosevelt so attractive a figure, qualities that he himself admired: "First, he has a clear brain, and second, he has a big heart. And all through his administration you can find running that milk of human kindness that comes from a big heart, a heart that thinks for the cripple, for the sick, for the poor, for the weak and for the afflicted. . . . It is because of that that I believe he him-self has the great, strong strength of character." The arrogant young aris-tocrat had grown up and put his talents to work for others. Smith had become his biggest fan.

As Smith began his tour of the state on behalf of Roosevelt, his cam-paign generated tremendous enthusiasm. In Buffalo Smith drew 5,500 people to the Elmwood Music Hall, which was almost twice as many people as Roosevelt and his opponent, Charles H. Tuttle, had addressed there combined. The people came to hear Smith's traditional election-year dismantling of the New York Republicans, and they weren't dis-appointed. There was another crowd in excess of five thousand for his Rochester address; his appearance there and in Buffalo proved that two years in private life had not dimmed his star. "Mr. Smith's personal popularity up-State is as great or greater than when he was running for office," the *New York Times* reported.

The former presidential nominee encountered more large crowds as he traveled to Providence and Boston to give two national addresses. Traveling in Kenny's private car, the same car that had carried him around the country during the 1928 campaign, he found thousands of people waiting for him at the Providence train station. Thousands more lined Smith's route through the business district. One of those waiting to meet the New Yorker was a two-year-old whose parents were such strong supporters that they had named their son Alfred E. Smith Walsh. The proud parents presented Smith with a bouquet of flowers as he prepared to address an overflow crowd of 15,000. Smith opened with a mild joke at the Republicans' expense. "Under a Republican administration it is called a business depression. In a Democratic administration they call it a panic. Somebody the other day called it a cycle. They ought to call it a bicycle because both Democrats and Republicans are being taken for a ride on it." But he turned serious when he characterized the Republican record in meeting the Depression: "The Republican party stands indicted on three counts, and I will produce the indictments. The first is that they definitely promised continued prosperity, knowing that they could not produce it. In the second place, they refused to face the bad business situation before it was forced upon them. Thirdly, they did not do what they could to relieve unemployment and hard times." Smith dismissed the Republican claim that the unemployed were benefiting from a speeding up of public works. In fact, he said, the federal budget for public works had been reduced by $26 million, and thousands of government workers were being laid off in an effort to save money.

In Boston, Smith's speech was supposed to concentrate on the tariff and Prohibition. But he was more interested in driving home the lessons of the 1928 campaign:

> What has happened to the Republican Party in this instance is nothing more or less than the result that might be expected when false issues are injected into a campaign. Lack of sincerity or even honesty behind a false campaign pledge not only wrecks itself but tends to bring about the destruction of those who issue it. . . . There is one thing of lasting benefit that will come from the situa-

tion under which we are suffering; and that is the American people for a good many years to come, if ever, will not again be fooled
by false propaganda, by misleading statements and by the promotion of what are really not issues and should have no place in
American political campaigns.

Religion was not mentioned, but his audience knew what he was talking
about.

At the conclusion of the 1930 campaign, Smith had a right to feel that
he had secured a measure of personal vindication. His defeat in 1928 had
done nothing to diminish his personal popularity. Most of the state reforms he had proposed were being carried to fruition by a successor who
shared a similar philosophy of government and who had become a close
friend. It appeared that the Republican Party was about to be punished
for its sins. Whether the success of the Democratic Party would spur
Smith to seek the presidential nomination again was a question that now
began to torment Roosevelt, but Smith showed no signs of abandoning
his successful new career in business. In October Smith had rejected a
suggestion that he tour Massachusetts. "I am not a candidate for office
now," he said. "I am a business man and am anxious to avoid the appearance of a hippodrome." Still, Roosevelt was well aware that by helping reelect him, Smith had also helped himself. The Happy Warrior was back
in the public spotlight.

# 10 ❋ RETURN OF
# THE HAPPY WARRIOR

Al Smith could not have been more pleased by what he was hearing as he sat with Franklin and Eleanor Roosevelt listening to the returns on election night, 1930. The Democratic Party was about to win enough seats to control the U.S. House of Representatives and to threaten Republican control of the U.S. Senate. Smith saw in the returns the possibility that the Democratic nominee in 1932 would defeat Herbert Hoover. The defeat of Thomas Heflin, the virulently anti-Catholic senator from Alabama, was especially satisfying. There were also signs that opposition to Prohibition was growing. In 1930, thirty candidates pledged to the modification or repeal of the Eighteenth Amendment were elected to the House, while the voters of Illinois, Rhode Island, and Massachusetts all approved referenda calling for change. While the "soaking wet" representatives and senators who favored repeal of the Eighteenth Amendment were still a minority, many nominally dry Congressmen were beginning to support a change in the Volstead Act that would permit the consumption of wine and beer. As the man who had done more than any other to put the Democratic Party behind the movement for change, Smith felt a justifiable pride.

Franklin Roosevelt's successful campaign for reelection completed Smith's happiness. Smith left Roosevelt headquarters before the arrival of a telegram of concession from Tuttle, at 9 p.m., but it was already apparent that Roosevelt would receive a record plurality. The final tally showed that Roosevelt had surpassed Smith's best showing by more than 300,000 votes and had even managed to top his biggest plurality in New York City by almost 40,000 votes. Most impressive, he had carried upstate New York by a plurality of 165,000, an unprecedented feat for a Democrat. Roosevelt's success at the polls naturally made him a potential nominee for president. The *New York Times* warned him to continue to address himself to the problems of New York and not to become involved in presidential intrigue. "What may come after is not for him but for the moving finger to write on the scroll of his political destiny," it observed. While Roosevelt denied that he had any presidential plans, he was not the kind of man to wait for destiny to decide.

Despite its improved electoral prospects, the Democratic Party remained deeply divided. Roosevelt knew that he would have to move cautiously to capture the presidential nomination. His major asset as a candidate was his proven ability to appeal to both urban and rural voters. Although opposition to Prohibition was growing quickly in the Democratic Party, victory seemed to depend on finding a candidate who could appeal to voters in areas where sentiment favoring Prohibition remained strong. Roosevelt supporters claimed he could win the dry voters in the South. Shortly after his reelection, the *Atlanta Constitution* described Roosevelt as a "cool and an authoritative apostle of Jeffersonian and Jacksonian Democracy, the Democracy of delegated and limited Federalism, sovereign State rights and the inalienable American privilege of home rule." These were the principles that would draw Southerners to his candidacy for president, it said. Roosevelt's advocates pointed to this editorial to prove that the South was now ready to vote for a wet candidate as long as the candidate was Roosevelt.

But the squire of Hyde Park could not depend on his appeal as a Protestant of good birth and rural background to win the backing of Southern and Western Democrats. Friendly editorials in the *Atlanta Constitution* notwithstanding, he could not hide that he was a Northerner, a wet, and a friend of Al Smith. At least one key Southern leader believed that he would have to do more to earn the support of the South. Cordell Hull, a former chairman of the Democratic National Committee from Tennessee, was a strong supporter of Prohibition who was bitterly opposed to Smith and Raskob. In Hull's view, Roosevelt needed to do something dramatic to establish his independence of Smith and show qualities of national leadership. Roosevelt knew Hull and was quick to acknowledge the receipt of a telegram of congratulations, congratulating him in turn for his election to the U.S. Senate. "I am so glad about your promotion," Roosevelt wrote. He and Louis Howe were already convinced that he would have to back away from the advanced position he had taken on Prohibition. They were also sure that he would have to do something that was even more dangerous. Roosevelt would have to dump Al Smith without alienating his supporters. The job would have to be done in stages and with great subtlety. It was John Raskob who gave Roosevelt his first chance.

Raskob was determined to force the Democratic Party to face the Prohibition issue. He drew a different lesson from the 1928 election than Roosevelt and Howe. He believed that the popularity of Smith's candidacy proved that millions of Americans were demanding a resolution of the Prohibition question. The party could not ignore the issue without risking the loss of the new support that it had found in the cities. Raskob also felt that the Democrats' success in the 1930 elections put him in a position to urge the party to make an early declaration of its intention to become the party of Prohibition reform in 1932. Under his direction and at his expense, the Democratic National Committee had hired a full-time staff in 1928 to initiate a sustained attack on the policies of the Republican Party and Herbert Hoover. Even many of Raskob's former critics in the party were singing his praises. As a result, soon after the 1930 elections, Raskob decided to hold an unusual meeting of the Democratic National Committee to endorse resolutions, including one supporting a new constitutional amendment giving the states the authority to decide if liquor would be sold within their borders. It was natural for him to share his plans with Roosevelt, for he considered him a friend as well as a political ally. On December 3, he wrote Lieutenant Governor Lehman that he had something important he wanted to tell Roosevelt and him: "I am very anxious to talk to you about national affairs and very much wish that I could see you sometime when you are in New York for an hour or so. I will promise not to ask you for money but I do want you to be fully acquainted with what I am doing and we are about to take some most important steps with which you and Franklin should be thoroughly familiar." Raskob told Roosevelt of his plan to call a national committee meeting when they met in mid-December.

But the party chief had misjudged his confidant. If Roosevelt had really been a friend, he would have tried to dissuade Raskob from calling a meeting that he had every reason to believe would provoke the Southerners. Seeing the national committee meeting as his opportunity to begin distancing himself from Smith, Roosevelt informed Hull of Raskob's plans. On February 22, 1931, Hull wrote Roosevelt what he had been doing with this information: "I have discussed the situation as you and I both understand it with numerous senators, congressmen and other leading Democrats. There is a growing feeling of protest against either of the two proposals which you repeated to me as being on the program for affirmative action at the coming national committee meeting." But betraying confidences alone would not have satisfied Hull. Roosevelt also prepared to make a public gesture, instructing New York state Democratic chairman James A. Farley to call a special meeting of the state Democratic committee to adopt a resolution opposing Raskob's plan. Farley also began soliciting proxies from members of the Democratic National Committee who were not planning to attend the March 5 meeting that could be used against Raskob if the vote was close.

Roosevelt did not tell Smith that he was personally opposed to the course that Raskob was pursuing. As late as February 20, Roosevelt wrote Smith without discussing the subject of the national committee meeting. It wasn't until five days before the meeting that Roosevelt made an effort to inform Smith of his views. In a letter to Smith, Roosevelt wrote:

> I have been trying to get you on the telephone. I do not know what the plans for next Thursday's meeting of the Democratic National Committee are, but the more I hear from around the country, the more certain I am that it would be very contrary to the established powers and precedents of the National Committee, were they to pass resolutions of any kind affecting party policies at this time.

Even then, Roosevelt did not reveal that the state Democratic committee would meet two days later to consider the issue.

On March 2, the New York State Democratic Committee adopted a resolution opposing any statements of policy by the Democratic National Committee. The Southerners were jubilant. "I am very much pleased," Senator Cameron Morrison of North Carolina said. "I think it was not only a piece of political acumen, but the right thing to do." Meanwhile, Roosevelt supporters attempted to deflect any criticism of their leader by accusing Raskob of plotting to renominate Smith. "Mr. Raskob, in seeking to make the Democratic party officially wet, was inspired by the hope that if such action were taken Mr. Smith would become the logical Presidential nominee," one unnamed partisan charged. By such reasoning, Roosevelt was not being disloyal by siding with the Southerners: he had been forced to act to protect his own presidential prospects. Certainly, Hull was convinced that Smith would be a candidate again. In his memoirs he wrote, "After Roosevelt's withdrawal from the Smith organization, all or most of those opposed to the Smith movement were gradually and ultimately to turn to Roosevelt as the most effective way of killing off Smith." If Smith had received a mortal blow, he was too busy to notice. With the opening of the Empire State Building only two months away, he was engaged in a desperate effort to prevent it from becoming a colossal financial flop.

The Empire State Building could not have opened at a worse time. With the Depression gaining momentum every day, there was almost no one to fill its over two million square feet of rentable space. On Christmas Eve 1930, Robert C. Brown, vice president of Empire State, Inc., wrote John Raskob that, based on a 25 percent rate of occupancy, he and Smith were projecting a deficit of nearly $600,000 for the first six months of the building's operations. He explained, "I am in hopes that there will be additional savings which will wipe out the apparent deficit of $593,000 but I do not think, at this writing, it is safe to count on them." Smith insisted publicly that all was proceeding according to plan. "The leasing of the Empire State Building is proceeding rapidly," he said. Business only grew worse in 1931. Smith and his staff would succeed in renting only 400,000 square feet by the end of the year, giving the building an occupancy rate of 22 percent. Nearly half of the space was rented by the County Trust Company, du Pont subsidiaries, and the Empire State Club, which was owned by Empire State, Inc. The company wasn't even making money from its handful of outside tenants, because many of them had left their old offices before their leases expired and Empire State, Inc., had agreed to assume them. By December 1931, the losses would be nearly twice Brown's estimate, and the deficit would reach $2.2 million.

Smith was up to his elbows in red ink when the Democratic National Committee meeting was announced. Raskob had undoubtedly told Smith about his plans, and Smith may even have endorsed them, but he was probably not paying attention. If he had initially approved the plan, by early March 1931 the controversy that it had stirred convinced him that it would be a mistake to try to press for resolutions. Smith and Norman Mack, the former state chairman, told Raskob that he must abandon his plan even though he had the votes to win. When Smith was reached by reporters who wanted his reaction to the state committee meeting, he surprised them by agreeing with the substance of the resolution: "Certainly a Democrat has a right to speak up and say what he thinks about any problem, but I know of nothing giving the committee the power to determine party policies. The convention is the supreme body of the party. That's fundamental." He also hinted that Raskob might not press for a vote on his resolutions. "I do know that he is going to the meeting with an open mind," Smith said.

In an interview the following day, Smith elaborated on his view of the controversy. He said he was not angry at the New York state committee for its vote, although it had been a mistake to condemn a proposal that hadn't actually been made. "The only fault is that those members started to talk before they knew what they were talking about, and indicated they acted without knowledge," Smith said. He defended the right of anyone to make any proposal in a Democratic Party meeting. "That is open to anybody in the Democratic party, even the dustman who removes ashes from this hotel," he explained. But he refused to commit himself on the question of whether the national committee should make a recommendation on Prohibition. "[I]t is up to the committee," he said. Smith had given a speech in North Carolina the night before, and reporters asked him to comment on the fact that Southerners saw that as a sign of an impending candidacy. "Well, they cannot discern something from nothing," Smith replied. But he added that he was not closing the door on another run for the presidency. It was too soon to say. "That is like crossing a bridge 17 miles ahead," he explained. Then you're not out of politics altogether? a reporter asked. "Well, not altogether," Smith replied, laughing.

When the Democratic National Committee finally met on March 5, it once again appeared that divisions in the party would kill any hope for victory. Raskob opened the meeting by making a number of policy recommendations intended to return the party to Jefferson's vision of a government of limited powers. In an effort to take "government out of business," Raskob proposed steps to make it easier for companies to merge and to remove the tariff from partisan politics. On the issue of Prohibition, he recommended his "home rule plan," which he insisted would protect dry states even if a majority of the other states authorized the sale of liquor. He did not ask for an immediate vote on his proposals, although he indicated that the committee could "suggest" them to the platform committee at some later time. But the Southerners were not satisfied. They had come to the meeting with the intention of finally settling their score with Raskob. "You cannot inscribe on the banner of the Democratic party the skull and cross bones of an outlawed trade," thundered Joseph Robinson, Smith's running mate in 1928. Senator Morrison brought the meeting to the verge of disintegration. "You'll never tie the Democratic party to death and destruction," Morrison said.

Smith attempted to restore a sense of perspective to the meeting. He criticized the Southerners for their attacks on Raskob: "I believed firmly when I became a member of the Democratic party . . . that there would be no Democratic gathering where anybody would be jumped all over for expressing their individual opinion." Attacks like Robinson's hurt the party. They were particularly hard to understand because Raskob had not recommended repeal, Smith said. He had actually recommended against it. But Smith agreed that the Democratic National Committee could not set party policy: "I know it is the supreme body of the party, and all this talk about platforms and platform declarations coming from committee, or from gatherings of any kind, is the negation of the very theory of Democratic platform making, because I have been brought up in the Democratic party to believe that the platform comes from the people." Smith also distanced himself from the substance of Raskob's recommendations. "As far as the declarations of political principle enunciated in Chairman Raskob's speech are concerned, I am not sure that I am for them all," he explained. Smith insisted that the meeting had a purpose larger than the settling of any particular issue:

> I knew this meeting was going to attract nation-wide attention. I knew it, and not for the reason that is in the minds of some of the delegates. But another, and to my mind a great reason, and that is, that I really believe that the American people are looking strongly to the Democratic party for relief from the chaotic condition that this country finds itself in midway in the term of the present President.

Following the meeting, Smith hosted a reception on the platform. Many congratulated him on his speech, and some said they hoped he would run again. Smith replied with a smile.

Many political observers were convinced that the Democratic National Committee meeting would mark a parting of the ways between Roosevelt and Smith: Roosevelt's decision to oppose Raskob was clearly part of a strategy that would establish his independence of Smith, at least while the Happy Warrior was a receptive candidate for the 1932 nomination. But one party to the purported break was sure they were wrong. "There is no split between Governor Roosevelt and myself," Smith insisted. "There is nothing to this newspaper talk about trouble." In his view, the action of the New York state committee had been ill-advised, but he accepted Roosevelt's explanation that what he objected to was the departure from party tradition. There had been no betrayal: Smith believed that Roosevelt was still committed to Prohibition reform; that they were still friends; that Roosevelt would seek his endorsement for president; and that he would give it.

Smith's inability to read Roosevelt's intentions requires some explanation. Despite his experience, Smith was not always a good judge of men. To some extent, this was the consequence of the openness and candor that were among his most appealing personal traits. Frances Perkins observed that if Al Smith considered you his friend, he held nothing back from you and assumed that you were completely honest with him. "I think he was unable to comprehend a friendship that was political, but that didn't admit you to any of the secret recesses of the mind and heart," she said. Proskauer put it another way: "[H]e trusted overmuch the integrity of those with whom he dealt." Smith was not completely naive. He did trust Roosevelt, but he also believed he could control him. Smith had been a great popular leader, and he counted on his charisma to hold his followers in line. It was inconceivable to him that Roosevelt could run for president without the enthusiastic support of the millions of new voters that he had brought to the polls in 1928. He believed his endorsement was the magic wand that would transform them into Roosevelt supporters.

Smith should have known better, because his magic had already failed once. In 1927 he had been so anxious to defeat Hearst's mayor, John Hylan, that he had reluctantly supported the candidacy of Jimmy

Walker. The two men were friends and had even shared an apartment in Albany for a time during their years in the legislature. (Smith said the tall, thin Walker reminded him of a peppermint stick in his striped pajamas.) As a result, Smith was well acquainted both with Walker's great political gifts—his intelligence, good looks, and charm—and with his loose morals—his disinclination for hard work, his love of nightlife, and his marital infidelity. Smith made Walker promise that he would reconcile with his wife and keep his nose to the grindstone, but he still felt the need for more insurance. He asked Joseph Proskauer to accept appointment as the city's corporation counsel to keep an eye on things. Proskauer had no illusions about the new mayor: "I said, 'Al, what makes you think that Jimmy Walker would ever appoint me as his corporation counsel?' 'Because I'd tell him to.' I said, 'You've got another thing coming.' What the event showed was that from the day Jimmy Walker became Mayor, Al could never talk to him on the telephone." It had been one of the worst miscalculations in Smith's political career. Walker did nothing to arrest the political corruption that had begun to grow again after the death of Boss Murphy in 1924. It would eventually engulf his administration and force him to resign. Smith had counted too much on his friendship with Walker—and also on his power as party leader. He was making the same mistake with Roosevelt.

When Smith and Roosevelt met on May 1, 1931, at the dedication of the Empire State Building, nothing appeared to have changed between them. The governor's presence was essential because the ceremonies that Smith had planned were more appropriate to the dedication of a public monument than the baptism of a commercial building. On hand were thousands of New Yorkers, milling in the streets, although they would have no chance of seeing the inside of the new building until the next day. In Washington, Herbert Hoover paused on his way to a cabinet meeting to throw a switch that lit the building for the first time. Ceremonies in the morning and at night were carried live by radio. Smith addressed the invited guests and the many thousands listening to the ceremonies on radio: "The Empire State Building stands today as the greatest monument to ingenuity, to skill, to brain power, to muscle power, the tallest thing in the world today produced by the hand of man." He recalled a cartoon in the *New York Evening Post* depicting a mother and her child observing the progress of the building from the roof of their tenement on the Lower East

Side. The mother tells the child, "Tony, your old man is building that!" "And Tony's old man had a large part in the building of it," Smith said, "and the mother had a justified pride and we share it with her. I am for the mother, and I am for Tony and for Tony's old man."

Then Roosevelt spoke, paying tribute more to Smith than to his building: "I think that its name is most highly fitting because it typifies the service that the principal backer and principal builder has rendered to the State of New York during all these years." Later, a photographer captured the two men on the observation floor as Smith gestured toward the seemingly limitless horizon. After the ceremony, the two men met for a conference. "We talked like two very old friends for an hour and a half last night," Roosevelt said. Nobody believed him when he said they did not discuss national politics, but it was probably the truth. They had met frequently over the past two years, but their conversations had concerned state affairs.

As the Depression deepened, the subject of politics was the only one that Smith could discuss with any degree of optimism. Many of his friends and business associates had been badly hurt by the decline in business activity. Millionaires like Raskob and Kenny had suffered huge paper losses, but his heart went out to the men of smaller means. Four members of the County Trust's board of directors were in serious financial trouble, and two would eventually declare bankruptcy, including the president of a small coal company who would die leaving only enough money to cover the cost of his funeral. Smith's personal finances had also been severely damaged by the collapse of stock values. Early in 1932, Fred French asked Smith if he would buy stock in Knickerbocker Village, a limited dividend corporation that was building subsidized housing in the Fourth Ward. Although Smith had introduced the law providing for this kind of housing project, he told French that he couldn't afford to invest:

> During the last six months I have scratched and scraped everything I had to margin up loans, collateral to which are high grade stocks and would be sold at a time like this at great sacrifice. Were it not for my salary it would be difficult to get along. Every dollar that I lay my hand on, I must use to reduce my bank indebtedness and I do not see any bright spot ahead and cannot carry the interest charges much longer.

Smith was clinging to stocks that he had purchased on margin when their price was high, trapped in the same vicious cycle with other investors: as the price of stocks had fallen, so had their value as collateral; to keep his stocks, he was forced to come up with more and more cash. He estimated that the Warner Brothers stock that he owned had fallen in value by at least $48,000.

Things would have been bad enough if he had been responsible only for his own losses, but he told Edward J. Flynn that he was also trying to help members of his family who had lost heavily in the market. Flynn, the boss of the Bronx Democrats, was an old friend of Smith's whom Roosevelt had appointed secretary of state. At some point after the Democratic National Committee meeting in March, Flynn decided that he had to tell Smith that he intended to begin working on Roosevelt's presidential campaign. When he committed himself to Roosevelt, he had relied on Smith's statement that he would not be a candidate for president. The rumors of a Smith candidacy in the wake of the Democratic National Committee meeting, however, convinced him that he should make sure that Smith understood his position. During a meeting at Smith's office in the Empire State Building, Flynn asked him directly if he intended to run again. Smith replied by reaching into his desk drawer and pulling out a number of papers that he spread before him:

> "Ed, these are all debts I must clear up. Financially I am in an extremely bad position." Then he told me that various members of his family had been in the stock market without his knowledge, had suffered great losses, and were heavily in debt. This situation had been brought about by Jim Reardon [sic], who was President of the Country Trust Company. . . . [I]t was only after Reardon's death that Smith learned of his family's involvement. Smith felt that in honor he must assume the obligations his relatives had incurred and he assured me that it would probably take him the rest of his life to clear up these financial burdens.

Not long afterward, Herbert Lehman called on Smith with the same errand and was told substantially the same thing.

By the middle of June 1931, it began to appear that Roosevelt would inherit all of Smith's supporters. In Massachusetts, where Smith was considered practically a native son, a drift to Roosevelt was apparent. Colonel

Edward House had recently hosted a luncheon for Roosevelt and state party leaders at his summer home near Manchester by the Sea. "I have always been an admirer of what Governor Roosevelt stands for," U.S. Senator David I. Walsh, a strong Smith supporter, said later. "I can only repeat what I said some time ago. It is high time we had a Roosevelt in the White House." Massachusetts Governor Joseph B. Ely was reported to be backing Roosevelt, as were Republican Senator Marcus A. Coolidge and Boston Mayor James Michael Curley, who had just dropped Owen Young.

The press remained watchful for any sign of a Smith candidacy. In October, when Smith announced his opposition to a proposed amendment to the state constitution that Roosevelt was supporting, many saw it as confirmation of the split that they had anticipated since March. Smith made several speeches against the amendment, which provided for mandatory annual appropriations for reforestation, and he may well have been angry at Roosevelt for endorsing a bill that he believed raised serious policy and constitutional problems. His biggest criticism of Roosevelt, however, was that he had fallen silent on Prohibition. Roosevelt had said nothing on the issue since April, when he signed two bills urging Congress to call for a national referendum on changes in the Eighteenth Amendment. Privately, Roosevelt was doing everything he could to prevent the Democrats from becoming the party of Prohibition reform. Louis Howe told Hull, "The entire West is in thorough sympathy with subordinating the Prohibition issue to the economic questions. Even the dry States, such as Kansas, have expressed the desire to keep this from obscuring matters such as the tariff and utility regulation. New York will, of course, do what the Governor says and I have assurances from Pennsylvania that they will go along the same lines." Even if New Jersey, Massachusetts, and Illinois joined to insist on a wet plank, Howe predicted that Roosevelt's control of New York and Pennsylvania would permit the South and West to write the kind of platform they desired.

Roosevelt's silence on Prohibition was only part of what was bothering Smith. He was also waiting for Roosevelt to ask for his support for his presidential candidacy. As the party standard bearer four years before, as his predecessor as governor, and as his friend, Smith naturally assumed that Roosevelt would want his endorsement. Roosevelt's unofficial campaign for president was under way, and a formal announcement was expected early in the new year. Yet he and Roosevelt had not met since the opening of the Empire State Building. Smith had not given up hope, however, when an invitation arrived from the governor during the second week of November: "The first trial balance of the budget will be done next Wednesday, the 16th. I'm coming to New York that night;—don't you want to run in any time on Tuesday or Wednesday the 17th or 18th and talk with me about it?" Smith was sure that Roosevelt would finally ask for his help in winning the presidency. The press also thought the meeting might be important. Was this a conference to try to set things straight between them? Roosevelt denied there was anything out of the ordinary about the meeting: "During the 20 years I have known Al Smith, we never have had what could be called a conference. We see each other frequently to discuss things in general, and that is just what is going to happen this time. Why I see Al pretty nearly every time I go to New York. Sometimes the papers learn about it and sometimes they don't." As he arrived at Roosevelt's house, Smith also played down the importance of the meeting. "I have come simply in response to an invitation to take luncheon with the Governor," Smith said. "I'm here to eat." The reporters followed Smith up to Roosevelt's second-floor library, where the old allies greeted each other. "Hello, Governor. How are you?" Smith said. "Hello, Al. I'm mighty glad to see you." The reporters were shown out. Two hours later, Smith emerged. What had they talked about? "We discussed State finances," Smith declared.

That was all they discussed. Roosevelt had not asked Smith for his support. Even then, Smith tried to deny the evidence that his friend was preparing to break with him. A week later, Smith sent Roosevelt a jocular note over a newspaper clipping that showed a picture of Herbert Hoover and companions mistakenly placed under a headline describing the November meeting between Smith and Roosevelt. But Smith's disappointment soon turned to anger. Two weeks after his meeting with Roosevelt, Smith told Clark Howell, the publisher of the *Atlanta Constitution*, how he felt during a meeting in his office. Howell had been a strong supporter of Smith in 1928. Now, he asked Smith to support Roosevelt. "The country expects you to support him, and it will not believe that you can possibly do otherwise," Howell said. "The hell I can't," Smith shot back. Smith said that he was not opposed to Roosevelt, but he rejected Howell's contention that he was clearly the best candidate. Howell said Roosevelt would carry the South. Smith replied that he doubted that he would be as successful in the North and East. "He then went on to say that 'millions' of people in this section resented 'the way he had been treated'—'that no Democrat had ever polled as many votes as he had,' etc.," Howell recalled.

Howell asked Smith if there were some personal reason for his hostility to Roosevelt. Smith denied it:

> "No," he said—"socially we are friends. He has always been kind to me and my family, and has gone out of his way to be agreeable to us at the Mansion at Albany, but"—then he arose, stamped his foot, and said—"Do you know, by God, that he has never consulted me about a damn thing since he has been Governor? He has taken bad advice and from sources not friendly to me. He has ignored me!" And then with increased fervor, and slamming his fist on the table, he said—"By God, he invited me to his house before he recently went to Georgia, and did not mention to me the subject of his candidacy."

Howell lamely explained that Roosevelt did not want to declare himself as a candidate yet. He asked Smith why he hadn't raised the question himself during their meeting. Howell told Roosevelt that Smith insisted that "it was up to you to broach the subject."

Smith told Howell that he was angry about Roosevelt's recent "dodging" on Prohibition. "Why the hell don't he speak out—he has been more outspoken on the question than even I have been, and now ain't the time for trimming." Howell asked if he was insisting on a platform plank calling for repeal. "No," he said. "But we should demand a referendum." Howell sought to assure Smith of Roosevelt's sincerity on Prohibition. "I quite agreed with him as to the wisdom of his policy, stating that it was wise from every standpoint. . . . I felt sure you would support such a declaration," Howell wrote to Roosevelt. With no substantive difference between the two men on Prohibition, Howell felt sure they could still patch up their differences. He concluded, "My recommendation is that you see him upon your return and talk with him on the subject. I think it will go a long way toward getting him in line. By handling him diplomatically I believe he will come around all right." But Howell was wrong in assuming that Roosevelt wanted Smith's support.

Roosevelt did not meet with Smith on his return to New York, nor did he make an effort to win his support in the months that followed. In Roosevelt's view, Howell did not understand the importance of the symbolism of Prohibition. It was not just another issue: it was the battlefield of a struggle for power between Smith and his opponents in the party. Smith had reminded Howell of these larger conflicts when he referred to the still-aching grievances of the 1928 election. Al Smith was himself a symbol of the divisions within the Democratic Party and the country. Roosevelt had made the decision that he must remain aloof from Smith in order to emerge as the unity candidate in 1932. He could not go back. He could not be the champion of repeal, and he could no longer be Al Smith's friend. This strategy ran the risk of subjecting him to attack as a Southern candidate, a collaborator with the bigots who had sold out their party in 1928. But Roosevelt was willing to take this risk. In the months to come, his supporters would portray the break as the result of Smith's desire to run for president again. But it was Roosevelt who had the guilty conscience. As he traveled north at the conclusion of his vacation in Warm Springs, Roosevelt told Farley that he was thinking about offering Smith a seat in his cabinet.

Smith's feeling toward Roosevelt soon became even more bitter. There had always been a danger that in attempting to build his own reputation, Roosevelt would do something to damage Smith's. Frances Perkins recalled how Roosevelt once tried to get her to admit that he was more liberal than Smith on the issue of appointing women to public office. (She believed Smith had displayed greater courage.) It was not the last time that Roosevelt would denigrate Smith's achievements. According to James Farley, Roosevelt did it again in the summer of 1931 during a visit to James Cox, the former Ohio governor who had been Roosevelt's running mate in 1920. Cox told *New York Times* columnist Arthur Krock that Roosevelt had corrected him when he said Smith possessed a genius for administration. According to Krock, Roosevelt said, "On the contrary, Smith was a poor Governor. He left things in a mess at Albany, and I have had great difficulty in trying to straighten them out." Smith had somehow learned of the remark by the time he arrived in Washington to speak at a Jackson Day celebration on January 9, 1932. Cox was also in town for the meeting, and Smith invited him to his hotel room. "He seemed to be somewhat in liquor and offered me a drink," Cox told Krock. When Smith asked if the report was true, Cox confirmed it and tried to swear him to silence. When the affair was reported by *Collier's* magazine, Roosevelt reacted with outraged innocence. "The man who says anything of the kind is not only a liar but a contemptible liar," Roosevelt said in a statement released to the press. For Smith, Roosevelt's denial was only proof of his dishonesty and disloyalty.

It did not take Smith long to decide that he would again seek the Democratic nomination. He had counted on Roosevelt to lead the fight against Prohibition and religious bigotry. Now that Roosevelt declined to play this part, Smith felt it was up to him to defend the interests of his supporters. By the middle of January 1932, Belle Moskowitz had received the order she had long awaited and was hard at work on the new campaign. Not long afterward, George Van Schaick, Roosevelt's superintendent of insurance and a friend of Smith's, called on the former governor at his apartment in the hope of clearing up the "misunderstanding" between Smith and Roosevelt. It was cocktail time, and Smith mixed a couple of old-fashioneds and sat down. Van Schaick recalled, "I said that the matter on my mind was the animosity that had developed between him and FDR and that as a friend of both I would like to straighten it out." "I'll tell you what the trouble is," Smith replied.

[T]hen [said Van Schaick] he began to enumerate a number of things which had hurt him at the time shortly after FDR assumed the governorship. They were small, trivial and petty. As he went along, he became quite heated and then came to his campaign for the Presidency. This was the high point of his lament. He reviewed the campaign against him based largely because of his religion and spoke very bitterly of the narrowness and bigotry which had developed in certain sections. He spoke with deepest feeling. Continuing, he said that having been defeated on such narrow and un-American grounds in 1928, that now in 1932 when it was quite likely an auspicious Democratic year, all should stand aside and give him another chance to overcome the prejudice he had faced in 1928. He said further that FDR should recognize it and not attempt to take the nomination away from him. This was the major and by far the most important grievance.

By this point in the conversation, Smith was talking loudly and pounding the table. "I was sorry I had raised the question," Van Schaick said.

Smith was fighting nearly impossible odds. Roosevelt had the support of most of the state organizations, which meant that he was going to win an overwhelming majority of the primaries in the coming months. There was a good chance that he would enter the convention with enough delegates to win on the first ballot. Smith's desire to announce his candidacy worried Raskob and his lieutenant, Jouett Shouse. They were anxious to see Roosevelt beaten and had been working since August 1931 to encourage favorite-son candidates in an effort to tie up enough votes to block Roosevelt's nomination. But they recognized that it would be suicide for Smith to make an active fight and tried to persuade him to follow a different course. In late January, Shouse asked New Hampshire committeeman Robert Jackson to honestly evaluate Smith's chances of winning the New Hampshire primary. Shouse explained that he would try to talk Smith out of running if his prospects were slim. Jackson replied that Smith would be so "decisively beaten" that he would be humiliated. Shouse asked Jackson to repeat his opinion to Smith that same afternoon at the Empire State Building. Smith was not pleased, Jackson recalled. "I saw Smith and told him what I had said to Shouse. He became angry and questioned the accuracy of my prediction. I suggested that if he was in doubt, John Curtin could substantiate my appraisal of the situation in a two days visit to New Hampshire. He said he might adopt the suggestion. At this point it became clear to me that he intended to become a candidate." Curtin was dispatched to make the fact-finding trip and apparently confirmed Jackson's assessment on his return. Smith agreed to adopt the favorite-son strategy to block Roosevelt's nomination. After that, it would be every man for himself.

Smith finally made a statement at his office on February 7, two weeks after Roosevelt had declared his candidacy. The reporters were waiting when he entered and seated himself in a green leather armchair behind his desk. "Well, here it is boys," Smith said, handing his secretary a stack of mimeographed press releases, which were marked for publication the following day. As she distributed them, the newsmen eagerly scanned the short statement:

> If the Democratic National Convention, after careful consideration, should decide it wants me to lead I will make the fight; but I will not make a pre-convention campaign to secure the support of delegates. By action of the Democratic National Convention of

1928, I am the leader of my party in the nation. With a full sense
of the responsibility thereby imposed I shall not in advance of the
convention either support or oppose the candidacy of any aspirant
for the nomination.

Moments later, the reporters were clamoring for clarification. What exactly did the statement mean? Was Smith a candidate or wasn't he? Smith
refused to describe himself as a candidate. The reporters insisted that he
would be a candidate even if he didn't campaign because others would
campaign for him. The rules in most states prevented undeclared candidates from winning delegates, Smith replied. "Without a pre-convention
campaign I don't see how a man can get delegates." The reporters coun-
tered that not all states required that a candidate be official. Would he try
to stop a Smith campaign in those places? "I don't see how I could stop
anyone from doing that," Smith said. "I think any man who tried to stop a
thing like that would be biting off more than he could chew, and I won't
do it." Smith said he didn't know what the dominant issue would be in
the upcoming campaign.

    In early April, it appeared that Smith's statement would have no ef-
fect. Although Smith's supporters put him on the ballot in several states,
they found it hard to solicit support in the absence of an active campaign
by their candidate. As predicted, Roosevelt swept the New Hampshire primary, carrying not only the rural portions of the state but the cities where
immigrants and Catholics were a significant minority. The *Stamford Advocate* reported that in Connecticut, the initial enthusiasm for Smith following his statement was on the wane. "The way in which Smith has
been fading out of the picture has been a surprise to nearly everyone," the
paper reported. In California, the trend seemed to be favoring Roosevelt.
Smith supporters in Pennsylvania were not having much success in their
effort to secure votes for an uninstructed delegation of Smith supporters.

    But Roosevelt could not ignore Smith. The Happy Warrior was out-
lining a concrete program for dealing with the economic emergency that
was putting pressure on him to clarify his own fuzzy proposals. Smith had
begun to lay out his own ideas in January 1932 during an address on Jackson Day, the Democrats' annual celebration of Andrew Jackson's birthday. At a Washington dinner, he told two thousand of the party faithful
that the time had come for the federal government to help the unemployed. "If I speak for nobody else I at least speak for myself when I say

that the administration's plans for the relief of unemployment are inde-
fensible," Smith said. Hoover had passed the relief problem to state and
local governments, which had already nearly bankrupted themselves trying to care for the unemployed. Even then, "We are only going to be able
to take care of a little less than half of the heads of families that find
themselves idle in the city of New York," Smith said. He called on the
federal government to immediately issue bonds for public works projects
that would put the unemployed to work. Smith anticipated an immediate
objection to the use of federal credit for unemployment relief by insisting
that it was no different from providing credit to businesses and banks
through the Reconstruction Finance Corporation, which had been created by the Hoover administration to restore the economy by making
loans to business. "Now if it is all right to put the credit of the government
behind business, let the credit of the government be used to keep the wolf
of hunger away from the doormat of millions of people." The bond issue
was indeed the most controversial part of his speech. Newspaper editors
around the country deplored the measure as an extravagance and an unprecedented extension of federal authority.

Smith renewed his call for federal action to fight unemployment several days later during a speech in Boston. Hoover had still not recognized
the severity of the country's problem, Smith charged. "You have got to say
that we are in a state of war—war against unemployment, malnutrition
and the disease and the suffering that grow from it," he said. At least two
things are needed in the emergency, Smith said. First, a federal public
works administrator should be appointed, "clothed with that plenary
power we gave to men during wartime, to carry this war on, to cut
through, slash, tear out the red tape." Second, the federal government
must issue bonds to raise funds for state and local governments. The
country was crying for leadership: "The people of this country are entirely
tired of inaction, of timidity and vacillation. They are crying out loud for
leadership. . . . Self-confidence is the greatest foe of depression. Let the
American people 'pep up'! Let them support this party of ours. Put us in
position to give them the leadership they need, and we will come out of
this trouble."

Roosevelt could no longer afford to remain vague about his plans for
recovery. Smith was working out the details of his proposal for a federal
bond issue, using his weekly syndicated newspaper column to advocate a
$3 billion program whose funds would be split among federal, state, and

local projects. Even Hoover could claim to have a plan for ending the Depression since the creation of the Reconstruction Finance Corporation. On April 7, Roosevelt delivered a radio speech that was intended to outline his approach to the economic crisis. Like Smith, he criticized the view that the RFC could lead the recovery: "These unhappy times call for the building of plans that rest upon the forgotten, the unorganized but the indispensable units of economic power, for plans like those of 1917 that build from the bottom up and not from the top down, that put their faith once more in the forgotten man at the bottom of the economic pyramid." But Roosevelt was no less critical of Smith's plan:

> It is the habit of the unthinking to turn in times like this to the illusions of economic magic. People suggest that a huge expenditure of public funds by the Federal Government and by State and local government will completely solve the unemployment program. But it is clear that even if we could raise many billions of dollars and find definitely useful public works to spend these billions on, even all that money would not give employment to the 7 million or 10 million people who are out of work. Let us admit frankly that it would be only a stop gap. A real economic cure must go to the killing of the bacteria in the system rather than to the treatment of symptoms.

Despite Roosevelt's scathing criticism, his own recommendations for dealing with the Depression were sketchy and intended to appeal mainly to the Southern and Western wings of the party. Roosevelt insisted that government action should be directed in the first instance to restoring the purchasing power of farmers: "How much do the shallow thinkers realize, for example, that approximately one-half of our population of 50 or 60 million people earn their living by farming or in small towns where existence immediately depends on farms?" He also proposed providing relief to small banks and home owners and advocated reducing tariff rates, but offered no steps to alleviate urban unemployment.

Roosevelt's speech was condemned by newspapers for its radical tone and its lack of specifics. To appeal to "the forgotten man" without suggesting what government should do struck many observers as a political trick to win the votes of the suffering. "Why the Governor should feel it necessary to say things which, coming from another, would be called demagogic claptrap, it is hard to understand," the *New York Times* commented. His speech "was of a sort to make his friends sorry and the judicious grieve." Many wondered how Smith would respond to Roosevelt's harsh criticism. They did not have long to wait. He delivered a strong counterattack five days later at another Washington dinner held by the Democratic National Committee.

Smith's speech was the kind a candidate for president was expected to give. It presented a detailed view on a wide range of issues. The problem with those running for office is that nobody wants to get specific about solutions to our problems, Smith said. "The country today is sick and tired of listening to political campaign orators who tell us what is the matter with us. Few, if any, of them know what the cure is. . . . It is a perfectly easy thing to say we must restore the purchasing power of the farmer. Fine! Of course, we must. But how are we going to do it?" His boldest proposal aimed at restoring world trade by declaring a twenty-year moratorium on repayment to the United States of the war debts of the European nations. The money these countries saved as a result could be used to purchase goods around the world. To further encourage the Europeans to resume their import of American goods, Smith proposed to give them a credit against their debts of 25 percent of the value of Americans goods they imported each year. As a further step, Smith called for the creation of a tariff commission that would set American duties on "a scientific basis."

Smith defended his proposal for a public works program as a necessary step for dealing with a prolonged economic crisis. He was not one of those who believed that a federal public works program would quickly restore the nation to prosperity, Smith said. While the public works program would "stimulate industry and promote employment," its main purpose was to provide public jobs for the unemployed as long as the Depression lasted. Smith noted that there had been criticism of the program because its primary goal was relief: "Exception to this has recently been taken in a nation-wide speech by a prominent Democrat on the theory that it is a stop-gap. Who ever said it was anything else? It is at least better than nothing, and infinitely better than the disguised dole in States and municipalities encourage by the Federal government." Having made it clear that it was Roosevelt he was talking about, Smith delivered his hardest blow:

I have recently stated that while I would accept a nomination for the Presidency if it were tendered me by the Convention, that until the Convention assembled, I would not be for or against any candidate. I announce tonight an exception to that statement. I will take off my coat and fight to the end against any candidate who persists in demagogic appeals to the masses of the working people of this country to destroy themselves by setting class against class, rich against poor.

Smith's speech was widely praised. The *New York Times* hailed the resurrection of the Happy Warrior:

People who feared that this Presidential campaign was going to be stale, flat and unprofitable left "Al" Smith out of their reckoning. His speech at the Jefferson dinner in Washington last night did more than flutter the dovecotes. It made even the eagles of the party hide their heads under their wings in fright. For nothing so trenchant and terribly frank was ever uttered on a similar occasion. . . . Upon the toes of all pussy footers he trod remorselessly.

Smith was praised by some Southern newspapers as well. Where the *Times* discerned a new fighting spirit, the *Dallas News* portrayed Smith as the bearer of the party's conscience: "You expect no idealism from Fulton Fish Market, the gas house district and Tammany Hall, but it was their product Al Smith, who voiced the one sure note of idealism at the Democratic Jefferson Day dinner." "Gov. Smith's voice may be the voice of one crying out in the wilderness but like John he may be preparing the way for the return of soundness, sanity and courage in public life," Joseph P. Tumulty wrote in a letter to the *Newark Evening News*.

Smith gained more credibility two weeks later in the Massachusetts and Pennsylvania primaries. The Roosevelt leader in Massachusetts, Mayor Curley of Boston, had badly underestimated Smith strength in the state and committed Roosevelt to a primary fight he could only lose. The Roosevelt candidates were crushed by an average vote of nearly three to one for Smith. "The figures as revealed by the [Boston] Post naturally make me feel very happy and full of gratitude to all my friends in Massachusetts," Smith said. There was more good news from Pennsylvania, where returns showed Smith running even with Roosevelt, though the uninstructed slate had run candidates in only half the constituencies.

Roosevelt would eventually be declared the winner, but Smith had scored a psychological victory. "Al Smith ran an amazing race considering the handicaps he was under," Arthur Krock observed. "His vote was by no means negligible." Of course, Smith heartily agreed. "It ought to put a chock under the Roosevelt band wagon and stop people from jumping on it, on the theory that there is nowhere else to go," he said. Two weeks later, Roosevelt lost the California primary in a stunning upset to Texan John Nance Garner, the Speaker of the U.S. House of Representatives, who was running with the support of McAdoo and Hearst. Garner won convincingly, gaining 211,913 votes to Roosevelt's 167,116. Smith placed third with 135,981, but this didn't prevent him from proclaiming a moral victory: "The vote I got in California is a personal tribute to me and can be regarded in no other light. I had no organization of my own in that State and the regular Democratic organization was against me. I carried the city of San Francisco over both of the other candidates and that without any organization." Now, even Roosevelt's supporters acknowledged that they had lost any chance of an easy victory. "It was obvious that for the first time they envisage a real struggle at Chicago for the nomination," the *New York Times* reported.

While Roosevelt stumbled toward the Democratic convention, Smith appeared to be gaining momentum as a result of a rapid change in the country's attitude toward Prohibition. The strong sentiment for repeal of the Eighteenth Amendment was evident in a New York City demonstration on May 14, when as many as two million people, led by Mayor Jimmy Walker, marched down Fifth Avenue in a "beer parade." Among the marchers were many prominent people, including boxer Gene Tunney, industrialist Walter Chrysler, financier E. F. Hutton, and Mrs. William Randolph Hearst. Three weeks later, John D. Rockefeller announced that he had changed his mind and now opposed Prohibition. Then McAdoo, the hero of the dry forces in 1924, announced his support for a referendum on the issue. Will Rogers noted the rush to change sides: "Why, the drys are diving off the springboard so fast there won't be any room in the water for the original wets. Will H. Hayes, the old Presbyterian circuit rider, went off the sixty-foot board into the deepest part yesterday. Bishop Cannon is just now trying to find a bathing suit that will fit him." The last barrier to Prohibition repeal seemed to crumble when the Republicans, meeting in the same Chicago hall that the Democrats would occupy several weeks later, approved a plank calling for a national referendum on Prohibition.

Smith had reason to believe he had the wind at his back as he boarded the Twentieth Century Limited at Grand Central for the trip to Chicago. A crew of railroad workers led the cheers from the crowd of three hundred that had gathered to see him off. Two small boys pushed their way to the front to shake hands with the former governor. In an interview with reporters on the platform, Proskauer insisted that Smith was a candidate. "We are going to Chicago to obtain the nomination of Alfred E. Smith. Our mission is not to stop anyone or to nominate anyone else," he said. Smith himself had little to say. He was asked to reply to a prediction by Farley that all but four New York delegates would vote for Roosevelt. "That's just some of Jim Farley's ballyhoo," Smith said. Farley's claim that Massachusetts, Rhode Island, Connecticut, and New Jersey would fall in line for Roosevelt was "a bedtime story," he added. Smith refused comment when asked if he was prepared to switch his delegates to Newton Baker. "I'll have a statement when I get to Chicago," Smith said. A reporter asked if he would issue the statement immediately after arriving. "Well, I may take time out to shave and wash up first. I'm an old-fashioned razor man, and I hate to try it on the train." As the train departed, a poster of Smith's face regarded the receding crowd.

In Chicago, Smith plunged back into the political world that he knew so well. As he strode through the lobby of the Congress Hotel, he impressed observers as a vigorous man in the prime of life. Dressed in a conservative blue suit and sporting a white boater hat, the fifty-nine-year-old wore on his face "a ruddy glow of health." After his shave, he proved this appearance of vigor was no illusion, inviting three hundred reporters to "fire away." Smith denied being interested only in blocking Roosevelt. "I do not know anything about the 'Stop Roosevelt movement,'" he said. "I am here to combat a 'Stop Smith' movement which commenced a year and a half ago. I am here to get myself nominated." He was asked for his prescription for Democratic success. "Write an honest, straightforward, to-the-point platform and nominate me for President." The reporters pressed him for an explanation of how he could win. Would he meet with McAdoo to discuss strategy for blocking Roosevelt? "After I finish with you gentlemen, I haven't anything on."

Reaching an agreement with McAdoo, who was managing the Garner campaign, was a vital prerequisite for Smith's plan. Smith and

McAdoo had no reason to like one another. Both were proud, but McAdoo had a reputation for arrogance. Still less did Smith like Hearst, the man behind Garner's candidacy. Nevertheless, Smith and McAdoo met on the same day that Smith had told reporters he had no plans to see the California leader. After a long conference, it was reported that the hatchet had been buried, and it seemed clear that they had buried it in Roosevelt. The day was capped off by a presentation of a five-pound bass by a Chippewa, Chief Man of the Heavens. "Thanks, Chief, I am glad to meet you," Smith remarked. He balked at posing with the fish, however. "I've been posing for nine hours today," Smith told the photographers. "Take one of the other pictures and paint a fish on it."

The 1932 Democratic National Convention opened amid a welter of uncertainties on the evening of Monday, June 27. The platform committee was torn as the wets insisted on a plank advocating repeal. In the convention hall itself, Roosevelt's forces seemed badly outnumbered. The galleries were full of Smith supporters, who greeted their candidate with an ovation. As the applause thundered, Smith shook hands with John F. Curry, the Tammany boss. The first night was auspicious for the Stop Roosevelt movement. The keynote speaker, who had been chosen by the Roosevelt managers, made a long, boring speech. "This was no note. This was in three volumes," Will Rogers complained. Kentucky Senator Alben Barkley's speech also drew attention to the strength of the wet forces. Although a coauthor of the Eighteenth Amendment, Barkley announced that he favored resubmitting the amendment, prompting wild applause and an impromptu demonstration that attracted the standards of all but eight states.

But wet strength didn't necessarily benefit the anti-Roosevelt forces. They lost several decisive votes before the night was over, including their challenges to the credentials of the Roosevelt delegations from Louisiana, Minnesota, and Puerto Rico. William Allen White saw sectional divisions as decisive in the voting. "[T]he Roosevelt bloc . . . as it developed after three ballots in today's convention is obviously a vote of the rural Democracy," White wrote.

Although Roosevelt and his allies had won the first round, Smith and his supporters were soon celebrating a smashing victory on Prohibition. The opening of the third day of the convention was postponed until evening because the platform committee was still fighting over the Prohibition plank. As the convention finally convened shortly before 8 p.m., no one could be sure how the vote on repeal would go. A week earlier, the wets would have been satisfied by the adoption of the "home rule" plank that Smith had supported four years before, which urged that wet states be allowed to legalize the sale of liquor. The platform committee, however, had finally approved a plank advocating repeal. The outcome of the battle was apparent soon after the balloting finally began early Thursday. The first four states to announce their vote in favor of repeal were Kentucky, Louisiana, South Carolina, and Texas. When the ballot was concluded only eight states—Alabama, Arkansas, Georgia, Kansas, Mississippi, Nebraska, North Carolina, and Oklahoma—had backed the minority plank. The majority plank had been adopted 934¾ to 213¾ . The vote stunned even the proponents of change. Raskob feared that he had been too successful. "It's too wet," he said. The vote outraged the drys. "They have adopted a barroom plank," Senator Carter Glass of Virginia complained. Cordell Hull's reaction revived his aching grievance against Smith and Raskob:

> This is a culmination of four years of use of the Democratic organization, with affiliated organizations, equipped with vast monies to quietly hand-pick many delegations and pack the Democratic National Convention with sole reference to the anti-prohibition movement. No serious thought about the Democratic party and vital panic and other public questions is permitted. The purpose is to take over the Democratic party and use it as a pack horse or agency solely to advance the cause of repeal of the Eighteenth Amendment.

Hull's explanation couldn't begin to account for such a wholesale rejection of Prohibition, but it did measure the drys' appetite for revenge.

But would the victory help Smith win the nomination? Except for the wet plank, Roosevelt was largely successful in attaining the platform that he wanted. Smith had hoped to see a plank embodying his plan for canceling much of the European countries' war debts, but in a close vote the resolutions committee backed Roosevelt's position opposing cancellation. Smith had also wanted an unemployment relief plank supporting a federal bond issue for public works. The plank that was finally approved described in general terms an "extension of Federal credit to the States" and

"expansion of the federal program of necessary and useful construction."
A bond issue was not recommended.

Following the late session on Wednesday, the delegates assembled
again on Thursday night to listen to nominating speeches and begin balloting for their nominee. Governor Joseph Ely of Massachusetts gave a
strong speech on Smith's behalf, touching off a demonstration that appeared to outshine the nominating speech for Roosevelt. "A roar with
greater volume than a steamship whistle rose from 20,000 throats," reported the *Times*. Delegates from Massachusetts, Connecticut, Rhode Island, New Jersey, and two territories, the Philippines and the Canal
Zone, trooped into the aisles. Smith supporters in the galleries opened
banners, waved flags and handkerchiefs, and rained confetti upon the
delegates below. The demonstration lasted for a little more than an hour.
"With a flag waving above the entire cast, it looked the finale of a bur-
lesque show," a reporter wrote.

Nevertheless, those in the convention hall at the time of the demonstration saw something that Smith could not see. "[I]t was noticeable that
the enthusiasm was far more marked among the visitors than among the
delegates," a reporter for the *New York Times* observed. William Allen
White put the point bluntly: "[F]or all its glow, Governor Ely's oration
moved the delegates not at all. The modern political convention of 1,000
men, each picked largely because he is a realist and follows orders under
fire, cannot be swept off its feet." Smith listened to Ely's speech and the
roar of the crowd on the radio in his suite at the Congress Hotel. What he
heard convinced him that he was not a has-been.

It was well after midnight when the convention finally turned to the
business of selecting the presidential nominee. The 1,154 delegates were
prepared for an all-night session. The general wisdom was that if Roosevelt was going to be stopped, it would not be until after the second ballot. If he had not attained the 769¼ votes needed for nomination at that
point, it was predicted that his support would begin to erode. The first
ballot was something of an anticlimax as a result. When it concluded at
6:45 a.m., Roosevelt had received 666½ votes; Smith, 201¾; Garner, 90¼;
and Governor Albert C. Ritchie of Maryland, 21. Six favorite sons split
the rest. The anti-Roosevelt forces immediately sought to test the strength
of Roosevelt's control over his delegates. The second ballot showed Roosevelt with 677 delegates, a gain of only eleven. Smith's floor leader Frank

Hague of New Jersey believed that the third ballot would fulfill the prediction that Roosevelt would now begin to lose support. Apparently, Farley was afraid of the same thing. The Roosevelt forces moved for an
adjournment, but the motion failed and the third ballot began. It showed
no dramatic change: Roosevelt gained another five delegates. It seemed
clear that another ballot would not be productive Friday morning. The
delegates needed sleep. The two sides needed time to seek support behind the scenes. An adjournment until 9 p.m. was approved.

The possibility of a deadlock that would deny Roosevelt the nomination grew late Friday afternoon. Roosevelt had hoped to make a deal with
Hearst. He had withdrawn his support for the League of Nations largely
to make himself more acceptable to the isolationist publisher; his opposition to the cancellation of war debts was another step away from "interna-
tionalism." He had offered Garner the vice presidency in a bid for
Hearst's support, but late Friday afternoon Roosevelt learned that Hearst
would not accept him.

Roosevelt was not ready to take no for an answer. Hearst was operating under the assumption that a deadlock between Smith and Roosevelt
would yield a candidate he could support. Roosevelt sent his emissaries to
Hearst once again to describe a different scenario:

> Mr. Hearst had decided not to plump for the Governor, believing
> that, in the event of Mr. Roosevelt's defeat, "the worst he could get
> would be Governor Ritchie of Maryland." Accordingly, the Roo-
> sevelt strategists sent word that the defeat of the Governor would
> be more likely to bring about the nomination of Newton D. Baker,
> anathema to Mr. Hearst because of his views on international af-
> fairs.

Hearst began to have second thoughts about the desirability of deadlock.
After all, it was possible that Smith himself might emerge as the nominee.
This was a possibility too painful to contemplate, for in addition to his dis-
taste for Smith's foreign policy, Hearst had a deep personal enmity that
grew from his long personal feud with Smith. Recognizing that he would
not have the pleasure of nominating his own candidate, Hearst decided to
take what satisfaction he could from smothering Smith's hopes.

Smith learned that California and Texas would vote for Roosevelt about an hour before the convention reconvened. He was shocked. The Mississippi delegation had voted to abandon Roosevelt on the fourth ballot. Roosevelt's defeat appeared to be at hand. He was also angry: friends would later insist that McAdoo and Smith had made a solemn promise to inform one another before announcing a decision to release their delegates. The agreement was designed to prevent either party from being embarrassed. In the minutes before the resumption of the convention, Smith tried to reach McAdoo. When McAdoo refused to take his call, he called Garner. The manager of the hotel informed him that Garner did not wish to speak with him about the obvious subject of his call. There was nothing left to do but take his seat in front of the radio. As the fourth ballot began, McAdoo left his seat in the California delegation and advanced to the podium. Smith turned to Kenny and had a brief, whispered conversation. The office staff began packing as Smith waited to hear McAdoo's speech, his eyes fixed on one of his posters that hung above the radio.

The delegates in the convention hall were slower than Smith to grasp the significance of McAdoo's appearance at the podium. They had heard rumors of a break to Roosevelt by California and Texas, but they had heard many rumors. Most expected another long night of balloting. As McAdoo began to speak, the convention hall grew quiet:

> We believe . . . that California should take a stand here tonight that will bring this contest to a swift and, we hope, satisfactory conclusion—a stand, we hope, which will be promotive of party harmony, a stand taken with the utmost unselfishness and regardless of our own views of the situation—a stand prompted by the fact that our belief in Democracy is such that when any man comes into this convention with the popular will behind him to the extent of almost 700 votes . . .

McAdoo was interrupted. During the last moments of his speech, the hall had grown as "silent as a great cathedral during mass," a reporter observed. As the delegates suddenly realized the import of his words, cheering erupted on the floor and booing began in the balconies. The American flag began to wave above a dozen delegations at once. A *New York Times* reporter described the scene:

Suddenly a rebel yell split the air, and the delegates from Texas . . .
were out of their seats waving the standard of their State and above
it their Lone Star flag. . . . A Texan, who probably won't remember
what he did, half ran, half fell through the aisle to the rostrum and
surrendered the . . . flag of Texas to Mr. McAdoo, who received it
with a grim but satisfied smile. Like knights raising their petards
[*sic*] before their king, the standard bearers gathered before the
tall, straight Mr. McAdoo and held aloft the standards of their
States.

As the demonstration died out, the people in the galleries began to make
themselves heard.

The galleries refused to permit McAdoo to finish his speech. As he approached the microphone, "there rolled down from the overcrowded balconies an ominous and sonorous roar of disapproval." McAdoo waited for
several minutes for the booing to subside. At last he turned to Senator
Walsh, who called on Anton Cermak. "I appeal to the Mayor of the city
of Chicago to control this convention," Walsh demanded. Cermak tried.
"Please, I appeal to you, allow this great gathering to go back home with
nothing but pleasant memories," he implored. The crowd listened quietly
to their mayor, some even applauded, but the booing resumed as soon as
McAdoo moved toward the microphone. Convinced that the opposition
of the galleries was implacable, McAdoo pushed ahead, placing his lips
against the microphone. His final comments were delivered over a roar of
opposition:

> I intend to say what I propose to say here without regard to what
> the galleries or anybody else thinks. . . . I want to create no
> wounds. I had a very ineffectual part in the wounds that were cre-
> ated against my wish in 1924. . . . The great State of Texas and the
> great State of California are acting in accord with what we believe
> best for America and for the Democratic Party. I would like to see
> Democrats fight Republicans, and not Democrats, unlike 1924.
> Our decision represents the will of these delegates.

By the end of his speech McAdoo was shouting to be heard. "California
casts 44 votes for Franklin D. Roosevelt," he said at last. The convention

had reached its climax. As the balloting continued, states began to switch their votes to Roosevelt. Even Mississippi recorded a unanimous delegation for Roosevelt. Only the Smith states refused to make the nomination unanimous. By the end of the balloting the Smith headquarters had been disassembled and packed away.

It was immediately clear that the nomination of Franklin D. Roosevelt on July 1, 1932, marked a new stage in the struggle between Southern and Western Democrats on one hand, and Democrats from the North and East on the other. Though McAdoo had portrayed the switch by California and Texas as a step toward party unity, it was actually a move to consolidate the strength of the South and West.

Given the long-standing sectional conflict and the personal animosities between Smith and his recent allies, McAdoo and Hearst, it became difficult to understand how Smith ever expected to defeat Roosevelt. Smith was not around to explain. He had refused to comment on Roosevelt's nomination on Friday night. The next day, his friends described him as "exceptionally cheerful" at breakfast. "He even sang while he ate," one of them said. But his bitterness was too plain to be denied. He was returning to New York on a 12:30 p.m. train and would therefore miss Roosevelt, who was flying to Chicago to deliver his acceptance address. Smith left the Congress Hotel by a side door to avoid the crowd that was arriving to greet Roosevelt. The nominee appeared conciliatory as he arrived at the Chicago airport. As he was assisted to his car, several in the crowd called, "Don't forget to make up with Al Smith." "I'll do that," Roosevelt promised. But Roosevelt's thoughts were on his acceptance speech. Before an enthusiastic crowd in the convention hall, he promised, "I pledge you—I pledge myself—to a new deal for the American people." Almost half of the delegates had already left for home. Their seats and the galleries were filled with invited guests. Like Smith, many of those who had left believed that in this New Deal they had been dealt out.

# 11 ✳ REPEAL AND REFORM

There had always been a risk in Roosevelt's strategy for capturing the Democratic nomination. To win the delegates from the South and West he had rejected Smith's endorsement, gambling that he could win the nomination without alienating Democrats in the North and East. In the days after the Chicago convention, this was a bet that Roosevelt appeared to have lost. The *Times* of London observed:

> Mr. Roosevelt has only secured the election after a struggle which has left a large section of his party in a mood of bitter resentment. . . . A few months ago the Democratic victory in the Presidential election appeared inevitable. Since then, open dissensions in the party have weakened its chances and at the moment President Hoover's chances would seem to be at least as good as Mr. Roosevelt's.

Roosevelt had achieved an important victory over his foes, but now he had to unite the party, and Smith's endorsement appeared to be crucial. In the general election, the Happy Warrior's supporters numbered in the millions. As Smith's train sped home, many believed that only he could persuade them to vote for Roosevelt.

Bitterness against Roosevelt ran deep. In the first place, he had benefited from what many perceived to be a corrupt deal with McAdoo and Hearst that not only defeated but humiliated Smith. Smith supporters insisted that Smith and McAdoo had an ironclad agreement not to release their delegates without consulting one another. This would give either party the opportunity to make the best possible deal and withdraw gracefully. McAdoo's apparent insincerity in his agreement with Smith raised questions about the honesty of the Garner candidacy itself. The sense of betrayal was compounded by the fact that the vice presidential nominee was a Texan whose loyalty to the ticket in 1928 had been suspect. To some it seemed that Roosevelt had made a deal with the devil. Peter E. Laughlin wrote to Frank P. Walsh, a Missouri native, describing the reaction of Kansas City Catholics:

> I am amazed at the widespread resentment among many of "our" people over the turn down of Smith and the intrusion of Mr. McAdoo in such a spectacular fashion. Only yesterday, I ran into eight votes in two houses, always strong Democrats, but vowing they would vote for Hoover. Upon my effort to placate them, the reply came with force, "The damn Kluckers [sic] foisted Hoover upon the country in 1928, and we will try to inflict him back on the — — —."

Laughlin insisted that unless some effort were made to appease them, "many thousands" of Catholics in Missouri would abandon the Democratic ticket. In late August, Massachusetts Senator David I. Walsh confirmed that New England Democrats still felt "considerable disappointment" over the convention's failure to nominate Smith and were only gradually reconciling themselves to Roosevelt. The *New York Times* reported two months later that while Boston men were beginning to rally around Roosevelt, Boston women remained bitter: "Their attitude appears to be that the party at Chicago notified their sons that they no longer need apply for a Presidential nomination. It will be more difficult to deal with that primal emotion."

At first Smith was as angry as his supporters. The man who was said to have been cheerful and singing at breakfast on the morning of his departure for New York was reported to have discussed with several of his party on the train the possibility of a trip to Europe, which would keep him out of the country during the fall campaign, quietly depriving the Democratic ticket of his support. Smith asked Proskauer what he should do. Proskauer pointed out that in his acceptance address Roosevelt had committed himself wholeheartedly to the platform. He had specifically promised to repeal Prohibition. It was impossible to oppose a candidate who had taken such a strong stand in support of Smith's position, Proskauer said. Smith agreed, but he told Proskauer to make a note to himself in his notebook—six months after inauguration the platform would be in the "trash can," Smith said.

Smith waited five days before announcing his support for the Democratic ticket. He was receiving thousands of letters and telegrams urging him to continue his race for the presidency. His statement addressed this hope directly:

> To them I say it is not practical in our country to start a third party at this time, as it would simply register a negative vote which would accomplish nothing for the people in their hour of need. . . . The question before us today for decision is, shall the record of the last 12 years of Republican administration be approved at the polls in November? As far as I am concerned, I am totally dissatisfied with that record and shall do nothing to lend it countenance. I shall therefore support the Democratic party.

Reporters followed up the statement with questions. He was asked about his rumored trip to Europe. "That's a joke," he replied. Did he plan to meet with Roosevelt? "I'm not going to speak about that today," Smith said. He pointed to the statement. "That is all there is. You asked for it and you got it." For the next three months, Republicans would try to exploit Catholic discontent by feigning sympathy over the treatment of the Happy Warrior. But any hope Smith would help them died in early October when the Democratic Party announced his speaking schedule for the campaign. Smith was indeed preparing to settle old scores—but it was the Republican Party that would be the target. On October 24, crowds estimated at 250,000 greeted him as his motorcade left the Holland Tunnel and carried him to Newark's 113th Regiment Armory, where 30,000 waited to hear him. Smith quieted the crowd with a reminder that the Democratic Party was paying to broadcast his speech nationally. "Well, now we will go after them," he told the audience, which responded with laughter.

Smith measured the distance that the country had traveled in four years. "[W]e are all four years older, but we are certainly at least 40 years wiser," he said. Four years before, the American people had gullibly accepted the Republican Party's promise of perpetual prosperity. Smith had always limited himself to the prosperity issue in discussing the ways that the Republicans had deceived the voters in 1928. But he now addressed the religious issue publicly for the first time since his Oklahoma City speech. While the Republicans had never raised the issue of his Catholicism directly, they had used defense of the Eighteenth Amendment as a symbol of opposition to a Catholic president, Smith charged. The anti-Catholic campaign began the minute he sent his telegram to the Democratic convention restating his intention to seek a modification of the Prohibition amendment: "And as a result of that, after the convention was over, there sprang up all over the country a wide-spread opposition to me because of that telegram, which we all found out afterward was nothing more nor less than a cloak for bigotry."

Smith drew his charge carefully. He was not complaining about the bigotry that arose from ignorance but about its exploitation by people who knew better: "[W]hat I found particular fault with was that the Republican party, with its money, its power and its influence, incited and encouraged that spirit of bigotry. They should have discouraged it. But it meant votes and dissension within the Democratic ranks, and it is a matter of record that it was encouraged." Smith reminded his audience of Mabel Willebrandt's speech to the Methodist Conference in Ohio. Since the election, Mrs. Willebrandt had written a book in which she alleged that the Republican National Committee had ordered her to give that speech and had specifically approved the text of her address, including her call for the churches to use their influence to defeat Smith. "All the bigotry and intolerance that arose throughout the country because of her remarks can be directly charged to that political committee," Smith said.

Smith charged that the Republicans were continuing to use Prohibition to attract anti-Catholic votes. The Republican plank promised a referendum on Prohibition without committing the party to do anything, even if a majority favored repeal: "Consequently, it is easy for them to receive the approval of the Anti-Saloon League, the Woman's Christian Temperance Union, the Ku Klux Klan and the aggregation of bigots that make up what we call the dry forces." The Republican plank was barely an improvement over the planks of the past. "[I]t leaves the Republican party today where it was in 1928, the party of bigotry, of deceit and of hypocrisy," Smith said. By contrast, the Democratic plank was unequivocal in its commitment to repeal. "I wrote that plank," Smith said. He concluded by plugging the Democratic nominees by name for the first time, calling for the election of "Roosevelt, Garner and the entire Democratic ticket."

The reaction to Smith's speech by both Democratic and Republican party officials was mixed. The Republicans sidestepped Smith's indictment of their 1928 campaign and criticized his remarks about Prohibition. " 'Give us beer, give us something to drink.' What a magnificent political creed," Senator William E. Borah said. Borah also attacked Smith for damning all Prohibitionists. "He denounced as bigots, cranks, hypocrites and intellectual crooks all who are not in favor of tearing down all barriers against the return of the liquor traffic," he said. Privately, Republicans expressed delight at Smith's charge of intolerance against the dry forces, believing that it might create dissension among the Democrats. It was reported that some Democrats were concerned about this too. Democratic headquarters received complaints from Democrats in the South and West. Even the friendly *New York Times* defended Smith halfheartedly. "It was personal, but pardonable," an editorial concluded. Democratic leaders were more concerned that Smith had not given Roosevelt a stronger endorsement. Clearly, Smith must do more to persuade Catholics not to vote for Hoover. He had to give them a reason to vote for Roosevelt.

Smith opened his next speech in Boston with the fullest expression yet of his desire to deliver his supporters to Roosevelt. Massachusetts had supported Smith in 1928 more strongly than any other state, including New York, and he returned its affection. But he immediately made it clear that his speech was about the future, not the past: "I came here for the purpose and I propose to show that the purpose was well-founded and that purpose is to come into New England and ask for the unqualified full and complete support of Franklin D. Roosevelt." "The Republican Failure," as Smith described it, was a failure of leadership. Hoover was blaming the Democrats in Congress for thwarting his plans for recovery. But other political leaders had conquered hostile legislatures, including Roosevelt, who "made a record of achievement that made him prominent enough throughout the United States to be nominated for President." Smith's old nemesis, the Kansas journalist William Allen White, had recently tried to score points for his candidate by raising doubts about Roosevelt's upper-class background. Smith reminded the audience that in 1928 White had extolled Hoover as a man of cultural accomplishment. "In 1928 Hoover was the cultured man and I was the fish peddler; in 1932 Frank Roosevelt is the cultured man and poor Herbert is the little boy around his father's blacksmith shop."

But this was not the most dramatic shift in Republican propaganda. Smith denounced Republican efforts to curry favor with Catholics by appearing to mourn the failure of the Chicago convention to nominate him. "Now, I am not a suspicious person by nature, was not born that way," he explained. "I have the kindliest feelings for every living being." But "I am a little suspicious when Senator Moses gets so terribly excited and wrought up and speaks with a sob in his voice because I wasn't nominated and what a terrible thing it was." Smith insisted that he didn't want sympathy from the Republicans. He had accused them of exploiting religious prejudice in 1928 and that was exactly what they were attempting in 1932. Playing the religious card wouldn't work this time, Smith said. The Republicans in 1928 had forgotten the principles upon which the country was established, but Catholics could not. "There can be no bigotry, there can be no resentment in the Catholic heart," Smith said. Catholics would demonstrate their gratitude for America's promise of equal opportunity and religious freedom by doing the right thing for their country. "[T]he salvation of the country, the progress that it must make to get away from the stagnation of business and unemployment, lies upon the success of the Democratic ticket under the leadership of Franklin D. Roosevelt and John Garner," he concluded.

The reception that Smith received on his way back to New York showed the evident relief of all Democrats, including his supporters, that the party was united again. His path took him through the larger cities in western Massachusetts. Although suffering from a cold, he spoke several times from the back of the train. Once again the people showed that they adored him. A man who had managed to force his way through the crowd to shake Smith's hand was observed kissing his palm as he retreated. Catholic priests anxious to express their approval of Smith's speech were prominent in the crowd. There were also many children. As his train pulled out of Worcester, a cigar fell from Smith's pocket, touching off a brawl among the children trying to retrieve it. Smith encountered his biggest crowd at Springfield: "Watchers filled the windows of a score of factories for a half mile before the station was reached," the *New York Times* reported. "They packed the roofs of train sheds, they swarmed on the tracks. In waiting trains windows were flung open." The crowd was estimated at 30,000. Another five thousand were waiting at Pittsfield. Smith was clearly enjoying himself. Someone in the passing crowd wanted Smith's view of Mabel Willebrandt. "How about Mabel?" he asked. "She's alright," Smith replied with a smile. Finally, his train crossed into New York and headed for Albany.

Although it was late when Smith arrived, he went directly from the train station to the Executive Mansion. Smith was led to the library, where he and Roosevelt promptly lit up, Roosevelt a cigarette and Smith a cigar. They talked privately for an hour before inviting in the newspaper reporters. Both men were at pains to demonstrate their friendliness. Could this meeting be described as an old-fashioned "Frank and Al get-together"? one reporter asked. "Go as far as you like," Smith replied. "If we were a couple of Frenchmen, we'd kiss each other. As it is, we have to rely on a handshake." There is absolute friendliness? "Well, you don't see any blood, do you?" Smith replied. Smith joked that he had been so engrossed in campaigning that he had forgotten it was Friday. "I came near eating meat today," he said.

On the stage of the Brooklyn Academy of Music, Smith and Roosevelt gave the public visible proof that their friendship had been restored. The theater was small compared to other arenas, but it had traditionally served as one of the final forums in any state campaign. On the evening of November 4, a capacity crowd of four thousand was waiting to see Smith and Roosevelt together for the first time since their reconciliation. Only slowly did the noisy crowd become aware of the remarkable scene unfolding before it. Roosevelt was entering, walking slowly with the assistance of his son Elliot. As soon as the crowd realized that the other man assisting the governor was Smith, pandemonium erupted.

> When the crowd realized fully that the Happy Warrior and the man who gave Mr. Smith that appellation in placing him in nomination for the Presidency in 1924, were giving concrete evidence of the reconciliation, effected last week at the Executive Mansion

at Albany, the men and women in the audience went wild. Not a person in the hall remained seated. All jumped up and cheered the spectacle of the two old friends, again united in friendship, smiling down upon them.

The crowd quieted only when Smith insisted. "The hour is late and the 'raddio' is costly," he joked. Smith's humor appeared to confirm the return of good feeling: "At Madison Square Garden on Monday night the President made the extraordinary statement that if we did anything to the tariff the churches, the schools and the hospitals would decay and grass would grow on the principal streets of our great city. So what do you think I did about it? I immediately made arrangements for a putting green."

On election night, it was almost possible to forget there had ever been a split between Smith and Roosevelt. Smiling broadly and waving his brown derby, Smith arrived at Democratic headquarters at the Biltmore Hotel shortly after 9:30 p.m. By then, Roosevelt's victory was assured. The victorious campaign of the Democrats seemed to have dissolved all bitterness. Even John Raskob appeared to have recovered. He wrote Farley, "There never was a candidate fighting for the presidency who conducted himself with greater dignity, and kept in a happier mood than did Governor Roosevelt, who, too, refrained from mud-slinging or in any other way losing his self-respect for a single instant." For the moment at least, all Democrats shared a feeling of deep satisfaction over Roosevelt's victory.

It would be four long months before Roosevelt took office. Meanwhile, the country's suffering continued. In New York City, unemployment had reached 750,000—30 percent. There had been 280,000 evictions in the preceding eight months, and it was estimated that between 150,000 and 200,000 families were in need of relief. City government did not have enough money to provide relief to all because tax receipts had fallen as unemployment rose. Property tax collections were $35 million behind the previous year. The city was caring for only 126,000 families, providing a bare $23 per family monthly. Nearly 900,000 people were depending on private charity. The city had requested $25 million in loans from the city's banks to cover the cost of an expanded relief program through the spring, but the bankers balked, worried by the city's rapid approach to insolvency. Making matters worse, New York City was in the midst of a political crisis as Tammany and its critics battled to see who would replace Jimmy Walker, who had been forced to resign over charges that he had taken bribes from companies doing business with the city.

Al Smith helped fill the leadership vacuum in New York. When, at the end of October, the bankers refused to loan the city any more money for relief, Smith lectured them publicly. City officials had asked for $25 million in loans to cover six months of relief, hoping to avoid the anxiety of the previous winter, when loans were made month by month, often at the last minute. The bankers were unwilling to make such a large commitment. They argued that the city's finances could not justify such a large bond offering and that it made no difference that the loans were for purposes of relief. Smith rejected good business practice at a time of emergency. "I regard the question of relief as aside from organized business," he said as he committed the County Trust to purchasing $100,000 in municipal bonds. When the bankers continued to resist, Smith suggested the appointment of a small committee "to thrash out the problem." Acting Mayor Joseph V. McKee named a committee including Smith, officials of the National City and Chase Banks, the comptroller, and the president of the Board of Aldermen.

Smith was more than an advocate for New York. He was its spiritual leader. When a meeting of the bankers' committee conflicted with a previous commitment to the New York Infirmary for Women and Children, Smith abandoned the bankers to lead a sing-along at Town Hall. "Today I started the block canvass for unemployment relief, so I don't know of anything more appropriate than 'The Sidewalks of New York,' " he explained. The singing began badly. Smith missed his cue, forcing the orchestra to begin again. As he struggled to be heard, he looked nervous. Flashbulbs popped in his face, but he gained confidence as the song progressed. As he finished the chorus, he resumed his accustomed role. "With one hand," according to the *Times*, "he waved the orchestra back into the chorus and with the other and his knees he invited the audience to come along. It did." He was completely at home as he led the singing of "The Bowery": "Bending over like a cheerleader, Mr. Smith came up suddenly on the second word, and he continued through the leading of the chorus to jump around like one. The song ended with a roar. And thundering applause could not woo the singer back."

The applause of a large crowd must have sounded particularly good to

Smith just then. He was the president of one company and the chairman of another—and both posts brought him little but heartache. Every day Smith went to his office at the Empire State Building to make calls in a vain effort to attract new tenants. Bankruptcies had thrown millions of square feet of office space on the market during 1932, forcing landlords to slash rents in a desperate effort to stave off their own creditors. With the financial backing of the du Ponts, Smith did not have to worry about bankruptcy. But he could only have felt helpless as he knocked on doors that wouldn't open. The presidency of the Empire State Building in 1933 amounted to little more than leading celebrities on tours and urging the staff to pinch pennies.

The chairmanship of the Country Trust was hardly less painful. Although the bank was not threatened with collapse, it was involved in an embarrassing lawsuit against two of Smith's friends, Timothy J. Mara, a sports promoter, and Patrick F. Kenny, a contractor. When campaign money was running low in 1928, County Trust president James Riordan had persuaded Mara, Kenny, and a dozen of Smith's close friends to "borrow" money from the Country Trust and give it to the campaign. Riordan told them the loans would be repaid from campaign contributions received after Smith won the election, but soon after Riordan's suicide the bank began efforts to collect the loans. Mara and Kenny refused to pay, forcing the bank to sue them. Smith had known nothing of the loans at the time, but this did not spare him publicity that suggested his campaign had benefited from illegal contributions. Nor did it relieve him of the responsibility of collecting the loans from men who had been trying to help him—many of whom were already in financial trouble.

As the inauguration neared, Smith could hardly have escaped the hope that he would be rescued from the business world by an appointment in the new administration. His personal relationship with Roosevelt had continued to improve as they worked together in the weeks following the election in an effort to persuade the New York state legislature to adopt a plan for charter reform for New York City. They also had a common interest in the success of the administration of the new governor, Herbert Lehman, whose candidacy they had both supported. The idea that Smith would soon be moving to Washington did not seem farfetched. In January there was a rumor that Smith might be asked to reorganize the Reconstruction Finance Corporation.

Belle Moskowitz had never believed that Roosevelt would put Smith in his administration. A Roosevelt hater for the past four years, she would have cautioned Smith against getting his hopes up, but Moskowitz died suddenly on January 2 at the age of fifty-six. The news reached Smith in Albany during Lehman's inauguration. He was overwhelmed with grief. Unable to answer reporters' questions as he boarded the train to return to New York, he could only reply, "She had the greatest brain of anybody I ever knew." On arrival in New York, Smith walked slowly through Grand Central, his head bowed. He explained later, "When I was asked in Albany to comment on the death of my friend, I had to refuse, because it was simply impossible to collect my thoughts. The sad news put a damper on everything that had happened in Albany. It would not have been possible for any news to have come that would have distressed me more. I regard the passing of Mrs. Moskowitz as a disaster." Frances Perkins sent Smith her condolences. "I have your letter. I read it carefully," he replied. "The loss of Mrs. Moskowitz was a severe blow. She was a loyal, faithful and devoted friend and we are going to miss her very much."

In the months that followed, the idea of Smith's joining the administration seemed more and more plausible. There was more in Smith's favor than his proven administrative ability. There was the perception that Roosevelt would choose from both the more radical wing of the party, which included men like Huey Long and Senator Burton Wheeler of Montana, and the leaders from the East, who had always opposed the inflationary policies of the rural Democrats. Smith was obviously the most prominent Eastern leader, and he may well have believed that he had a good chance to be appointed to some top post. His official position was that he was "too busy" to join the cabinet or head the RFC. It appeared that Smith and Roosevelt were on the verge of a permanent reconciliation at a dinner given in Roosevelt's honor at the Manhattan Club on February 20. In remarks there, Smith urged the party to unite behind the new president. Turning to Roosevelt, he pledged his own support, touching off a standing ovation.

If Smith had any hopes for himself, they collapsed suddenly two days later when Roosevelt's cabinet appointments were announced. The president-elect confounded the political pundits by choosing men almost exclusively from the Southern and Western wing of the party. Not only did he fail to recognize party leaders from the North and East, he selected several men who were well-known enemies of Smith. The new secretary of state was to be Cordell Hull. While Hull's appointment could be justified by his experience in foreign affairs, there was no fig leaf to cover the selection of Daniel C. Roper as secretary of commerce. Roper, who had supported Hoover in 1928, had been forced on Roosevelt by McAdoo, who had originally hoped to make him secretary of the Treasury. Roper had no industrial experience and was obviously a political appointee. Two Catholics were named to the cabinet: Farley became postmaster general and Thomas J. Walsh, attorney general. But when Walsh died on his way to the inaugural, Roosevelt chose a McAdoo man as his replacement. The Republicans immediately tried to use the cabinet appointments to exacerbate divisions within the Democratic Party. Calling it the "small-time cabinet," they asked, "Where are Young, Baruch, Smith and Baker?"

Smith was worried about the direction of the new administration. There were growing demands for radical action to end the Depression, and many of them originated in the rural wing of the Democratic Party. This wing of the party had a long history of supporting panaceas like making silver legal tender as a way of solving complex economic problems. Recently it had given the country Huey Long, the Louisiana demagogue who proposed to end the Depression by confiscating all fortunes over $1 million and redistributing them to the poor. As an urbanite, Smith was naturally suspicious of inflationary schemes that raised prices for the farmer by taking the money out of the pockets of urban workers who received fixed wages. But he was even more opposed to the rhetoric of populism, which portrayed a world divided between the people and their exploiters. This was the same kind of language that Hearst used, and Smith opposed it for the same reason that he had opposed the publisher: it led the poor to attack the only system that gave them a chance to escape poverty. He was also convinced that it was Bryan's use of this rhetoric that had frightened the urban middle class away from the Democratic Party.

At the root of Smith's dislike for the populists was a deep distrust of their honesty. Men like Bryan and Hearst claimed to be for "the people," but what seemed to interest them most was power. This distrust had been reinforced only a year earlier when Long had visited Smith at his apartment. Sitting with a drink in his hand, Long had urged Smith to soften his position on Prohibition so that he could support him for president. "Don't spoil my chances of putting you in the White House," Long said. He acknowledged that the South was no drier than any other part of the country. Southerners supported the ban on liquor because "there are some people we don't want to get it," he explained, apparently referring to African-Americans. Smith excused himself and made a telephone call to the man who had set up the meeting. "John, come and get this fellow. Otherwise, I'm going to throw him off the roof," Smith said.

By March 1933 a growing number of Democrats appeared to be joining Huey Long in embracing radical measures. Smith had recently been appointed editor of the magazine *New Outlook*, and he used the March issue to portray the Democratic Party at a crossroads. "The radical and conservative elements in the party are widely and deeply at variance," Smith wrote. He left no doubt about which side he was on: "The Democratic Party, in my opinion must rid itself of the counsels of the minority of bigots, fanatics, populists, demagogues, mountebanks and crackpots who masquerade as leaders and give the party a bad name with sensible people." He condemned "the fanatics who dragged religion and liquor into politics" and "the populists who blighted the party for so many years with their free silver and other economic heresies." Without naming Long, Smith slammed him along with "the mountebanks with their clownish tactics and their irresponsible ravings against millionaires and big business."

Despite his misgivings, Smith attended Roosevelt's inauguration and marched with the Tammany delegation in the Democratic victory parade. As the New Deal got under way, his doubts began to ease, and he was soon expressing strong support for Roosevelt's legislative program. In the April issue of *New Outlook*, he praised Roosevelt for acting quickly to take control of the situation: "It is wise for the new Administration to take full advantage of its large majorities in the new Congress and of the popular approval at the very beginning of the special session, to drive through emergency legislation. A great many things can be done now which cannot be done later." Specifically, he approved of the banking legislation that had been introduced. "We must work toward a unified banking system under national control," Smith said. He also supported the administration's proposals on currency reform, reorganization of the federal government, reduction of veterans' benefits, taxation of beer (soon to be legal with the repeal of Prohibition), and the farm problem. Smith was satisfied that Roosevelt had chosen the right path:

> I said last month that the Democratic party was at the crossroads. I will say now that it has taken the right turn, and that every one in the country, irrespective of party, or other affiliations, should support the new Administration loyally and patriotically in the path on which it is now moving—because I am satisfied that it is the path back to economic health and happiness.

Smith's approval of the general course of the New Deal did not mean he agreed with all of Roosevelt's programs. In the same issue in which he called on the country to support the new administration, he expressed a lack of enthusiasm for the proposed Tennessee Valley Authority and other regional planning programs. He said he was generally opposed to resettlement schemes, believing people should be allowed to remain on their native land if that was what they wanted. But Smith's biggest objection was that these plans had little to do with boosting employment, which was what the cities needed most. Even the proposed reforestation programs that would transport urban youths to the wilderness were off target. Smith was impatient for a new deal in the cities.

Three months later, near the end of Roosevelt's historic first hundred days, Smith found himself in strong support of the New Deal. The gains that had been made by the inflationists were small compared to the triumph that supporters of public works appeared to have achieved. In a column on inflation, Smith indicated that he was not unalterably opposed to monetary inflation but made it clear that it should be used only as a last resort. First, let the administration try to inflate the economy through public works, Smith said. By the beginning of June, Smith had become convinced that Roosevelt agreed with him. By then the administration had introduced the National Industrial Recovery Act. Although Smith was skeptical about the act's effort to boost employment through government-enforced trade agreements, he supported fully the part of the bill that provided for the issuance of public works bonds. "There are heartening evidences that there is to be an entirely new deal in public works," he said. On June 22 Smith defended the New Deal in an address at the Harvard commencement. While frankly acknowledging the experimental nature of much of the New Deal legislation, he insisted that it was operating under firm democratic control:

> We need not worry too much about a dictatorship because of this drastic and revolutionary legislation that we have had in the last two months. It took long hours to write down, to draw it up and put it into legal phraseology, but the shortest statute in this country is a repeal. All you have to say is, "Chapter 619 of the laws of 1923 is hereby repealed." That is easy. The page boys and the assistant sergeant at arms in either the House of Representatives or the Senate can draw up a repeal act.

Although a dissenter on details, the Happy Warrior was a New Dealer in spirit on June 22, 1933.

Even as Smith called for support for the Roosevelt administration's experiments, however, he was growing increasingly conservative. He had always had a keen appreciation of the danger posed by arbitrary government. As a leader of the permanent minority in the state legislature, he had seen the Republicans abuse power, turning government into a tool for benefiting their communities and friends simply because they could get away with it. But there was more at stake than money. Arbitrary government could punish a man for his personal beliefs by denying him free speech. It could control his form of worship. It could, in short, deprive him of the individual liberties that are at the core of American freedom. During his legislative and gubernatorial careers, this sensitivity was balanced by his desire to see the power of government grow to protect the health and safety of workers. As governor, Smith had dismissed the Republicans' charge that public housing and government ownership of waterpower were socialistic because he knew that expanding the power of the state in these instances was enhancing democracy, not threatening it. He also believed that his reforms had made New York government more democratic. But Smith's fear of arbitrary government grew in the years after 1928.

The first sign of the change in Smith's thinking occurred on March 7, 1931, when he announced in his syndicated column that he no longer supported the direct primary. This was a major reversal. As governor,

Smith had made restoration of the primary, which had been repealed by the Republicans in 1921, one of his legislative priorities. "It is a fundamental policy that no one can question, unless he is prepared to make the charge that the people who elect are incapable of nominating," Smith said in the annual message to the legislature in 1923. But the Republicans continued to block the primary for statewide offices, and in his column in March 1931, Smith said the Republicans had been right. The main problem was that turnout for the primaries had never lived up to expectations, Smith said. As a result, small groups of voters with fanatical views on particular subjects had been able to gain control of the nominating process. As the price of their support, they demanded that the candidate vote their views, even when a majority of his constituents believed otherwise. It was Prohibition that had revealed the danger in direct primaries:

> In New York State and, for that matter, throughout the country, men are elected to Congress who do not believe the presence of the Eighteenth Amendment in the Constitution to be in the best interests of all the people. In some states these men know that the overpowering majority of the rank and file of the people of their own states are opposed to it. Their own district may even be opposed to it, but they are compelled to be for it because the active minority of the district, which may constitute a majority of the participants in the primary, controls the result.

Smith believed that the primary had made it possible for a minority to impose Prohibition on the majority in New York and other states. The only way to restore democracy was to return to a system under which nominations for office were made by party leaders. "If we are to have success under our system we must have the assumption of responsibility by political parties," he wrote.

Smith's desire to prevent abuses of power soon led him to an even more significant—and painful—reversal, when he withdrew his support for the proposed Child Labor Amendment. He had long advocated the adoption of the amendment, which gave Congress the power to "limit, regulate and prohibit" the labor of minors under eighteen. It was a natural extension of his pioneering role in the limitation of child labor in New York State. When the Depression revived interest in the amendment, however, Smith gave serious consideration to the arguments against it. As he deliberated, he began to see similarities between the amendment and Prohibition. A single national standard could work to the disadvantage of some groups more than others, he wrote in the *New Outlook* in October 1932: "[F]reedom of persons under 18 from labor is not an absolute, basic human right. It is a relative matter of age, race, climate, family and economic conditions, and local sentiment. In other words, it is a matter to be settled by the conscience and common-sense of each community and not by Federal mandate."

Smith expressed doubts about whether the federal government could enforce a child labor amendment any better than it could the Prohibition amendment. But the fundamental issue was whether the federal government could be trusted with another broad grant of power. The amendment was vague. What did it mean by "limit" and "regulate" labor? Would Congress seek to take advantage of this vagueness as it had exploited the term "intoxicating liquors" in the Eighteenth Amendment? "Who knows what kind of laws will be passed by Congress under the authority to limit and regulate?" Smith asked. Some critics were saying it would give the federal government power over education. Smith hated child labor, but he feared a new constitutional amendment more. "After careful, and I may say almost prayerful, consideration of these arguments for and against the child labor amendment, I wish to be recorded in the negative," Smith announced.

> I find it difficult and distressing to oppose now my loyal comrades of these early battles. I have, however, learned in recent years the bitter lessons of the Eighteenth Amendment. I devoutly hope that the people of this country will not permit themselves to be deluded by sentiment, tricked by false logic, coerced by minorities, or stampeded by rhetoric, into a repetition of their recent monumental folly in attempting to legislate morality into the United States Constitution.

As the end of Prohibition finally came into view, Smith became increasingly preoccupied by its "lessons."

His countrymen were not so philosophical. By the fall of 1932, the only thing they could say for sure about Prohibition was that they wanted it gone. Roosevelt's election on a repeal platform sealed its fate. In February 1933 Congress approved a new constitutional amendment repealing the Eighteenth Amendment and sent it to the states for ratification. The Twenty-first Amendment was approved less than a year later.

Smith received much of the credit for repeal. In April, soon after Congress approved the sale of beer, the Anheuser-Busch brewing company sent a wagon drawn by its famous Clydesdale horses to the front door of the Empire State Building where Smith was presented with a case of beer. "My only regret is that the wagon load is not all mine," Smith joked. More formal recognition followed in June when Smith was elected chairman of the New York convention called to ratify the repeal amendment. As he arrived in Albany for the convention, Smith was greeted by thousands of happy supporters. Accompanied by a marching band, the triumphant wets paraded to the grounds of the Capitol where Lieutenant Governor Herbert H. Lehman welcomed Smith. "To him, more than any one in the country, belongs the credit for the victory which is now in sight," Lehman told the cheering crowd.

Smith took great satisfaction in repeal, but he remained deeply concerned that its significance be understood. In an editorial in the August issue of the *New Outlook*, he declared that government should never again attempt to regulate personal morality. The United States was a diverse nation consisting of "millions of people scattered over a great continent, with all sorts of traditions and habits handed down from countless generations of ancestors." To protect the rights of these culturally distinct groups from invasion by a strong central government, the founding fathers had adopted the federal system of government. But Prohibition violated the spirit of the Constitution, Smith said.

> It invaded a field which belonged exclusively to the states and to the people. It allowed a minority to impose a moral code of its own upon the majority. It set up a tyrannical bureaucracy as outrageous, as wicked, and as contemptuous of human rights as any bureaucracy which ever existed abroad. It gave functions to the Federal government which that government could not possibly discharge, and the evils which came from the attempts at enforcement were infinitely worse than those which honest reformers attempted to abolish.

Smith had always believed that Protestant extremism was behind the Prohibition movement. But he had interpreted the passage of the Eighteenth Amendment as an aberration—the result of war fever. Now, in the place of Smith's customary optimism, there was a new fearfulness. The 1928 election had convinced him that he had been wrong to believe that religious tolerance was growing. He was no longer sure that repeal of the Eighteenth Amendment would end the threat to the rights of ethnic and religious minorities. In a country where immigrant Americans were not fairly represented, Smith saw a serious possibility that militant Protestants or some other group would once again make the federal government an instrument of oppression. He began to believe that the danger of giving new power to the federal government outweighed any good it might do. Without fully realizing it, Smith was abandoning the expansive view of federal power that he had expressed in his 1928 acceptance speech. He was putting himself on a collision course with the New Deal.

Smith's personal limitations also played a role in alienating him from the national administration. He had only a limited knowledge of large parts of the United States. With the exception of his trips to Democratic conventions around the country, he had not traveled much outside of New York. Had he been elected president, he would not have been handicapped by this disadvantage for long. Smith would have applied the same inductive method that had enabled him to conquer the arcane rules of the New York Assembly to the task of acquiring this broader knowledge. In the absence of an opportunity to learn about new problems, however, Smith's usual approach worked against him. He had neither the time nor the resources that were available to the New Dealers. He knew little more than what he read in the newspapers about undertakings like the Tennessee Valley Authority, which was a bold effort to remake the economy of a huge region that had long suffered from underdevelopment and poverty. It was an attempt to improve the lives of millions of working people with whom Smith would have been likely to identify. His limited knowledge of the program led Smith to view it merely as a resettlement scheme. Smith was also suspicious of the prominent role that academics played in Roosevelt's "Brain Trust" and the new federal agencies that were being created to administer the New Deal. He had acquired his knowledge of politics from the ground up, and he distrusted those who claimed to be able to solve a problem based on their knowledge of a theory.

Despite the obvious differences between Smith and some of the more radical voices in the new administration, he remained a sincere if skeptical supporter of Roosevelt during the first months of the New Deal. Through the fall of 1933, his biggest criticism of the administration was that it was not doing enough to help the unemployed. On the surface, he continued to enjoy a friendly relationship with the president. In October Roosevelt spoke at the closing dinner of the National Conference of Catholic Charities. As he passed Smith on his way to the rostrum, Roosevelt stopped and whispered something to him. Smiling broadly, Smith replied by slapping the president on the back. In November, Smith and Raskob had tea with the president and Eleanor at the White House. The "ice was broken," an unnamed friend reported.

The situation changed suddenly when the administration began experimenting with currency manipulation in an effort to drive down the value of the dollar. The hope was that a cheaper dollar would make American agricultural products look more attractive in foreign markets, and their prices would rise. Most business leaders opposed the policy. A few days after Smith's White House tea, a Treasury Department adviser resigned to protest what he considered "a drift into unrestrained inflation." The Chamber of Commerce sent a letter to some of the nation's leading citizens, including Smith, asking them for their views.

Smith's response was blunt. A policy of inflation was nothing more than a surrender to the rural wing of the Democratic Party, he said. "Is the Democratic Party fated to be always the party of greenbackers, paper money printers, free silverites, currency managers, rubber dollar manufacturers and crackpots?" he asked. There was no proof that the purchase and sale of gold could restore the nation to prosperity. "In the absence of anything definitely known to be better, I am for a return to the gold standard," he said. "I am for gold dollars as opposed to baloney dollars."

I am for experience as against experiment. If I must choose between private management of business and management of business by a government bureaucracy, I am for private management. I am ready to go through a certain amount of deflation if the choice is between this and outright money inflation. If I must choose between the leaders of the past, with all the errors they have made and with all the selfishness they have been guilty of and the inexperienced young college professors who hold no re-

sponsible public office but are perfectly ready to turn 130 million
Americans into guinea pigs for experimentation, I am going to be
for the people who have [made] the country what it is.

Smith insisted that this did not mean that he opposed change, but human
nature was at the root of this and all economic depressions and that could
not be changed overnight. "It cannot be done by magic, fiat, hocus pocus
and mere experimentation," he said. The *New York Times*, which supported sound money, hoped Smith's letter would cause "new and deep
searchings of heart everywhere, especially among the common folk in
daily work who have come to look upon the ex-Governor as their champion and spokesman."

The indictment of Roosevelt's monetary policy was followed by more
bitter words in the December issue of *New Outlook*. In the same issue in
which he reprinted his letter to the Chamber of Commerce, Smith published his first extended criticism of the administration's public works program. Smith noted that the administration had recently created a Civil
Works Administration to replace the Public Works Administration. The
CWA was supposed to speed the jobs program by introducing a new cate-
gory of project. "Halfway between a lemon and an orange is a grapefruit,"
Smith explained. "Halfway between a public work and a relief work is a
civil work." It was all mere wordplay designed to deceive the American
people, he charged.

> It looks as though one of the absent-minded professors had played
> anagrams with alphabet soup. The soup got cold while he was un-
> consciously inventing a new game for the nation, a game which
> beats the crossword puzzle—the game of identifying new depart-
> ments by their initials. The reason for the new CWA is, however,
> as clear as crystal. It was created to hide the failure of another ex-
> isting agency. It was set up because the PWA, or Public Works Ad-
> ministration, had broken down.

The public works program would fail without a complete reorganization,
Smith said. He insisted that he was criticizing CWA not because he opposed putting more men to work but because the CWA would fail to do
what it was supposed to do. Many public officials were aware of this but

were afraid to speak out, Smith said. "No sane local official who has hung up an empty stocking over the municipal fireplace is going to shoot Santa Claus just before a hard Christmas," he wrote.

It was inevitable that Smith would be answered with rebukes that were no less stinging than his own. Yet no one expected that the sharpest criticism would come from a Catholic priest. The Rev. Charles E. Coughlin had already attained national prominence through his weekly radio sermons from Detroit. Coughlin was a fanatical supporter of monetary inflation whose anger at Eastern bankers would later lead him to reveal a virulent anti-Semitism. His first blow at Smith was struck in his radio address on November 27, three days after the release of Smith's letter to the Chamber of Commerce. He reminded his audience that Smith's opposition to inflation was entirely consistent with his position as a banker: "Are we forgetful that Mr. Smith is a wealthy banker? Naturally he makes at least a portion of his living from the County Trust Bank of New York. Naturally, he is interested in the maintenance of the national war debt bonds, as is every banker." With little ammunition for his attack, Coughlin resorted to charges of conspiracy and personal betrayal: "My friends this is but part of the organized attack on our leader who is trying to redeem us from the money changers. This famous letter, which will go down in national political history as an obituary notice, could have been handed to Mr. Roosevelt during the well-advertised White House tea party last week. It had already been written." Coughlin was only warming up. The next day he boarded a train to carry his attack on Smith into New York itself.

On his arrival in New York, Coughlin revealed a sensational new charge against Smith. In the intervening twenty-four hours, he had discovered the real reason why Smith was opposing currency inflation. He explained that a bishop whom he refused to identify had told him that he and New York bishop John J. Dunne had accompanied Smith in a car to the offices of J. P. Morgan and waited while Smith paid a brief visit there. Coughlin gave an account of what allegedly transpired: "Mr. Smith entered Morgan's very much disturbed. . . . He emerged wreathed in smiles and gave them the impression that he had just arranged an immense loan for the Empire State Building." "I am just as much grieved as if I'd had to say it about my own father," Coughlin said later, during an interview at the New York Athletic Club. "But when anyone stands in the way of President Roosevelt, and it's either Roosevelt or ruin, I've got to take a stand. This is war." That evening Coughlin was to address a crowd of seven thousand at the Hippodrome. The audience zeroed in on Smith before Coughlin even spoke. They booed when former Oklahoma senator Robert L. Owen, the Democrat who had abandoned his party in 1928, mentioned "crackpotism, whatever that means." They booed again when another speaker referred to "baloney dollars." Coughlin delivered the final insult. "Two more years of this lying commodity system as advocated by Smith, Morgan, Woll, Acheson and the rest of them would leave us a nation of carcasses," he charged.

Smith did not rise to the bait. He said he respected Coughlin's right to disagree with him. "I insist on the right of free speech for myself, and I would be the last one in the world to attempt to deny it to anyone else," he explained. Nevertheless, he added,

> I do very deeply resent any statement about me made by Father Coughlin which is not true, and the charge that my position on the monetary question was in any way affected by any loan from J. P. Morgan is absolutely false. So, too, the suggestion that I borrowed money from the house of J. P. Morgan, or anybody connected with it, to progress construction of the Empire State Building or for any corporation with which I am connected, is absolutely false.

Smith seemed far more concerned with Coughlin's charge that he was opposed to the president. The next issue of the *New Outlook* was full of praise for Roosevelt and seemed to suggest that Smith's words had taken him farther than he meant to go. Through the summer of 1934, Smith worked hard to prove that he was still a supporter of the New Deal. As the pain of the Depression continued, however, the country was becoming increasingly polarized between the supporters of Coughlin and Long and the businessmen who were unhappy with the New Deal. Consequently, when it was revealed in August that Smith was among the founders of a new group being organized by John Raskob and the du Ponts to fight radicalism, many observers believed that he was finally going to break with the administration.

The new group, the American Liberty League, may have been one of the most misguided efforts to influence public opinion in American history. The idea was to create a group that would build support for "individual and group initiative and enterprise" and property rights as a bulwark against the increasingly radical proposals for restoring the nation's prosperity. The Liberty League would be nonpartisan, and its executive committee would include both Democrats and Republicans. A number of politicians served on the board of directors, including Smith, John W. Davis, the 1924 Democratic presidential nominee, and two Republicans, former New York governor Nathan L. Miller and James W. Wadsworth, Jr. The other board members were wealthy businessmen, which immediately raised the suspicion that the Liberty League would be used as a weapon against the New Deal. "It looks to me as if the League was organized to stop the New Deal," Senator James P. Pope of Idaho said. Senator Elmer Thomas of Oklahoma agreed. "The organizers of the League are die-hards and stand-patters who have always been opposed to the New Deal," he said. The administration itself immediately seized on the formation of the League as an opportunity to discredit Roosevelt's opponents as men who were defending their self-interest. In an interview with reporters who were not allowed to quote him directly, Roosevelt was said to have praised the League "with faint damns." Creating a league to defend property was like defending two of the Ten Commandments, he told them. He noted that Wall Street had welcomed the formation of the League as "little short of an answer to a prayer."

Smith was soon sorry that he had joined the Liberty League. While he had agreed to join the group at Raskob's request, he had no intention of aligning himself with an organization that was opposed to the president. Despite his criticisms of the New Deal, Smith still considered himself a supporter of the administration. His conception of the group was spelled out in a statement of purpose prepared by a subcommittee on which he served:

> There appears to be . . . a real chance to secure the support of millions who represent the backbone of the nation, from small to large property owners, to align themselves on a broad platform upon which they will be willing to fight for the preservation of the present system. It is such a platform that must be aimed at—a platform which should straddle no issues but which, at the same time, should not hurt its cause by being highly controversial.

Once the Liberty League came under attack from the Roosevelt administration, its organizers abandoned the hope that it might be a popularly based organization and converted it into a business group that opposed all the major programs of the New Deal.

In trying to explain why Smith had become associated with the Liberty League, some speculated that he had fallen under the spell of his wealthy new friends. While it was true that some of his friends like Raskob and Kenny were wealthy, most of his business associates were men of small means who had been hit hard by the Depression. Smith had joined the board of directors of the Consolidated Indemnity and Insurance Company at the behest of "Johnny" Gilchrist, a freckle-faced classmate at St. James School. The company was on the verge of bankruptcy and in danger of being taken over by the New York State Department of Insurance. Smith served on the boards of two other companies that closed their doors, the National Surety Company and the Federal Broadcasting Company. He was also chairman of the Meenan Oil Company, a heating oil firm where his son, Arthur, was a vice president.

Smith himself was far from wealthy. He had lost most of the money that he had invested. Although he had received five thousand shares of common stock in the Empire State Building, the value of these shares was only $25,000. His earnings were enough to allow him to continue to live on Fifth Avenue, but he remained a salaried employee. In 1933 there was a rumor that Smith would head the new state liquor board at a salary of $12,000, but he denied it. "I'm not a rich man," he explained. Arthur had been successfully settled, but Smith continued to look for a better job for his youngest son, Walter, who was working for him at the County Trust. Young Al couldn't find enough work as a lawyer to be self-supporting and was living with his parents.

Being dependent on wealthy men like Raskob and the du Ponts for his job certainly made it harder for him to say no when they asked him for something. In May 1935 the U.S. Supreme Court struck down the National Industrial Recovery Act on grounds that threatened much of the New Deal's legislative program. Roosevelt denounced the "horse and buggy Court," prompting a great deal of criticism. Raskob asked Smith to join the attack on Roosevelt at a public meeting in Chicago that would be held under the auspices of the Liberty League. Smith resisted. Although he was willing to make a private speech to the members of the

League, he opposed the plan for a public rally. In June, during a meeting of the League executive committee, Smith again refused a request that he speak publicly against Roosevelt. Under pressure from Irénée du Pont, Smith momentarily relented, but when the League publicity man called to arrange a press conference in Chicago, Smith refused to participate or even issue a statement.

Smith's effort to remain neutral was made more difficult as the New Deal became increasingly radical. In the days following his attack on the Supreme Court, Roosevelt fought a bill that embodied Long's Share the Wealth plan. But in June, just two days after defeating Long's bill, the administration introduced its own tax bill, providing for stiff inheritance taxes, higher rates on large incomes, and higher business taxes, and Long promptly took credit for the measure. Roosevelt even sounded like the Louisiana Kingfisher as he explained his proposal: "Great accumulations of wealth cannot be justified on the basis of personal and family security. In the last analysis, such accumulations amount to the perpetuation of great and undesirable concentration of control over the employment and welfare of many, many others." Although Smith had held himself apart, between Roosevelt and his critics, for a year and a half, he could not support his lonely posture forever. He finally agreed to speak at a dinner of the American Liberty League at the Mayflower Hotel in Washington on January 25, 1936, two days after the start of Roosevelt's reelection campaign.

The moment seemed to be right. The New Deal was sliding in public opinion polls. Preliminary results from a *Literary Digest* poll showed that 60 percent disapproved of the New Deal, and Roosevelt's support seemed shaky outside the South. Roosevelt was already having trouble with Tammany, which blamed him for his role in Walker's resignation. But there was weakness in other cities as well, as the *New York Times* pointed out.

It is not the case merely of New York, but of other large cities like Chicago and St. Louis and San Francisco. In several of them the Democratic organization and control are not satisfactory to the party authorities at national headquarters. Evidence of dissension and factions and disloyalty trickles out from large centers of population. The rural heart is said still to be true to the Administration but the urban pulse is not so steady.

The Democratic majorities had largely been won in the cities. "If their votes drop off, the Presidential election may be closer than any Democratic prophet has hitherto admitted," the *Times* concluded. Although still predicting an electoral total of 325 votes, Farley was privately concerned by the continuing slippage in the president's popularity. "My own feeling is that right at this time the President is as weak as he has ever been and there is some significance to these polls," he confided to his diary.

In an effort to shore up support, Roosevelt indirectly attacked the Liberty League in an address at the opening of Congress on January 3. The enemy was the "power-seeking minority" that had struggled to dominate democratic government since the founding of the republic. Lately, the would-be usurpers had been "financial and industrial groups, small but politically dominant," he said. These interests had now taken over reputable business groups and spawned new associations: "They steal the livery of great national constitutional ideals to serve discredited special interests. . . . [T]hey engage in vast propaganda to spread fear and discord among the people—they would gang up against the people's liberties." No one missed the obvious reference to the League. Roosevelt went on to accuse the League and other groups of masking their desire for a return of the old order in generalized criticisms of New Deal legislation. Why didn't they simply call openly for overturning the new laws? In fact, "our resplendent economic autocracy does not want to return to that individualism of which they prate." They coveted the power now being exercised by the government, Roosevelt said. "They realize that in 34 months we have built up new instruments of public power. In the hands of a people's government, this power is wholesome and proper. But in the hands of political puppets of an economic autocracy such power would provide shackles for the liberties of the people." The speech was a masterly effort by Roosevelt to discredit his critics by identifying himself with democratic government and painting his foes as enemies of equal rights. The Liberty League was a handy whipping boy.

Roosevelt had done everything he could to make it hard for Smith to appeal to his traditional constituency, "the rank and file" of working-class and middle-class Americans. The circumstances of Smith's January 25 speech made it harder. Six thousand people tried to get tickets for the dinner at the Mayflower. Twelve hundred crammed into a ballroom where Smith would speak, while another eight hundred would listen to loudspeakers in a room nearby. These were normal numbers for a Smith speech, but this was not the typical Smith crowd. Some observers commented on the beautiful dress and the high social standing of many of the attendees. With a few significant exceptions, they were all Republicans. Wearing white tie and tails, John W. Davis, Governor Albert C. Ritchie of Maryland, and the handful of other Democrats in the room were indistinguishable from the sea of Republican businessmen and politicians. Such elite company was not accustomed to being crammed together the way they were that night, but any price was worth paying to hear Smith attack Roosevelt. The speaker himself seemed far less eager. The newsreel cameras that day had caught none of his familiar humor as he got off the train at Washington. He was sullen and impatient at being made to wait while the cameras took another shot. He had a job to do, but it was clearly not a job he relished.

Smith began slowly. He did not want the reason for his speech misconstrued. It was not a desire for office. "I am not a candidate for any nomination by any party at any time," he explained. Nor had his need to speak grown out of bitterness: "I have no ax to grind. There is nothing personal in this whole performance in so far as I am concerned. I have no feeling against any man, woman or child in the United States. I am in possession of supreme happiness and comfort." After the speech, some commentators would criticize Smith for bragging about his personal comfort at a time when people were starving. They had missed the point. Smith was simply claiming to speak with disinterestedness. He did believe his speech would benefit one group particularly, "the great rank and file of the American people, in which class I belong."

Smith said he wanted the United States to remain a land of opportunity. "Now listen: I have five children and I have ten grandchildren, and you take it from me, I want that gate left open, not alone for mine; I am not selfish about it, not for a minute, but for every boy and girl in the country, and in that respect I am not different from every father and mother in the United States." He had joined the Democratic Party in part because it was committed to equal opportunity. "I was attracted to it in my youth because I was led to believe that no man owned it; further that no group of men owned it; but on the other hand, that it belonged to all the plain people in the United States." The painful truth was that a Democratic administration had undertaken a program that threatened the nation.

He listed three dangers. "The first is the arraignment [sic] of class against class," Smith said. This was an invitation to "civil strife." It was also an effort to hoax the poor: the rich are not immoral because they have money any more than the poor are virtuous because they have none. "I have met some good and bad industrialists; I have met some good and bad financiers. But I have also met some good and bad labor." The second danger was "government by bureaucracy instead of what we have been taught to look for, government by law." The third danger grew out of the second. The growth of bureaucracy was increasing the cost of government so much that it was drawing resources from the private sector and redistributing them, "not by any process of law, but by the whim of a bureaucratic autocracy."

Having outlined the problems briefly, Smith began to warm to his subject. "Well now, what am I here for? . . . What would I have my party do? I would have them reestablish and re-declare the principles that they put forth in that 1932 platform." The 1932 platform was the clearest expression of Democratic principles ever, Smith said. "And listen: No candidate in the history of the country ever pledged himself more unequivocally to his party platform than did the President." With the mention of Roosevelt, the audience sensed that Smith had reached the turning point. "Well, here we are," he said, pausing as if on the brink of a precipice. The audience cheered and applauded, urging him on. He continued:

> Millions of Democrats just like myself, all over the country still believe in that platform. And what we want to know is why it wasn't carried out. And listen. There is only one man in the United States of America that can answer that question. It won't do to pass it down to an under secretary. I won't even recognize him when I hear his name. I won't know where he came from. I will be sure that he never lived down in my district!

The audience laughed for the first time. They were sure now that Smith would not hold back in his attack on the administration.

Smith reviewed the administration's performance through a plank-by-plank examination of the 1932 platform. Putting on his glasses, he read: "First plank: 'We advocate immediate and drastic reduction of governmental expenditures by abolishing useless commissions and offices, consolidating departments and bureaus and eliminating extravagance. . . .' Well now, what is the fact? No offices were consolidated, no bureaus were eliminated; but on the other hand the alphabet was exhausted." The audience laughed and applauded again. "Another plank," Smith continued. " 'We favor maintenance of the national credit by a Federal budget annually balanced. . . .' " Yet federal indebtedness was at an all-time high. He explained that he did not oppose borrowing on principle. "[I]f it solved our problem and we were out of trouble I would say, 'All right, let 'er go.' " Smith himself had advocated a larger federal role in unemployment relief. But the administration's effort was largely a failure. "They started out to prime the pump for industry in order to absorb the ranks of the unemployed, and at the end of three years their employment affirmative policy is absolutely nothing better than the negative policy of the administration that preceded it." He had the same objection to the new social welfare legislation. While he favored the goal of these bills, he predicted that the administration's "haphazard, hurry-up" legislation would fail to accomplish its purpose.

For Smith, Roosevelt's "betrayal" of the Democratic platform involved more than a failure to honor campaign pledges. It was a repudiation of the Democratic Party's tradition of hostility to a strong central government. He proposed as an experiment taking copies of the Democratic and Socialist platforms, obscuring their party identification and laying them side by side. "Then study the record of the present Administration up to date," Smith instructed. "After you have done that, make your mind up to pick up the platform that more nearly squares with the record, and you will put your hand on the Socialist platform. You don't dare touch the Democratic platform. And, incidentally, let me say that it is not the first time in recorded history that a group of men have stolen the livery of the church to do the work of the devil." It was the New Deal's effort to implement socialist ideas that was causing all the problems. "This country was organized on the principles of a representative democracy, and you can't mix Socialism or Communism with that. They are like oil and water. They are just like oil and water. . . . How do you suppose all this happened? Here is the way it happened: the young Brain Trusters caught the Socialists in swimming and they ran away with their clothes." Smith had trouble making himself heard over the laughter. "Now it is all right with me—it is all right with me if they want to disguise themselves as Norman Thomas or Karl Marx, or Lenin, or any of the rest of that bunch, but what I won't stand for is to let them march under the banner of Jefferson, Jackson, or Cleveland."

The New Deal was illegitimate because it had lost touch with the central problem of democracy: how to limit the power of government. Smith reminded his audience that the nation's founders were men who had emigrated to find freedom. "Always have in your minds that the Constitution and the first ten amendments to it were drafted by refugees and by the sons of refugees." The Constitution protects freedom by restricting the power of the federal government, by separating power within the federal government between branches and by providing a process for amending the Constitution. But all of these safeguards were being undermined. "Congress has overstepped its bounds. It went beyond the constitutional limitation, and it has enacted laws that not only violate that, but violate the home rule and the state's [sic] rights principle." The threat to liberty was even greater because Congress had ceded its ill-gotten powers to the president, who now ruled with virtually no check. "In the name of heaven, where is the independence of Congress? Why, they just laid right down. They are flatter on the Congressional floor than the rug on the table here." Government must change over time, but Smith insisted that these changes were not legitimate unless they were approved by the people.

The Democrat who was loyal to his party's traditions had few choices as another election approached. "There is only one of two things we can do," Smith said. "We can either take on the mantle of hypocrisy or we can take a walk, and we will probably do the latter." Still, he was not ready to announce his decision. The speech concluded with a series of recommendations for the Democratic Party. "I suggest to the members of my party on Capitol Hill here in Washington that they take their minds off the Tuesday that follows the first Monday in November." They should resurrect the 1932 platform and make it their program. They should stop trying to change the form and structure of government without recourse to the people. "This country belongs to the people and it doesn't belong to any administration." Smith reminded the members of Congress that they had sworn an oath before God and the people to protect the Constitution. The Constitution should receive the same respect as the Bible. They should reread the parable of the prodigal son and apply it to their own lives. "Stop! Stop wasting your substance in a foreign land, and come back to your Father's house." Finally, he issued a solemn warning:

There can be only one capital, Washington or Moscow. There can
be only one atmosphere of government, the clear, pure, fresh air
of free America, or the foul breath of Communistic Russia. There
can be only one flag, the Stars and Stripes, or the Red Flag of the
Godless Union of the Soviet. There can be only one National An-
them, The Star Spangled Banner or the Internationale. There can
be only one victor. If the Constitution wins, we win. But if the
Constitution—stop! Stop there. The Constitution can't lose. The
fact is, it has already won, but the news has not reached certain
ears.

The audience stood and gave Smith an ovation. They had come for the
show, and Smith had given a good one.

But Smith's reasons for opposing the New Deal were very much his
own. His audience was made up of insiders who opposed the New Deal
as a threat to their privileges. Smith thought he was speaking for the outsiders. He believed that Roosevelt had given in, first to the Southerners
and then to the Brain Trusters. He had abandoned the poor by undermining economic growth, while building federal power to the point
where it threatened individual rights. Under Roosevelt, the Democratic
Party had abandoned its finest traditions. But Smith's speech showed that
he, too, had changed. He had always been the most pragmatic of men.
Under the pressure of grave problems, he had taken the lead in expanding the power of government. Had he been elected president in 1928, he
probably would have availed himself of the same policies that Roosevelt
was trying. But Smith had not been elected, and his fear of government
power had grown so great that it led him to overlook the great need of the
people he wanted to help. To the millions who were unemployed, the
New Deal offered the only hope of avoiding starvation. There is no question that its promises were grandiose and that four years of the New Deal
had failed to end the Depression. But what were the alternatives? For
Smith to suggest a return to the 1932 Democratic platform and a national
government of limited powers seemed not just dangerous but silly. Many
of his friends and supporters were stunned: Al Smith had become an
ideologue.

## 12 ❋ MINORITY LEADER

Al Smith didn't have to gamble everything on the success of his Liberty League speech. He could have confined his remarks to an attack on the New Deal. He could even have gone further in his criticism of Roosevelt personally without jeopardizing the loyalty and affection of his followers in the party. But Smith believed that the Democratic Party had cast off the lifeline of Jeffersonian tradition and was in danger of drowning in unfamiliar currents. As a regular Democrat for over thirty years, he knew the probable fate of a man who turned his back on his party: he would not only redouble the fury of his enemies, he would lose the respect of many friends. This was a chance he believed he had to take. After all, who else was big enough to attempt a one-man rescue of the Democratic Party? The Democrats were shocked by his threat to oppose the party that had made him its presidential candidate only eight years before. They were also alarmed by Smith's vow to fight for the voters of small means, the very core of the New Deal's support. While nobody could doubt the difficulty of Smith's task, many believed he was a serious threat. "A bolt led by him will hurt, and seriously," Arthur Krock wrote. "The effect of it will be to jeopardize further for the President the populous seaboard States."

This didn't stop party leaders from pretending Smith's attitude was unimportant. When the U.S. House of Representatives opened on Monday, Smith's speech was the main topic of debate. Representative Clifton A. Woodrum of Virginia told the House that a walkout by Smith would have no effect because he had ceased to be a Democrat years before:

He took a walk some time ago, for I submit you can't walk out of a place you have never been in. In fact, he is the party's best walker-outer. How well do we remember the little walk he took in Chicago, he and little Johnny Raskob, and little Jouett Shouse, and those other spoiled little boys who can't take it. No, he took the walk in Chicago and is still walking and he just happened to stop in Washington the other night on his hike.

Woodrum's speech touched a spring in his fellow Democrats, who stood and cheered. But Smith could not be dismissed so easily. Representative Hamilton Fish of New York, a Republican, rose to his defense: "The gentleman from Virginia . . . spent one half hour, or more, denouncing Alfred E. Smith personally, ridiculing him, and did not answer at any time in his speech a single one of the criticisms made by Governor Smith." The *New York Times* noted that the Democrats seemed to protest too much. "If the blow he struck wasn't a hard one, why get so hot about it?" On the other hand, the editorial doubted a claim that the "minimum strength" of Smith's following was two to three million.

The first effective counterattack came three days after the Liberty League speech. Roosevelt had chosen Joseph Robinson, Smith's running mate in 1928, to deliver the administration's response. Although outclassed by Smith as a speaker, Robinson marshaled both the details of the Liberty League dinner and the accomplishments of Smith's own record to raise doubts about his motive in attacking the New Deal. He began by quoting a news report that described the diners as "jammed elbow to elbow, tailcoat to tailcoat, fluttery bouffant dress to sleek black velvet dress." Clearly, this was not the average Democratic clambake. A "billion dollar audience" watched Smith with adoring eyes, Robinson said. "It was the swellest party the du Ponts ever gave." Robinson's message was obvious. Smith had changed sides. "The brown derby has been discarded for the high hat; he has turned away from the East Side with those little shops and fish markets, and now his gaze rests fondly upon the gilded towers and palaces of Park Avenue." It was a damning portrait, but it was not enough. Smith could not be discredited unless it could be demonstrated that he had broken with his earlier views.

Al Smith had "advocated and championed every basic principle that has been written into law by the Roosevelt administration," Robinson said.

As proof, Robinson quoted from Smith's speech to the Harvard Alumni Association in June 1933. In that address Smith had sought to calm fears about the emergency legislation of the early New Deal. He recalled that he himself had once been labeled a radical for supporting workmen's compensation, child welfare laws, factory codes, and public ownership of waterpower. It was Smith who called for a "more equal distribution of property" during the 1928 campaign, Robinson said. Nor was Smith's "radicalism" a thing of the distant past, he added. Smith had supported the National Recovery Act. He had taken the lead in demanding jobs for the unemployed and had called on Congress to surrender authority to a public works czar, the very delegation of power to the executive that he now condemned. Robinson's staff had done a thorough research job. They had even found an address that Smith had given to the Catholic Conference on Industrial Problems in which he had recommended taking the Constitution, wrapping it up, and putting it on a shelf for the duration of the emergency. Robinson gloated, "Just think of that! Alfred E. Smith proposed in 1933 that we wrap up the Constitution and put it on the shelf until the depression was defeated, and then coming down here in 1936 to lecture Democratic leaders on constitutional government!" Having apparently proven that Smith's views had completely changed in a matter of four years, Robinson was ready to render his verdict: Al Smith was a traitor who had thrown in with the forces of evil. "The list of directors and officers of the American Liberty League reads like a roll-call of the men who have despoiled the oil, coal and water-power resources of the country." To speak comfort to such men amounted to desertion in time of war.

> Yes, Governor Smith, it was as difficult to conceive of you at the Liberty League banquet as it would be to imagine George Washington waving a cheery good-bye to the ragged and bleeding band at Valley Forge while he rode forth to dine in sumptuous luxury with smug and sanctimonious Tories in near-by Philadelphia.

"The policies of the Liberty League have become the platform of the unhappy warrior," Robinson concluded.

Robinson had made an effective speech, but for a while it almost appeared that Smith had attained his objective. Once again he had captured the nation's attention and established the political agenda. Smith's desertion threatened to reduce Roosevelt's plurality in New York City and thus to cost him the electoral vote of the state. There seemed a strong possibility that Massachusetts, Rhode Island, and Connecticut might follow Smith. James Michael Curley, who was now governor of Massachusetts, appeared worried. He was reported to have amazed a meeting of businessmen by calling on Roosevelt to "drop some of his recovery activities" and to "say something definite and reassuring" to business. Smith had been stung by Robinson's attack, but his good humor returned several days later when reporters stopped him as he left Mayor Fiorello La Guardia's office. "Did you ask the Mayor to join the Liberty League?" he was asked. "No, I didn't have any blanks with me," Smith said. "Do you think you'll ever wind up in that [mayor's] office?" "Not a chance unless I drop dead in there." At moments like this, it almost appeared that Smith might have a chance of unhorsing an incumbent president. But the negative reaction to Smith's speech had only begun to be felt.

Roosevelt's plan to counter the effect of Smith's speech was to avoid direct attacks on the Happy Warrior that might anger Catholics and to pour fire on the Liberty League. Farley was dispatched on a cross-country speaking tour to drive home the iniquity of the League. In Topeka, he called it "an organization of multi-millionaires which is run as a subsidiary of the Republican National Committee." Obviously, its only motive was to elect a Republican president: "A brilliant editorial writer said it ought to be called the American Cellophane League and he gave two good reasons. He said first, it's a du Pont product, and, second, you can see right through it." If the administration was circumspect, there were many New Dealers who attacked Smith freely. He was hung in effigy by one hundred men at the Grand Coulee Dam the day after Farley's speech. Even H. L. Mencken wanted to get in on the fun. He wrote a Roosevelt supporter in Kentucky:

> Calling Al "the Landlord's Agent" will do him more harm than 10,000 arguments by Joe Robinson. The epithet is a masterpiece, and with your kind permission I shall lift it. As you know, I am in favor of Al, but I must confess that he seems to have lost all of his political cunning. The speech he made at Washington should have been made in New York at a meeting of fishpeddlers, police sergeants and other lowly but honest men.

By the end of February, Farley was able to report progress to Roosevelt. Not only had the president not lost support, he seemed to be gaining in strength. "I told him the Smith speech had driven back thousands to his support—people who had been drifting away," Farley said.

Smith and his allies had hoped to encourage the election of uninstructed delegations to the Democratic National Convention in Philadelphia, which could then provide a platform for criticizing the New Deal. But these hopes soon collapsed even in Massachusetts. By the middle of June, Smith lacked any delegates, pledged or unpledged, and there seemed little point in attending the convention in Philadelphia. It was also reported that Smith was afraid that there would be a hostile demonstration if he appeared. On June 21, Smith joined Bainbridge Colby, Joseph A. Reed, Joseph B. Ely, and Daniel F. Cohalan in sending a telegram to the convention that called on the Democrats to repudiate Roosevelt and the New Deal. "If you fail, then patriotic voters of all parties will know unhesitatingly to what standard they must rally in order to preserve the America of the great leaders of the past," they wrote. The meaning was unmistakable: Smith was ready to support the Republican Party.

The Democrats in Philadelphia responded with scorn to the missive from their former leaders. The first thing noticeable about the telegram was the absence of the names of a number of prominent Democrats who were known to be critical of the New Deal and who might have been expected to sign. The support of Bernard M. Baruch, Owen D. Young, James M. Cox, John W. Davis, and Lewis Douglas would have given the telegram greater credibility. Smith knew this. He was reported to have argued with Baruch over the latter's failure to sign. Critics of the telegram were quick to dismiss its significance. McAdoo was disdainful. "These gentlemen have been so long effaced as Democrats that I think their suggestions will be ignored," he said. Nor was this sentiment a sectional one. "Why don't these guys get wise to themselves?" asked John F. Carew, a New York Supreme Court justice. "They are as dead as John Quincy Adams." Farley, meanwhile, linked the signers to the now thoroughly discredited League. "No one is surprised by a report that certain people, prominent in organizations like the Liberty League will send telegrams to the convention or issue statements," he said. Even the *Boston Herald*, a Republican paper, warned Republicans not to overestimate the significance of the telegram. The only effect of the protest was to provide the convention with some entertainment. Entertainer Eddie Dowling "wowed" the convention with his parody of "Three Blind Mice":

Five blind men; five blind men.
They want to run, they want to run.
They're not here, but they sent a note, (Men who once were considered wise,)
Trying their hardest to rock the boat. (Now the tops for the booby prize.)
It looks like the donkey has got the goat (Of course, you can't see if you shut your eyes.)
Of five blind men. (Five blind men.)

The next day it was the Republicans who provided the fun by unfurling three banners in the galleries reading "Al Smith—We Want Al Smith." They were subdued with fists.

After the June 21 telegram, Smith's status as a party pariah was firmly established. A Democratic club in Syracuse removed his picture from the place of honor it had occupied for eighteen years. Yet there was still a question of whether Smith would campaign for the Republican candidate, Alfred M. Landon. Smith was reluctant because it meant he would have to oppose his friend, Herbert Lehman, whose reelection as governor of New York was vital to the president's success. Even after it was announced in late September that Smith would make four or five speeches during the campaign, there was still no indication of what he would say. Although he had had several conferences with the Republican national chairman, party officials doubted he would endorse Landon and questioned whether he was even prepared to attack Roosevelt.

Smith's first speech was delivered at Carnegie Hall on October 1. Standing on the stage where he had faced down Hearst, establishing his mastery of New York politics, he found himself on the defensive. He was angry that he had been called a traitor to the interests of the average American. This was a favorite tactic of the New Deal, Smith said. "Unless you're ready to subscribe to the New Deal 100 per cent and sign your name on the dotted line, you're a Tory, you're a prince of privilege, you're a reactionary, you're an economic royalist." Name-calling was part of the strategy to set class against class, he said. It was also a tactic for avoiding questions that you didn't want to answer. In the Liberty League speech, he had demanded an explanation for why the Democratic platform was abandoned:

> Well, did anybody attempt that? Ha—they did not! But one of the Democratic leaders undertook to make a reply to it. And what was the reply? Al's gone high-hat. That's a perfectly good excuse for disregarding the sacred promise of the party given to the people in 1932. There's another mistake about it. I have a high hat. So has every other man that ever goes to a wedding or a funeral. But I also have a brown derby.

The audience cheered the reference to the brown derby. "And listen," he quickly added, "I grew up to the derby from no hat—I didn't reach down and get it." The jab at Roosevelt's patrician origins brought more applause. Next, he rebutted the charge that "when Al moved away from the fish market" he turned his back on his old neighbors. Many of them were present in the hall, he said. And all of them knew that they could see him in his office at the Empire State—"just the same as it was when I sat in the clubhouse night after night to meet them."

Smith also attempted to dispose of the accusation that his new business "associates" had changed his views. "In the true sense of the word I have no business associates," he insisted. "I'm a salaried man. I've never been anything else. . . . There ain't no difference between me and any other salaried employee." He told the audience he was not making an apology for going into business. "There's nothing dishonorable about business, whether it be large or whether it be small, or about business men, whether they be big or whether they be little," he said. Even Roosevelt had been in business, he said.

There was a still more serious charge that Smith was eager to address. He claimed that it was being "more or less whispered" that "Al has a grudge." "Nothing could be as stupid and nothing could be as silly as that," he said. His differences with the New Deal were matters of principle. What could be more principled than a debate over whether platform promises had been kept? "My fault with them is that they've betrayed the party—they've fooled me and they've fooled the millions of Democrats that I suggested vote for them," he charged. Nor was it true that he was personally angry with Roosevelt: "As far as the President himself is concerned, why certainly I entertain no grudge or no ill feeling. I supported him every time he was a candidate. He didn't always support me, but I don't feel bad about that." If anybody was guilty of holding a grudge, it was the administration, which had enshrined its hostility to its Democratic opponents by favoring those who were FRBC (For Roosevelt Before the 1932 Chicago Convention).

Now came the heart of his speech. It was not he who rejected the Democratic administration, but the New Dealers who rejected Democratic tradition and everyone faithful to it. The New Dealers belonged to parties all over the political spectrum. "Why even a Communist with wire whiskers and a smoking bomb in his hand is welcome as long as he signs on the dotted line," Smith charged. "Now, is La Guardia a Democrat? If he is, I'm a Chinaman with a haircut." Smith insisted he wasn't alone in believing this. Prominent Democratic newspapers were criticizing the New Deal. "Seven or eight" Democratic members of the U.S. Senate, including Carter Glass of Virginia, had opposed many New Deal measures. Defections from the administration since 1932 were legion. The only difference among the critics was over how far to go in opposition. Smith said he had made up his mind. Paraphrasing a recitation on Roman citizenship, Smith said, "America, you have been a tender friend to me, you have been God's gift of opportunity to me, and to be an American is greater than to be a King, and I am an American before I am a Democrat, before I am a Republican or before I'm anything." The audience interrupted with cheering and applause. He told them that in his long public career he had never "ducked, dodged," or "pussyfooted" about recommending remedies for the problems he saw. "I firmly believe that the remedy for all the ills that we are suffering from today is the election of Alfred M. Landon," he said.

Smith's endorsement of Landon evoked more pity than shock. Landon himself presented the endorsement as a victory of principles over partisanship. "I deeply appreciate the support of Alfred E. Smith, a great Democrat and a great American. He has placed country above partisanship," he said. The Democrats expressed little concern. Speeches like the Carnegie Hall address were no threat at all because the case against Roosevelt appeared rooted in a personal grievance. "We were prepared to answer Governor Smith if he had discussed issues," a staff member at the

Democratic National Committee explained. "But now what is there to answer?" The *New York Times* agreed that the endorsement of Landon seemed "more a matter of personalities than of principles": "Protesting that he cherished no grudge or grievance against the President, he made it all too clear that he was deeply resentful of the slight put upon him and the hurts he has received. . . . [H]is hearers could not but feel that he was venting a long-cherished wrath." The speech struck even longtime foes like Curley as pathetic. "I am sorry for Smith," Curley said. "He is really a victim of circumstance."

Sensing Smith's vulnerability, members of the administration abandoned their careful approach and began attacking him directly. "Al's plume is a bedraggled white feather," declared Hugh S. Johnson, the former head of the National Recovery Administration. According to Daniel and Edward O'Connell, the Democratic leaders in Albany, Smith had angered so many Democrats in the town where he was once beloved that it would be necessary to post the largest police guard in the city's history when he came to give his final speech. The O'Connells were exaggerating for political effect, but Smith was beginning to hear criticism from the rank and file. As he stepped from the train at the La Salle Street Station in Chicago, wearing his brown derby, he was met by both applause and boos from a crowd of five thousand. "You were all right in 1928, not so good in 1932 and lousy now," one man shouted. Another yelled: "Go on home—you're wasting your time out here." Even Jack Dempsey, the boxer, threw a punch. Smith "reminds me of a fighter who had a chance to win the title but was beaten and then he starts to holler that he was framed, robbed and sold out," Dempsey said.

Despite the O'Connells' prediction, Smith was not stoned as he arrived at the Albany station at the end of his speaking tour. The crowd that had gathered to greet him sang "Should Auld Acquaintance Be Forgot." The song had a special poignance at that moment, he said. "It has within it a signally sorrowful note to me because I am coming within the shadow of the building, where I helped to make Democratic history, to talk against that party, because I am convinced in my heart and soul it is not my Democratic party that I have known all during my years of service." Smith charged the New Deal with undermining the solidarity of the American people, which was based on a belief that their form of government provided equal access to economic opportunity. The administration had questioned that faith by suggesting that wealth was not the reward of skill and hard work but something that had been stolen through a manipulation of the system. Smith did not believe that Roosevelt was intentionally undermining American institutions, but he did accuse the president of helping the socialists and Communists encourage class hatred "by arraigning class against class, by starting people against each other, by leading large numbers of a community to believe that there is some hidden and some unseen power that is attempting to crush them to the earth."

The 1936 election was not between two political parties but two views of the social order, Smith concluded. Supporting Roosevelt were those who believed in the inevitability of class conflict and revolution. It was no wonder that the Comintern, the Soviet-dominated organization that was attempting to spread Communism around the world, was supporting him for reelection. On the other hand, there were those like Smith who believed that the United States was the one country in the world where a man's religion, race, or creed did not prevent him from rising to the level set by his talent. Smith had always believed that God had selected the United States as the country that would most closely approach His perfect justice. He refused to believe that the Depression had proven that there was something fundamentally wrong with capitalism, and he was determined to fight those who believed that government would be more just in its division of rewards than the economic system. In his view, he was attempting to do what he had always done—defend equal opportunity.

Smith appeared to be relieved when the end of the campaign finally arrived. While nobody could accuse him of being halfhearted in his opposition to the Democratic ticket, his support of the Republican candidate had always seemed less than enthusiastic. In none of his speeches had he praised Landon's qualifications. He did make the obligatory prediction of victory in a ceremonial meeting with the candidate in New York in October. When Roosevelt was reelected in another landslide, Smith hastened to put the campaign behind him: "The American people have spoken, and the cardinal principle of democracy is the will of the majority. Every citizen, every real American, must put his shoulder behind the wheel and stand behind the President." Smith believed he had been right to oppose Roosevelt. "I firmly believe we were right; time will establish that," he wrote Joseph Ely. "A strong and vigorous minority, under our form of government is the only real check on the tyranny of a majority," he wrote in another letter. Smith nevertheless expressed his willingness to work with Roosevelt. "I am ready and willing to be helpful to the new administration if any help is desired," he said. Nor did Smith appear bitter during his traditional birthday interview on December 30. While he had criticized the federal public works program, he indicated that he supported a program of federal grants for public housing if the partnership of public and private sectors proved ineffective. He was wistful rather than bitter when asked if he would choose politics as a career again: "I'd be glad to. I enjoyed every minute of it and the greatest pleasure of my life was as an Assembly member. If I had plenty of money and didn't have to work for a living, I would be satisfied to spend the rest of my life as minority leader in the Senate." It was not surprising that Smith felt a yearning for the days when he had led the minority in the Assembly. The 1936 election had left him a minority leader without a party.

This doesn't mean that Smith wasn't still in great demand as a dinner speaker. He was present in New York every year on St. Patrick's Day for the dinner given by the Friendly Sons of St. Patrick. At the 1937 Friendly Sons dinner, Smith gave a typically funny speech, but a tape reveals that his voice was deeper than normal and his words were slurred. It seems clear that he had been drinking. Was this an isolated incident, a case of someone overindulging on a festive occasion? Or does it suggest something more serious? It is not an issue that is easily addressed. The allegation that Smith was an alcoholic was made frequently by his enemies. During the 1928 campaign, the Democratic Party went to great lengths to prove that accounts like the one about Smith at the New York State Fair were apocryphal. Another rumor claimed that Smith had been caught driving drunk when the truth was that he didn't know how to drive. Investigating Smith's drinking habits doesn't lend credence to these obvious falsehoods, and it can give us a deeper understanding of the forces with which he was struggling in the 1930s.

Of course, Smith drank. Before 1920, saloons were one of the important centers of social life in all urban areas. Not only was there no stigma attached to drinking, as there was in rural areas that had been influenced by the Prohibition movement, it was an integral aspect of manhood. The saloon was where Smith met his friends when he was in New York and where he staved off the loneliness of his bachelor existence is Albany. It is also clear that Smith did not stop drinking with the advent of Prohibition. Historian Robert Slayton reports that Smith kept a cache of liquor on the second floor of the Executive Mansion that was served to friends and family, and, on the night of Smith's presidential nomination, even to members of the press. Slayton concludes that Smith was "a light to moderate social drinker who enjoyed an occasional beer" and switched to cocktails during Prohibition—"the tall, diluted highballs that so many sophisticates took up." Smith's son Walter told the author that his father would have two drinks before dinner and never drank during the day or after dinner.

There is evidence, however, that Smith drank heavily during at least some periods of his life. In 1924 Louis Howe, a former Albany newspaper correspondent, had lunch with some of his old colleagues, who told him that Smith was drinking less than he used to. "[T]hey told me in some ways at least Smith is much drier than he used to be," Howe wrote Roosevelt. "How long he has sworn off for this time God knows." The Albany reporters were credible witnesses. Smith had always enjoyed an unusually close relationship with reporters. With the exception of the reporter who turned him in for wanting to "blow the foam off," they respected his confidences, and he was frank with them. His sharing a drink with reporters on the night of his nomination for president gives further proof of that intimacy. Howe's reporter friends may well have been in a position to know that he drank heavily. Howe's implication that Smith had "sworn off" before must be viewed skeptically, in light of his hostility to Smith, but it can't be dismissed altogether. There is also James Cox's testimony that Smith was "somewhat in liquor" when he asked Cox whether Roosevelt had called him a poor governor. This was the story that Cox told *New York Times* columnist Arthur Krock in January 1932 after *Collier's* reported Roosevelt's unflattering remarks about Smith. A year and a half later, Krock described his conversation with Cox to James Farley using a more emphatic description of Smith's state of inebriation. Cox said Smith was "extremely drunk" on the night they spoke, Krock told Farley. This fragmentary evidence suggests that at times during his life Smith drank heavily, perhaps even compulsively, although it is not possible to draw conclusions about how deep an impact this had on him, his family, or his career.

It seemed for a time during 1937 that Smith might become a leader in the growing anti-Communist movement. Civil war had broken out in Spain only a few months before, throwing Catholics and Communists into violent confrontation there. In New York, the Rev. Edward Lodge Curran of Brooklyn had founded the American Association Against Communism to fight the battle at home. In April Smith was a guest speaker at an anti-Communism rally sponsored by the association in the Hippodrome. A crowd of four thousand cheered Queens borough president George U. Harvey, a Republican candidate for mayor, when he promised that as mayor he would get rid of Communists in two weeks by authorizing the police to use "a liberal supply of rubber hose." Curran himself seemed to threaten violence by suggesting that "if they wanted it the way it was in Spain, let them have it." Smith's speech did not endorse violence but indicated an appreciation of the seriousness of the problem. Things had changed since he was a boy, he explained: "I spent years of my life in a neighborhood where we heard crackpots, Socialists and all kinds of agitators, but we paid no attention to them. What is the need for such a gathering as this tonight, these contributions, this impassioned argument; it must be because communism is dangerous." Communism posed no serious threat of taking over through the ballot box, Smith acknowledged. The Communist candidate for president, Earl Browder, had flopped at the polls. "Nobody voted for him," Smith said. "I'm not sure that he even voted for himself." The man in the street recognized that Communism had defrauded the very people it was supposed to benefit. "Done away with the aristocracy," Smith snorted. "Yes, by taking everything away from them. But in taking it away they set up another aristocracy of privilege —the commissars." Nevertheless, Communists remained a threat and "should be sent back to the country from which they came."

Some believed that Smith's speech showed that his break with the New Deal had made him a reactionary. When it was announced that Smith would meet the pope during his first trip to Europe in the spring of 1937, it was immediately asserted that Smith was answering a Vatican summons to discuss strategy for fighting Communism and labor unrest in the United States. But Smith denied the report of a Vatican summons. On his arrival in Italy, he insisted that he had come for personal reasons. "For years, I've been wanting to come to Italy, but either I didn't have the money or I didn't have the time," he said. "Now I've got both. I'm coming to Europe to fulfill a lifelong ambition." A loyal son of the church did not need any other reason to visit the pope. It was a pilgrimage, he explained in a speech to the North American College in Rome: "So this is Rome! That was about the only thing I could say when I came to Rome. I've read about it, I've heard about it and I've thought a great deal about it. I was even unjustly accused at one time of attempting to take His Holiness away from it. Imagine my amazement when I beheld the Eternal City." In the first of a series of syndicated columns he wrote during his trip, Smith underlined the spiritual purpose of the journey. "[T]he sole and only reason for my trip was to receive the blessing of the Holy Father," he explained. The Catholic church saw the visit as an opportunity to honor a hero of the faith. On the street, priests cheered the American celebrity. But it was Pius XI himself who expressed the depth of the church's grati- tude when he met Smith in his private chambers. The pope did most of the talking. "It pleased me greatly to hear him speak so well and so affec- tionately of America," said Smith, "and I was indeed embarrassed by the tribute he paid me as 'a loyal son of the Church.' " The pope gave Smith gifts, including a picture of himself for Mrs. Smith and a rosary. Smith had brought a gold replica of the Empire State Building. In presenting it, he managed to offer some explanations about the building. (The pope had never been in anything taller than the Eiffel Tower.) But for the most part, Smith was tongue-tied. "I never have been taken aback for want of something to say in my whole life and I have met many prominent peo- ple. But for the first time in my life there was nothing I could say. And af- ter I left His Holiness must have said to himself, 'How did that fellow make all those speeches?' " But the pope did not let him get away soon. At his public audience, Pius XI introduced Smith as a representative of the American people, who were very near to his heart. Smith was over- whelmed. "I have always been proud of being a Catholic," he said. "I was never prouder than today when I called him 'Father' and he call me 'Son.' "

Ireland was another emotional high point of the trip. On his way back to Dublin from a visit to the cottage of his grandmother in Westmeath, Smith sang "My Wild Irish Rose," "Come Back to Erin," and other "Irish" songs, the *New York Times* reported. Smith was bursting with pride:

> Am I pleased with Ireland? I should say so. . . . When I saw so many well-kept farmsteads, all so bright and clean and such hand- some cottages for the rural laboring folk, I found it hard to recon-

cile this lovely pastoral country with the poor Ireland that we had heard so many stories about in America. I saw no evidence of poverty. I think we have poorer homes in the Southern States of America than I saw in my travels today.

Smith was surprised to have encountered so little poverty throughout his trip. "Everywhere I went I met contented people," he said. These sanguine views offended some back home. One irked editorial writer dismissed him as the "traditional ten-day tripper": "Al Smith saw only contented people wherever he went. Really, one expected better of him. Did he imagine that Mussolini would send out invitations for all the discontented people in the concentration camps and the orphan asylums and the Italian population generally to meet Mr. Smith formally at 5 o'clock in front of Il Duce's office?"

But Smith was a far keener observer of foreign affairs than some of his comments suggested. He had interviewed Mussolini and found him an attractive leader who appeared to have the support of most Italians. But he was not blind to the growing threat of war or attracted by fascism. "[I]n my opinion, no such form of government could obtain in the United States until you did two things: (1) Tear up the Declaration of Independence, and (2) throw the Constitution into the ash can." The traveler returned with a renewed appreciation for American institutions. "We who are going home have seen what they have in Europe," Smith said in a speech to his fellow steamship passengers. "It may be all right for them, but not for us. Thanks to God, we are on the way back to America, which still has the best form of government ever devised by the brain of man." His final newspaper column repeated the sentiment: "On the last day of the boat trip at Mass I thanked God for permitting me to be born in His country, the United States of America."

By September 1937 Al Smith had lost thousands of admirers and friends, but he was not a reactionary. There were some who questioned his decision in 1934 to accept the chairmanship of the newly appointed Legion of Decency of the archdiocese of New York. It seemed inconsistent with his strong defense of free speech and suggested that he was being increasingly influenced by the conservative views of the Catholic church. But there was nothing hypocritical in Smith's insistence that he still opposed censorship. As governor he had called for the repeal of the state statute banning the exhibition of any movie that had not been approved by a government board. "[C]ensorship of thought . . . abridgment in any way of the freedom of speech . . . unquestionably encourage . . . intolerance and bigotry," Smith wrote in calling for the abolition of movie censorship. But he had never advocated the abolition of laws against obscenity. He treated speech with sexual content differently from political speech.

Smith also continued to support reform at the state and local levels. As a delegate to the New York State Constitutional Convention in 1938, he pushed for an amendment that authorized state and local governments to issue bonds for the construction of public housing. The Republicans had succeeded in withholding this power when his state housing law had been approved, and little housing had been built. Smith was determined to correct this problem. He also favored amendments that would facilitate the consolidation of counties, provide state funds for eliminating dangerous railroad crossings, remove from the legislature its power to pass special and local bills, and establish a system of biennial legislative sessions. He joined the Republicans in pushing an amendment that authorized citizens to seek a court review of the decisions of quasi-judicial administrative boards. Although the Democrats opposed the measure as likely to paralyze the effectiveness of these boards, Smith insisted it was necessary to check abuses of power by the bureaucracy. He did join the Democrats in opposing an effort to limit individual rights. When Congressman Hamilton Fish rushed through an amendment barring Communists from taking civil service exams, it was Smith who moved that the measure be reconsidered. (Smith's motion was carried after Fish, in his haste to head off the challenge, mistakenly amended his amendment so that only those who advocated the violent overthrow of the government could take the exam.)

A year after the constitutional convention, the people of New York City were given an opportunity to express their feelings toward Al Smith when his son, Alfred, ran for City Council. Smith had always worried about the futures of his three sons. When Arthur graduated from Manhattan College, his father helped him find a position at the Meenan Oil Company. He also loaned him $63,000, which Arthur probably used to buy an interest in the company. Arthur later became a vice president. Walter had also graduated from Manhattan College. At thirty, he was the

Smiths' youngest child and was working for his father at the County Trust Company. Smith was anxious to find a better job for Walter and had recently written to a du Pont official in an effort to help Walter secure some du Pont insurance contracts that would enable him to join an insurance company as a partner. "He has a family to take care of and I want him set up before anything happens to me as I have to help him now," he explained.

Smith's deepest concern was for young Al, his oldest son. Not surprisingly, Alfred's marriage to Betty in 1924 following a four-week courtship had not been a success. They finally separated in 1932 but not before Betty withdrew the money in two of their bank accounts, claiming the $14,000 was hers. Things went from bad to worse when Alfred became the target of a blackmail plot that grew out of a one-night stand with a woman he met at a party. During the next three years he paid the blackmailers over $12,000. Finally, he asked his father for help, and the police were called. The scandal became public when the blackmailers were indicted in 1936. Three months later, Betty Smith sued Alfred for divorce, generating still more bad publicity.

Young Al's behavior undoubtedly put a strain on his relationship with his parents, but they forgave him, and he continued to live with them happily. George Van Schaick was visiting the Smiths' apartment one morning when Alfred stopped on his way to work and kissed his father good-bye "much as a little boy would do." Alfred was still living with his parents when he announced his candidacy for City Council in 1939. Smith was beaming with pride when his son filed his nominating petitions. "You're starting your own political career," Smith announced. "If you achieve any part of the success I did, you'll keep the name alive." He posed for photographers with his arm around his son. At times during the campaign, it seemed as if it was the Happy Warrior who was running for City Council. At a party to promote his son's candidacy held in the Empire State Club, Smith was asked what it felt like to be the candidate's father. He replied, "It's all the same. I can't feel any difference. This is my son. When he is elected I will keep after him. We see each other every morning at the breakfast table, we have plenty of time to exchange views." In a radio speech for Alfred he outlined the problems confronting the city and promised to help: "All of these problems, with my assistance, will be studied by Alfred E. Smith, Jr." On the eve of the election, he confided that he had never hoped for victory for himself as fervently as he was hoping for it for his son. He made a final appeal to his friends: "To the people of New York who have been my friends for so many years I want to express my personal thanks for whatever support they see fit to give my son on election day." On Election Day, New Yorkers responded by electing young Al.

By that time, Smith had already returned to the national stage, propelled by the issues surrounding the imminence of war in Europe. He was an early and vocal critic of Nazi Germany. When Hitler became chancellor in March 1933, Smith joined Newton D. Baker and John W. Davis, among others, in signing an interfaith appeal on behalf of German Jews and then addressed a protest rally at Madison Square Garden. Smith opposed those like Secretary of State Cordell Hull who urged the country to adopt a wait-and-see policy toward the Nazis:

> Well, all I can say about that is that where there is a good deal of smoke there must be some fire. And the only thing to do with it, not in our interest alone but in the interest of the future of the German people, is to drag it out into the open sunlight and give it the same treatment that we gave the Ku Klux Klan. . . . And it don't make any difference to me whether it is a brown shirt or a night shirt.

In November 1938, following the violence and destruction of Kristalnacht, he rose to protest again. In a radio address, Smith acknowledged that the United States like Germany was troubled by religious and racial bias. "We have not yet won that battle, as too frequently there are revivals of religious and racial prejudices arising in America," Smith said. But there was an important difference between the United States and Germany: "Whatever may be the shortcomings of the American scene, it is undeniably true that we have never by law recognized these private hates. It is equally true that in every community the underlying and leading opinion has frowned upon—although sometimes without complete success—all manifestations of persecution and forced inferiorities." In fact, America's segregation laws clearly embodied private hates. But Smith's point was that in the United States even bigots were forced to pay lip service to the promise of equality.

Once war broke out in Europe, Smith was an early and outspoken advocate of measures to aid Great Britain and to prepare the United States for the possibility of war with Germany and Japan. In October 1939 he delivered a radio address supporting an amendment to the neutrality laws to permit the Allies to purchase supplies for cash and to transport them from U.S. ports in their own ships. Roosevelt had requested the amendment as necessary to keep American ships from carrying goods to Europe and becoming targets. Smith supported Roosevelt's argument that a policy of cash and carry did not violate the nation's neutrality. Far from increasing the risk of American involvement in the war, it removed Americans from harm's way by restricting the trade to European ships. If such a law had been in place in 1917, American shipping would not have been sunk and the United States might have avoided the war, Smith said. Those who argued against the amendment seemed to be inviting the very attacks that would make war more likely. Roosevelt's policy was the one best designed to preserve America's peace.

> It is because I firmly believe in my heart and soul that the amendments suggested by the President are the best calculated to save us from the scenes that we witnessed in 1917 when our American boys were starting for France that I am at this microphone tonight, appealing to the American people to stand solidly behind the President because he is so clearly right, so obviously on the side of common sense and sound judgment and of patriotism that only those who lack an understanding of the issue will oppose him.

Isolationist sentiment was strong in many parts of the country, and Smith's speech was harshly criticized. Many expressed surprise that he was now supporting Roosevelt. Pickets at CBS headquarters hoped to intercept Smith on his way in to make the speech. They marched with signs reading "Al—Why have you changed your color?" and "Al—Are you going with the other crowd now? Why?" Later, the Rev. Edward Lodge Curran, president of the Catholic Truth Society, whose anti-Communism rally Smith had addressed two years before, found fault with Smith's foreign policy deviation. "This was not the time for Mr. Smith to arise and defend the President's policy," he said. Curran also accused the Roosevelt administration of using Smith "to drown out the voice of Father Coughlin," a leading isolationist. Smith had entered another controversy that was likely to lose him friends, but it was one that would soon prove that he and Roosevelt were right and the isolationists were wrong.

Despite Smith's support for the administration's foreign policy, he was still adamantly opposed to its domestic policies. Two weeks after Roosevelt was nominated for an unprecedented third term, Smith endorsed Republican nominee Wendell Willkie, a former Democrat. Smith campaigned for Willkie, whom he knew and liked. In his first speech of the campaign, at the Brooklyn Academy of Music, Smith attacked Roosevelt for attempting to violate the tradition that a president serves for only two terms. The Democratic convention had called Roosevelt an indispensable man. Smith bridled. "Indispensable to who? And to what? To the recipients of political patronage and of political favor. And that's the group that made up the so-called Democratic convention that was held at Chicago." Smith campaigned hard for Willkie. By the end of the campaign he believed the Republican had a good chance to win and was surprised when Roosevelt was elected by virtually the same vote that he had received in 1936.

But he did not spend much time bemoaning the election results. The pace of world events gave him little time for morose reflection. In his birthday interview at the end of December, he swung back into line behind the Allies and Roosevelt's efforts to help them. Roosevelt had recently called for "dynamic non-belligerence" in the form of additional aid to Britain. Smith said the president had made "a very courageous, straight-hitting speech," although it flew in the face of public sentiment. "It remains to be seen whether the American people will regard it as something for them or just another speech." Did Smith believe the country's situation was serious? "I don't think there is any doubt about it. The whole world looks to this country for leadership and the day of the silent leader is past." He went on to urge less public agitation on the issue, clearly directing his remarks to the isolationists. "[T]here is too much 'where-as-ing' and too much 'be it resolved.' " These groups should be satisfied with communicating their view to Congress. What kind of aid should be given to Britain? His answer was no less infuriating to isolationists: "When you promise to help a fellow it is hard to stop when he is going down for the last time. . . . We should lend the production facilities of this country to Great Britain. She is struggling pretty hard to say the least."

Smith's support was appreciated in Britain. In January 1941 Winston Churchill sent Smith a telegram thanking him for a fifteen-minute speech he had just delivered to a national radio audience, urging support for the administration's Lend-Lease legislation. The two men had met for the first time in 1929 when Churchill was in New York visiting financier Bernard Baruch. Churchill asked Baruch to invite Smith to dinner and later accompanied him to a meeting at Tammany Hall. (Smith's daughter Emily remembered hearing the Englishman cry "Hear, hear!" during Smith's address.) The two men became friends. Smith even smuggled a bottle of Scotch into Churchill's hospital room after he had been injured in a car accident during one of his prewar trips to the United States. Still, Smith was surprised to receive Churchill's telegram. "Delighted to read your stirring speech," Churchill wrote. Smith was touched. "It is a rather remarkable thing . . . that a man with the worries . . . that must be Mr. Churchill's would take time to read a speech," Smith told Emily.

Smith provided more support for Britain during the spring. Robert Moses had been urging Smith to confront the Irish-Americans who were earnestly praying for Britain's defeat in the hope that this would free the northern counties of Ireland from British rule. At the Friendly Sons of St. Patrick dinner on St. Patrick's Day, Smith insisted that the German propagandists were lying when they said that Irish-Americans opposed the Allies: "The dictators believe they can stir up class hate, magnify differences. They will find it won't work. The last group in all America that will fall for that bunk will be the Irish; first, because they are patriotic; second, because they have a sense of humor and, third, because they have a sense of religious faith." At the end of May, Smith joined John W. Davis and James M. Cox on a radio program supporting Roosevelt's proclamation of a national emergency. As a spokesman for immigrant Americans, Smith was able to make a direct appeal to recent arrivals who felt a conflict of loyalty between their new home and their native countries. Disunity was the greatest threat the country faced— "a greater peril than even Adolf presents," Smith said. He demonstrated his own commitment to unity by putting aside the bitter enmity of the last five years and resurrecting his friendship with the president of the United States.

The personal relationship between Smith and Roosevelt resumed with little of the fanfare that marked its break. On June 9, 1941, during a visit to Washington to attend the graduation of a friend's son from Georgetown University, Smith met with Roosevelt at the White House. It was the first time that the two men had seen each other since Smith had called for tea in 1933. Smith played down the significance of his latest visit. "It is just a friendly call," he told reporters who were waiting for him at the White House. Wearing a straw boater and clenching a cigar in his teeth, he listened to the inevitable question. Had he come to bury the hatchet with Roosevelt? "There never was a hatchet," Smith insisted. When he next visited Washington six weeks later, he visited Roosevelt again. The half-hour meeting was another personal call, Smith said. When, in September, Roosevelt ordered the Navy to take action against any Axis ship that threatened national security, Smith stood firmly behind the president: "The President's speech was a perfectly lucid explanation of the present world situation. I am unable to understand what could be the basis for any exception to the clear, concise, strong presentation made by him."

Once the United States entered the war, Smith became a leader on the home front. Only three weeks after Pearl Harbor he spoke confidently of the future. "Going on the experience of the past, I don't see any great trouble ahead," he said. The country was unified. "I cannot see the slightest bit of politics coming from Washington today; they are pretty united." He added that after victory the world would need an international organization to prevent future wars—"some form of organization to weld the democracies together, and if some dictator sticks his head over the fence we'll all sock him."

Smith was rewarded for his efforts to rally the country behind the war effort. The British were extremely grateful to him for his early support. In March 1943 he met with Foreign Secretary Anthony Eden and Lord Halifax, the British ambassador, at their embassy in Washington. Following their discussions, the two men drove Smith to another White House meeting with Roosevelt. Smith told reporters there that he had accepted the ride to save "taxi fare." As usual, he was uncommunicative on the reasons for his visit with the president. "I just came in for a little talk," he said. Otherwise, he planned to "hang around" Washington "for a little and talk to some personal friends about something." But Smith had some real business with the president. Soon after his meeting, Smith entered into negotiations with Harold D. Smith, the director of the budget, over the possible sale of the Empire State Building to the federal government. In a letter to the budget director in May, Smith reported that the asking price was $38 million. The negotiations would continue over the coming months, serving as concrete evidence of the reconciliation of Roosevelt and Smith, at least on the personal level.

Smith had also repaired most of the damage his reputation had suffered in his hometown. In New York City, Smith was second only to Mayor Fiorello La Guardia in his leadership on the war. In June 1943 he was the grand marshall of one of the biggest parades the city had seen in years. Seated in a jeep ahead of mounted policemen riding nine abreast, Smith led the parade, which was organized to encourage participation in the Civilian Defense Volunteer Organization. As he rode down lower Broadway he acknowledged the cheers of 500,000 amid a swirl of ticker tape. At City Hall Park, Smith joined La Guardia in addressing the crowd. Smith hit the enemies of the United States, describing them as "our crackpot friend and paperhanger from Vienna, shovel-faced Benito and the little yellow skunks in Asia." Smith also was a frequent speaker at war bond rallies. "You are going to have to do some walking and talking and pound the sidewalks as they never have been pounded before," he told 2,400 volunteer bond salesmen at the beginning of the third bond drive in August.

Four months later Al Smith celebrated his seventieth birthday. He did not seem quite himself that day as he arrived at the office, his secretary, Mary Carr, told his daughter Emily. His usual good humor was absent. Perhaps he was saddened by how quickly time was passing, Emily suggested. But he had many reasons to be cheerful. The bitterness over the break with the president was a thing of the past. On top of a stack of congratulatory telegrams and letters on his desk sat a short typed note on heavy blue stationery from Roosevelt, who apologized for his inability to attend the reception that was being given in Smith's honor later that day. There were letters from New York's political leaders in both parties, including Governor Thomas E. Dewey, who sent Smith a paperweight made from the paneling of the governor's office. Dewey called it a reminder "that 13 million people have not forgotten your loyalty to them and that they will love and respect you for so long as men revere great qualities in other men." There were also the greetings from national leaders—justices and judges, senators and representatives—and private individuals, including many people whom Smith had never met. Many boxes of cigars arrived, although Smith's doctor had ordered him to cut down. "The doctor said three a day, but I amended that and made it four, and then I always sneak one, so that's five," Smith explained.

During his traditional birthday interview with reporters, Smith demonstrated a firm intention to avoid any criticism of Roosevelt. Although he warned that high taxes would impede recovery at the conclusion of the war, he had no desire to talk about politics. "I really believe the great big interest today is the war. Let's polish off Adolf and Hirohito and then go back to politics." What about a possible fourth term for Roosevelt? He shook his head: "I don't know anything about it, and I think it's not well to talk about it now." This didn't mean that he had nothing critical to say. The American people were too complacent about the war. It might take a "good-sized casualty list" from an invasion of Western Europe before it "sinks into the minds of the American people." He struck an indignant pose when asked if he was going to retire. "From what?" He was working harder than ever on the war bond, Red Cross, and other fund-raising drives. He seemed fit enough to continue. The *New York Times* reporter noted that the former governor looked even healthier and more vigorous than the year before.

Later in the day, Smith attended a reception in his honor sponsored by the archbishop's Committee on the Laity. Before hundreds of members of the committee and leaders in all areas of New York life, Archbishop Francis Spellman praised Smith as "the exemplification in one person of all that is noblest in man, in an American, in a patriot, and in a Catholic." The apostolic delegate to the United States delivered a special benediction from Pope Pius XII. Smith responded that he could not think of better birthday presents than the words he had received from the archbishop and the pope. There were more presents at a family party in his apartment, where Smith helped cut two cakes for his thirteen grandchildren. Everyone in the family was present except young Al and Emily's husband, John Warner, who were both in the military. Unfortunately, young Al's life had continued to be troubled after his election to the City Council. Ethical lapses had forced him to stop practicing law, but he had been commissioned as an Army captain, and he remained close to his parents. Having received permission to return home for his father's birthday party, he burst into the apartment just as the photographer had managed to get the twenty-six members of the family posed.

In the new year Smith continued to speak out when asked. In January he broadcast a radio appeal for volunteer salesmen for the fourth war bond drive. As always, he made the goal intelligible for the rank and file:

> I'm asking you to volunteer to get out and pound the pavements of old New York—yes, the East Side and the West Side—to buy galoshes for the boys in the foxholes. Not big bonds; galoshes don't cost a million dollars. Just small bonds. Here is an assignment that will bring victory perhaps just that many days nearer. Don't go on day after day without the satisfaction of having given so short a time to the direct service of your country.

In February 1944 Smith joined his close friend Joseph M. Proskauer and John Foster Dulles on an NBC radio program promoting "inter-faith and inter-racial" harmony. At the Friendly Sons of St. Patrick dinner on St. Patrick's Day, he reiterated his message: "This is a national hook up and to the nation I say—forget bigotry, intolerance and racial and religious hatred."

Smith was uncomfortable at times with all of the attention that he was receiving. It had been decided that the first major housing project undertaken by New York City on the Lower East Side would be named the Alfred E. Smith Houses. The project, housing eight thousand people, would rise between the Brooklyn and Manhattan Bridges in the heart of the Fourth Ward. In November 1943 Moses had sent Smith the language that was to be engraved on the plaque dedicating the project. Smith approved the plaque but expressed some nervousness about the groundbreaking ceremony, which was scheduled for October 15, 1944. "I am looking forward to it with a good deal of anxiety," he wrote Moses. Other times, he was willing to indulge the mood of nostalgia. At the Legislative Correspondents' Dinner in Albany in March 1944, Smith joined former Speaker of the Assembly Joseph McGinnies, a Republican, on the stage. As a soloist sang "Put Your Arms Around Me, Joe, For You Belong to Me," even the hard-boiled pols grew misty-eyed. "Many of the 400 political leaders wept as they extended a five-minute ovation to the two men, among the best loved ever to tread Capitol corridors," the *New York Times* reported. In April, he did make one apparent concession to age, quitting as president of the board of trustees for the New York State College of Forestry at Syracuse University. Otherwise, it seemed nothing but death would prevent him from continuing his activities.

In May, however, Smith was struck by tragedy. Katie had developed pneumonia in April and had been hospitalized at St. Vincent's. She appeared to be recovering when she died suddenly on the morning of May 4. Smith was stunned by the news. "The stroke is cruel," the *New York Times* observed. "The presses swarm with novels and romances. In none can be found anything as pleasant and as touching as the game of cards that Mr. and Mrs. Smith played every night before bedtime." The funeral of Mrs. Smith filled St. Patrick's Cathedral with five thousand mourners. Another three thousand stood outside. She was buried in Calvary Cemetery, Queens.

Katie's death threw Smith into a deep depression from which he would never recover. "The Governor looks pretty tired and old," Robert Moses wrote a friend. "Maybe the children and the grandchildren can make it up." Nevertheless, he did not immediately curtail his activities. Less than a week after the funeral, he signed a letter to *Time* magazine defending Moses from some criticism. On May 24, Smith fulfilled a commitment to lead a party of press back to his old neighborhood to walk the site of the future Alfred E. Smith Houses. His former neighbors called out to him. "We know why you're down here, Governor; we know you came here to do something for us," one said. Two days later, he hosted a press conference in the Empire State Building to publicize reports of mass exterminations of civilians by the Nazis. The statement, signed by Smith, the governors of eighteen states, Associate Supreme Court Justice Frank Murphy, members of Congress, and business and labor leaders, called on the United States and its allies to repeat their warnings to the Germans "that no person who participates in crimes against the Jews and other minorities shall escape punishment." During the press conference, Smith said that all available radio facilities should be used to broadcast this message to the Germans. The message also demanded that the Allies pay more than lip service to the welfare of threatened groups by opening their borders to refugees and setting up temporary refuges.

Despite the tragedy of war and his personal grief, Smith was still capable of the humor that had always been his trademark. In June he traveled to the Sixty-ninth Regiment Armory to address four thousand New York Life Insurance Company employees who had volunteered to sell bonds during the fifth war bond drive. As he was introduced, the band began to play "The Sidewalks of New York" and the audience rose for a standing ovation. "I've heard that song before," Smith replied after the salesmen had sat down again. He told them that his fellow directors on the New York Life board had been delighted by a report of their employees' success in selling bonds. "You ought to see how those old birds were tickled to death." Speaking only a week after the Allies had landed in France, Smith spoke about victory as if it had already been won:

> There never was any doubt in anybody's mind that we would eventually win the war. Why? Because we were fighting for something. We were fighting for a great cause. We were fighting to establish the equality of man, the brotherhood of man, under the fatherhood of God. And the other fellows are not able to say that. What about the little Japs? What are they fighting for? To build up what they call an empire. . . . And what about Adolph [sic]? Adolph is trying to promote what he calls the superiority of the Aryan race. Well, I don't know what you know about it; maybe some of you might have met some Aryans in the business of life insurance, but in the long days I spent in public office, I never saw an Aryan. . . . And if there was one down there, he never voted, because if he did, that would have been different. We would have had to know.

Smith told the salesmen to stress the importance of the cause, but he added the practical advice that they remind people that they were only lending their money and that the borrower was completely trustworthy. "[W]hen the day comes that the United States Government bond isn't any good, then nothing is good. We are all finished! We are all washed up!" He concluded by reminding his audience that God would never abandon the United States. "He made it a haven of repose and a harbor of refuge for the downtrodden and poor and the oppressed of every land." Another standing ovation rolled through the cavernous armory as Smith left center stage. It was his final public appearance.

In August Robert Moses took Smith and Raskob fishing on his boat. During the outing, Moses became convinced that Smith was suffering from more than depression: "The Governor is in bad shape. Of course, he is depressed about Katie but there is something radically wrong with him on the physical side. John Raskob is obviously very much worried about it." Over the next four days Smith's condition deteriorated. "I am really worried about Governor Smith. He feels miserable and is home today," Raskob wrote Moses. Soon after, Smith was admitted to St. Vincent's Hospital. At first it appeared that he was not seriously ill. Raskob wrote Moses that he hoped that Smith would be released within a week to ten days. Smith's doctor, Raymond Sullivan, told the press that his patient had suffered from the excessive heat and had merely entered the hospital for "a rest." He would be out by the middle of the week, Sullivan promised.

But the patient was suffering from cirrhosis, and his liver was beginning to fail. In October the world learned that Al Smith was dying. From Rome, Archbishop Francis Spellman sent Smith a telegram, transmitting an apostolic benediction. In all the churches in the New York diocese, priests read a special prayer for Smith's rapid recovery or "happy death." The Rockefeller Institute Hospital was besieged by calls about the former governor's condition. Hundreds showed up at the hospital personally, including Alfred E. Smith, a thirteen-year-old African-American boy who showed reporters the letter that his namesake had sent to his parents at the time of his birth, expressing his gratitude for naming their child for him. Smith seemed to improve briefly. He was weak but alert when Raskob visited him on October 2. At the end, Smith realized that he was dying and was praying constantly. Death came at dawn on October 4. The roses sent by Franklin and Eleanor Roosevelt had just arrived.

# EPILOGUE

Not everything said about Smith immediately following his death was kind. There was still a great deal of misunderstanding about the reasons for his break with Roosevelt. During the Democratic convention in July, for example, a quiz show asked what Democratic leader threatened to "take a walk" after a previous Democratic convention. Many people believed that Smith had broken with the Democratic Party following the Democratic convention in Chicago in 1932. It made sense to those who saw Smith's 1936 bolt as the action of a disappointed candidate for president. The *New York Times* reinforced this view in its obituary. "Mr. Smith's failure to realize his foremost ambition, election to the Presidency, led to his break with Franklin D. Roosevelt, long his friend," it said. The *Washington Post*'s appraisal of Smith was patronizing:

> That in normal times Al Smith, despite his imperfect understanding of national issues and his even more imperfect understanding of foreign affairs, would have made an extremely successful President of the United States may be granted. That he was the man for the job in such times as these may be strongly doubted. He fell short, though perhaps not far short, of the qualities necessary to great statesmanship in a time of world crisis.

Would Smith have lived up to the challenges of the Depression and world war? The answer can be only speculative. I believe that Smith would have followed a course very similar to Roosevelt's. Despite his inexperience in foreign policy, he was a consistent supporter of an active American involvement in world affairs. An advocate of the League of Nations and the World Court, Smith recognized the danger of Nazism from the beginning and supported the fight against the isolationists. On the domestic side, there can be no question that the American people would have been better off if Al Smith had been elected president in 1928: the federal government would have started providing relief to the unemployed three years before the inauguration of the New Deal. It also seems likely that he would have followed Roosevelt in extending the reforms achieved in New York to the entire country. Smith's conservatism was a reaction to the evidence of the deep religious and ethnic divisions in American society revealed by the 1928 campaign. Had he been elected, his fear of government abuse of minorities would not have emerged, and he may well have become one of the country's great presidents.

Despite the sour notes from the *Washington Post*, the anger that Smith had aroused by taking a walk in 1936 had largely vanished by 1944, and his death provided an occasion for old friends who had been separated from him to celebrate the qualities and accomplishments that they had always admired. A White House statement praised Smith's honesty and cited his courage as well: "To the populace he was a hero. Frank, friendly, warm-hearted, honest as the noonday sun, he had the courage of his convictions, even when his espousal of unpopular causes invited the enmity of powerful adversaries. . . . In his passing the country loses a true patriot." Roosevelt had been Smith's most powerful adversary, but the attack on the New Deal had been forgiven as an outgrowth of the very qualities of honesty and courage that had produced his greatest victories for the common man. "With the passing of Alfred E. Smith the common people of America and the workers especially lose their warm and unselfish friend," labor leader David Dubinsky said.

In the years to come, Smith would be caught in the crossfire of the debate over the role of government in American life that had begun during the New Deal. Liberals could not champion a man who attacked the New Deal, while conservatives could not warm to someone who played such a prominent role in the founding of the American welfare state. Inevitably, his reputation dwindled. But Smith was never in any doubt about his role in American history. On Flag Day in 1939, he gave a speech at the Betsy Ross home in Philadelphia that constitutes a fitting epitaph, although he did not intend it that way. Smith was trying to explain what he believed to be the distinctiveness of American democracy. Roosevelt had recently characterized it as America's commitment to the rule of the majority. That was wrong, Smith said. The essence of American democracy lies not only in its dedication to the equality of men but in its protection of the rights of the minority. "The fact of the matter is that the Constitution is intended to protect the rights of the minority and we should all thank God for it in the name of every minority in the country." It was the opportunity for personal freedom that had drawn his ancestors to the United States, he explained. At first these freedoms had been denied to the newcomers, and they had been forced to fight for them. But their fight had compelled America to fulfill the promise of equality contained in the Declaration of Independence. "The fight [for] political and religious freedom and for racial tolerance has been the biggest part of the development of our American democracy," Smith said. He was proud of what he had achieved as a minority leader.

Smith did not believe that the fight for equal rights was over. In February 1939, in an address at Lincoln University, a black college, Smith predicted that African-Americans would be the next minority to expand American freedom. Whites must face up to their role in the "Negro problem," Smith said. Blacks were not asking for more than the immigrants had. "Opportunity is all they ask. They can and are solving their own problem and working out their own destiny." This didn't mean that whites shouldn't help:

> We can help them work out their economic future if we provide more adequate education opportunities for them. We should stop crowding them into slums, both country slums and city slums. The Negro problem would be much more quickly solved, too, if better health and medical service were available to the race, and that is one of the things we must give attention to along with education, housing, jobs and better working conditions in the future. And education is not merely to end illiteracy, but to give them school and college education, especially to those who have it in them to become leaders among their own people.

Clearly, government would have to play a role in aiding African-Americans, but Smith believed that like other immigrant groups they would take control of their own destiny. Through institutions like Lincoln University, they would develop their own leadership. "They can help raise their own race's level of intelligence, self-respect and self-support," he said. In the final analysis, they would win equal rights for themselves.

Robert Moses would later claim that like him, Smith was a gradualist on the issue of civil rights for African-Americans. Smith told him a story about the first black patrolman in the Fourth Ward and how long it had taken him to win acceptance from the white officers. In addition, Smith was "disturbed and disgusted" by "extravagant promises to minorities here and abroad," Moses said. Yet in 1941 Smith resigned from the Society for Preservation and Encouragement of Barber Shop Quartets when the organization refused to allow a black quartet, the Grand Central Red Caps, to perform at its national competition in St. Louis. How could Smith have failed to support Martin Luther King, Jr., and the civil rights movement? This was the same fight he had waged for his own people.

New Yorkers demanded the opportunity to say good-bye to Al Smith. The family had originally planned to keep the casket closed during the period that it was on display in St. Patrick's Cathedral. But in deference to public sentiment, it was left open. Outside, in a drizzling rain, the line of mourners wound around the cathedral, growing from three and four abreast in the church itself to more than ten abreast outside. When the doors opened at 2 p.m., Smith's casket was located in one of the chapels. At 8:30 p.m. it was moved to the main aisle. As they passed the casket, the mourners saw Smith lying in formal dress with the Medal of the Knights of Malta on his chest and the rosary he received from the pope in his hands. By 1 a.m., when the last mourner left, it was estimated that 160,000 had viewed the body. After the doors were closed, an honor guard from the Sixty-ninth Regiment and the Catholic War Veterans watched over Smith's body in the empty cathedral.

The crowds were back for the funeral the next day. An estimated 35,000 filled the sidewalks on both sides of Fifth Avenue for six blocks in either direction from St. Patrick's Cathedral. As they watched the dignitaries arrive and enter the church, they could easily recall the most dramatic moments of a great life. Jimmy Walker, Robert Wagner, Herbert Lehman, and James Farley were there. So was Eleanor Roosevelt, representing the president, who was ill. (He would die six months later.) Mayor La Guardia arrived in a police car. More than five thousand people squeezed into the cathedral. The Catholic church was represented by a magnificent procession:

> Cross bearers and acolyte brothers, regular clergy, secular clergy, provincials of religious communities, diocesan curia, very reverend monsignori, right reverend monsignori, right reverend abbots with chaplains, knights in attendance, Passionists in severe black robes lined with white, the Franciscan Brothers in brown, the Carmelites in white lace surplices, the Monsignori and Bishops in purple robes, purple birettas with black tassels and black birettas with purple tassels.

In the eulogy, Monsignor Joseph P. Donahue, vicar general of the New York archdiocese, explained Smith's importance to the church:

> He can in all justice be called the boast of the Catholic American laity. His leadership exerted powerful influence, not merely in the political world but in the wider and vastly more important realm of Catholic ideals. He did not limit himself only to the open and fearless profession of his faith, but in every circumstance he gave evidence of the joy which was his in the possession of the greatest possible gift—his faith.

Smith's faith encompassed more than a belief in God. He also believed in the equality of men, the institutions of democratic government, and the destiny of the United States. His faith had prevented him from falling into cynicism and despair when the people abandoned him to follow a new leader. It was the reason they continued to love him. Nothing could extinguish the optimism of the Happy Warrior.

# NOTES

## PROLOGUE

3 *"I just can't understand it"*: Frances Perkins, *The Roosevelt I Knew* (New York: Viking, 1946; reprint, New York: Harper Colophon, 1964), 157.

## 1: GREAT EXPECTATIONS

8 *"Here comes the son of a bitch"*: Adrian Cook, *Armies of the Streets: The New York City Draft Riots* (Lexington: University Press of Kentucky, 1974), 59.

8 *"Prisoners? Don't take any"*: Ibid., 74.

9 *Over six feet tall*: Alfred E. Smith, *Up to Now: An Autobiography* (New York: Viking, 1929), 4–5.

10 *His father, Emanuel*: It was Frances Perkins who identified the nationality of Al Smith's paternal grandfather. Matthew and Hannah Josephson, *Al Smith: Hero of the Cities; A Political Portrait Drawing on the Papers of Frances Perkins* (Boston: Houghton Mifflin, 1969), 13–15.

10 *"They are the children of God"*: Ibid., 17.

11 *"Carriages, wagons, carts"*: James D. McCabe, *Lights and Shadows of New York Life; Or, the Sights and Sensations of the Great City* (Philadelphia: National Publishing House, 1872; reprint, New York: Farrar, Straus and Giroux, 1970), 130.

13 *"This is like the view"*: Norman Hapgood and Henry Moskowitz, *Up from City Streets: Alfred E. Smith: A Biographical Study in Contemporary Politics* (New York: Grosset & Dunlap, 1927), 13.

14 *"The spirit of pulling down"*: Charles Lockwood, *Manhattan Moves Uptown: An Illustrated History* (1976; reprint, New York: Barnes & Noble, 1995), 13.

14 *"Overturn, overturn, overturn"*: Allan Nevins, ed., *The Diary of Philip Hone, 1828–1851* (New York: Dodd, Mead, 1927), 730.

14  *"Why should it be loved"*: Lockwood, *Manhattan Moves Uptown*, 11.

14  *"For years I walked"*: Jacob Riis, *How the Other Half Lives: Studies Among the Tenements of New York* (1890; reprint, New York: Sagamore, 1957), ix.

16  *"Your senses ache"*: Junius Henri Browne, *The Great Metropolis: A Mirror of New York* (Hartford: American Publishing, 1869), 274.

16  *"His earliest memories"*: Martin Green, *New York Evening World*, October 16, 1922.

17  *"[H]e himself would not be contented"*: Smith, *Up to Now*, 5.

17  *"When I was growing up"*: Ibid., 25.

18  *"No gymnasium that was ever built"*: Ibid., 17.

19  *"given chocolate to drink"*: Ibid., 6–7.

20  *"I went to the Dime Museum so often"*: Ibid., 49.

20  *"Hats off, youse"*: Armond Fields and L. Marc Fields, *From the Bowery to Broadway: Lew Fields and the Roots of American Popular Theater* (New York: Oxford University Press, 1993), 43.

21  *"On a warm night in summer"*: Smith, *Up to Now*, 37–8.

22  *"The undulating of the bridge"*: David McCullough, *The Great Bridge* (New York: Simon & Schuster, 1972; paperback, New York: Touchstone, 1982), 398.

22  *"I remember Mother"*: Josephson and Josephson, *Al Smith*, 24.

23  *"That was my first view of a great calamity"*: *New York Evening World*, Oct. 16, 1922.

23  *"We had good food"*: Josephson and Josephson, *Al Smith*, 19.

24  *"I don't know where to turn"*: Emily Smith Warner, *The Happy Warrior: A Biography of My Father, Alfred E. Smith* (New York: Doubleday, 1956), 27.

24  *"a great mischief"*: Josephson and Josephson, *Al Smith*, 35.

25  *"If anybody made a hostile demonstration"*: Ibid., 36.

26  *"He was talking all the time"*: Ibid., 53.

26  *"On Sundays"*: unidentified newspaper article in scrapbook, Alfred E. Smith collection, Museum of the City of New York.

27  *"I think I may well say"*: Smith, *Up to Now*, 15.

27  *"receiving clerk"*: Hapgood and Moskowitz, *Up From City Streets*, 24.

## 2: MAKING IT

29  *"Unfortunate tenants"*: "Noted Men in the Public Eye," *Bayside Review*, August 1901, Smith collection, Museum of the City of New York.

30  *"If [Mayor Grant] had instituted a search"*: *New York Tribune*, December 18, 1890, 6.

32  *"[T]his campaign of mine is a sort of uprisin' "*: *New York Herald*, October 15, 1894, 4.

33  *"One individual, who had interviewed the bar too assiduously"*: Ibid., October 16, 1894, 3.

34  *"Why that man's been to Congress enough"*: Ibid., October 18, 1894, 4.

34 *"Ully smoke!"*: Ibid., October 17, 1894, 4.

35 *"I had a choice"*: Smith, *Up to Now*, 56.

36 *"I propose to do what I can"*: New York Times, July 2, 1895, 1.

37 *"Here you are, Al"*: Smith, *Up to Now*, 45.

39 *"If Al had gone on being a clerk"*: New York Times, May 5, 1944, 19.

41 *"In those days a penny looked big"*: Smith, *Up to Now*, 59.

42 *"Prior to that time, nominations"*: Ibid., 58.

42 *"It was not only the Stars and Stripes"*: New York Times, September 3, 1901, 1.

44 *"[A]t no time since the days of William M. Tweed"*: Ibid., September 18, 1901, 1.

46 *"He said that a man who went to the legislature"*: Smith, *Up to Now*, 67.

46 *"[S]o that while contemplating my coming nomination"*: Ibid., 66.

47 *"You see it's this way"*: Henry F. Pringle, *Alfred E. Smith: A Critical Study* (New York: Macy-Masius Publishers, 1927), 137–8.

48 *"Al went up to Albany"*: Hapgood and Moskowitz, *Up from City Streets*, 50–1.

## 3: STRANGERS AT THE DOOR

50 *"I casually observed"*: Smith, *Up to Now*, 74.

50 *"The great metropolis of our State"*: New York Times, January 6, 1904, 2.

51 *"So consistently have the Republicans controlled"*: Ibid., January 3, 1904, 8.

53 *"The average citizen in the rural district"*: Revised Record, New York State Constitutional Convention, 1894, vol. 4, 10.

53 *"We of the minority"*: Ibid., vol. 4, 17.

53 *"There are men here"*: New York Times, September 14, 1894, 1.

53 *"Thirty years of Republican Assemblies"*: New York World, November 5, 1922, Editorial Section, 1.

53 *"The state constitution of 1894"*: Gordon E. Baker, *Rural Versus Urban Political Power: The Nature and Consequences of Unbalanced Representation* (New York: Doubleday, 1955), 32.

56 *"The hayseeds think"*: William L. Riordan, *Plunkitt of Tammany Hall: A Series of Very Plain Talks on Very Practical Politics*, (1905; reprint, with an introduction by Peter Quinn, New York: Signet Classics, 1995), 21.

56 *"It says right out in the open"*: Ibid., 21.

56 *"I cannot conceive of the Republican Party"*: New York Times, February 3, 1904, 5.

56 *"It abolishes everything"*: New-York Daily Tribune, February 5, 1904, 4.

57 *"I can tell a haddock from a hake"*: Hapgood and Moskowitz, *Up from City Streets*, 55–6.

58 *"[H]e has stories today"*: Ibid., 73–4.

59 *"If there is such a thing as hell"*: New York Times, January 17, 1905, 1.

60 *"Was it not better"*: Ibid., March 28, 1905, 1.

60 *"I knew nothing about banking"*: Smith, *Up to Now*, 74–5.

60 *"I just hated the idea"*: Ibid., 74–5.

61 *"I worked very hard"*: Ibid., 76.

61 *"I would sooner have a short shakehand"*: Speech of the Hon. Alfred E. Smith, April 13, 1932, Alfred E. Smith Papers, New York State Library, Albany.

61 *"Mr. Wende said"*: Smith, *Up to Now*, 111–12.

65 *"Everybody in the Assembly knew"*: James W. Wadsworth Reminiscences, Oral History Project, Columbia University, New York (hereafter cited as Columbia Oral History), 67.

65 *"I felt that I had made so much headway"*: Smith, *Up to Now*, 76.

65 *"inconspicuous"*: Citizens Union Committee on Legislation, *Report*, 1905.

65 *"intelligent and active"*: Ibid., 1906.

65 *"We would have our executive sessions"*: Beverly Robinson Reminiscences, Columbia Oral History, 42.

66 *"We might get into a long wrangle"*: Ibid., 42–3.

67 *It was better for boys to be at the ballpark*: Pringle, *Alfred E. Smith*, 151.

68 *"I discovered that Al Smith"*: Robinson Reminiscences, Columbia Oral History, 43.

68 *"I had so well established myself"*: Smith, *Up to Now*, 84.

68 *"increased ability"*: Pringle, *Alfred E. Smith*, 151.

69 *"The Republican leaders said"*: Lawrence Veiller Reminiscences, Columbia Oral History, 211.

69 *"[W]ithin the last week or two"*: *New-York Daily Tribune*, March 11, 1909.

70 Smith *"made one of the worst records"*: Citizens Union Committee on Legislation, *Report*, 1909.

71 *"They tell us that his bill"*: *New York Evening Post*, June 30, 1910.

71 *"The present occupant of the Executive Chamber"*: Ibid.

71 But he had *"voted and worked against the public interest"*: Citizens Union Committee on Legislation, *Report*, 1910.

## 4: DOING GOOD

72 *"Senator Wagner and Assemblyman Smith to see"*: Warner, *Happy Warrior*, 27.

73 *"It would be impracticable and unfair"*: *New York Times*, November 25, 1910, 10.

74 *"His voice was the lowest and gentlest"*: Warner, *Happy Warrior*, 86.

74 *"I would have just as soon"*: Nancy J. Weiss, *Charles Francis Murphy, 1858–1924: Respectability and Responsibility in Tammany Politics* (Northampton, MA: Smith College, 1968), 9–10.

74 *"After the failure to-day"*: *New York Times*, February 9, 1911, 2.

75 *"Kings [County]"*: Ibid., November 11, 1910, 2.

75 *"The decision to throw over Senator Grady"*: Frank Freidel, *Franklin D. Roosevelt: The Apprenticeship* (Boston: Little, Brown, 1952), 100.

76 *"The business of the House"*: New York World, January 4, 1911, 6.

76 *"For years men"*: New York Times, January 14, 1911, 10.

77 *"[T]he votes of those who represent the people"*: Ibid., January 17, 1911, 1.

77 *"Never in the history of Albany"*: Geoffrey C. Ward, A First-Class Temperament: The Emergence of Franklin Roosevelt (New York: Harper & Row, 1989; reprint, New York: Harper Perennial, 1990), 134.

77 *"Gradually the struggle"*: Ernest K. Lindley, Franklin D. Roosevelt, A Career in Progressive Democracy (Indianapolis: Bobbs-Merrill, 1931), 84.

78 *"Those who looked closely"*: New York Times, January 22, 1911, V, 11.

78 *"handkerchief box young man"*: Geoffrey C. Ward, Before the Trumpet: Young Franklin Roosevelt (New York: Harper & Row, 1985; reprint, New York: Perennial Library, 1986), 251.

78 *"This, combined with his pince-nez and great height"*: Perkins, The Roosevelt I Knew, 11.

79 *"Accordingly, E. R. and I hurriedly dressed"*: Ward, A First-Class Struggle, 128.

79 *"It is safe to predict"*: New York Times, January 22, 1911, V, 11.

80 *"I know I can't make you change your mind"*: Lindley, Franklin D. Roosevelt, 92.

81 *"Those who called themselves"*: Raymond Moley, 27 Masters of Politics (New York: Funk & Wagnalls, 1949), 34.

81 *"Germans and Scandinavians"*: Ward, Before the Trumpet, 141–2.

81 *"I am anxious to hear"*: Ward, First-Class Temperament, 59.

81 *"very charming in spite of the fact"*: Ibid., 138, footnote 10.

82 *"I might almost say"*: Ibid., 93, footnote 7.

82 *"This is absolutely untrue"*: Freidel, Franklin D. Roosevelt, 106.

82 *"Why is the business"*: New York World, January 26, 1911, 1.

83 *"Gentlemen, this is a most uncalled for"*: Freidel, Franklin D. Roosevelt, 107.

83 *"[T]he party was scarcely"*: New York Times, February 28, 1911, 1.

84 *"The insurgents had said"*: Ibid., April 8, 1911, 24.

84 *"I pick up ideas"*: Josephson and Josephson, Al Smith, 85.

85 *"considerable ability in floor leadership"*: Citizens Union Committee on Legislation, Report, 1911.

86 *"It seemed that three-fifths"*: New York World, April 6, 1911, 6.

87 *"We have tried you citizens"*: New York Times, April 3, 1911, 3.

88 *"That's what he does"*: George Martin, Madame Secretary, Frances Perkins (Boston: Houghton Mifflin, 1976), 81.

88 *"You're in favor of the bill"*: Ibid., 83–4.

89 *"These fellows in the Assembly"*: Ibid., 89.

90 *"got a firsthand look"*: Perkins, The Roosevelt I Knew, 17.

90 *"It's uncivilized"*: Martin, Madame Secretary, 119.

91 *"There is a Commandment"*: Louis D. Silveri, "The Political Education of Alfred E. Smith" (Ph.D. diss., St. John's University, 1963), 132.

92 *"[A]mong all the hundreds"*: Warner, Happy Warrior, 69.

92  *"the peak of my political prominence"*: Smith, *Up to Now*, 124.

93  *"Al Smith was sitting"*: Robert Binkerd Reminiscences, Columbia Oral History, 33.

93  *"He hopes that by using"*: Robert F. Wesser, *A Response to Progressivism: The Democratic Party and New York Politics, 1902–1918* (New York: New York University Press, 1986), 114.

94  *"William Sulzer was impeached"*: *New York World*, October 18, 1913, 4.

95  *"My friends, this is"*: "Speech of ex-Governor Sulzer, at the Progressive Club of the Second Assembly District, Saturday Evening, November 1st," Alfred E. Smith Papers, New York State Library, Albany, NY.

96  *"I remember that we walked"*: Jonah Goldstein Reminiscences, Columbia Oral History, 10.

96  *"There'll be another day"*: Wesser, *Response to Progressivism*, 132.

96  *"wanted to fix it"*: *New York Times*, November 11, 1913, 7.

97  *"Give the people everything"*: Wesser, *Response to Progressivism*, 136.

97  *"Show me the bill"*: Ibid., 140.

97  *"more constructive legislation"*: Ibid., 141.

97  *"We are at the end"*: Ibid., 164.

98  *"Nobody has to put"*: Josephson and Josephson, *Al Smith*, 148.

99  *"This is the entering wedge"*: Silveri, "Political Education," 131.

99  *"The State of New York"*: Alfred E. Smith, *Progressive Democracy: Addresses and State Papers of Alfred E. Smith* (New York: Harcourt, Brace, 1928), 160.

100  *"The most corrupt legislature"*: Silveri, "Political Education," 132.

101  *"I will stop talking"*: New York State Constitutional Convention, *Revised Record* (Albany, NY: J. B. Lyon, 1916), vol. 1, 632.

101  *"You want an appeal"*: Ibid., vol. 3, 2975.

102  *"I would sooner be"*: Ibid., 2974.

102  *"law in a democracy"*: Silveri, "Political Education," 143.

103  *"I am frank to say"*: Hapgood and Moskowitz, *Up from City Streets*, 130.

103  *"to one sect"*: Alvin P. Stauffer, Jr., "Anti-Catholicism in American Politics, 1865–1900" (Ph.D. diss., Harvard University, 1933), 93.

103  *"Al Smith knows more"*: Paula Eldot, *Governor Alfred E. Smith: The Politician as Reformer* (New York: Garland Publishing, 1983), 10.

## 5: RECONSTRUCTION

106  *"It is difficult to talk"*: *New York Times*, October 17, 1918, 15.

107  *"a man of quite unusual ability"*: Ibid., September 3, 1915, 5.

107  *"The proposed nomination"*: Ibid., October 29, 1915, 4.

107  *"His address was a succession"*: *New York Evening World*, October 19, 1922.

108  *"Ten minutes after Al Smith began"*: Ibid., October 20, 1922.

109  *"This tunnel, now"*: Pringle, *Alfred E. Smith*, 36.

110  *"In my judgment"*: New York Times, April 8, 1918, 8.

111  *"Mr. Smith is the best representative"*: Ibid., July 25, 1918, 1.

111  *"Al Smith seemed as pleased"*: Ibid., 6.

112  *"Only a miracle, it was thought"*: Joseph M. Proskauer, A Segment of My Times (New York: Farrar, Straus, 1950), 42.

112  *"He knows this city"*: New York Times, September 19, 1918, 12.

116  *"The only question"*: Ibid., October 23, 1918, 12.

117  *"He is wrong again"*: Ibid., October 30, 1918, 7.

117  *"In the closing hours"*: Ibid., November 2, 1918, 8.

119  *"Don't be frightened, Governor"*: Warner, Happy Warrior, 102.

119  *"To me, it was a palace"*: Ibid., 102.

119  *"I had never rung bells"*: Ibid., 103.

120  *"I was eager"*: Smith, Up to Now, 171.

121  *"If democracy is worth"*: New York Times, October 26, 1919, 18.

121  *"We must enact"*: Alfred E. Smith, Public Papers of Alfred E. Smith, Governor, 1919 (Albany: J. B. Lyon, 1920), 31.

122  *"a sort of unreality"*: New York Times, January 2, 1919, 10.

123  *"It has been said here"*: Ibid., February 19, 1919, 4.

123  *"They seemed to imply"*: Smith, Up to Now, 177.

124  *"Home, to them, has always meant"*: Catherine Smith, "How I Brought Up My Five Children," Woman's Home Companion 52 (March 1925), 29.

125  *"He told the mothers of our country"*: New York Times, March 5, 1919, 1–2.

126  *"What I am afraid of"*: Smith, Public Papers, 1919, 752.

128  *"There are two things"*: New York Times, June 21, 1919, 15.

## 6: THE VOCATION OF POLITICS

130  *"Politics is a strong and slow boring"*: H. H. Gerth and C. Wright, eds., From Max Weber: Essays in Sociology (New York: Oxford University Press, 1946; reprint, New York: Galaxy Books, 1958), 128.

132  *"I have been particularly careful"*: W. A. Swanberg, Citizen Hearst; A Biography of William Randolph Hearst (New York: Scribner, 1961), 327.

133  *"does nothing while thousands"*: Ibid.

134  *"it was so stupid"* and *"[T]his foolish attack"*: Smith, Up to Now, 196.

134  *"Just this time a year ago"*: New York Times, October 19, 1919, 2.

135  *"It is a particularly easy thing"*: Ibid., October 23, 1919, 1.

135  *"I do not have to meet him"*: Swanberg, Citizen Hearst, 329.

135  *"All that was savage in him"*: Pringle, Alfred E. Smith, 27.

136  *"Of course I am alone"*: New York Times, October 30, 1919, 2.

137  *"I cannot think"*: Ibid.

138  *"I have more reason"*: Ibid.

140  *"I contend there is no disorder"*: Ibid., November 3, 1919, 1.

141  *"Each and every adherent"*: Robert K. Murray, Red Scare: A Study of Na-

*tional Hysteria* (University of Minnesota, 1955; reprint, New York: McGraw-Hill, 1964), 219.

142 *"Much of the dissatisfaction"*: Alfred E. Smith, *Public Papers of Alfred E. Smith* (Albany, NY: J. B. Lyon, 1921), 29.

143 *"It is therefore quite evident"*: New York Times, January 8, 1920, 1.

143 *"Although I am unalterably opposed"*: Smith, *Progressive Democracy*, 273.

145 *"I have a keen understanding"*: Ibid., 270.

145 *The five Socialist assemblymen were "all right"*: New York Times, February 24, 1920, 17.

145 *"some highbrow college stuff"*: Proskauer, *Segment of My Times*, 46.

146 *"It deprives teachers"*: Smith, *Progressive Democracy*, 276.

146 *"The clash of conflicting opinions"*: Ibid., 278.

146 *"Law, in a democracy, means"*: Ibid., 281.

146 *"[T]he safety of this government"*: Ibid., 278.

148 *"Everybody writes to me"*: Smith, *Public Papers*, 1920, 620.

148 *"All I can do"*: Ibid., 634.

148 *"Now, whom do the people"*: Ibid., 615.

149 *"I would say today"*: Ibid., 630.

149 *"The real fact is"*: Smith, *Public Papers*, 1919, 793.

150 *"We must banish from our minds"*: Ibid., 794.

150 *"Meet the King"*: Hapgood and Moskowitz, *Up from City Streets*, 225.

150 *"I am well supplied"*: Smith, *Public Papers*, 1920, 619.

151 *"The utter disregard"*: New York Times, April 26, 1920, 1.

152 *"I nominate here today"*: Ibid., July 1, 1920, 4.

153 *"He threw his whole heart"*: Smith, *Up to Now*, 210.

153 *"a demonstration that will stand out"*: New York Times, July 1, 1920, 2.

153 *"Men who have visited"*: Ward, *First-Class Temperament*, 508.

154 *"it converted a man"*: New York Times, July 1, 1920, 2.

154 *"I had accomplished"*: Smith, *Up to Now*, 210.

155 *"The thing I intend to do"*: New York Times, September 29, 1920, 8.

155 *"[T]he welfare of every man"*: Ibid., October 13, 1920, 5.

155 *"And I want to say"*: Ibid., October 31, 1920, 1.

156 *"Governor Smith, defeated"*: Ibid., November 3, 1920, 10.

156 *"Even in defeat"*: Smith, *Up to Now*, 221.

156 *"After Governor Glynn's speech"*: New York Times, December 31, 1920, 4.

## 7: THE KLAN RIDES AGAIN

157 *"Do we have to go"*: Warner, *Happy Warrior*, 129.

157 *"It was definitely fixed"*: Smith, *Up to Now*, 228–9.

158 *"Our whole family had accepted"*: Warner, *Happy Warrior*, 131.

159 *"They enjoyed heckling"*: Smith, *Up to Now*, 226–7.

159 *"I am going to stay"*: New York Times, April 7, 1922, 19.

160 *"Smith was determined"*: Ibid., May 22, 1985, B2. The chapter of Chadbourne's autobiography in which he claims to have supported Smith was not published with the rest of the memoir in 1985, and the family refused requests to release it. However, the *New York Times* obtained a copy.

161 *"That was certainly a magnificent Tuesday"*: Franklin D. Roosevelt to Alfred E. Smith, November 9, 1922, Smith Papers, New York State Library, Albany.

161 *"My Mother was opposed"*: Smith to Roosevelt, November 15, 1922, Smith Papers, New York State Library, Albany.

163 *"Are the people"*: Smith, *Public Papers, 1920*, 33.

163 *"The Republican majority"*: *New York Times*, January 31, 1919, 6.

164 *"We are watched"*: Alfred E. Smith, *Addresses of Alfred E. Smith, 1922–1944* (New York: Society of the Friendly Sons of St. Patrick, 1945), 55.

165 *"I am of the firm opinion"*: Smith, *Progressive Democracy*, 305.

165 *"Wouldn't you like"*: Pringle, *Alfred E. Smith*, 318.

166 *"Every State official"*: *New York Times*, May 17, 1923, 1.

166 *"The State has a perfect right"*: Ibid., May 18, 1923, 18.

167 *"composed of equal parts"*: Pringle, *Alfred E. Smith*, 330.

167 *"the South . . . has long been"*: *New York Times*, June 2, 1923, 2.

167 *"Generations yet unborn"*: Lawrence W. Levine, *Defender of the Faith: William Jennings Bryan, the Last Decade, 1915–1925* (New York: Oxford University Press, 1965; reprint, Cambridge, MA: Harvard University Press, 1987), 123.

167 *"the women whose husbands"*: *New York Times*, June 10, 1923, VIII, 1.

168 *"Mr. Bryan knows"*: Ibid., June 11, 1923, 1.

169 *"I am going to make the best of it"*: Robert K. Murray, *The 103rd Ballot: Democrats and the Disaster in Madison Square Garden* (New York: Harper & Row, 1976), 44.

171 *"You command me to accept"*: *New York Times*, February 19, 1924, 1.

171 *"[I]n New York"*: Ibid., October 21, 1923, 3.

172 *"The so-called Volstead Act"*: Ibid., February 21, 1924, 4.

172 *"It's strange"*: Ibid., April 4, 1924, 8.

173 *"If I were to tell you"*: Ibid., April 16, 1924, 1.

173 *"The Governor was affected"*: Ibid., April 26, 1924, 1.

174 *"[W]ith what good public cause"*: Ibid., April 28, 1924, 14.

175 *"It was the first real sorrow"*: Smith, *Up to Now*, 283.

175 *"The intellectual superiority"*: John Higham, *Strangers in the Land: Patterns of American Nativism, 1860–1925* (New Brunswick, NJ: Rutgers University Press, 1955; corrected with a new preface, New York: Atheneum, 1978), 276.

176 One analysis of employment: Heywood Broun and George Britt, *Christians Only: A Study in Prejudice* (New York: Vanguard, 1931), 231–2.

176 *"Now let the Niggers"*: David M. Chalmers, *Hooded Americanism: The His-*

*tory of the Ku Klux Klan* (New York: Watts, 1981; reprint, Durham, NC: Duke University Press, 1987), 33.

177 *"Indianapolis, Dayton, Portland"*: Kenneth T. Jackson, *The Ku Klux Klan in the City, 1915–30* (New York: Oxford University Press, 1967; reprint, New York: Oxford University Press, 1973), 236.

177 *"a quasi-secret order"*: Michael Williams, *The Shadow of the Pope* (New York: Whittlesey House, McGraw-Hill, 1932), 152.

177 *"Come on, stand up"*: Murray, *103rd Ballot*, 123.

178 *"For God's sake"*: Joseph M. Proskauer Reminiscences, Columbia Oral History, 5.

178 *"Joe, this is"*: Robert A. Caro, *The Power Broker* (New York: Knopf, 1974), 286.

179 *"This faith in him"*: *New York Times*, June 27, 1924, 4.

181 *"Are you a Protestant?"*: Williams, *Shadow of the Pope*, 164.

182 *"Saturday will always remain"*: Murray, *103rd Ballot*, 162.

183 *"It certainly was not"*: Smith, *Up to Now*, 287–8.

183 *"I am the Democratic governor of that state"*: Ibid., 288.

184 *"If I were to tell anybody"*: *New York Times*, July 10, 1924, 1.

184 *"Al's not yet ready"*: Pringle, *Alfred E. Smith*, 314.

185 *"If monkeys had votes"*: Murray, *103rd Ballot*, 212.

185 *"There must come a time"*: *New York Times*, July 15, 1924, 2.

186 *"I don't take the Ku Klux Klan"*: Ibid., October 8, 1924, 1.

186 *"This is the sixteenth time"*: Smith, *Up to Now*, 296.

## 8: PROTESTANT TRIUMPH

187 *"I'm all right"*: *New York Times*, January 16, 1925, 2.

189 *"At that time"*: Smith, *Up to Now*, 340.

189 *"There is no comparison"*: Eldot, *Governor Alfred E. Smith*, 132.

191 *"Alfred E. Smith today"*: *New York Times*, November 5, 1925, 1.

191 *"He holds these crowds"*: Walter Lippmann, *Men of Destiny* (New York: Macmillan, 1927), 7.

194 *"I'm not going to answer"*: Proskauer, *Segment of My Times*, 55.

194 *"[Y]ou 'impute' to American Catholics"*: Smith, *Progressive Democracy*, 255.

195 *"good plain Americanism"*: *New York Times*, April 18, 1927, 1.

195 *"Even on the train"*: Ibid., April 22, 1927, 3.

196 *"The revulsion of feeling"*: Ibid., January 29, 1928, III, 1.

196 *"Politicians had once more"*: Reuben H. Maury, *The Wars of the Godly* (New York: McBride, 1928), quoted in Williams, *Shadow of the Pope*, 182.

196 *"practically dead"*: *New York Times*, June 11, 1928, 4.

197 *"It was the biggest crowd"*: Warner, *Happy Warrior*, 177.

197 *"gave an aspect of majesty"*: Ibid., June 10, 1928, 1.

198 *"He is weeping"*: Louis Howe to Roosevelt, n.d., Louis Howe Papers, Franklin D. Roosevelt Library, Hyde Park, NY.

198 *"is more inclined to impatience"*: Pringle, *Alfred E. Smith,* 278.

198 *"I was in a position"*: Goldstein Reminiscences, Columbia Oral History, 28.

198 *"Jefferson gloried"*: *New York Times,* June 28, 1928, 1.

199 *"I offer one"*: Ibid., 3.

199 *"A delegate from Texas"*: Ibid., June 29, 1928, 2.

200 *"My nomination"*: Ibid., 1.

200 *" 'Move the arm' "*: Ibid., August 22, 1928, 3.

201 *"That old-fashioned statesman stuff "*: Ibid.

201 *"The greatest privilege"*: Alfred E. Smith, *Campaign Addresses of Governor Alfred E. Smith, Democratic Candidate for President,* 1928 (Washington, D.C.: Democratic National Committee, 1929), 1.

203 *"Mr. Smith's record"*: Roy V. Peel and Thomas C. Donnelly, *The 1928 Campaign; An Analysis* (New York: Richard R. Smith, 1931), 114.

205 *"for the defeat"*: *New York Times,* June 30, 1928, 1.

205 *"It's the only thing"*: Josephson and Josephson, *Al Smith,* 370.

206 *"[T]here is no doubt"*: *New York Times,* July 13, 1928, 16.

206 *"a man of unusual intelligence"*: Ibid., 4.

206 *"Let's take the worst"*: Ibid., July 15, 1928, 16.

207 *"No one in all"*: Ibid., August 21, 1928, 1.

207 *"The statement has been made"*: Ibid., September 4, 1928, 1.

208 *"It never occurred to me"*: Catherine Smith, "How I Brought Up My Five Children," *Woman's Home Companion* 52 (March 1925), 29.

208 *"I have spent"*: "Electing a President's Wife: Mrs. Alfred E. Smith in the White House," *Woman's Home Companion* 55 (March 1928), 10.

209 *"I cannot say very much"*: *New York Times,* July 13, 1928, 16.

209 *"Can you imagine"*: Edmund A. Moore, *A Catholic Runs for President: The Campaign of 1928* (New York: Ronald Press, 1956), 159.

209 Her *"weakness"*: *Outlook* 148 (April 25, 1928), 662.

209 *"Leave Katie alone!"*: Oscar Handlin, *Al Smith and His America* (Boston: Little, Brown, 1958), 130.

210 *"Governor Smith has a constitutional right"*: Williams, *Shadow of the Pope,* 192.

210 *"not more than one-half "*: Ibid., 195.

210 *"Shall we have a man"*: Ibid.

210 *"To call them intolerant"*: Ibid., 196.

210 *"a large corps"*: *New York Times,* July 15, 1928, 16.

211 *"It is time"*: Williams, *Shadow of the Pope,* 227.

211 *"To Murder Protestants!"*: Ibid., 254.

211 *"Obituray"*: Ibid., 256.

211 *"10 Reasons Why"*: Ibid., 273.

212 *"I see a very dark cloud"*: Ibid., 269.

212 *"Here, Sam"*: Ibid., 267.

212 *"Insolence"*: Ibid., 272.

212 *"by blood and conviction"*: Allan J. Lichtman, *Prejudice and the Old Politics: The Presidential Election of 1928* (Chapel Hill: University of North Carolina Press, 1979), 62.

212 *"The Republican Headquarters"*: Ibid., 66.

213 *"First they will try"*: Moore, *A Catholic Runs*, 179.

213 *"Whether this letter is authentic"*: Ibid., 146.

213 *"a very live and vital issue"*: Lichtman, *Prejudice*, 67.

214 *"There are 2,000 pastors"*: New York Times, September 8, 1928, 1.

215 *"She said you were"*: Ibid., September 9, 1928, 5.

215 *"outrageous"*: Ibid., September 13, 1928, 26.

215 *"We all felt"*: Lichtman, *Prejudice*, 68.

216 *"It will look like"*: New York Times, September 10, 1928, 3.

216 *"as we stepped down"*: Proskauer, *Segment of My Times*, 62.

217 *"The audience was always"*: New York Times, September 21, 1928, 2.

217 *"In this campaign"*: Smith, *Campaign Addresses*, 51.

219 *"Doesn't this look like"*: New York Times, September 23, 1928, 1.

219 *"I have been agreeably surprised"*: Ibid., September 24, 1928, 2.

219 *"The foundations of America"*: Williams, *Shadow of the Pope*, 291.

219 *"Would you vote"*: Ibid., 328–9.

220 *"Since it is immaterial"*: Lichtman, *Prejudice*, 157.

220 *"by an anti-Negro South"*: Robert A. Slayton, *Empire Statesman: The Rise and Redemption of Al Smith* (New York: Free Press, 2001), 286.

221 *"The behavior of the crowd"*: Frances Perkins Reminiscences, Columbia Oral History, vol. 2, 643.

221 *"[W]e are confronted"*: New York Times, October 23, 1928, 2.

222 *"We shall use words"*: Smith, *Campaign Addresses*, 203.

223 *"I think you will see"*: New York Times, October 27, 1928, 2.

223 *"It looks like"*: Ibid.

224 *"Wonderful, wonderful!"*: Ibid., November 3, 1928, 1.

224 *"A subway crush"*: Ibid., November 4, 1928, 3.

225 *"It has been many years"*: Ibid., October 28, 1928, III, 1.

225 *"He is an extraordinary man"*: Ibid., November 4, 1928, III, 1.

226 *"The hands are"*: Ibid., November 7, 1928, 29

226 *"I remember him saying"*: Perkins Reminiscences, Columbia Oral History, vol. 2, 645.

226 *"She said, 'You're absolutely wrong' "*: Ibid., 689.

227 *" 'Herbert' "*: Warner, *Happy Warrior*, 226–7.

227 *"The Governor's ruddy face"*: New York World, November 7, 1928, 4.

227 *"It's God's will"*: Warner, *Happy Warrior*, 228.

228 *"Nothing embarrasses me"*: Perkins Reminiscences, Columbia Oral History, vol. 2, 691.

228 *"Losing his own state"*: Walter Lippmann Reminiscences, Columbia Oral History, 131.

228 *"Well, we're rid"*: New York Times, November 9, 1928, 24.

228 *"I'll never forget"*: Perkins Reminiscences, Columbia Oral History, vol. 2, 691.

228 *"Al looked hurt"*: Ibid., 693.

228 *"I will never lose"*: New York Times, November 8, 1928, 1.

229 *"No one can say"*: Ibid., 24.

229 *"the miserable tradition"*: Ibid., November 7, 1928, 24.

229 *"My, oh my"*: Olive Sullivan to Frank P. Walsh, November 7, 1928, Frank P. Walsh Papers, Rare Book and Manuscript Division, New York Public Library.

230 *"The greatest element"*: New York Times, November 10, 1928, 3.

230 *"Governor Al Smith's philosophy"*: New York World, November 9, 1928, 1.

230 *"He said finally"*: Perkins Reminiscences, Columbia Oral History, vol. 2, 699.

## 9: GATEWAY OF OPPORTUNITY

231 *"It's all right"*: New York Times, November 9, 1928, 2.

231 *"There is one thing"*: Ibid., November 8, 1928, 1.

232 *"He paused"*: Ibid., November 9, 1928, 1.

232 *"[N]o political party"*: Smith, Campaign Addresses, 321.

233 *"The flag stands for"*: Hapgood and Moskowitz, Up from City Streets, 141–2.

233 *"I read about that"*: New York Times, December 11, 1928, 37.

233 *"It's all news to me"*: Ibid., January 27, 1929, 26.

234 *"And let me tell you"*: Ibid., January 3, 1929, 3.

235 *On January 18*: John J. Raskob to Alfred E. Smith, January 18, 1929, John J. Raskob Papers, Hagley Museum, Wilmington, DE.

235 *He apparently had*: Bernard M. Baruch to Alfred E. Smith, May 9, 1933, Bernard M. Baruch Papers, Princeton University Library, Princeton, NJ.

235 *"[A]fter living in a mansion"*: New York Times, March 1, 1933, 10.

236 *"I presented Roosevelt's"*: James A. Farley, Memorandum, n.d., James A. Farley Papers, Library of Congress, Washington, D.C.

237 *"Impossible"*: Frances Perkins to Florence Shientag, April 15, 1959, Frances Perkins Papers, Rare Book and Manuscript Library, Columbia University, New York, NY.

237 *"I was an awfully mean cuss"*: Perkins, The Roosevelt I Knew, 12.

237 *"I have a vivid picture"*: Ibid., 11.

237 *"Frank, you ought to"*: Ward, First-Class Temperament, 154.

238 *"Awful arrogant fellow"*: Perkins, The Roosevelt I Knew, 11.

238 *"[T]here was a tendency"*: Proskauer Reminiscences, Columbia Oral History, 2.

238 *"I love him"*: New York Times, July 1, 1920, 2.

239 *"picking up a fish"*: Ibid., July 8, 1920, 1.

239 *"I was treated"*: Ward, *First-Class Temperament*, 787.

240 *"[D]on't be so sure"*: Ibid., 780.

241 *"Okay, you're the doctor"*: Ibid., 790.

241 *"The policies of the state"*: New York Times, October 3, 1928, 12.

241 *"He has been in the front line"*: New York World, October 4, 1928, 2.

242 *"[A] Governor does not have to"*: New York Times, October 3, 1928, 1.

242 *"Mr. Roosevelt intended"*: Ibid., December 1, 1928, 3.

242 *"All talk that Mr. Smith"*: Ibid., December 14, 1928, 1.

242 *"Well, I'll tell you Frank"*: Ibid., January 1, 1929, 2.

242 *"I recommended"*: Perkins Reminiscences, Columbia Oral History, vol. 3, 27.

243 *"Oh, yes. I'll be here"*: Ibid., vol. 2, 718–19.

243 *"I can't tell Guernsey Cross"*: Ibid., vol. 3, 32.

244 *" 'Hello, Frank' "*: New York Times, March 12, 1929, 10.

245 *"I'm working hard now"*: Ibid., September 11, 1929, 18.

248 *"He acted with great boldness"*: Ibid., January 9, 1930, 26.

250 *"probably the greatest attainment"*: Theodore James, *Empire State Building* (New York: Harper & Row, 1975), 91.

250 *"You will be happy to know"*: Roosevelt to Smith, January 14, 1930, Franklin D. Roosevelt Papers, Franklin D. Roosevelt Library, Hyde Park, NY.

251 *"We are interpreting the outcome"*: Walter Lippmann to Roosevelt, January 14, 1930, Roosevelt Papers.

251 *"Hearty congratulations"*: Smith to Roosevelt, January 15, 1930, Roosevelt Papers.

251 *"By the way"*: Roosevelt to Smith, February 4, 1930, Roosevelt Papers.

251 *"Letter received"*: Smith to Roosevelt, n.d., Roosevelt Papers.

251 *"I spent considerable time"*: Smith to Roosevelt, May 22, 1930, Roosevelt Papers.

252 *"[I]f there is a man"*: New York Times, October 1, 1930, 22.

252 *"Mr. Smith's personal popularity"*: Ibid., October 26, 1930, 15.

253 *"Under a Republican administration"*: Ibid., October 28, 1930, 2.

253 *"What has happened"*: Ibid., October 29, 1930, 2.

254 *"I am not a candidate"*: Ibid., October 27, 1930, 18.

## 10: RETURN OF THE HAPPY WARRIOR

256 *"What may come after"*: New York Times, November 5, 1930, 20.

256 *"cool and an authoritative apostle"*: quoted in New York Times, November 7, 1930, 3.

257 *"I am so glad about"*: Roosevelt to Cordell Hull, November 10, 1930, Roosevelt Papers.

257 *"I am very anxious to talk to you"*: John J. Raskob to Herbert H. Lehman, December 3, 1930, Herbert H. Lehman Papers, Lehman Library, Columbia University, New York.

258 *"I have discussed the situation"*: Hull to Roosevelt, February 22, 1931, Roosevelt Papers.

258 *"I have been trying"*: Roosevelt to Smith, February 28, 1931, Roosevelt Papers.

258 *"I am very much pleased"*: New York Times, March 3, 1931, 14.

259 *"Mr. Raskob"*: Ibid., March 2, 1931, 4.

259 *"After Roosevelt's withdrawal"*: Cordell Hull, *The Memoirs of Cordell Hull* (New York: Macmillan, 1948), vol. 1, 145.

259 *"I am in hopes"*: Robert C. Brown to Raskob, December 24, 1930, Raskob Papers.

259 *"The leasing of the Empire State Building"*: New York Times, December 30, 1930, 26.

260 *"Certainly a Democrat"*: Ibid., March 3, 1931, 14.

260 *"The only fault"*: Ibid., March 4, 1931, 16.

260 *"government out of business"*: Ibid., March 6, 1931, 16.

261 *"I believed firmly"*: Ibid.

262 *"There is no split"*: Ibid., March 5, 1931, 1–2.

262 *"I think he was unable"*: Perkins Reminiscences, Columbia Oral History, vol. 3, 357.

262 *"[H]e trusted overmuch"*: Proskauer, *Segment of My Times*, 47.

263 *"I said, 'Al' "*: Proskauer Reminiscences, Columbia Oral History, 24.

263 *"The Empire State Building"*: James, *Empire State Building*, 99.

264 *"I think that its name"*: Ibid., 101.

264 *"During the last six months"*: Smith to Fred French, February 29, 1932, Smith Papers, New York State Library, Albany.

265 *He estimated that the Warner Brothers stock*: Smith to William H. Kelley, March 9, 1932, Smith Papers, New York State Library, Albany.

265 *"Ed, these are all debts"*: Edward J. Flynn, *You're the Boss* (New York: Viking, 1947), 86.

266 *"I have always been"*: New York Times, June 14, 1931, 2.

266 *"I can only repeat"*: Ibid.

266 *"The entire West"*: Howe to Hull, August 24, 1931, Cordell Hull Papers, Library of Congress, Washington, D.C.

267 *"The first trial balance"*: Roosevelt to Smith, November 11, 1931, Roosevelt Papers.

267 *"During the 20 years"*: New York Times, November 17, 1931, 2.

267 *"I have come simply"*: Ibid., November 19, 1931, 25.

267 *"The country expects"*: Clark Howell to Roosevelt, December 2, 1931, quoted in Elliott Roosevelt, ed., *F.D.R., His Personal Letters*, (New York: Duell, Sloan and Pearce, 1950), v. 3, 229.

269 *As he traveled north*: James A. Farley, Memorandum, December 10–11, 1931, Farley Papers.

269 *Frances Perkins recalled*: Perkins, *The Roosevelt I Knew*, 55.

269 *"On the contrary, Smith was a poor Governor"*: Arthur Krock, Private Office

Memorandum, January 15, 1932, Arthur Krock Papers, Princeton University Library, Princeton, NJ.

269 *"The man who says anything of the kind"*: *New York Times*, January 16, 1932, 14.

270 *"I said that the matter on my mind"*: "Notes of George S. Van Schaick as to His Recollections of Governor Alfred E. Smith," Perkins Papers.

271 *"decisively beaten"*: [Robert Jackson], "Suggestions for J.A.F.," n.d., Farley Papers.

271 *"If the Democratic National Convention"*: *New York Times*, February 8, 1932, 12.

272 *"The way in which Smith has been fading"*: *Stamford Advocate*, April 1, 1932, Smith Papers, New York State Library, Albany.

272 *"If I speak for nobody else"*: *New York Times*, January 9, 1932, 10.

273 *"You have got to say"*: Ibid., January 15, 1932, 17.

274 *"These unhappy times"*: Ibid., April 8, 1932, 1, 10.

274 *"Why the Governor should feel"*: Ibid., April 9, 1932, 14.

275 *"The country today"*: "Speech of the Hon. Alfred E. Smith, April 13, 1932," Smith Papers, New York State Library, Albany.

276 *"People who feared"*: *New York Times*, April 14, 1932, 20.

276 *"You expect no idealism"*: quoted in *New York Times*, April 15, 1932, 10.

276 *"Gov. Smith's voice"*: Joseph P. Tumulty to Editor, *Newark Evening News*, April 15, 1932, Joseph P. Tumulty Papers, Library of Congress, Washington, D.C.

276 *"The figures as revealed"*: *New York Times*, April 27, 1932, 1.

277 *"Al Smith ran an amazing race"*: Ibid., May 1, 1932, III, 5.

277 *"It ought to put a chock"*: Ibid., April 28, 1932, 2.

277 *"The vote I got"*: Ibid., May 5, 1932, 3.

277 *"Why, the drys are diving off"*: Ibid., June 11, 1932, 17.

278 *"We are going to Chicago"*: Ibid., June 22, 1932, 8.

278 *"I do not know anything"*: Ibid., June 23, 1932, 10.

279 *"Thanks, Chief"*: Ibid., June 24, 1932, 13.

279 *"This was no note"*: Ibid., 16.

279 *"[T]he Roosevelt bloc"*: Ibid., June 29, 1932, 15.

280 *"It's too wet"*: Ibid., June 30, 1932, 16.

281 *"A roar with greater volume"*: Ibid., July 1, 1932, 15.

281 *"[F]or all its glow"*: Ibid., 16.

282 *"Mr. Hearst had decided"*: Ibid., July 2, 1932, 4.

283 *"We believe"*: Ibid., 5.

284 *"Suddenly a rebel yell"*: Ibid.

285 *"exceptionally cheerful"*: Ibid., July 3, 1932, 10.

285 *"Don't forget"*: Ibid., 9.

## 11: REPEAL AND REFORM

286 *"Mr. Roosevelt has only secured"*: quoted in *New York Times*, July 4, 1932, 3.

287 *"I am amazed"*: Peter E. Laughlin to Frank P. Walsh, August 18, 1932, Walsh Papers.

287 *"considerable disappointment"*: *New York Times*, August 24, 1932, 6.

287 *"Their attitude appears to be"*: Ibid., October 25, 1932, 10.

288 *"100 percent"*: Proskauer Reminiscences, Columbia Oral History, 7.

288 *"To them I say"*: *New York Times*, July 7, 1932, 1.

288 *"That's a joke"*: Ibid., 8.

288 *"Well, now"*: Ibid., October 25, 1932, 15.

290 *" 'Give us beer' "*: Ibid., October 26, 1932, 11.

290 *"It was personal"*: Ibid., 16.

290 *"I came here for the purpose"*: Ibid., October 28, 1932, 12.

292 *"Watchers filled the windows"*: Ibid., October 29, 1932, 4.

292 *"Go as far as you like"*: Ibid., 1.

292 *"When the crowd realized"*: Ibid., November 5, 1932, 1.

293 *"The hour is late"*: Ibid., 11.

293 *"There never was a candidate"*: Raskob to James A. Farley, November 10, 1932, Raskob Papers.

294 *"I regard the question"*: *New York Times*, November 1, 1932, 3.

294 *"Today I started"*: Ibid., November 10, 1932, 1.

296 *"She had the greatest brain"*: Ibid., January 3, 1933, 1.

296 *"I have your letter"*: Smith to Frances Perkins, January 6, 1932 [1933], TLS, single manuscript, Collection 15673, New York State Library, Albany.

296 *"too busy"*: *New York Times*, January 29, 1933, 1.

297 *"small-time cabinet"*: Ibid., February 23, 1933, 2.

298 *"Don't spoil my chances"*: Walter Smith, interview by author, White Plains, NY, September 12, 1985.

298 *"The radical and conservative elements"*: *New Outlook*, March 1933, 9.

298 *"It is wise"*: Ibid., April 1933, 9.

299 *"There are heartening evidences"*: Ibid., June 1933, 10.

300 *"We need not worry"*: Alfred E. Smith, Address at Harvard Commencement, June 22, 1933, Smith Papers, New York State Library, Albany.

301 *"It is a fundamental policy"*: Alfred E. Smith, *The Public Papers of Alfred E. Smith, Governor of New York, 1923* (Albany: J. B. Lyon, 1924), 57.

301 *"In New York State"*: *New York World-Telegram*, March 7, 1931, Smith Papers, New York State Library, Albany.

302 *"[F]reedom of persons under 18"*: *New Outlook*, October 1933, 12.

303 *"My only regret"*: *New York Times*, April 8, 1933, 3.

303 *"To him, more than any one"*: Ibid., June 27, 1933, 19.

303 *"millions of people"*: *New Outlook*, August 1933, 10.

305 *"ice was broken"*: *New York Times*, November 15, 1933, 2.

305 *"Is the Democratic Party"*: New Outlook, December 1933, 9.
306 *"new and deep searchings of heart"*: New York Times, November 24, 1933, 14.
306 *"Halfway between a lemon and an orange"*: New Outlook, December 1933, 11.
307 *"Are we forgetful"*: New York Times, November 27, 1933, 2.
307 *"Mr. Smith entered Morgan's"*: Ibid.
308 *"I insist on the right"*: press release, November 29, 1933, Smith Papers, New York State Library, Albany.
309 *"individual and group initiative"*: American Liberty League, press release, August 21, 1934, Raskob Papers.
309 *"It looks to me"*: New York Times, August 24, 1934, 2.
309 *"with faint damns"*: Ibid., August 25, 1934, 1.
309 *"There appears to be"*: Alfred E. Smith, et al., "Report to the Executive Committee of the American Liberty League," December 20, 1934, Raskob Papers.
310 *"I'm not a rich man"*: New York Times, March 31, 1933, 1.
311 *Smith refused to participate*: Jouett Shouse to Raskob, June 12, 1935, Raskob Papers.
311 *"Great accumulations of wealth"*: New York Times, June 20, 1935, 1.
311 *"It is not the case merely of New York"*: Ibid., January 22, 1936, 18.
312 *"My own feeling"*: James A. Farley, Memorandum, January 19, 1936, Farley Papers.
312 *"power-seeking minority"*: New York Times, January 4, 1936, 8.
313 *"I am not a candidate"*: Ibid., January 26, 1936, 1.

## 12: MINORITY LEADER

318 *"A bolt led by him"*: New York Times, February 2, 1936, IV, 3.
319 *"He took a walk"*: Ibid., January 28, 1936, 1.
319 *"The gentleman from Virginia"*: Congressional Record, January 27, 1936, 1029.
319 *"If the blow he struck"*: New York Times, January 28, 1936, 18.
319 *"jammed elbow to elbow"*: Ibid., January 29, 1936, 12.
321 *"drop some of his recovery activities"*: Ibid., February 2, 1936, IV, 4.
321 *"Did you ask the Mayor"*: Ibid., February 5, 1936, 3.
321 *"an organization of multi-millionaires"*: Ibid., February 7, 1936, 2.
321 *"Calling Al 'the Landlord's Agent' "*: H. L. Mencken to Colonel P. H. Callahan, February 18, 1936, Farley Papers.
322 *"I told him the Smith speech"*: James A. Farley, Memorandum, February 29, 1936, Farley Papers.
322 *"If you fail"*: New York Times, June 22, 1936, 1.
322 *"These gentlemen have been"*: Ibid., 3.

323 *"Five blind men"*: Ibid., June 25, 1936, 12.

323 *"Unless you're ready to subscribe"*: New York Herald Tribune, October 2, 1936, 12.

325 *"I deeply appreciate"*: New York Times, October 2, 1936, 1.

326 *"more a matter of personalities"*: Ibid., October 3, 1936, 16.

326 *"I am sorry for Smith"*: Ibid., 2.

326 *"Al's plume is"*: Ibid., October 13, 1936, 22.

326 *"You were all right"*: Ibid., October 23, 1936, 19.

326 *"reminds me of a fighter"*: Ibid., October 14, 1936, 16.

326 *"It has within it"*: Ibid., November 1, 1936, 43.

327 *"The American people"*: Ibid., November 5, 1936, 3.

327 *"I firmly believe"*: Smith to Joseph B. Ely, November 5, 1936, Smith Papers, New York State Library, Albany.

327 *"A strong and vigorous minority"*: Smith to Rt. Rev. John L. Belford, November 5, 1936, Smith Papers, New York State Library, Albany.

328 *"I am ready and willing"*: Smith to Raoul E. Desvernine, November 5, 1936, Smith Papers, New York State Library, Albany.

328 *"I'd be glad to"*: New York Times, December 31, 1936, 36.

328 At the 1937 Friendly Sons dinner: NBC recording, Friendly Sons of St. Patrick dinner, Astor Hotel, New York, March 17, 1937, Recording Division, Library of Congress, Washington, D.C.

329 *"a light to moderate social drinker"*: Slayton, *Empire Statesman*, 193.

329 *"Smith's son Walter"*: Walter Smith, interview with author, September 12, 1985, White Plains, NY.

329 *"[T]hey told me"*: Howe to Roosevelt, February 25, 1924, Howe Papers.

329 *"extremely drunk"*: James A. Farley, Memorandum, August 11, 1933, Farley Papers.

330 *"a liberal supply of rubber hose"*: New York Times, April 14, 1937, 1.

330 *"For years, I've been wanting to come"*: Ibid., May 23, 1937, 29.

331 *"So this is Rome!"*: Ibid., 1.

331 *"[T]he sole and only reason"*: New York Herald Tribune, May 30, 1937, 1.

331 *"I never have been taken aback"*: New York Times, May 29, 1937, 1.

331 *"I have always been proud"*: New York Herald Tribune, May 30, 1937, 1.

331 *"Am I pleased"*: New York Times, June 30, 1937, 21.

332 *"Al Smith saw only"*: Ibid., July 1, 1937, 26.

332 *"[I]n my opinion"*: New York Herald Tribune, June 13, 1937, 18.

332 *"We who are going home"*: Ibid., July 5, 1937, 5.

332 *"On the last day"*: Ibid., July 11, 1937, 17.

333 *"[C]ensorship of thought"*: Smith, *Progressive Democracy*, 284.

334 *"He has a family"*: Smith to William F. Raskob, April 22, 1938, Raskob Papers.

334 *"much as a little boy would do"*: "Notes of George S. Van Schaick," Perkins Papers, 6.

334 *"You're starting your own"*: New York Times, November 3, 1939, 18.

334 *"All of these problems"*: Alfred E. Smith, Radio Speech, November 3, 1939, Smith Papers, New York State Library, Albany.

335 *"To the people of New York"*: New York Times, November 5, 1939, 45.

335 *"Well, all I can say"*: Ibid., March 28, 1933, 13.

335 *"We have not yet won"*: Ibid., November 12, 1938, 6.

336 *"It is because I firmly believe"*: Smith, Radio Speech, Nov. 3, 1939, Smith Papers, New York State Library, Albany.

336 *"Al—Why have you changed"*: New York Times, October 2, 1939, 1.

336 *"This was not the time"*: Ibid., 10.

337 *"Indispensable to who?"*: Ibid., October 24, 1940, 18.

337 *"a very courageous, straight-hitting speech"*: Ibid., December 31, 1940, 6.

338 *"Hear, hear!"*: Warner, Happy Warrior, 245.

338 *"Delighted to read"*: Ibid., 301.

338 *"The dictators believe"*: New York Times, March 18, 1941, 16.

338 *"a greater peril than even Adolf"*: Ibid., May 29, 1941, 1.

339 *"It is just a friendly call"*: Ibid., June 10, 1941, 19.

339 *"The President's speech"*: Ibid., September 13, 1941, 3.

339 *"Going on the experience of the past"*: Ibid., December 31, 1941, 15.

339 *"taxi fare"*: Ibid., March 17, 1943, 15.

340 *"our crackpot friend and paperhanger"*: Ibid., June 3, 1943, 23.

340 *"You are going to have to do some walking"*: Ibid., August 26, 1943, 19.

341 *"The doctor said three a day"*: Warner, Happy Warrior, 309.

341 *"I really believe"*: New York Times, December 31, 1943, 17.

341 *"the exemplification in one person"*: Warner, Happy Warrior, 311.

342 *"I'm asking you"*: New York Times, January 4, 1944, 19.

342 *"This is a national hook up"*: Smith, Speech to the Friendly Sons of St. Patrick, March 17, 1944, Smith Papers, New York State Library, Albany.

342 *"I am looking forward to it"*: Smith to Robert Moses, Robert Moses Papers, New York Public Library, New York.

342 *"Many of the 400"*: New York Times, October 5, 1944, 13.

343 *"The stroke is cruel"*: New York Times, May 5, 1944, 19.

343 *"The Governor looks pretty tired"*: Moses to Eddie Bates, May 8, 1944, Moses Papers.

343 *"We know why you're down here"*: New York Times, May 25, 1944, 14.

343 *"that no person who participates in crimes"*: Ibid., May 26, 1944, 19.

344 *"I've heard that song before"*: Smith, Speech to New York Life Insurance Employees, 69th Regiment Armory, New York, June 13, 1944, Smith Papers, New York State Library, Albany.

345 *"The Governor is in bad shape"*: Moses to Jim?, August 4, 1944, Moses Papers.

345 *But the patient was suffering from cirrhosis*: Robert Moses reported this fact to Frances Perkins in an undated letter in the Perkins Papers. It was con-

firmed by Walter Smith, interview with author, White Plains, NY, September 12, 1985.

## EPILOGUE

346  *"take a walk"*: New York Times, July 2, 1944, VI, 37.

346  *"Mr. Smith's failure"*: Ibid., October 4, 1944, 1.

346  *"That in normal times"*: Washington Post, October 5, 1944, Moses Papers.

347  *"To the populace"*: New York Times, October 5, 1944, 13.

347  *"With the passing of Alfred E. Smith"*: Ibid., 12.

348  *"The fact of the matter is"*: Alfred E. Smith, Address on WOR, June 29, 1939, Smith Papers, New York State Library, Albany.

348  *"Opportunity is all they ask"*: Alfred E. Smith, Address to Lincoln University E.S. Club, February 1, 1939, Smith Papers, New York State Library, Albany.

349  *"disturbed and disgusted"*: Robert Moses, "In Memory of Governor Smith," Moses Papers.

350  *"Cross bearers and acolyte brothers"*: New York Times, October 8, 1944, 42.

# BIBLIOGRAPHIC ESSAY

Al Smith did not write many letters, and the ones that he did write seldom reveal much about what he thought or felt. Most of his correspondence resides in Albany, where his papers are split between the New York State Archives, the repository of his gubernatorial papers, and the New York State Library, which houses personal papers relating mostly to his career after 1928. There is also a collection in the Museum of the City of New York that consists mainly of memorabilia donated by the Smith family.

Among the papers of Smith's close associates, the best sources of information are the Frances Perkins Papers in Columbia University's Rare Book and Manuscript Library and the John J. Raskob Papers, Hagley Library, Greenville, Delaware. The Perkins Papers contain a partial manuscript for a book that she projected as a sequel to *The Roosevelt I Knew*. Some of this material was published in Matthew and Hannah Josephson's *Al Smith: Hero of the Cities*. Where Perkins is an invaluable source of information about Smith's early career, Raskob's papers are key to understanding the years after 1928. Raskob served as chairman of the Democratic National Committee from 1928 to 1932, provided the inspiration and much of the financing for the Empire State Building, and was the moving force behind the American Liberty League. The papers of these Smith associates were also consulted: Robert Moses (New York Public Library), Belle L. Moskowitz (Connecticut College Library), Herbert Lehman (Lehman Library, Columbia University), Robert F. Wagner (Joseph Mark Lauinger Library, Georgetown University), and Pierre S. and Irénée du Pont (Hagley Library, Greenville, Delaware).

The papers of other leading Democrats of the period were helpful, particularly those gathered at the Franklin D. Roosevelt Library, Hyde Park, New York. In addition to Roosevelt's papers, the library has those of Louis Howe; George Graves, who was Smith's secretary; and Edward J. Flynn and Samuel I. Rosenman, who started by working for Smith and went on to work for Roosevelt. These collections were consulted at the Library of Congress: Newton D. Baker, Cordell Hull, James A. Farley, Joseph P. Tumulty, James W. Wadsworth, and Thomas J. Walsh. There is some relevant material in the Lillian D. Wald Papers and the Frank P. Walsh Papers in the New York Public Library. At the Princeton University Library, I consulted the Bernard M. Baruch Papers and the Arthur Krock Papers.

In the absence of any substantial collection of Smith correspondence, it is nevertheless possible to recapture the sound of his voice from documentary records. Although the debates of the New York Assembly were not recorded, stenographers took down the give-and-take at the New York State Constitutional Convention in 1915, giving us a picture of Smith as a debater at the peak of his legislative career. To a lesser extent, Smith's voice also emerges from the record of the Page commission, of which he was a member. The Page commission, officially known as the Commission to Inquire Into the Courts of Inferior Criminal Jurisdiction, held hearings in 1909 that led to a complete revamping of the lower courts in New York and other large cities. On December 1, 1932, Smith provided extensive testimony on reorganizing the government of New York City to the Joint Committee to Investigate the Affairs of New York. From 1931 through early 1934, Smith expressed himself regularly in print: first as a weekly columnist for the McNaught Syndicate, and after October 1932 as editor of the *New Outlook* magazine. Some of these pieces were dictated by Smith; others were drafted by Robert Moses. Taken together, they present a clear picture of his views on a wide range of political subjects. Also indispensable are Smith's St. Patrick's Day addresses to the Friendly Sons of St. Patrick, collected in *Addresses of Alfred E. Smith Delivered at the Meeting of the Society of the Friendly Sons of St. Patrick, 1922–1944* (New York: Society of the Friendly Sons of St. Patrick, 1945).

In the absence of much primary material, the reminiscences of Smith's family and friends become critical for understanding the way he thought and felt. In addition to the memoirs cited in the text, Robert Moses published A *Tribute to Governor Smith* (New York: Simon and Schuster, 1962) and "Al Smith," *New York Times Magazine*, January 21, 1945, 18–19, 52–3. I was fortunate to be able to interview Smith's youngest son, Walter, at his home in White Plains, New York, on September 12, 1985. I also benefited enormously from the recollections that were systematically recorded by the Oral History Project at Columbia University. The Perkins reminiscences run to several volumes and are undoubtedly the most important for understanding Smith. But almost all of the interviews conducted with people who knew Smith provide important details. I consulted the reminiscences of Eddie Dowling, James A. Farley, Edward J. Flynn, Jonah J. Goldstein, Herbert H. Lehman, Walter Lippmann, Jeremiah T. Mahoney, John Lord O'Brien, Joseph M. Proskauer, Samuel I. Rosenman, Francis R. Stoddard, George S. Van Schaick, James W. Wadsworth, and Emily Smith Warner.

There are many useful Ph.D. dissertations on Smith's career. Louis Silveri's "The Political Education of Al Smith: The Assembly Years, 1904–1915" (St.

John's University, 1964) was particularly helpful because it is the only study devoted to Smith's legislative career. The following are also important: David R. Colburn, "Alfred E. Smith: The First 50 Years, 1873–1924" (University of North Carolina, 1971); Charles N. Donn, "The World Beyond the Hudson: Alfred E. Smith and National Politics, 1918–1928" (University of Michigan, 1973); Martin I. Feldbaum, "An Abstract of the Political Thought of Alfred E. Smith" (New York University, 1963); and Louis C. Zuccarello, "The Political Thought of Alfred E. Smith" (Fordham University, 1970). My own dissertation focused on the years after 1928: "Fallen Hero: Alfred E. Smith in the Thirties" (Columbia University, 1992). Smith also made an appearance in my master's thesis, "The Fight for Minority Rights: New York City's Age of Reform, 1931–1947" (Columbia University, 1979). Leona Becker's master's thesis is worthwhile: "Alfred E. Smith: A Personality Study of a Political Leader" (University of Chicago, 1938).

Several other dissertations helped on particular subjects: Earland I. Carlson, "Franklin D. Roosevelt's Fight for the Presidential Nomination, 1928–32" (University of Illinois, 1955); William J. Jackson, "Prohibition as an Issue in New York State Politics, 1836–1933" (Columbia University, 1973); David E. Kyvig, "In Revolt Against Prohibition: The Association Against the Prohibition Movement and the Movement for Repeal, 1919–1933" (Northwestern University, 1971); and Roy H. Lopata, "John J. Raskob: A Conservative Businessman in the Age of Roosevelt" (University of Delaware, 1975).

In addition to the books and articles cited in the Notes, the following have been useful:

## SMITH BIOGRAPHY

Robert L. Duffus, "Al Smith: An East Side Portrait," *Harper's* 152 (February 1926), 320–7; Frank Graham, *Al Smith, American: An Informal Biography* (New York: Putnam, 1945); Samuel B. Hand, "Al Smith, Franklin D. Roosevelt, and the New Deal: Some Comments on Perspective," *Historian*, 27 (May 1965), 366–81; Denis T. Lynch, "Friends of the Governor," *North American Review*, 226 (October 1928), 420–4; Henry Moskowitz, *Alfred E. Smith: An American Career* (New York: Seltzer, 1924); Donn C. Neal, *The World Beyond the Hudson: Alfred E. Smith and National Politics, 1918–1928* (New York: Garland, 1983); Richard O'Connor, *The First Hurrah: A Biography of Alfred E. Smith* (New York: Putnam, 1970); Jordan A. Schwarz, "Al Smith in the Thirties," *New York History* 45 (October 1964), 316–30.

## OTHER BIOGRAPHICAL MATERIAL

David Burner, *Herbert Hoover: A Public Life* (New York: Knopf, 1979); Blanche Wiesen Cook, *Eleanor Roosevelt, 1884–1933* (New York: Viking, 1992); William H. Harbaugh, *Lawyer's Lawyer: The Life of John W. Davis* (New York: Oxford

University Press, 1973); Mark D. Hirsch and Louis M. Hacker, *Proskauer: His Life and Times* (University: University of Alabama Press, 1978); James McGurrin, *Bourke Cockran: A Free Lance in American Politics* (New York: Scribner, 1948); Richard O'Connor, *Courtroom Warrior: The Combative Career of William Travers Jerome* (Boston: Little, Brown, 1963); Elisabeth Israels Perry, *Belle Moskowitz: Feminine Politics and the Exercise of Power in the Age of Alfred E. Smith* (New York: Oxford University Press, 1987); Norman Podhoretz, *Making It* (New York: Random House, 1967); Henry F. Pringle, "John J. Raskob: A Portrait," *Outlook* 149 (August 22, 1928), 645–9; Alfred Rollins, *Roosevelt and Howe* (New York: Knopf, 1962) and "Young F.D.R. and the Moral Crusaders," *New York History* 37, no. 1 (January 1953), 3–16; Joan Hoff Wilson, *Herbert Hoover: Forgotten Progressive* (Boston: Little, Brown, 1975).

## GENERAL

David Burner, *The Politics of Provincialism: The Democratic Party in Transition* (New York: Knopf, 1967); Zechariah Chafee, Jr., *Free Speech in the United States* (Cambridge, MA: Harvard University Press, 1954); John Kenneth Galbraith, *The Great Crash* (1954; reprint with new introduction by the author, Boston: Houghton Mifflin, 1961); William E. Leuchtenburg, *The Perils of Prosperity, 1914–1932* (Chicago: University of Chicago Press, 1958); Walter Lippmann, *Interpretations, 1931–1932* (New York: Macmillan, 1932); Samuel Lubell, *The Future of American Politics*, 2d ed. (Garden City, NY: Doubleday, 1956); Paul L. Murphy, *World War I and the Origin of Civil Liberties in the United States* (New York: Norton, 1979); Fred D. Ragan, "Justice Oliver Wendell Holmes, Jr., Zechariah Chafee, Jr. and the Clear and Present Danger Test of Free Speech: The First Year, 1919," *Journal of American History* 58 (June 1971), 24–45; Frederick Rudolph, "The American Liberty League, 1934–1940," *American Historical Review* 56, no. 1 (October 1950), 19–33; Arthur M. Schlesinger, Jr., *The Age of Roosevelt: The Crisis of the Old Order, 1919–1933* (Boston: Houghton Mifflin, 1957); George Wolfskill, *The Revolt of the Conservatives: A History of the American Liberty League* (Boston: Houghton Mifflin, 1962).

## IRISH-AMERICANS

Jack Beatty, *The Rascal King: The Life and Times of James Michael Curley, 1874–1958* (Reading, MA: Addison-Wesley, 1992); Thomas Beer, *The Mauve Decade: American Life at the End of the Nineteenth Century* (Garden City, NY: Garden City Publishing, 1926); Louis Filler, ed., *Mr. Dooley: Now and Forever* (Stanford, CA: Academic Reprints, 1954); Andrew M. Greeley, *That Most Distressful Nation: The Taming of the American Irish* (Chicago: Quadrangle Books, 1972); Oscar Handlin, *Boston's Immigrants, 1790–1880* (1941; revised and enlarged edition, New York: Atheneum, 1977).

## NATIVISM

Ray Allen Billington, *The Protestant Crusade, 1800–1860* (New York: Macmillan, 1938; reprint, Chicago: Quadrangle Books, 1964); Glenn Feldman, *Politics, Society, and the Klan in Alabama, 1915–1949* (Tuscaloosa: University of Alabama Press, 1999); John Higham, *Send These To Me: Immigrants in Urban America* (New York: Atheneum, 1975; revised edition, Baltimore: Johns Hopkins University Press, 1984); Richard Hofstadter, *The Paranoid Style in American Politics and Other Essays* (New York: Knopf, 1965); David A. Horowitz, ed., *Inside the Klavern: The Secret History of a Ku Klux Klan of the 1920s* (Carbondale: Southern Illinois University Press, 1999).

## NEW YORK CITY

Iver Bernstein, *The New York City Draft Riots: Their Significance for American Society and Politics in the Age of the Civil War* (New York: Oxford University Press, 1990); Amy Bridges, *A City in the Republic: Antebellum New York and the Origins of Machine Politics* (Ithaca, NY: Cornell University Press, 1984); Robert A. Caro, *The Power Broker: Robert Moses and the Fall of New York* (New York: Random House, 1975); Robert Ernst, *Immigrant Life in New York City, 1825–1863* (1949; reprint, Syracuse, NY: Syracuse University Press, 1994); Gene Fowler, *Beau James: The Life and Times of Jimmy Walker* (New York: Viking, 1949); Timothy J. Gilfoyle, *City of Eros: New York City, Prostitution, and the Commercialization of Sex, 1790–1920* (New York: Norton, 1992); David C. Hammack, *Power and Society: Greater New York at the Turn of the Century* (New York: Russell Sage Foundation, 1982); Alfred Hodder, *A Fight for the City* (New York: Macmillan, 1903); Thomas Kessner, *The Golden Door: Italian and Jewish Immigrant Mobility, 1880–1915* (New York: Oxford University Press, 1977); Herbert Mitgang, *Once Upon a Time in New York: Jimmy Walker, Franklin Roosevelt and the Last Great Battle of the Jazz Age* (New York: Simon and Schuster, 2000); Gustavus Myers, *The History of Tammany Hall* (1901; reprint with a new introduction by Alexander B. Callow, Jr., New York: Dover, 1971); Leon Stein, *The Triangle Fire* (Philadelphia: Lippincott, 1962); Bayard Still, *Mirror for Gotham: New York as Seen by Contemporaries from Dutch Days to the Present* (1956; reprint with new introduction by James F. Richardson, New York: Fordham University Press, 1994); Lawrence Veiller, *Three Years of Progress in New York's Police Courts* (New York: Charity Organization Society, 1913).

## NEW YORK STATE

Gordon E. Baker, *Rural Versus Urban Political Power: The Nature and Consequences of Unbalanced Representation* (New York: Doubleday, 1955); Malcolm E. Jewell, ed., *The Politics of Reapportionment* (New York: Atherton, 1962);

William Kennedy, *O Albany! Improbable City of Political Wizards, Fearless Ethnics, Spectacular Aristocrats, Splendid Nobodies and Underrated Scoundrels* (New York: Viking, 1983); Howard A. Scarrow, *Parties, Elections and Representation in the State of New York* (New York: New York University Press, 1983); Edmund R. Terry, "The Insurgents at Albany," *The Independent* 71 (September 7, 1911), 534–40; Robert F. Wesser, *Charles Evans Hughes: Politics and Reform in New York, 1905–1910* (Ithaca, NY: Cornell University Press, 1967).

## 1928 ELECTION

David Burner, "The Brown Derby Campaign," *New York History* 46 (October 1965), 356–80; Paul A. Carter, "The Campaign of 1928 Re-examined: A Study of Political Folklore," *Wisconsin Magazine of History* 46 (1963): 263–72, and "The Other Catholic Candidate: The 1928 Presidential Bid of Thomas J. Walsh," *Pacific Northwest Quarterly* 55 (1964): 1–8; William F. Ogburn and Nell Snow Talbot, "A Measurement of the Factors in the Presidential Election of 1928," *Social Forces* 8 (December 1929):175–83; Roy V. Peel and Thomas C. Donnelly, *The 1928 Campaign: An Analysis* (New York: Richard R. Smith, 1931); Ruth Silva, *Rum, Religion, and Votes: 1928 Re-examined* (University Park: Pennsylvania State University Press, 1962).

## PROGRESSIVISM

Louis Filler, *Crusaders for American Liberalism: The Story of the Muckrakers*, 2d ed. (Yellow Springs, OH: Antioch Press, 1964); Louis Filler, ed., *Late Nineteenth Century Liberalism: Representative Selections, 1880–1900* (New York: Bobbs-Merrill, 1962); Richard Hofstadter, *The Age of Reform: From Bryan to F.D.R.* (New York: Knopf, 1955); J. Joseph Huthmacher, *Senator Robert F. Wagner and the Rise of Urban Liberalism* (New York: Atheneum, 1968), and "Charles Evans Hughes and Charles Francis Murphy: Metamorphoses of Progressivism," *New York History* 46 (June 1965): 25–40; Clifford W. Patton, *The Battle for Municipal Reform: Mobilization and Attack, 1875–1900* (Washington, D.C.: American Council of Public Affairs, 1940); Lincoln Steffens, *Autobiography of Lincoln Steffens* (New York: Literary Guild, 1931) and *Shame of the Cities* (1904; reprint, New York: Hill and Wang, 1957).

## PROHIBITION

Fletcher Dobyns, *The Amazing Story of Repeal: An Exposé of the Power of Propaganda* (Chicago: Willett, Clark, 1940); Mark Edward Lender and James Kirby Martin, *Drinking in America: A History* (New York: Free Press, 1982; revised and expanded, New York: Free Press, 1987); Andrew Sinclair, *Prohibition: The Era of Excess* (Boston: Little, Brown, 1962).

# INDEX

# PrairyErth

## (a deep map)

By William Least Heat-Moon

Blue Highways:
A Journey into America

PrairyErth (a deep map)

# William
# Least Heat-Moon

# PrairyErth

## (a deep map)

A PETER DAVISON BOOK

Houghton Mifflin Company

BOSTON

For information about permission to reproduce selections
from this book, write to Permissions, Houghton Mifflin
Company, 2 Park Street, Boston, Massachusetts 02108.

Library of Congress Cataloging-in-Publication Data
Heat-Moon, William Least.
PrairyErth : (a deep map) / William Least Heat-Moon ; [maps and
Kansas petroglyphs drawn by author].
p.    cm.
"A Peter Davison Book."
ISBN 0-395-48602-5
1. Chase County (Kan.) — Description and travel.    2. Chase County
(Kan.) — History, Local.    3. Heat-Moon, William Least — Journeys
— Kansas — Chase County.    I. Title.
F687.C35H44    1991    91-23250
917.81'59 — dc20    CIP

Printed in the United States of America

HAD 10 9 8 7 6 5 4 3

Book design by Robert Overholtzer

Maps and Kansas petroglyphs drawn by the author.

This book is printed on acid-free paper.

*PrairyErth* speaks in many voices. The author thanks
the numerous writers, alive and dead, whose descriptions
of Chase County and Kansas and the American prairie,
indeed the globe itself, have informed and advised
him — and contributed to the scope and substance of
the Commonplace Books.

Acknowledgments for the use of lengthy quotations
from previously published works are given on page 624.